THE ECONOMICS OF RISING INEQUALITIES

Centre for Economic Policy Research

The Centre for Economic Policy Research is a network of over 550 Research Fellows and Affiliates, based primarily in European universities. The Centre coordinates the research activities of its Fellows and Affiliates and communicates the results to the public and private sectors. CEPR is an entrepreneur, developing research initiatives with the producers, consumers and sponsors of research. Established in 1983, CEPR is a European economics research organization with uniquely wide-ranging scope and activities.

CEPR is a registered educational charity. Institutional (core) finance for the Centre is provided by major grants from the Economic and Social Research Council, under which an ESRC Resource Centre operates within CEPR; the Esmée Fairbairn Charitable Trust and the Bank of England. The Centre is also supported by the European Central Bank, the Bank for International Settlements, the European Investment Bank; 23 national central banks and 41 companies. None of these organizations gives prior review to the Centre's publications, nor do they necessarily endorse the views expressed therein.

The Centre is pluralist and non-partisan, bringing economic research to bear on the analysis of medium- and long-run policy questions. CEPR research may include views on policy, but the Executive Committee of the Centre does not give prior review to its publications, and the Centre takes no institutional policy positions. The opinions expressed in this report are those of the authors and not those of the Centre for Economic Policy Research.

Centre for Economic Policy Research
90–98 Goswell Road
London EC1V 7RR
UK

Tel: +44 (020) 7878 2900   Fax: +44 (020) 7878 2999
Email: cepr@cepr.org   Website: www.cepr.org

The Economics of Rising Inequalities

Edited by
DANIEL COHEN, THOMAS PIKETTY,
and
GILLES SAINT-PAUL

OXFORD
UNIVERSITY PRESS

This book has been printed digitally and produced in a standard specification
in order to ensure its continuing availability

OXFORD
UNIVERSITY PRESS

Great Clarendon Street, Oxford OX2 6DP

Oxford University Press is a department of the University of Oxford.
It furthers the University's objective of excellence in research, scholarship,
and education by publishing worldwide in

Oxford New York

Auckland Cape Town Dar es Salaam Hong Kong Karachi
Kuala Lumpur Madrid Melbourne Mexico City Nairobi
New Delhi Shanghai Taipei Toronto
With offices in
Argentina Austria Brazil Chile Czech Republic France Greece
Guatemala Hungary Italy Japan South Korea Poland Portugal
Singapore Switzerland Thailand Turkey Ukraine Vietnam

Oxford is a registered trade mark of Oxford University Press
in the UK and in certain other countries

Published in the United States
by Oxford University Press Inc., New York

ISBN 978-0-19-872773-6

Contents

Introduction

Discussions about rising inequalities often boil down to the following question: to what extent are rising inequalities the mechanical consequence of changes in economic fundamentals (such as changes in technological or demographic parameters), and to what extent are rising inequalities the contingent consequences of country-specific and time-specific changes in institutions? Needless to say, both the 'fundamentalist' view and the 'institutionalist' view have some relevance. For instance, the decline of traditional manufacturing employment since the 1970s has been associated in every developed country with a rise of labour-market inequality (the inequality of labour earnings within the working-age population has gone up in all countries), which lends support to the fundamentalist view. But, on the other hand, everybody agrees that institutional differences (minimum wage, collective bargaining, tax and transfer policy, etc.) between Continental European countries and Anglo-Saxon countries explain why disposable income inequality trajectories have been so different in those two groups of countries during the 1980s–90s, which lends support to the institutionalist view. The chapters in this volume show the strength of both views. Through empirical evidence and new theoretical insights it will show that institutions always play a crucial role in shaping inequalities, and sometimes preventing them, and yet, that with a vergeace, inequalities across age, sex and skills often come back through the window. From Sweden to Spain and Portugal, from Italy to Japan and across the Atlantic, the volume will explore the diversity of the interplay between market forces and institutions. No simple message will emerge but it would be foolish to bet that one is more important than the other.

I. MARKETS AND INSTITUTIONS

The chapter by Bover, Bentolila and Arellano looks at earnings inequality in Spain. Using data from Spanish Social Security records, they find that Spain, unlike France and Germany, has experienced a substantial rise in inequality in the 1980s and 1990s. This, despite the fact that wages are determined by collective agreements as in France and Germany. The authors investigate the determinants of the returns to skills in Spain, paying substantial attention to labour-market institutions. They find that unions tend to compress wage inequality: the returns to skills are lower in sectors with greater union coverage. Thus, part of the rise in wage inequality may be ascribed to the decline in union power that Spain has experienced as in many other countries. But on the other hand, firm-level agreements tend to push the returns to skills up, thus partly offsetting the compression effects of union agreements at the sectoral level. That is, employers tend to negotiate wages to bring them more in line with worker productivity. Another important finding is that long-term unemployment tends to increase the returns to skills. As argued by the authors, this is evidence of loss of skills during unemployment spells. A higher share of long-term unemployment therefore reduces the total supply of skills in the economy, which pushes the returns to skills up. Massive unemployment then contributes to raise wage inequalities.

The comparison of Portugal and Spain is one of the most fascinating exercises in the field of labour economics. Here are two neighbouring countries, which have shared many developments in the past three decades and which stand as opposite cases regarding unemployment. Portugal's unemployment is among the lowest in Europe, Spain's among the highest. If one were to take Paul Krugman's famous line that rising wage inequalities and rising unemployment are mirror images of the same trends, one should expect the Portuguese economy to have traded off low unemployment against large inequalities, at least when compared to Spain. The chapter by Canto, Cardosa and Jimeno finds that this is indeed the case. Yet it argues that the difference is not as large as one could have expected *a priori* and not for the reasons that are expected. For one thing, the statutory minimum wage (as a proportion of the average wage) is higher in Portugal than in Spain, and the incidence is correspondingly higher in Portugal. Furthermore, the premium which is paid in Spain to fixed-term employment is larger than in Portugal. Finally, the coverage rate of collective bargaining is not different (around 80 per cent in both cases). All this tends to make Portuguese institutions no more conducive to unequal outcome than the Spanish one.

Furthermore, the driving forces regarding the composition of employment across and within sectors are broadly similar. The major difference appears to originate in the difference across sectors (rather than within sectors). Portugal has maintained low-wage, labour-intensive industries where low-skill workers can still be employed, while, in contrast, Spain has experienced relatively high wages in the types of industries which have resulted in high unemployment among low-skill workers. The fact that the statutory minimum wage is higher in Portugal casts doubt on the fact that institutions are the only factors at stake here.

Other chapters in this volume focus upon institutional forces. In particular, the chapters by Daron Acemoglu ('Changes in Unemployment and Wage Inequality: An Alternative Theory and Some Evidence') and by Giorgio Brunello and Tsuneo Ishikawa ('Does Competition at School Matter? A View Based Upon the Italian and Japanese Experiences') both look at the interplay between educational institutions and firm hiring policies. Both chapters emphasize that different institutional equilibria can exist, and that these different institutional equilibria can have important implications for the dynamics of wage inequality. Acemoglu shows that small variations in the supply of skills can lead to qualitative changes in the composition of jobs offered by firms. For instance, an increase in the proportion of skilled workers can induce firms to stop creating a single type of job, and can lead to an endogenous increase in the demand for skills and in wage inequality, which may or may not be efficient. Brunello and Ishikawa show that the same parameter values can give rise to multiple equilibria: one equilibrium in which schools are very competititve and academic degrees are highly rewarded by the private sector (which the authors identify as Japan), and another equilibrium in which schools are more 'flexible' and the private sector relies mostly on internal training (which the authors identify as Italy). Such models could be used in order to account for the wide cross-country variations in inequality trends.

The chapter by Etienne Wasmer ('The Causes of the "Youth Unemployment Problem": A (Labour) Supply Side View') basically argues that we should take demographics seriously. Wasmer argues that changes in fundamental demographic parameters can account for a large fraction of the rise in youth unemployment rates observed in Europe since the 1970s. More specifically, the fact that large cohorts of workers born during the post-World War II baby-boom entered the labour market during the 1970s induced a large labour supply shock: the supply of low-experience labour increased suddenly, which could easily explain why the labour-market position of these workers deteriorated so quickly. Wasmer also argues that rising female participation induced an additional labour supply shock which played an important role in the story.

The fact that distribution of income may be affected by labour-market frictions has been largely ignored in the previous literature. Such types of interactions may be magnified if one allows for migration. In his contribution to this volume, Javier Ortega develops a model of two countries with labour markets that are both subject to search frictions but differ in the sense that one country has a more efficient labour market. He shows that multiple equilibria may arise. In one equilibrium there is no migration, while in another there is migration from the country with the least efficient to that with the most efficient labour market. Furthermore, this equilibrium Pareto dominates the other since all workers end up in the best functioning labour market. Mutiplicity arises because migrants have higher search costs, so that their outside option in bargaining is reduced. This generates downward wage pressure, which increases incentives to post vacancies, and thus the attractiveness of the recipient country's labour market. In Ortega's model, migration is the sole outcome of differences in labour-market efficiency. Migrants do not move to earn more, but to end up in a better labour market. But they do affect wages and the distribution of income.

II. LIFE LONG INEQUALITIES AND THE SCOPE FOR REDISTRIBUTION

Labour-market outcomes are usually pointed out as the critical factors underlying the rise of inequalities. Yet, the picture is not one for one. One reason is that a rising dispersion of income may reflect short-run fluctuations of an individual lifetime. This is the topic that is taken on by Preston and Blundell (on British data). They show that inequality in both income and consumption was sharply greater in the late 1980s for all cohorts than it had been for preceding cohorts at a similar age. On the other hand, they also show that the variance of permanent shocks (as opposed to the variance of transitory shocks) does not appear to have risen for any cohort. How can we then account for rising consumption inequalities? The authors argue that it can be attributed in part to an ageing population and in part to new cohorts facing higher levels of initial income inequality. The younger cohorts are indeed particularly hit. They face not only an increase in the variance of transitory components of their income (by comparison with older cohorts when they were at a similar age) but in their permanent inequality as well.

The work by Bjorkland and Palme on Swedish data starts from the same problem as Preston and Blundell. To the extent that studies of income inequalities blend two conceptually different sources of income inequality namely, transitory variation of individual incomes over time and variation over long run lifetime incomes, it is difficult to see what it is that redistributive policies are really achieving. One of the insights of the analysis by Bjorkland and Palme is that two distinct redistributive mechanisms are actually at work. One is straight taxation which redistributes income at any point in time from high to low incomes, the other one is the welfare system which redistributes income over the life cycle. While the former is a powerful element for redistribution of average life-time incomes, the second appears to be specifically efficient in reducing income variability (although means tested welfare programmes also contribute positively to reducing long-run inequalities). To the extent that income variability is the highest among those with low long-run income, they conclude that the equalizing effect of taxes and transfers within the life cycle is also the largest in this group.

Income is also bound to be mutualized within each household. This is shown in the survey on Italy in the paper by Brandolini, Cippollone, and Sestito. The last decades have unleashed what they call a 'decompression' of the wage structure, originating from factors already at work in other advanced countries. Egalitarian practices regarding the response to rising inflation in the 1970s have been dismantled; the distribution of those not earning which narrowed from the late 1970s until the end of the 1980s widened abruptly in the early 1990s. As in other advanced economies the young, females, and more generally, persons who are not heads of households are all over-represented among the low paid. Low-paid workers are part-time workers, often not the breadwinner. The result is that low-paid Italian workers are usually not living in poor households: only 1/5 of them do.

Income is one crucial element of the welfare of a family but other factors driven by home production also count. Gottschalk and Mayer ask whether including the value of home production affects the trend in income inequality. This is clearly a very relevant question: a significant part of the inequality trend can be accounted for by the rising number of high-wage two-earner families, and one indeed expects the inclusion of home production in inequality measures to moderate the inequality trend. That is, one very important socio-demographic change observed since the 1970s is the rise of the participation rate of women married to high-wage men (such women have traditionally had lower participation rates than other women). In other words, top income households need to rely more than ever on other households to do their cleaning, cooking, etc., and this needs to be taken into account in order to have a proper view of the overall process. This effect is however not strong enough to undo the inequality trend: Gottschalk and Mayer find that income adjusted for the value of home production is indeed more equally distributed than unadjusted income, but that inequality of adjusted income also grew during the 1980s–1990s (regardless of the method used for adjusting income). These results are hardly surprising (one indeed expects the wages of high-skill wives who choose to go to work to be much higher than the value of their home production), but it was important to quantify these effects in a rigorous way.

The chapter by Bénabou explains another difference in institutions between Europe and the US, namely that redistribution is greater on the east side of the Atlantic. Traditional Political Economy theory views redistribution as the outcome of a political process by which the decisive voter increases his welfare at the expense of the rest of society. One prediction is that there will be more redistribution when the median is poorer relative to the mean, i.e. when there is more inequality. This line of explanation does not square with the US versus Europe evidence; in fact it does not do very well empirically. Bénabou shows theoretically how greater inequality may be associated with less, rather than more, redistribution. To the extent that the decisive voter is richer than the median (but not necessarily richer than the mean), the support for redistribution may, over some range, decrease when inequality increases. The reason is that redistribution is opposed by a group of richer agents, who contribute more than what they get out of it. At low levels of inequality this group is small, because taxes are not very different across agents and most of them benefit from the welfare-enhancing effect of redistribution. At higher levels of inequality, however, the group of agents who contribute more than their benefits in terms of higher aggregate welfare is greater; hence there is more opposition to redistribution. Bénabou shows that, to the extent that capital market imperfections make inequalities more persistent, this phenomenon may lead to multiple steady states. A high inequality society will remain so precisely because it redistributes less, which prevents the poor from investing in human capital. Conversely, a low inequality society will redistribute more, which allows the poor to invest, thus increasing their relative income. Depending on initial conditions, the economy may converge to a high inequality/low redistribution equilibrium or to a low inequality/high redistribution one. This may contribute to explain transatlantic differences in both the distribution of income and societal options.

Hassler, Rodriguez, Storeletten and Zilibotti develop a theoretical model of voting for unemployment benefits. They argue that greater unemployment benefits induce people to take greater risks when acquiring skills, in that they choose to become more specialized. This is because they suffer less from a negative demand shock affecting their specific skill, as unemployment benefits allow them to maintain their income level. By contrast, if unemployment benefits are low, people will not put all their eggs in the same basket and will rather acquire general skills that allow them to minimize the income loss associated with shocks that hit specific skills. What the authors show is that this process is self-reinforcing: once workers are locked in their skills, they will vote for the level of unemployment benefits consistent with their earlier choice. Thus, specialized workers will support generous unemployment benefits, while less specialized ones will not be so generous. The economy may, therefore, end up in a steady-state equilibrium where people are specialized and unemployment benefits are high, or in an equilibrium where the reverse occurs. According to the authors, this may contribute to explain why unemployment benefits are higher in Europe than in the US. This highlights the main theme of this volume. Market forces and institutions act together: not only independently from one another but most often in response to one another. Single minded reforms of institutions are bound to fail if they ignore the logic that has brought them to life.

The chapters in this volume were the results of a research project launched at CEPR jointly with the Instituto de Estudios Economicos de Galicios. They were presented during two workshops held at La Coruña, in February 1997 and April 1998. We are grateful to Guillermo de la Dehesa for his effort in making this project come through.

List of Contributors

Daron Acemoglu

Manuel Arellano, CEMFI

Ronald Bénabou

Samuel Bentolila, CEMFI

Anders Björklund, Swedish Institute for Social Research, Stockholm University, S-106 91 Stockholm, Sweden
E-mail: anders@sofi.su.se

Richard Blundell

Olympia Bover, Banco de España

Andrea Brandolini, Bank of Italy, Economic Research Department

Giorgio Brunello, Department of Economics, Padua University, Italy, IZA Bonn and CESifo Munich

Olga Cantó, Universidad de Vigo

Ana R. Cardoso, Universidade do Minho

Piero Cipollone, Bank of Italy, Economic Research Department

Peter Gottschalk, Boston College

John Hassler

Tsuneo Ishikawa, Department of Economics, University of Tokyo, Japan

Juan F. Jimeno, Universidad de Alcalà, FEDEA and CEPR

Susan E. Mayer, University of Chicago

Javier Ortega

Mårten Palme, Stockholm School of Economics, Box 6501, 5-113 83 Stockholm, Sweden
E-mail: stmp@hhs.se

Ian Preston

José V. Rodríguez Mora

Paolo Sestito, Bank of Italy and Ministry of Labour

Kjetil Storesletten

Etienne Wasmer, ECARE, ULB; CEPR, London

Fabrizio Zilibotti

PART I

MARKETS AND INSTITUTIONS

1

The Distribution of Earnings in Spain during the 1980s: The Effects of Skill, Unemployment, and Union Power

OLYMPIA BOVER, SAMUEL BENTOLILA, AND MANUEL ARELLANO

1.1. INTRODUCTION

Since the early 1980s, the UK and the US have witnessed significant increases in wage inequality. In contrast, there has been little change in other countries such as France or Germany. Increases in Anglo-Saxon countries have been traced back to rising returns to education and experience, but also to higher differences in remunerations for workers with comparable schooling and seniority. Forces often mentioned as underlying these developments are changes in demographics, changes in labour quality, skill-biased technological change, rising returns to unobserved ability, growing international trade flows, and changes in institutions such as declines in minimum wages in real terms or deunionization.

In this chapter, we provide the first detailed account of the evolution of wages in Spain during the 1980s, distinguishing between changes in inequality arising from changes in the returns to skill and experience and changes in dispersion within observable categories of workers.

We analyse changes in the conditional distributions of male earnings in Spain during the 1980s, using a new database of Social Security records. We employ a sample of monthly earnings for more than 30,000 male employees for the period 1980–87. It is a matched employer–employee data set, although with a limited number of characteristics recorded for each agent. The data set has the structure of an unbalanced panel subject to censoring due to top and bottom coding in the Social Security records. We first describe the behaviour of various quantiles

We wish to thank the Ministerio de Trabajo y Seguridad Social for providing the main data, Francisco de Castro and Pilar Velilla for research assistance, and Thomas Bauer for help in locating German data. We are also grateful for comments from participants in the CEPR workshop on 'Rising income inequalities' at La Coruña, and in seminars at the Research Department of the Banco de España and Universitat Pompeu Fabra. Any errors are our own responsibility. The last two authors gratefully acknowledge financial support from the Spanish Dirección General de Enseñanza Superior (DGES) (Grant PB96-0134).

summarizing the evolution of the distribution of real earnings. We then focus on the evolution of the returns to skill and experience, across sectors and over time, taking into account firm size. In a second stage, we attempt to account for the variation of these estimated returns by regressing them on a set of sectoral and national economic variables. The sectoral ones are the coverage of trade union collective agreements, the share of public employment, the hiring rate, and R&D expenditures, whereas the national variables are the share of long-term unemployment, unemployment rates by skill, and changes in the composition of the labour force.

The chapter is organized as follows. In Section 1.2 we briefly review some developments in the Spanish economy and its wage bargaining system, and introduce our database. In Section 1.3 we describe the econometric techniques used to analyse the data. In Section 1.4 we show our estimated returns to skill and experience by sector and period, for different firm size classes. We then turn to an empirical assessment of the economic forces behind the evolution of those returns. This is based on a stylized model of wage setting in unionized firms operating in imperfectly competitive markets, presented in Section 1.5. The estimation results from a specification inspired by the model are shown in Section 1.6. Section 1.7 contains our conclusions.

1.2. INSTITUTIONAL SETTING AND DATA DESCRIPTION

1.2.1. Background

Very little is known about the wage distribution in Spain, due to lack of microeconomic data.[1] Sectoral data from the main wage survey, the *Encuesta de Salarios* (which suffers from important shortcomings, for example in terms of coverage), suggest that there was a significant reduction in earnings dispersion across both occupations and sectors in the second half of the 1970s and a slow increase in the 1980s. The standard deviation in hourly earnings (including overtime and bonuses) across occupational categories fell from 0.587 in 1966 to 0.45 in 1977, and then slightly increased to 0.49 in 1987 (García Perea, 1991).[2,3]

The apparent fall in wage dispersion in the 1970s was probably the result of the explosion of pent-up demands for more equality at the time of the establishment of a democratic regime in 1975 coupled with increasing unemployment affecting especially low-wage workers. In the 1980s, several developments potentially affecting wages can be pointed out. The educational level of the labour force rose

---

[1] Recently, some studies on returns to education have been carried out with earnings data from decadal and quarterly family expenditure surveys; for a review see Oliver *et al.* (1999).

[2] Similar data appear in Jimeno and Toharia (1994). Melis and Díaz (1993) report an increase in nominal annual labour earnings inequality from 1986 to 1990, based on data on single-earner Spanish income tax returns.

[3] Abadie (1998) carried out a conditional quantile analysis of earnings using cross-sections from the Family Expenditure Surveys for 1980 and 1990. He found that returns to education fell at most quantiles, except for the younger college-educated cohorts.

and the average age of workers fell. The secular decrease in the share of agriculture in the economy was accompanied by a process of restructuring in manufacturing, in the aftermath of the oil shocks of the 1970s, which caused much employment turbulence. Restructuring allowed for technological catch-up in the midst of a long recession which only ended in the second half of 1985. The prospect of European Community membership favoured a steady increase in the degree of openness of the economy, which was strengthened after 1985. Wage bargaining institutions were definitely enshrined in the law in 1980, with the approval of the so-called Workers' Statute. In contrast with the decline of unionization experienced in Anglo-Saxon countries, over the first half of the 1980s union power was being established in Spain. Lastly, during this period, the unemployment rate increased dramatically, from around 11 per cent in 1980 to above 21 per cent in 1985, then falling only slightly to around 20 per cent in 1987. The increase in unemployment hit low-skill workers more than high-skill ones.

1.2.2. The Spanish Wage Setting System

In Spain, wages are essentially set by collective bargaining. Slightly less than 15 per cent of all employees are covered by firm-level agreements, while almost 70 per cent are covered by agreements with a broader scope. Most agreements are bargained for at a quite centralized level, usually applying to an economic sector, although for bargaining purposes sectors do not correspond to the usual standard sectoral classifications, and they may be broad or narrowly defined. Sectoral agreements usually apply to a whole province, which are sub-units of regions, although they can also cover one region, several regions, or even the whole country. The agreements determine the wage scale for different occupations.

There are two main unions, organized along economic sector and regional lines, and a few smaller unions typically with regional scope. Employer organizations are structured along the same lines as the major unions, within a single confederation of organizations. In order to be entitled to participate in collective bargains, a union needs to obtain at least 15 per cent of the votes in the elections for worker representatives (held every four years) in the sector of reference, or 10 per cent of the votes at the national level. Union density is very low, around 10 to 15 per cent. However, this is not very relevant, because the advantages of being a union member are scant: conditions agreed in collective agreements are legally binding, as minima, for all workers in the appropriate economic and geographical domain and occupation, regardless of union affiliation. Thus, affiliation is quite irrelevant in Spain and a better proxy for union power is the coverage of collective bargains as a percentage of the total number of employees in a sector, although it is not a high-quality measure. In the sample period spanned by our data, the aggregate number of collective agreements and their coverage increased steadily.

Sectoral union coverage ratios vary widely at the beginning of the sample period: it is low in Construction and Other services and high in Mining and

Manufacturing (see Table 1.9).[4] What explains this sectoral variability? As described above, coverage will be higher the wider the definition of the sectors for collective bargaining purposes (with some sub-sectors ending up not covered) and the wider the geographical area of applicability. It will also depend on the presence of public employment in the sector, because coverage is usually higher for public (non-tenured) employees and employees in public firms than for private employees. Lastly, coverage tends to be lower in Services than in other sectors (as is common in many other countries). Collective bargaining was already established in the Franco regime, in 1958, through a type of law called the *Ordenanzas laborales*. Somewhat surprisingly, the sectoral structure set during the dictatorship period did not vary much with the advent of democracy in 1977.[5] As to the time-series evolution of sectoral coverage ratios in our sample period, it can be interpreted as a quite mechanical drive by unions to increase coverage in all sectors. Over the 1980s, then, coverage tends to converge to very high proportions: by 1987 all sectors, except Other services, end up between 83 per cent and full coverage, with the average around 95 per cent (see Table 1.9).[6]

Collective bargains are much more relevant for low-skill than for high-skill workers. For instance, Dolado *et al.* (1997) find, from a 1990–91 survey, that no high-skill worker reported an average hourly wage which was below the minimum wage guaranteed in collective bargains for their corresponding sector and skill/ professional status (including seniority and overtime premia), while 41 per cent of the unskilled did. Similarly, the average wage reported by high-skill workers was 57 per cent higher than such minimum guaranteed wage, while it was only 0.2 per cent higher for low-skill workers. Thus, while wages may be formally bargained for all workers, bargained wages are seldom applicable to high-skill ones.

Sectoral collective bargains usually determine wages and annual hours of work only. Three-quarters of workers covered are under one-year agreements, while agreements for two years usually contemplate their conditions to be revised at the end of the first year. For all but the last two years covered by our database, 1980–87, there were also nationwide collective agreements setting wage growth rate bands (of 2–4 percentage points width, depending on the year) applicable to all Spanish workers.[7]

In the period covered by our data, there were three national legal minimum wage levels, for workers up to 16 years old, for 17 year olds, and for older workers. The relative values of the first and second to the third were around 39 per cent and

---

[4] It is also high in Finance, though there are problems with data on this sector at the beginning of the sample. Also, some sectors show coverage above 100 per cent, which stems from having different sources for the numerator and the denominator of the coverage ratio. This is discussed in the Appendix.

[5] For descriptions see Escobar (1995) or Abellán *et al.* (1995).

[6] As a result, we would not expect union coverage to depend much on observed wage growth or wage differentials, as might have been the case with union affiliation (if this was a relevant variable in the Spanish case).

[7] The actual bands were: 11–15 per cent (1981), 9–11 per cent (1982), 9.5–12.5 per cent (1983), 5.5–7.5 per cent (1985), and 7.2–8.6 per cent (1986). There were no agreements in 1984 and 1987. Further description can be found in Jimeno (1992) and Jimeno and Toharia (1994).

61 per cent, respectively.[8] Minimum wages were raised annually by the inflation rate expected at the end of the previous year.

1.2.3. Characteristics of the Database

We use a database of Spanish Social Security records. It contains the information provided monthly by firms when paying contributions for their employees. This information was matched, by the Spanish Ministry of Labour, with workers' and firms' individual records at the Social Security system. The matched database contains information on workers' characteristics, i.e., sex, age, occupation, and pre-tax monthly earnings, and on the firm they work for, i.e., its sector, region of location, and size (number of workers).

The type of data source determines some special characteristics of the earnings variable available. In particular, we observe the taxable earnings base, rather than actual earnings, which is subject to floors and ceilings which depend on the worker's occupation and vary over time. This causes the censoring of earnings for a fraction of the observations, most of them at the top. Moreover, this earnings variable excludes overtime payments, travel allowances, occasional payments, and fringe benefits.

There is another data problem. In Spain all employees are entitled to receive statutory bonuses, equal to one extra instalment of the regular monthly pay, in July and December.[9] In some sectors and firms, workers get additional bonuses. By law, in their declaration of taxable earnings for Social Security purposes, firms must evenly spread bonus pay amounts over the year. However, before January 1983 spreading was compulsory for the July and December bonuses only, not for any additional ones. As a consequence, reported earnings in our sample may be artificially low before 1983, for workers with three or more bonus payments per year.

The criteria followed to construct the final database are as follows.[10]

1. *Definition of earnings.* The database does not contain information on either days of work per month or hours of work per day, which precludes the computation of hourly wages. As a result, we analyse the behaviour of monthly earnings.

2. *Sex and age.* There is no information on workers' marital status or other family characteristics, such as the number of children. We deem these to be especially important for the labour supply of married women, so we analyse male earnings only. We also exclude from the sample workers aged 16–19, due to the instability of their attachment to the labour market, and men aged 65 or older, due to the importance of transitions to retirement at those ages. This leaves us with men aged 20–64.

---

[8] Their respective monthly values in 1985 were: 14,370; 22,800; and 37,170 pesetas.
[9] If the corresponding collective bargain allows it, workers can choose to spread receipt of these statutory bonuses evenly over the year.
[10] See the Appendix for details.

3. *Working time.* As a way to target full-time, full-month employees, we exclude workers with reported monthly earnings below the floor for the taxable earnings base in their occupation.
4. *Sector.* The data set covers private sector, non-tenured public sector, and State-owned enterprise employees. We analyse data on workers in the non-agricultural sector only, because the coverage of the sample for the agricultural sector in the database is quite limited. At the empirical estimation stage we distinguish between eight sectors, roughly corresponding to the usual one-digit classification.
5. *Period and frequency.* The data refer to the months of June and December, starting in December 1980 and ending in December 1987. We discard the June data, to suppress the effects of seasonality, and retain only those referring to December. In this section we provide descriptive statistics for 1980–87. Later on, in the econometric analysis, we drop the first year due to lack of availability of one sectoral variable used as a regressor.

The original database contains close to 6 million observations, on about 6,000,000 workers. After applying a set of filters described in the Appendix, we drew a random sample comprising 30 per cent of the remaining total, and were left with 140,545 observations from the filtered database, which refer to 32,291 workers.

The most relevant characteristics of the observations in such sample are contained in Table 1.7. Almost all of the 19 per cent censored observations are top-coded. The number of observations per individual varies, with 34 per cent of them being observed for the full seven years spanned by the sample.

A key variable is the skill level. As a measure of skill we use a grouping by education of occupational categories. The number of years of schooling is not observed, but the database provides information on occupation. There are ten occupational groups, but most do not correspond to educational levels. Thus we focus on three occupations which correspond to educational groups: workers with a *college* degree (*licenciados*, with at least five years of higher education), workers with a *junior college* degree (*diplomados*, with at least three years of higher education), and individuals working in *unskilled* jobs (*peones*). The remaining group, including all workers in between the last two groups, is labelled as *medium-skilled.*

Another variable we use later on is firm size. We distinguish between three classes: *small* firms, with up to 100 employees, *medium-sized* firms, between 101 and 1,000 employees, and *large* firms, above 1,000 employees. We do not, however, use the information on regions in the database, for reasons to be explained below.

1.2.4. A First Look at Earnings in Spain in the 1980s

The period 1980–87 was a relatively slow growth period, with an average annual GDP growth rate of 2.3 per cent. But this comprises part of a recession,

Table 1.1. *The distribution of real monthly earnings in 1980 and 1987*[a]

	Median monthly earnings			75th–25th percentile[b]		50th–25th percentile[b]	
	P50		Annual growth (%)	P75–25		P50–25	
	1980	1987	1980–87	1980	1987	1980	1987
All workers	91,785	90,592	−0.19	0.540	0.615	0.269	0.278
Skill							
College	186,588	205,300	1.37	n.a.	n.a.	0.454	0.538
Junior college	137,049	153,589	1.64	n.a.	n.a.	0.317	0.296
Medium-skill	91,534	90,653	−0.14	0.499	0.562	0.252	0.262
Unskilled	67,645	65,931	−0.37	0.338	0.342	0.139	0.141
Age (years old)							
20–29	78,709	69,651	−1.73	0.465	0.410	0.200	0.167
30–44	101,341	98,628	−0.39	0.493	0.594	0.295	0.307
45–64	97,066	106,620	1.35	0.503	0.507	0.262	0.297
Sectors							
Mining	104,107	112,169	1.07	0.435	0.512	0.264	0.341
Construction	74,183	69,917	−0.84	0.368	0.332	0.146	0.128
Manufacturing	96,815	96,990	0.03	0.466	0.546	0.256	0.286
Transport and p.u.	97,184	101,848	0.67	0.539	0.551	0.299	0.296
Trade	76,194	77,180	0.18	0.474	0.516	0.176	0.186
Finance	n.a.	n.a.	n.a.	n.a.	n.a.	n.a.	n.a.
Hotels	63,393	68,433	0.22	0.328	0.360	0.157	0.166
Other services	93,797	97,247	0.52	0.477	0.571	0.241	0.282

Notes

[a]Real earnings in 1985 pesetas (deflated by the national CPI).

[b]Quantile measures refer to log earnings.

Source: Own calculations on Social Security data set (see Appendix).

1980–85, with a 1.5 per cent growth rate, and part of a boom, 1986–87, with a 4.4 per cent growth rate. Over the whole period, wages bargained in collective agreements fell in real terms by 1 per cent per year, while owing to wage drift, real wages managed simply to stagnate, with a yearly growth rate of −0.02 per cent per year.

Our sample shows similar behaviour, with median monthly earnings for all workers, deflated by the national consumer price index (CPI), decreasing by 0.19 per cent per year.[11] As shown in Table 1.1, the evolution is quite different for workers with college education, whose median earnings increased by 1.37 per cent per year, than for unskilled workers, whose earnings fell by 0.37 per cent. Figure 1.1 shows these variables, normalized in 1980.[12] Patterns also differ by age: young workers' earnings fell by 1.73 per cent per year, while for the oldest

[11] Note that these facts refer to a sample whose demographic composition changes every year.

[12] The evolution of medians and dispersion measures is very similar for the 1983–87 period, which is free of potential measurement error arising from the change in the regulation on reporting of bonuses discussed in the previous subsection.

O. Bover, S. Bentolila, and M. Arellano

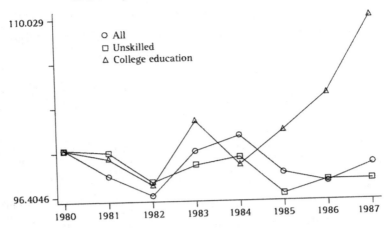

Figure 1.1. *Median earnings, by skill. 1980 = 100.*

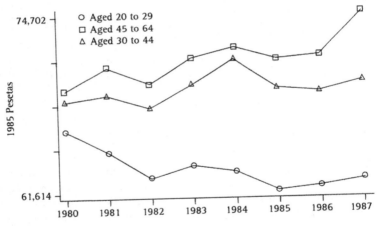

Figure 1.2. *Median earnings, unskilled, by age.*

group there was an increase of 1.35 per cent; Fig. 1.2 shows the evolution of medians by age group for unskilled workers.[13]

These differences suggest an increase in the returns to skill and experience. Table 1.2 helps make this general impression more precise. It shows a bigger increase in the earnings of college-educated workers vis-à-vis unskilled ones for middle-aged workers than for younger ones, while top censoring precludes

[13] Note also that due to variation in top codes, there may be censored earnings observations below the median, even if the median itself is not censored. The effect of this would be to downward bias the median. This is not an issue for the college, junior college, and unskilled categories, but may be so for the catch-all medium-skill one, and for aggregate earnings measures that do not control for the skill category.

Table 1.2. *Returns to education and experience*[a]

	1980	1987	Change 1980–87
Education			
Ratio of college-educated to unskilled workers median real earnings			
20–29 years old	1.82	1.94	0.12
30–44 years old	2.89	3.09	0.20
45–64 years old	3.03	n.a.	n.a.
Age			
Ratio of 45–64 to 20–29 years old median real monthly earnings			
College	1.74	n.a.	n.a.
Unskilled	1.05	1.19	0.14

Note: [a]Real earnings in 1985 pesetas (deflated by the national CPI).

Source: Own calculations on Social Security data set (see Appendix).

observation for older workers. It also shows a pronounced increase in the returns to experience for unskilled workers, while information for college-educated workers is again top censored. Table 1.1 highlights quite diverging earnings trends across sectors as well, with a range going from −0.84 per cent in Construction to 1.07 per cent in Mining (it is probably higher in Finance, but the median is top censored).

Due to censoring in our data, we cannot provide the usual measures of earnings dispersion (e.g., the Gini coefficient or the variance of log earnings). We can nevertheless show quantiles based on relative earnings categories. The most widely quoted measure, the (log) difference between the 90th and the 10th percentile, $P90-10$, is unfortunately also censored in our data. Table 1.1 shows two measures for log earnings: the difference between the 75th and the 25th percentile, $P75-25$, or interquartile range, which captures dispersion around the median, and the 50–25 percentile difference, $P50-25$, which measures dispersion in the lower half of the earnings distribution.

Earnings dispersion clearly increases when all workers are considered. Figure 1.3 shows kernel density estimates of the earnings distributions in the initial and final years. In comparison with 1980, in 1987 a significant amount of frequency mass moves away from the middle of the distribution, mostly to the upper half. In addition, Table 1.1 shows that inequality rises both around the median, by 7.5 percentage points according to the $P75-25$ measure, and below the median, by 0.9 percentage points according to the $P50-25$ measure.

We cannot fully characterize dispersion within skill cells, due to top-coding for higher skill groups. Nevertheless, Fig. 1.4 shows a clear shift to the right in the distribution of earnings for college-educated workers. For the bottom half of the distribution, Table 1.1 also indicates increased inequality among college-educated workers, but a fall among workers with a junior college degree. Inequality

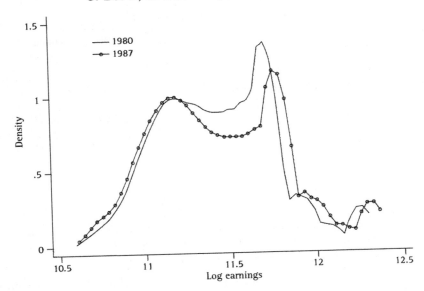

Figure 1.3. *Kernel density estimates.*

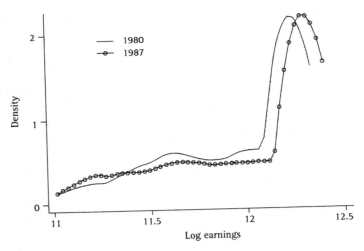

Figure 1.4. *Kernel density estimates: college education.*

also rises, slightly, among the unskilled. For this group, Fig. 1.5 shows lower mass at higher earnings (though not at the very top) of the 1987 distribution as compared with 1980, which is reflected in the increasing dispersion shown in Table 1.1 (see also Fig. 1.6). Moreover, the difference between the 90th and 10th percentiles, which is not censored for this skill group, rises from 0.652 to 0.674 over the period.

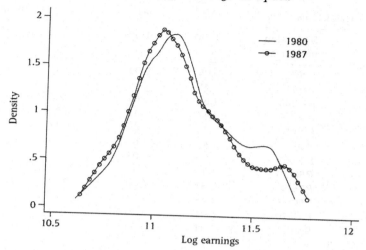

Figure 1.5. *Kernel density estimates: unskilled.*

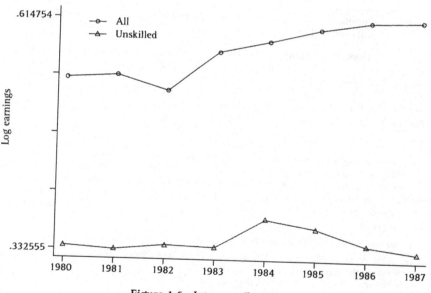

Figure 1.6. *Interquartile range.*

Regarding age, inequality drops among young workers but grows for older workers, especially among the middle-aged. Within sectors, inequality increases everywhere except in Construction and Transport and Public utilities, which suggests that a simple explanation of rising inequality based on a shift of employment shares towards sectors with higher dispersion cannot be the whole story.

O. Bover, S. Bentolila, and M. Arellano

Table 1.3(a). *Labour market variables for selected countries: Wage dispersion*[a]

Country	Dispersion measures	1980	1987	Equivalent seven-year change[b]
France	P90/50	2.05	2.09	0.04
	P50/10	1.45	1.33	−0.12
Germany[c]	P90/50	1.63	1.63	0.00
	P50/10	1.47	1.41	−0.07
UK	P90/50	1.72	1.89	0.17
	P50/10	1.47	1.61	0.14
US	P90/50	1.95	2.09	0.14
	P50/10	2.44	2.70	0.26
US[d]	P75/50	1.36	1.40	0.05
	P50/25	1.45	1.51	0.07
Spain	P75/50	1.31	1.40	0.09
	P50/25	1.31	1.32	0.01

Table 1.3(b). *Labour market variables for selected countries: Variables other than wage dispersion*[e]

Country	Population with a university degree		Share of employment in services		Unemployment rate	
	1989	Change 1979–89	1989	Change 1980–89	1989	Change 1980–89
France	11.1	3.5	63.5	8.1	9.4	3.1
Germany	11.0	5.6	51.4	5.2	3.2	6.9
G. Britain	17.4	5.4	68.5	8.8	6.1	0.0
US	21.5	4.9	70.5	4.6	5.3	−1.9
Spain	8.1	2.8	54.1	9.2	16.7	5.9

Notes: [a]Wage measures: (1) P90/50 and P50/10. France: Gross annual earnings of full-time workers. Germany: Gross monthly earnings plus benefits of full-time full-year workers. UK: Gross hourly earnings of persons paid on adult rates (the 1980 data refer to men under 21). US: Gross hourly earnings, computed as annual earnings divided by annual hours of work, of wage and salary workers.

Source: OECD (1993).

(2) P75/50 and P50/25. US: Gross hourly earnings of full-time workers.

Source: Juhn *et al.* (1993). Spain: Gross monthly earnings (social security taxable rates, own calculations, see the Appendix).

[b]Average change in a seven-year period. Original data multiplied by (7/6) in Germany and the second set of US ratios.

[c]For Germany, the first date is 1981.

[d]For the US, P75/50 and P50/25 are based on data for 1982–88.

[e](1) Population with college degree. France and Germany: Population aged 15 years old and older (for Germany, the change is from 1978 to 1989). G. Britain: Population aged 16–60. US: Population aged 18–64. Spain: Population aged 16–64. Sources for (1) and (2): Katz *et al.* (1995) for France, G. Britain and US; for Germany, Microzensus for 1978 and Statistical Yearbook of the Federal Republic of Germany (1994) for 1989; and EPA (INE) for Spain. (3) Unemployment rate. OECD-standardized rate from OECD Employment Outlook (1999).

How does the Spanish experience compare internationally? Some illustrative data are provided in Table 1.3 for male wages during our period of reference, 1980–87, in several countries. A rigorous comparison is difficult to carry out. First, different measures of wages are available for each country (hourly, monthly, etc.), and for this reason comparisons of levels are not fully appropriate. Secondly, for most countries only the $P90/50$ ratio, for dispersion above the median, and $P50/10$ ratio, for dispersion below the median are usually quoted, whereas in our data for Spain those ratios are censored. Thus, for all countries we present those two ratios, while for Spain and the US we also show the $P75/50$ and the $P50/25$ ratios.

Continental European countries show a pattern of a relatively small increase in dispersion above the median and a reduction in dispersion below the median. On the other hand, Anglo-Saxon countries show increased dispersion both ways. Spain follows a European pattern in that there is little change in dispersion in the lower part of the wage distribution.[14] On the other hand, Spain experienced a very significant increase in dispersion on the upper part, which is actually higher than that observed in the US over the same period.

We can set these observations against the evolution of the population of working age over the period. Table 1.4 presents some data for Spain, where we use the total population aged 16–64 as the reference. The table shows that there was an increase in the share of workers between 20 and 44 years old in the population, mostly at the expense of the eldest cohort (45–64 years old). There was also a uniform shift towards higher schooling which however, as shown in Table 1.3, is lower than in the most developed OECD countries. Thus, the reduced relative supply of older workers is consistent with the rising returns to experience, at least for the eldest group of workers, while the rising supply of educated workers suggests that increases in the demand for skilled workers must have also been at work in bringing about the observed rise in the returns to skill.

As to sectors, Table 1.4 reveals a very significant employment shift into services from all remaining sectors, especially from agriculture. As indicated by Table 1.3, this shift is relatively large by international standards. To the extent that employment in some services has a higher skill content than employment in other sectors, this may be a further factor helping account for the increase in the returns to skill. There may be, of course, increases in the demands for skill within sectors. Table 1.4 also reveals that from 1980 to 1987 the unemployment rate increased by about 6 percentage points for the college and junior college graduates, and by around 9.5 points for the lower skill categories. As is well known, the rise in unemployment in Spain is higher than in most other countries, and its evolution may have affected the wage distribution. In particular, it may have had an apparent wage compression effect through a change in the composition of employment, if workers with the least ability represent a disproportionate share of the pool of

---

[14] This is probably related to the operation of both the legal minimum wage and, especially, the relatively high minimum wages prevalent in sectoral collective agreements (see Bover *et al.*, 2000).

O. Bover, S. Bentolila, and M. Arellano

Table 1.4. Labour market changes in Spain, 1980–87[a]

	Percentage shares		
	1980	1987	Change 1980–87
1. Population by group as a share of population aged 16–64 years old			
Age			
16–19 years old	11.8	11.3	−0.5
20–29 years old	12.2	13.7	1.5
30–44 years old	37.5	38.5	1.0
45–64 years old	38.5	36.6	−2.0
Education			
Secondary or less of which	94.7	92.6	−2.1
– Primary or less	74.9	60.2	−14.7
– Secondary	19.8	32.4	12.6
Junior college	3.3	4.4	1.1
College	2.0	3.1	1.0
2. Sectoral shares in total employment			
Agriculture	19.0	15.5	−3.5
Industry	27.1	24.0	−3.1
Construction	8.9	7.9	−1.0
Services	44.9	52.6	7.6
3. Unemployment rates			
Total	11.4	20.5	9.1
Unskilled	10.7	20.2	9.5
Medium-skilled	11.7	21.1	9.5
Junior college	10.3	16.5	6.3
College	9.7	15.7	6.1

[a] Source: Spanish Labour Force Survey (EPA), first quarter, from INE website (http:// www.ine.es). Note: data not homogenized with post-1987:1 EPA definitions.

unskilled unemployed workers, since these workers' wages disappear from the observed wage distribution when they become unemployed.

The statistics above are suggestive but only have a limited descriptive value. In Section 1.4 we provide a more disaggregate analysis, by computing returns to skill and experience broken down by firm size, sector, and year employing a statistical model. At that stage we use a likelihood estimation procedure, described in Section 1.3, to overcome the problem of censoring. At a second stage, we also try more rigorously to elicit economic forces underlying the structure and evolution of estimated returns to skill and experience, presented in Section 1.6, as suggested by an economic model described in Section 1.5.

1.3. ECONOMETRIC TECHNIQUES

Our data set is an unbalanced panel subject to both left and right censoring, due to bottom and top coding in the Social Security records. Top coding, however, introduces a more severe form of censoring in our empirical conditional earnings distributions than bottom coding.

Letting w_{it}^* denote the underlying log earnings and w_{it} the observed censored log earnings variable, we have

$$w_{it} = d_{1it}c_{1t} + d_{2it}c_{2t} + (1 - d_{1it} - d_{2it})w_{it}^*,$$

where c_{1t} and c_{2t} represent the (log) top and bottom codes, respectively, and d_{1it} and d_{2it} are the censoring indicators

$$d_{1it} = 1(w_{it}^* \leq c_{1t}), \quad d_{2it} = 1(w_{it}^* \geq c_{2t}).$$

We conduct our empirical investigation in two stages. In the first one, we are interested in analysing, over time and across industries, the conditional distributions of log earnings given a set of individual and firm characteristics x_{it} (education—four groups, age—by year, and firm size—three groups). In our data, the censoring points depend on x, but we omit the dependence to simplify the presentation.

Obviously, only the non-censored portions of the conditional distributions of log earnings are non-parametrically identified, with the severity of censoring varying according to x_{it}. Specifically, the θth quantile of w_{it}^* given $x_{it} = \xi$, $Quant_\theta(w_{it}^*|x_{it} = \xi)$, is non-parametrically identified from the censored data provided

$$\theta_1^*(\xi) < \theta < \theta_2^*(\xi),$$

where

$$\theta_1^*(\xi) = \Pr(w_{it} \leq c_{1t} \mid x_{it} = \xi)$$
$$\theta_2^*(\xi) = \Pr(w_{it} \leq c_{2t} \mid x_{it} = \xi)$$

or alternatively, we can write

$$Quant_\theta(w_{it} \mid x_{it}) = \begin{cases} c_{1t} & \text{if } Quant_\theta(w_{it}^* \mid x_{it}) \leq c_{1t} \\ Quant_\theta(w_{it}^* \mid x_{it}) & \text{if } c_{1t} < Quant_\theta(w_{it}^* \mid x_{it}) < c_{2t} \\ c_{2t} & \text{if } Quant_\theta(w_{it}^* \mid x_{it}) \geq c_{2t}. \end{cases}$$

Here, we wish to focus on the modelling of single summary measures of position and dispersion of the conditional distributions of earnings. We proceed by adjusting a normal model with a heteroskedastic variance to the censored data. As an alternative, we could model the conditional median and the conditional interquartile range on the basis of the non-censored observations. Such procedure, however, while apparently more robust, would crucially rely on functional form assumptions when drawing conclusions about the entire median and interquartile regression functions. Log-normality, of course, imposes a strong, not fully testable, parametric assumption on the data, but relative to it, we can make an efficient use of the information to conduct specification searches about the conditional mean and variance of log earnings.

Assuming that log earnings in year t at industry s are conditionally normal,

$$w_{its}^* \mid x_{it} \sim N[\mu_{ts}(x_{it}), \sigma_{ts}^2(x_{it})],$$

an individual observation's contribution to the log-likelihood function for the censored panel takes the form

$$L_{its} = d_{1it} \, \log \Phi \left(\frac{w_{its} - \mu_{its}}{\sigma_{its}} \right) + d_{2it} \, \log \left[1 - \Phi \left(\frac{w_{its} - \mu_{its}}{\sigma_{its}} \right) \right]$$
$$- \frac{1}{2} (1 - d_{1it} - d_{2it}) \left[\log \sigma_{it}^2 + \frac{(w_{its} - \mu_{its})^2}{\sigma_{its}^2} \right].$$

In this expression, the first term represents the contribution to the likelihood if it is a bottom coded observation, the second term if it is top coded, and the last term if it is not censored.

In the empirical analysis, we use linear and exponential representations for μ_{its} and σ_{its}^2, respectively, allowing for firm-size specific returns to education, and linear and quadratic age effects

$$\mu_{its} \equiv \mu_{ts}(x_{it}) = z_{it}'\beta_{ts}$$
$$\sigma_{its}^2 \equiv \sigma_{ts}^2(x_{it}) = \exp(z_{it}'\gamma_{ts}).$$

The vector of variables z_{it} can be described as

$$z_{it}' = (s1, s2, s3, ed1 \times s1, ed2 \times s1, ed3 \times s1,$$
$$ed1 \times (s2 + s3), ed2 \times (s2 + s3), ed3 \times (s2 + s3), age, age^2)_{it}$$

where sj and edj ($j = 1, 2, 3$) denote, respectively, firm-size and education category dummy variables.

In the second stage, we investigate the relationship of the coefficients β_{ts} and γ_{ts} with aggregate and industry specific economic variables. From the point of view of estimation this can be regarded as imposing restrictions on the previous coefficients using minimum distance techniques.

Let the specification for the jth coefficient β_{jts} be of the form

$$\beta_{jts} = h_{ts}'\delta_j \quad (t = 1, \ldots, T; \, s = 1, \ldots, S)$$

where h_{ts} is a vector of aggregate and industry variables including a constant term (the presentation for the coefficients γ_{jts} in the conditional variance would be similar to this). In stacked form, we can write $\beta_j = H\delta_j$, where β_j is a TS vector containing the β_{jts} and H is a TS-rowed matrix whose rows are given by h_{ts}'. A minimum distance estimate of δ_j is

$$\hat{\delta}_j = (H'AH)^{-1}H'A\hat{\beta}_j$$

where $\hat{\beta}_j$ is the vector of the unrestricted estimates $\hat{\beta}_{jts}$, and A is a weighting matrix. Under the assumption of correct specification, the optimal choice of A is a consistent estimate of the inverse of the asymptotic variance of $\hat{\beta}_j$, but plim $\hat{\delta}_j$ is invariant to the choice of A. However, under misspecification the probability limit of $\hat{\delta}_j$ will depend on A.[15] Since in our setting we do not expect the h_{ts} variables to account for all the variation in the β_{jts}, 'misspecification' is to be expected. Thus, it seems appropriate to choose A in such a way that plim $(\hat{\delta}_j)$ represents an easily interpretable summary statistic. We considered two such choices for A leading to OLS $(A = I)$ and weighted least squares by industry size $(A$ equal to a diagonal matrix of industry weights). In both cases consistent standard errors robust to misspecification were obtained from

$$\widehat{Var}(\hat{\delta}_j) = (H'AH)^{-1}H'A\widehat{Var}(\hat{\beta}_j)AH(H'AH)^{-1}.$$

Note that our method in two stages could be reduced to one by considering a pooled log-likelihood function for all periods and industries, subject to the restrictions implied by the dependence of returns on sectoral variables:

$$L(\delta) = \sum_t \sum_s L_{ts}(\mu_{ts}, \sigma_{ts}^2).$$

We did not pursue such a method because of a computational disadvantage (i.e., having to maximize over the full data set), but more fundamentally because it would require to impose all the restrictions simultaneously. As a result the estimated effects would be more sensitive to misspecification. Moreover, we are interested in analysing first stage results *per se*, independent of our ability to relate them to economic variables in the second stage.

The assumption of conditional independence across workers is more plausible than that of independence over time of the observations for a given worker. In the event of autocorrelation, $L(\delta)$ will only be a pseudo log-likelihood, but our period specific log-likelihoods will remain unaltered. Nevertheless, the estimated $\hat{\beta}_{jts}$ for different periods will be correlated, which will potentially affect the consistency of the estimates of $Var(\hat{\beta}_j)$ that we employ.

1.4. THE EVOLUTION OF EARNINGS AND RETURNS TO SKILL AND EXPERIENCE

We now describe the results from our estimation of an earnings equation for each industry and year. Our aim is to obtain estimates of the returns to skill and experience. As described in Section 1.3, in a second stage these estimates are themselves regressed on a set of sectoral and aggregate economic variables.

Although the database included information on the firm's region of location, we do not use it. The reason is that there are hardly any data available on

---

[15] In general, for a fixed A: plim $\hat{\delta}_j = (H'AH)^{-1}H'A\beta_j$. If $\beta_j = H\delta_j$ then plim $\hat{\delta}_j = \delta_j$ for any A. But if $\beta_j \neq H\delta_j$, $(H'AH)^{-1}H'A\beta_j$ is a pseudo true parameter whose value depends on A.

economic variables varying simultaneously by region and sector and thus, having to choose, we considered the sectoral variation more important from an economic point of view than regional variation.

We introduce as regressors observable characteristics of workers and firms. Returns to potential experience are meant to be captured by the worker's *Age*, measured in years, and its square. All remaining regressors are dummy variables. Returns to skill are captured by the skill variable discussed in Section 1.2, which considers four groups: *College* graduates, *Junior college* graduates, *Medium-skilled* workers, and *Unskilled* workers. Employer size is captured through a breakdown into three categories: *Small*, *Medium-sized*, and *Large* firms.

We estimate the following specification for conditional mean log earnings for each industry $(s = 1, \ldots, 8)$ and year $(t = 1981, \ldots, 1987)$:[16]

$$
\begin{aligned}
\mu_{its} = {} & \beta_{1ts}\ Small + \beta_{2ts}\ Medium\text{-}sized + \beta_{3ts}\ Large \\
& + \beta_{4ts}\ College \times Small \\
& + \beta_{5ts}\ College \times (Medium\text{-}sized + Large) \\
& + \beta_{6ts}\ Junior\ college \times Small \\
& + \beta_{7ts}\ Junior\ college \times (Medium\text{-}sized + Large) \\
& + \beta_{8ts}\ Medium\text{-}skilled \times Small \\
& + \beta_{9ts}\ Medium\text{-}skilled \times\ + \beta_{10ts}\ Age + \beta_{11ts}\ Age^2
\end{aligned}
\tag{1.1}
$$

and a similar specification for the log of the conditional variance of log earnings.

Estimates of returns to skill from sectoral regressions may be biased if there is dynamic self-selection of workers to those sectors where their returns are higher. However, in our case we can essentially treat sectoral adscription as a fixed effect, since in our sample a very small proportion of workers change sector from one year to the next (below 1 per cent).

Unskilled workers constitute the reference (i.e. omitted) group, so that the β coefficients capture returns vis-à-vis that group. Equation (1.1) shows that returns to skill are allowed to vary between small firms and larger ones only, large and medium-sized firms having been pooled in these interactions so as to save on degrees of freedom. Average returns to a given characteristic are obtained by averaging the estimated β_{jts} coefficients across sectors, using the number of observations as weights. For instance, average returns to college in small firms in 1981 are given by

$$
\bar{\beta}_{1981}^{c,small} = \frac{1}{N_{1981}^{c,small}} \sum_s \hat{\beta}_{4,1981,s} N_{1981,s}^{c,small}
$$

where $N_s^{c,small}$ denotes the number of observations belonging to workers with a college education working at small firms in sector s.

---

[16] We lose the first year in the sample, 1980, due to the unavailability of one sectoral variable used at the second stage below—union coverage.

1.4.1. Estimated Earnings and Returns to Skill and Experience

The first stage provides us with estimates for four blocks of variables: (a) the common component of earnings for all workers or *basic earnings*, separately for small, medium-sized, and large firms ($\hat{\beta}_{1ts}$ to $\hat{\beta}_{3ts}$); (b) *returns to college*, separately for small and medium-large firms ($\hat{\beta}_{4ts}$ and $\hat{\beta}_{5ts}$); (c) *returns to junior college*, also for small and medium-large firms ($\hat{\beta}_{6ts}$ and $\hat{\beta}_{7ts}$); and (d) *returns to experience* (*age*) ($\hat{\beta}_{10ts} + 2\hat{\beta}_{11ts}Age$). We also obtain results for the medium-skill group, but we will hardly present them, given that the heterogeneity of education among workers within this group makes it difficult to provide an economic interpretation for them.

We discuss the results of the first stage estimation using graphs. Starting with earnings levels, Fig. 1.7 shows how they are affected by firm size, for different educational categories. The pictures portray the sum of basic earnings plus the interaction of the respective skill dummy with the firm size dummy. For example, the bottom line in panel (a) of Fig. 1.7 corresponds to college-educated workers in small firms, i.e. the weighted average of the sum $\hat{\beta}_{1ts} + \hat{\beta}_{4ts}$.

The figure indicates that, in general, larger firms pay their workers more than smaller firms at all educational levels, but particularly at the college level. This accords with the well-known employer size–wage effect described by Brown and Medoff (1989). Several factors may underlie this effect, ranging from neoclassical explanations (larger firms employ higher-quality workers, they have greater capital intensity, or they pay higher wages to reduce monitoring costs—which are presumably more important than in smaller firms—or to compensate for worse working conditions) to more institutional ones (larger firms have more monopoly power or, in the US, they pay higher wages in the non-union sector to avoid unionization). None of these explanations receives strong empirical support, so that no wide consensus has been reached yet on the most important sources of the size–wage effect, as indicated by the survey by Oi and Idson (1999), although these authors' reading of the evidence leads them towards the explanation based on workers being more able in large firms (Idson and Oi, 1999).

Aside from this difference in levels, the evolution is similar across firm sizes: earnings go down until 1985 and then recover in 1986–87 for all groups, except for college degree workers. But the size of the recovery varies. Basic earnings and earnings of medium-skilled workers end up lower in 1987 than in 1981 for all firm sizes. Workers with college or junior college degrees end up about level. The two outliers are workers in large firms with a junior college degree, whose earnings increase, and those in small firms with a college degree, whose earnings fall.

We now focus on the returns to college and junior college. The top panels of Figs 1.9–1.12 indicate that, as happened for total earnings, returns to college are larger in medium–large firms than in small firms, but returns to junior college are similar in both size classes.

As to their evolution, the top panels of Figs 1.10–1.12 show significant increases for both returns in medium–large firms. Returns to junior college in small firms are essentially flat, the mild increase apparent in Fig. 1.11(a) being the

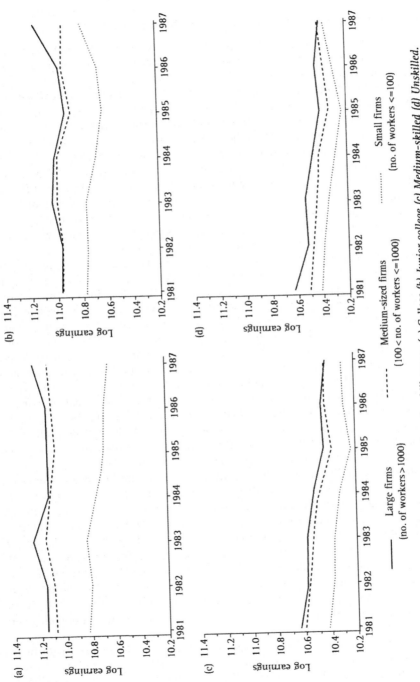

Figure 1.7. *Effect of firm size on earnings, by skill group: (a) College (b) Junior college (c) Medium-skilled (d) Unskilled.*

effect of an outlying sector. The most striking result is the decrease, for small firms, in the returns to college. We will discuss this finding below, in Section 1.6.1, once we have gathered further empirical results. For now, let us just say that this finding is consistent with the idea, advanced above, that employees in smaller firms are less productive than those in larger firms, and hence they command lower wages in the labour market. Alternatively, it may be an effect of composition. In small firms the proportion of clerical workers with college and junior college degrees is bigger than at large firms and, moreover, that proportion appears to have risen and this pulls down the mean. This composition effect might also explain in part why, in small firms, returns to junior college are about the same as returns to college at the end of the sample (cf. the top panels of Figs 1.9–1.11), and also the increasing difference between small and medium–large firms in the returns to college. This composition hypothesis receives some support when we estimate and explain the behaviour of conditional variances (see below).

It is instructive to look at these estimates at a disaggregated level, shown in Fig. 1.8 for small firms (patterns are similar across size classes). The Basic earnings are highest in Construction (1), where unskilled workers are valued the most, and lowest in Finance, insurance, and real estate (5). As to returns to college, the downward trend in small firms (Fig. 1.9) mainly reflects the falling returns in Transport and public utilities (3) and Finance (5), which, together with Mining (8),

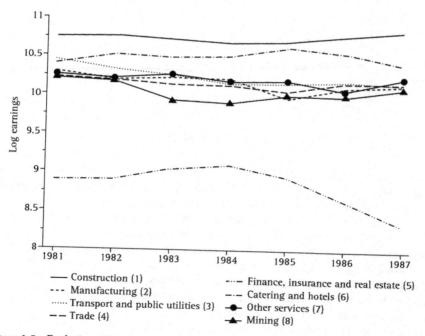

Figure 1.8. *Evolution of the common component of earnings, by sector: Small-sized firms.*

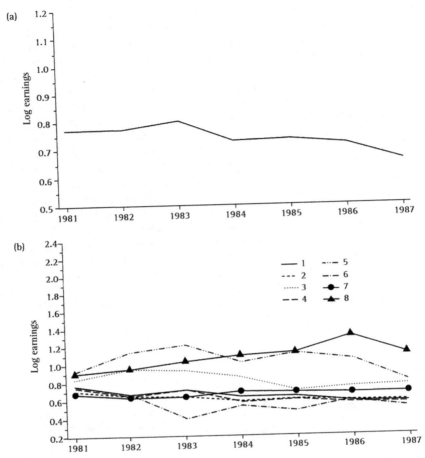

Figure 1.9. *Returns to college: Small firms. (a) Average (b) By industries.*

have been the sectors with the highest returns to college within that size class. Indeed, Mining is the only sector with a clear upward trend, a result which would be consistent with a compositional interpretation of the overall downward pattern in small firms (i.e., high-education workers are more homogeneous in this sector). As for medium–large firms, the upward trend in the returns to college is present in all sectors (Fig. 1.10). The mildly increasing average estimate of returns to junior college in small firms (Fig. 1.11) is fully driven by Transport and public utilities (3); it becomes constant when this sector is left out. In contrast, the upward trend in these returns in medium–large firms (Fig. 1.12) is widespread, and remains when Trade (4) is excluded.

Returns to potential experience, proxied by age, are shown in Fig. 1.13. As expected, these returns are higher the younger the worker; given concavity, the

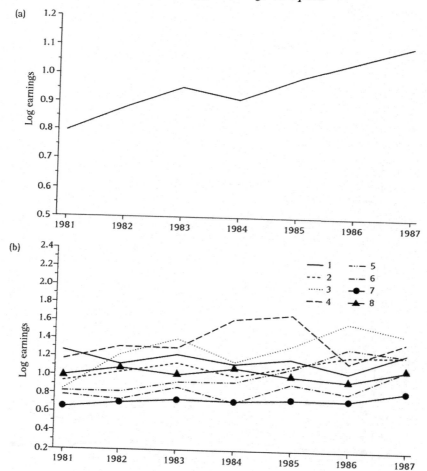

Figure 1.10. *Returns to college: Medium-sized and large firms. (a) Average (b) By industries.*

earnings profile peaks around 45–55 years old, depending on sector and firm size. Over the period, returns to experience remain roughly constant for the youngest workers (e.g., 22 years old) and increase for older ones. By sectors, it is in Finance (5) that young workers get the highest returns, although these decrease rapidly over the life-cycle so that this sector ends up having the lowest returns for older workers (cf. panels (b) and (d)). While specially acute in Finance, most sectors show an increase in the returns to experience over the whole period.

In conclusion, the main stylized facts arising from our estimates are as follows: (i) pay is positively related to firm size; (ii) basic earnings fall until 1985 and rise thereafter; (iii) in medium-sized and large firms, returns to both college and junior college rise; (iv) in small firms, returns to junior college remain essentially

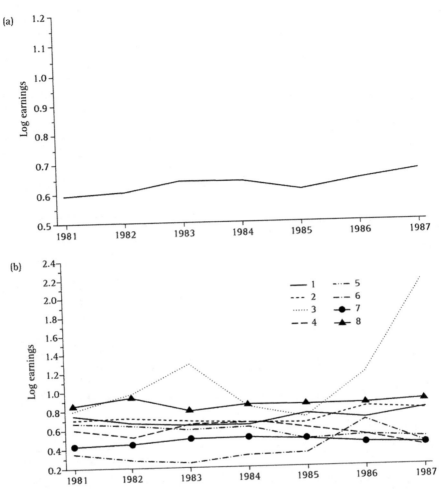

Figure 1.11. *Returns to junior college: Small firms. (a) Average (b) By industries.*

constant (except for Transport and public utilities, with a sharp increase in 1986–87) while returns to college clearly fall, and (v) returns to potential experience steadily increase over the period.

1.4.2. Estimated Conditional Variances

Our estimates, graphed in Fig. 1.14, show that the behaviour of the log conditional variance of log earnings varies with skill type.[17] For college and junior college

---

[17] This refers to the sum of the variance intercept estimate by size plus the coefficient on the interaction between the skill dummies and the size dummies.

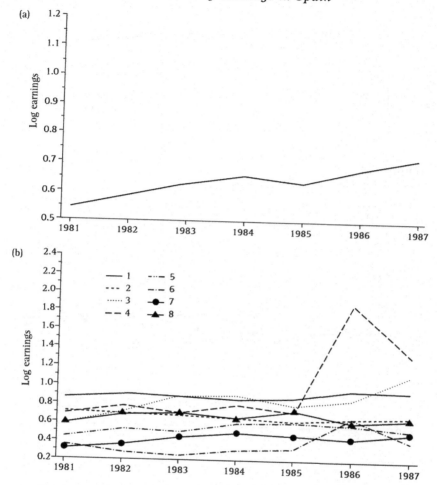

Figure 1.12. *Returns to junior college: Medium-sized and large firms.*
(a) Average (b) By industries.

earnings, the variance is in general lower the larger the firm; while for medium-skilled and basic earnings, it is smaller and similar for all firm sizes, with no stable ranking across size groups. The two high-skill groups experience an increasing variance over time, although for junior college graduates this is marked only in small firms, where it results from the behaviour of only one sector (Transport and public utilities), as discussed below. The lowest two skill groups show little change in variance over time.[18]

---

[18] Graphs for conditional variances by sector are not presented to save space, but are available upon request.

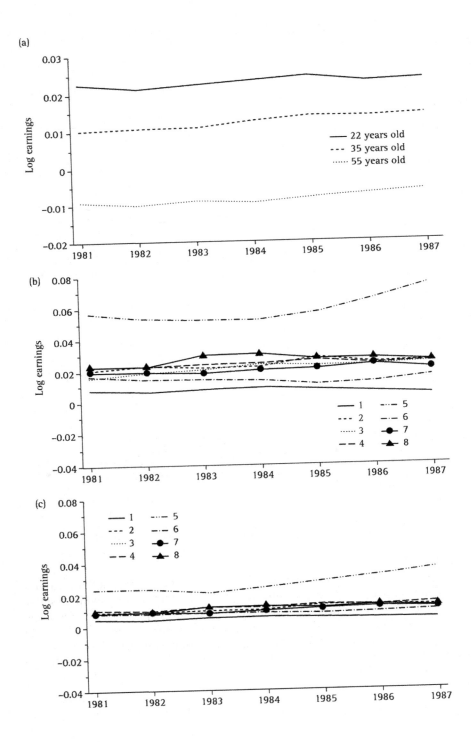

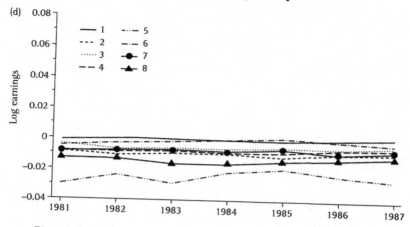

Figure 1.13. *Returns to age. (a) Average (b) By sectors 22 years old (c) By sectors 35 years old (d) By sectors 55 years old.*

Indeed, the conditional variance for college education increases significantly regardless of firm size (Fig. 1.15) and sector.[19] On the other hand, the variance for junior college increases mostly after 1985 (Fig. 1.16). This variance is plotted both including and excluding Transport and public utilities, in view of the enormous increase in variance experienced in small firms belonging to this sector in 1986–87. Overall, for all but medium-skill earnings, Transport and public utilities has the highest variance, whereas Mining is a high variance sector in basic earnings, as are Construction and Trade for junior college. Finance shows an increasing variance for college, which reaches high values from 1985 on.

Lastly, the variance is higher the younger the worker is, and shows no trend over the 1980s (Fig. 1.17). By sector, Trade has the highest variance for young workers and the lowest for older ones.

1.5. A STYLIZED MODEL OF WAGE SETTING

In the second stage of our empirical analysis we wish to study the determinants of the evolution of basic earnings and returns to skill and experience. In the literature this is typically done by examining changes in the supply of and the demand for labour of different types. Thus, for example, in the US a key issue has been to explain why, in the face of sizable increases in the supply of highly educated labour, the returns to skill have experienced a significant increase in the 1980s and 1990s. The key factors explaining this puzzle appear to have been the increase in physical capital, which is presumed to be complementary with skills, and skill-biased technological progress (see e.g. Katz and Murphy, 1992; or Mincer, 1991).

[19] This refers to the estimates for skill groups interacted with firm size groups, i.e. not considering the intercepts by size.

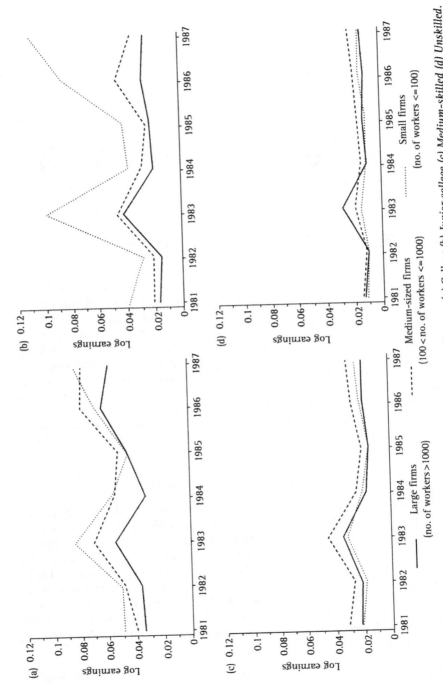

Figure 1.14. *Effect of firm size on the conditional log-variance, by skill group: (a) College (b) Junior college (c) Medium-skilled (d) Unskilled.*

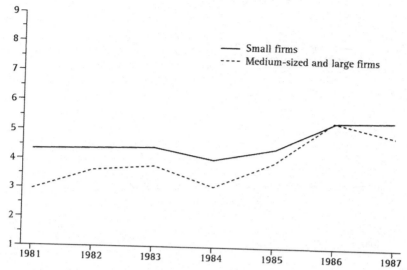

Figure 1.15. *Effect of college education on the conditional log-variance.*

In Section 1.2 we saw that some of the labour supply changes experienced in Spain conform, to a higher or lower degree, to those experienced in other OECD countries. Thus, in our empirical analysis we will consider such changes. However, our data set for Spain covers a relatively short period (seven years), spanning less than a full business cycle, rather than the long periods over which labour supply and demand interplay so as to determine equilibrium returns to skill. Our goal is to investigate other types of potentially relevant factors, considering in particular labour market institutions, which show enough variation over the sample.[20] As described in Section 1.2, wages are set in Spain in a relatively centralized way, with labour unions playing a key role. Thus, our next step is to develop a theoretical framework with union wage bargaining at the centre, which will serve as a guide for the empirical analysis of the evolution of the estimated returns to skill and experience presented in the preceding section.

There exists some literature on the effects of unions on returns to skill and wage inequality, most of which is empirical, generally finding that unions tend to compress the wage structure.[21] A recent theoretical model is provided in Acemoglu *et al.* (2000), which focuses on skill-biased technological change and assumes that unions play two roles: they set wages for both skilled and unskilled workers, thereby compressing wages, and they impede the firing of unskilled employees. The main result in that framework is that the increase in wage inequality is caused

---

[20] The interaction between union power and wage inequality has also been explored for the US by, e.g., Card (1992) and Freeman (1993).

[21] Acemoglu *et al.* (2000) provide a brief survey of the literature.

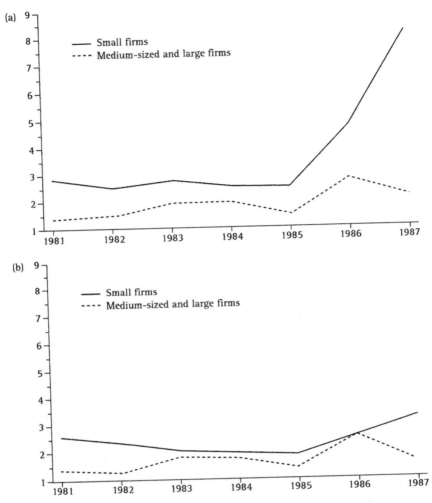

Figure 1.16. *Effect of junior college education on the conditional log-variance.*
(a) Average (b) Excluding Transport and public utilities.

by skill-biased technological change rather than by deunionization, but the latter does amplify the effects of the former. In contrast, in our model, unions only set wages for unskilled workers and do not play any role in firing decisions. These two features seem to us to be better suited to the features of the Spanish labour market, as described in Section 1.2.

We now present a simple model of wage bargaining at firms employing two types of labour, skilled and unskilled, and operating in imperfectly competitive product markets.

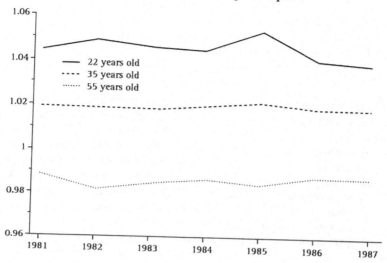

Figure 1.17. *Effect of age on the conditional log-variance.*

1.5.1. Product Market Structure and Labour Demand

For unskilled workers, wage setting is assumed to follow the right-to-manage structure, by which wages are set through bargaining between worker representatives and the firm's managers (hereafter called the firm).[22] Then, after the unskilled wage is set, the firm chooses the quantity of unskilled labour it wants to hire, as determined by its labour demand schedule. At this second stage the firm also decides how much skilled labour to employ. It can draw from a pool of skilled workers, but it is assumed to face a labour supply schedule, so that it has to pay a higher wage the higher the amount of skilled labour it wants to hire.

As usual, we solve backwards: first for skilled and unskilled labour demands, and then for the unskilled wage, which is determined by bargaining given agents' knowledge of those labour demand curves.

The firm maximizes real profits, π, subject to a Cobb–Douglas production function, an isoelastic product demand curve, and an isoelastic skilled labour supply curve, respectively:[23]

$$\pi = PY - W_u N_u - W_s N_s \tag{1.2}$$

[22] Although sub-optimal as compared with efficient bargains, the right-to-manage model appears to be a good description of wage bargains—especially once high-skill workers are excluded—in Europe in general, and in Spain in particular (see Layard *et al.*, 1991; Bentolila and Dolado, 1994, respectively).

[23] Note that the parameters δ and γ (with no subindex) used in this section are unrelated to the same parameters (typically with subindices) used in preceding sections. The same is true of parameter β in the next subsection.

$$Y = AN_u^\alpha N_s^{1-\alpha} \tag{1.3}$$

$$P = Y^{-\frac{1}{\eta}} \tag{1.4}$$

$$N_s = \delta^{-1} W_s^\delta \tag{1.5}$$

where P is the firm's product real price, in terms of an aggregate price index, Y is the output, A is total factor productivity, and N_s and N_u are, respectively, skilled and unskilled labour, which are paid real wages W_s and W_u. All coefficients are positive: α captures the unskilled labour intensity in production, η the price elasticity of product demand, and δ the wage elasticity of skilled labour supply. We assume that $0 < \alpha < 1$ and $\eta > 1$. The parameter A could also be interpreted as including a predetermined input like capital and, in general, we might allow for decreasing returns to labour, i.e., the sum of the coefficients on N_s and N_u being less than one; constant returns are just assumed for simplicity.

The first order conditions for the optimal choice of skilled and unskilled labour are given by

$$N_s = \left(\frac{\delta}{1+\delta} (1-\alpha) \kappa A^\kappa N_u^{\alpha\kappa} W_s^{-1} \right)^{-1/(1-(1-\alpha)\kappa)} \tag{1.6}$$

$$N_u = (\alpha\kappa A^\kappa N_s^{(1-\alpha)\kappa} W_u^{-1})^{1/(1-\alpha\kappa)} \tag{1.7}$$

where $\kappa \equiv 1 - 1/\eta$ captures the degree of competition in the product market. Operating on (1.2)–(1.7), we can obtain expressions for the optimal N_s and N_u as functions of the unskilled wage level W_u alone, which are used as constraints on the bargaining game.

1.5.2. Wage Bargaining

We assume that unskilled workers are represented by a labour union, which bargains with the firm so as to maximize the Nash product[24]

$$\Omega = (U_u - \tilde{U}_u)^\beta (\pi - \tilde{\pi}) \tag{1.8}$$

where U_u and β denote, respectively, the utility level and the bargaining power of the union, and $\tilde{U}_u$ and $\tilde{\pi}$ denote the agents' reservation values. $\beta \geq 0$ is a natural restriction.[25]

Labour union utility can be represented as being utilitarian, in the following way:[26]

$$U_u = N_u V_u[W_u] + (L_u - N_u)\tilde{V}_u$$

[24] We are therefore assuming away any strategic interactions among agents, which may give rise to alternative equilibria.

[25] The bargaining framework we assume follows Layard *et al.* (1991).

[26] This corresponds to maximizing the utility of the median voter once we assume that layoffs of unskilled workers are by random assignment.

where L_u is union membership and N_u the number of employed members. $V_u[W_u]$ and $\tilde{V}_u$ respectively denote utility obtained by employed and unemployed union members. The latter may be characterized as

$$\tilde{V}_u = \tilde{V}_u[u_u B_u + (1 - u_u)\tilde{W}_u)]. \tag{1.9}$$

In other words, it depends on the variables determining 'expected' income, namely: unskilled workers' unemployment rate, u_u, the wage they can obtain elsewhere, $\tilde{W}_u$, and the real unemployment benefit level, B_u.

Assuming $\tilde{U}_u = L_u \tilde{V}_u$, we can rewrite equation (1.8) as follows:

$$\Omega = ((V_u[W_u] - \tilde{V}_u)N_u)^\beta (\pi - \tilde{\pi}).$$

This objective function is maximized subject to the first order conditions (1.6) and (1.7). Setting the firm's status quo point, $\tilde{\pi}$, to zero for simplicity, we obtain the first order condition for W_u:

$$\beta \frac{V_u' W_u}{V_u - \tilde{V}_u} - \beta - (1 + \beta)s_u = 0$$

where $V_u' \equiv dV_u/dW_u$ and $s_u \equiv W_u N_u/\pi$.

With the additional assumption of isoelastic utility,

$$V_u = \gamma^{-1} W_u^\gamma$$

with $\gamma > 0$, the preceding equation can be rewritten in terms of a utility markup (M_u)

$$M_u = \frac{V_u - \tilde{V}_u}{V_u} = \frac{\beta \gamma}{\beta + (1 + \beta)s_u} \tag{1.10}$$

where $s_u = \frac{\alpha \kappa}{1 - \alpha \kappa - (1-\alpha)\kappa \delta/(1+\delta)}$. It is immediate from (1.10) that in this case $M_u \geq 0$, so that the participation constraint is satisfied.

Comparative statics are straightforward:

$$\frac{\partial M_u}{\partial \beta} > 0; \quad \frac{\partial M_u}{\partial \gamma} > 0; \quad \frac{\partial M_u}{\partial \alpha} < 0; \quad \frac{\partial M_u}{\partial \delta} < 0;$$

$$\frac{\partial M_u}{\partial \kappa} < 0; \quad \frac{\partial M_u}{\partial \tilde{V}_u} > 0. \tag{1.11}$$

In other words, the markup is higher: the lower the unskilled labour intensity in production (α), the higher the union's bargaining power (β) and workers' reservation value ($\tilde{V}_u$), and the more the union cares about wages (γ); the lower the wage elasticity of skilled labour supply (δ); and the lower the degree of competition in the product market (κ). These are all standard, except for δ. The higher δ, the less costly it is for the firm to increase its use of skilled labour, which should, *ceteris paribus*, hurt unskilled workers' wages.

Let us now turn to the log unskilled wage and the log skill premium, for which our empirical model is estimated. Equation (1.10) implies that

$$w_u \equiv \log W_u = \gamma^{-1} \log(\gamma(1 - M_u)^{-1} \tilde{V}_u). \tag{1.12}$$

Thus, for most parameters, the effects on M_u carry through to W_u : sign$(\partial w_u / \partial \lambda) = $ sign$(\partial M_u / \partial \lambda)$, for $\lambda = \{\beta, \alpha, \delta, \kappa, \tilde{V}_u\}$. The exception is the preference parameter γ: although it might be natural to expect the positive sign in (1.11) to also carry through, the actual effect is ambiguously signed. This happens because, due to the nonlinear relationship between W_u and M_u induced by the isoelastic preference specification, an increase in γ has two types of effects: it raises all the level terms but it also reduces the exponent (γ^{-1}).[27] In any event, in our numerical simulations mentioned below, the positive sign is always obtained.

Turning now to the skill premium, the combination of conditions (1.6) and (1.7) yields a very simple expression for the relative skilled–unskilled wage bill:

$$\frac{W_s N_s}{W_u N_u} = \frac{1 - \alpha}{\alpha} \frac{\delta}{1 + \delta}.$$

Clearly, this relative total remuneration does not depend on union activity. It depends on technology and on the elasticity of skilled labour supply. The skill premium does however depend on union activity, because there is a tradeoff between skilled–unskilled relative wages and relative employment or—given the labour forces—unemployment, and the union cares about such a tradeoff.

From conditions (6) and (7) plus the labour supply curve, we get the following expression for the skill premium as a function solely of W_u:

$$\frac{W_s}{W_u} = \left(\frac{1 - \alpha}{1 + \delta} \alpha^{\alpha\kappa} \delta^{2-(1+\alpha)\kappa} \kappa A^\kappa W_u^{-(1+\delta(1-\kappa))} \right)^{1/(1-\alpha\kappa+\delta(1-\kappa))}.$$

From this expression plus the solution for w_u in (1.12), we can compute the effects of the parameters on the log skill premium, $\omega_s \equiv w_s - w_u$. The parameters β, γ, and $\tilde{V}_u$ appear only through W_u, and so their effects are oppositely signed as those on W_u. The other parameters turn out to have ambiguously signed effects. This is due to the Cobb–Douglas production function plus the positive elasticity of skilled labour supply. Thus, we have carried out numerical simulations with $0 < \alpha < 0.5$ (as a way to distinguish unskilled from skilled labour) and parameter values which satisfy the appropriate restrictions.[28] For κ, α, and δ, depending on the parameter set, we get positive or negative effects, so that we cannot discard either. Perhaps the most unusual result we get is that skilled-biased technological change (a lower α) might in some cases reduce the skill premium.

---

[27] Note that, while we have not specified a functional form for $\tilde{V}_u$, it would be natural to use the isoelastic one: $\tilde{V}_u = \gamma^{-1} [u_u B_u + (1 - u_u) \bar{W}_u)]^\gamma$.

[28] Namely: $\beta \geq 0, \gamma > 0, \delta > 0, 0 \leq \kappa \leq 1, V_u > 0$. A is taken as a scale variable and set to 1.

Given the definition of reservation utility in equation (1.9), an increase in the unemployment rate prevailing among unskilled workers, u_u, would lower $\tilde{V}_u$ and W_u, thus raising ω_s. If we had considered a reservation utility level for the skilled, then it would be natural to expect that an increase in the unemployment rate among skilled workers (u_s) would lower the reservation value, thus lowering the skill premium.[29]

The model we have presented is very stylized. For instance, the Cobb–Douglas assumption imposes a unit elasticity of substitution between labour types, and some of the results are specific to this assumption. Additionally, our model is static, thereby neglecting any forward-looking behaviour or any dynamics in member-ship or employment. It also means that we ignore the influence of factors such as union bargaining power on the dynamic response of firms regarding, for instance, technology choice. Moreover, we have not considered the capital stock in the production function, and have thus ignored a potentially important source of wage inequality arising from capital–skill complementarity (see Krusell *et al.*, 1997).

Nevertheless, the model provides us with a framework for understanding the determinants of earnings and returns to skill. We therefore use it in the empirical section below as a guide for the choice of variables and for the interpretation of the signs obtained. Lastly, note that, by providing a single predicted value for the wage of each type of worker, the model leads to the interpretation of conditional variances of wages given skill as arising from unobserved heterogeneity within labour-type groups.

1.6. THE DETERMINANTS OF EARNINGS AND RETURNS TO SKILL AND EXPERIENCE

1.6.1. Basic Earnings and Returns to Skill

As mentioned before, the first stage provides us with estimates for the conditional means and variances of basic earnings (three firm size classes), returns to junior college and college (two firm size classes each), and returns to potential experi-ence. For each of these eight variables we have fifty-six estimated coefficients (i.e., 8 sectors × 7 years). The second stage consists of regressing these coefficients on a set of national and sectoral economic variables. We estimate the following type of regression for each set of coefficients j $(j = 1, \ldots, 8)$:

$$\hat{\beta}_{jts} = f(Union\ coverage_{ts}, Firm\text{-}level\ coverage_{ts}, Public\ employment_{ts},$$

$$Hiring\ rate_{t-1,s}, Long\text{-}term\ unemployment_t,$$

$$Unskilled\ unemployment_{t-1}, Skilled\text{-}Unskilled\ unemployment_{t-1},$$

$$R\&D_{t-1,s}, University\ degree\ population_t, Population\ 20\text{-}24_t, Sector_s).$$

$$(1.13)$$

---

[29] Considering capital would also imply that the wage markup would depend on the ratio of the firm's product demand relative to its capital, see Layard *et al.* (1991).

The regressors in equation (1.13) are intended to capture the determinants of earnings, as suggested by our theoretical model in Section 1.5. For each variable, we will discuss both how it relates to the theory and its estimated effect. In order to capture any variation in the estimated coefficients coming from forces left out of the model, we also include a few additional variables, listed below.

We start by presenting the results for the conditional means of basic earnings and returns to skill, leaving the discussion of returns to experience and conditional variances to subsequent sections. The estimates, from weighted least squares, are shown in Table 1.5.[30]

There are five blocks of variables, measuring: time-invariant sectoral characteristics, union bargaining power, reservation utility levels, technological change, and labour supply.[31] Let us take them in turn.

1. Time-invariant sectoral characteristics regarding technology (α), the degree of product market competition (κ), workers' bargaining power (β), etc., are represented by sectoral dummies. These may, however, also capture the fact that our measure of skill through the number of years of education may be a poor one, which could be refined if we observed the actual type of studies completed. In general, college graduates may correspond to different occupations in different sectors. It is more likely, for instance, to find college graduates with narrow job opportunities (e.g., with degrees in Philosophy) performing less skilled tasks in Other services than in Transport and public utilities (cf. Fig. 1.10, panel (b)). As a result, sectoral dummies may also capture skill composition effects.

The last line in Table 1.5 presents the goodness-of-fit statistic R^2 for regressions of the first-stage coefficients on sectoral dummy variables alone. These statistics are relatively high, which suggests that most of the variation in the dependent variables is of a cross-section rather than a time-series nature. Since, for the above reason, sectoral dummy variables are included alongside economic variables in these regressions, the latter not only capture any time-series variation but they also complement and/or compete with the dummies in explaining the cross-section variation. This fact, coupled with our having data for only seven years, may help explain why few economic variables attain high statistical significance.

Table 1.5 also shows the R^2 statistics for regressions with both sectoral dummies and a time trend. The full results of this specification are reported in Table 1.10, in which the trends are significant for all variables but one (returns to junior college in small firms). In several sectors, the R^2 statistics show that the trend already accounts for almost as much of the variation in the dependent variable as all the economic variables included together. Nevertheless, inclusion of economic variables obviously allows for an economic interpretation of the results which is precluded in the case of the trend, although, given lack of precision of the estimated effects, we will focus on their signs rather than their relative magnitudes.

---

[30] OLS estimates are very similar and are available from the authors upon request.

[31] Details on definitions and sources are given in the Appendix. The evolutions of sectoral and aggregate variables, and their sectoral breakdown, are shown in Tables 1.8 and 1.9, respectively.

Table 1.5. Determinants of basic earnings and returns[a]

	Basic earnings			Returns to junior college		Returns to college		Returns to experience
	Firm size			Firm size		Firm size		
	small	med.	large	small	med.–large	small	med.–large	
Union coverage (t,s)	−0.058 (0.41)	0.044 (0.30)	0.123 (0.81)	0.074 (0.60)	−0.033 (0.28)	−0.210 (1.85)	−0.106 (0.57)	—
Firm-level coverage (t,s)	0.888 (1.04)	1.082 (1.25)	0.806 (0.91)	1.963 (1.03)	0.134 (0.17)	−0.748 (0.87)	1.087 (0.90)	−0.0221 (2.98)
Public employment (t,s)	−0.010 (1.22)	−0.011 (1.26)	−0.015 (1.69)	−0.028 (0.81)	0.001 (0.14)	—	0.014 (0.93)	0.0003 (3.40)
Hiring rate (t−s)	0.006 (3.02)	0.007 (3.14)	0.010 (4.18)	—	0.006 (2.03)	—	—	−0.0001 (5.41)
Long-term unemployment (t)	−0.002 (0.29)	−0.005 (0.85)	−0.007 (1.16)	—	—	0.006 (1.11)	0.012 (3.16)	—
Unskilled unemployment (t−1)	−0.018 (2.35)	−0.022 (2.81)	−0.020 (2.46)	—	—	—	—	—
College − unskilled unemployment (t−1)	—	—	—	—	—	—	−0.006 (0.73)	—
J.coll.-unsk. unempl.(t−1)	—	—	—	−0.013 (0.92)	−0.021 (1.48)	—	—	—
R&D (t−1,s)	0.001 (0.11)	0.023 (1.81)	0.023 (1.77)	—	−0.033 (1.80)	0.002 (0.21)	—	—
University degree pop. (t)	—	—	—	—	—	−0.063 (1.91)	—	—
Population aged 20–24 (t)	—	—	—	—	—	—	—	0.7317 (11.43)
Constant	10.354 (52.56)	10.454 (51.73)	10.510 (51.00)	0.366 (1.15)	0.823 (3.67)	1.234 (5.77)	0.295 (1.42)	−0.0789 (9.91)
Construction	0.509 (2.45)	0.572 (2.67)	0.515 (2.33)	0.416 (1.06)	−0.256 (0.88)	−0.189 (0.97)	0.237 (1.04)	−0.0066 (3.97)
Transport & public utilities	0.329 (0.76)	0.527 (1.19)	0.922 (2.03)	1.142 (0.81)	−0.084 (0.20)	0.344 (1.33)	−0.776 (1.12)	−0.0060 (1.63)
Trade	0.108 (0.57)	0.242 (1.24)	0.306 (1.52)	0.070 (0.29)	0.093 (0.54)	−0.144 (0.84)	0.476 (2.39)	−0.0018 (1.44)
Finance, etc.	−1.186 (6.65)	−1.092 (5.96)	−1.076 (5.75)	0.063 (0.28)	−0.330 (1.80)	0.308 (2.01)	0.087 (0.54)	0.0126 (11.04)
Hotels and catering	0.467 (2.28)	0.616 (2.92)	0.529 (2.43)	−0.064 (0.23)	—	−0.235 (1.25)	−0.036 (0.17)	−0.0059 (4.32)
Other services	0.724 (1.44)	0.951 (1.85)	1.261 (2.39)	1.566 (0.76)	−0.541 (0.88)	−0.196 (1.18)	−1.061 (1.26)	−0.0189 (4.31)
Mining	−0.085 (0.96)	−0.070 (0.76)	−0.072 (0.76)	0.129 (0.94)	0.113 (1.04)	0.468 (5.34)	−0.218 (1.91)	−0.0006 (0.77)
R^2	0.964	0.944	0.944	0.655	0.801	0.853	0.799	0.947
R^2 trend + sec. dums.	0.962	0.941	0.935	0.629	0.816	0.833	0.772	0.937
R^2 sectoral dummies	0.955	0.930	0.929	0.606	0.761	0.818	0.660	0.883

Notes: [a]Weighted least squares estimates. The reference sector is manufacturing. Units: all variables in percentage terms except the share of the population of 20–24 years old, union coverage, and firm-level coverage.

Source: Own calculations on Social Security data set (see Appendix).

2. Union bargaining power (β) is meant to be captured by three sectoral variables.[32] *Union coverage* is the share of employees covered by any type of collective agreement. As predicted by the model, it is found to raise basic earnings and to lower returns to skill or, in other words, to reduce wage dispersion.[33] The second finding is more robust for returns to college than for returns to junior college.

In Spain, wage rates agreed to in sectoral bargains are in effect binding floors for any lower-level bargains. Consequently, the *share of employees covered by firm-level agreements* is expected to raise wages further, and our estimates for basic earnings confirm this prediction. It also raises returns to skill, a result which can be interpreted as follows. Individual firms have essentially no say in sectoral bargains. When there is a firm-level bargain, however, management will try to link wages more tightly with productivity levels. This can still be mutually advantageous: less skilled workers get more than the corresponding sectoral-agreement wage (which serves as their reservation level), while firms manage to mitigate wage compression typically imposed by sectoral agreements.

Thirdly, unions are more powerful in the public sector, but this should be largely captured by the union coverage variable. Thus, the empirical finding in Table 1.5 that the *share of employees working in the public sector* reduces basic earnings could be capturing the following compensating differential: even non-tenured public sector employees—the ones in our sample—have higher job security than private sector employees, and so they should earn lower wages. On the other hand, the public employment share is found to have a positive effect on returns to skill, which may reflect public sector pay schedules aimed at recruiting/retaining skilled workers with attractive alternative opportunities in the private sector, for whom job stability may be less important.

3. The reservation utility level $(\tilde{V}_u)$ is represented by several variables. First, when the *hiring rate*—as a share of sectoral employment—increases, prospects for incumbent employees improve, and so their wages should go up. We include this variable rather than the sectoral unemployment rate because the hiring rate, as a flow, may be a better indicator of labour market tightness (see Blanchard and Katz, 1995). The estimated positive effect on both basic earnings and returns to skill accords with our expectations.

The existing literature has pointed out that there are often negative effects of unemployment duration on employability (due to loss of skill, disenfranchise-ment from the labour force, discrimination, etc.). Thus, the higher the *long-term unemployment share* (one year or longer) in total unemployment, the better the prospects for current employees if they became unemployed, and so the higher their wages. However, this effect may not be the same for all employees: if the

---

[32] They could also capture the parameter determining the relative weight of wages vis-à-vis employment in union utility (γ).

[33] Empirically, unions have been found to reduce wage dispersion also in the US (e.g. Freeman, 1980, 1993; Card, 1992) and Canada (Lemieux, 1998).

cause of the negative duration dependence is loss of skill, then the average skill in the unemployed population falls, which may decrease competition faced by skilled workers while increasing competition faced by unskilled workers. Our finding in Table 1.5 that the long-term share does reduce basic earnings while raising returns to skill suggests that the latter effect dominates the former.

The last set of variables representing reservation utility are the *unskilled unemployment rate*, in the equation for basic earnings, and the corresponding *skilled–unskilled unemployment rate differentials*, in those for returns to college and junior college. For all of these variables we expect a negative effect, which is corroborated by our estimates.

4. Technological progress is represented by *sectoral R&D expenditures* as a share of value added. By increasing overall productivity, R&D should raise all earnings. If it is largely skill-biased, then it would reduce the intensity of unskilled relative to skilled labour in production (α) and we would expect a negative effect on basic earnings and a positive one on returns to skill, although we have shown in Section 1.5 that this need not happen.

Our estimates in Table 1.5 indicate that R&D intensity raises basic earnings, except at small firms. This is consistent with the hypothesis that labour unions redistribute the gains from improved technology to all workers and with the empirical findings in van Reenen (1993) for the UK. On the other hand, little uniformity is found for returns to skill: returns to college in small firms increase but there is no effect in medium–large ones, returns to junior college fall in the latter firms but there is no effect in small ones. Although compatible with the theory, these findings are somewhat surprising, and we can think of two potential reasons for them. The first one is that our measure of R&D is quite noisy and more aggregated than the other sectoral variables. The second reason is that R&D expenditures may mean very little in a country like Spain, that is more an adapter than a producer of technology. Indeed, Spanish R&D expenditures are very small (3 percent of value added in our sample period), so that most technological progress is generated by imported patent licences or is embodied in imported capital goods.[34]

5. We do not have any empirical measure for the wage elasticity of skilled labour supply (δ). However, we do control for such supply, as is typical in the recent literature on skill premia, by including as a regressor the *share of the population with a university degree*. By making skilled labour more abundant, this share should lower returns to skill. In fact, we do not find any effect on returns to junior college, while the expected negative effect is present for returns to college, though only in small firms. The latter is consistent with the composition effects we mentioned before, which we will now discuss further.

Some of the previous findings deserve a joint discussion. Table 1.5 indicates that firm-level coverage of wage bargains raises returns to skill except for college graduates working for small firms. We believe this is related to our hypothesis,

---

[34] Torres (2002) finds a similar lack of significance of R&D expenditures in trying to account for skill-biased technological progress in Spanish manufacturing.

advanced in Section 1.4.1, that the composition of skilled labour may differ across firm size classes. In particular, the skills of college graduates are more likely to be heterogeneous in small than in large firms. Several of our estimates give support to this idea. For instance, according to our first-step estimates, the variance of college earnings is lower the larger the firm (Section 1.4.2). And the second-step estimates indicate that a larger proportion of the aggregate population with a university degree reduces the average and raises the variance[35] of returns to college in small firms, but not in large ones.

Such differential heterogeneity could be the result of two factors. One is measurement error. We have aimed at measuring skill through the occupational groups most clearly linked to educational levels. Thus, one possibility is that small firms are more likely than large firms to employ college graduates to carry out tasks not requiring high skills[36] while reporting, for Social Security purposes, these workers as belonging to college-degree occupations.

An alternative, more compelling story is that employees at larger firms are more productive and hence command higher wages in the labour market. This is the leading explanation of the size–wage effect according to Idson and Oi (1999). This may happen because larger firms are able to screen job applicants better, possibly due to economies of scale in screening, and to attract and retain more capable workers through offering better opportunities and career ladders, due to their larger capital or other advantages.

Whatever the actual source, the higher ability of skilled workers in large firms would help account for two of our findings. First, if firm-level bargaining allows firms to associate wages more closely with productivity levels, then this type of bargaining should benefit college graduates working in large firms but could easily hurt those in small firms. Second, skill-biased technological change, to the extent that it is present, should benefit skilled workers in large firms, but not necessarily in small ones, helping to account for the diverging pattern of returns to skill in the two size classes over time.

We should report that we also tried with a few other variables suggested by either our model or recent research on wage inequality. First, as a measure of the degree of competition in the market (κ) we included the international trade balance and the import penetration rate by sector (for very broad sectors, due to lack of disaggregated data). Similar measures have been employed in other studies, mainly for the US, as an exogenous force creating competition against domestic unskilled labour from less developed countries and also reducing the demand for manufacturing goods. Second, returns to skill should be related to the capital–labour ratio if capital and skills are complementary factors, so we included such a ratio at the sectoral level (both for public and private capital stocks). Lastly, another potential source of an increase in the demand for skill is the shift from the primary and secondary sectors towards services. Thus, we also

---

[35] See Section 1.6.3.
[36] Typically, workers with college degrees with relatively low market demand.

included the share of services in national GDP. None of these variables was significant at all, and so they are not discussed any further.

1.6.2. Returns to Experience

For returns to experience, we estimate the second stage regression on the composite coefficient $(\hat{\beta}_{10ts} + 2\hat{\beta}_{11ts}Age)$ (see equation (1.13)). We choose a value of 35 for *Age*, which is a representative value, close to the average age in the sample (37.9 years old).

Our model does not address the issue of experience, so at this point our discussion must be more informal. A parsimonious specification includes, apart from sectoral dummies, the following four variables: (a) the coverage of *firm-level agreements*, whose coefficient should be positively signed if older workers carry a higher weight in unions' objective functions than younger ones (we also tried union coverage, but it was not significant at all); (b) the *hiring rate*, which should have a negative effect if the composition of newly hired employees is unbalanced in favour of younger workers; (c) the share of employees in the *public sector*, which should have a positive effect if seniority ladders are steeper in the public than in the private sector; and (d) the share of the *population of 20 to 24 years old*, which should bear a positively signed coefficient for straightforward labour supply reasons.

All of these expected signs are obtained, as shown in the last column of Table 1.5, except for the finding that a higher coverage of firm-level agreements tends to reduce returns to experience. This could again arise if in firm-level bargains wages are more tightly linked to productivity than at sectoral bargains and if younger cohorts of workers—as seems to be the case—possess higher skills than older ones, controlling for experience.

1.6.3. Conditional Variances

Lastly, we also explore the relationship between economic variables and the conditional variance of earnings, i.e., the variance within skill-firm size categories. As pointed out before, first-step estimates indicate little change in variances over time, except for workers with a college education. Since for all other skill groups sectoral dummies can be expected to capture most of the differences in conditional variances, here we only estimate a model with economic variables for college educated workers. Our theoretical model provides little guidance for this purpose, since it attributes conditional variances to unobserved heterogeneity of workers within skill-experience-firm size groups. Table 1.6 reports the results, in which the bottom rows show that again once sectoral dummies are included, adding economic variables does not much raise R^2 statistics over and above those obtained by simply including a time trend. The estimates indicate that higher dispersion in returns to skill is positively associated with a higher share of collective bargaining being carried out at the firm-level, with a higher

Table 1.6. *Regressions for the effect of college education on the conditional log-variance of earnings*[a]

	Small firms	Medium–large firms
Firm-level coverage (t,s)	—	10.022
	—	(2.59)
Hiring rate (t−1,s)	0.011	0.024
	(1.37)	(2.73)
Population with a	0.054	—
university degree (t)	(0.78)	—
Constant	1.023	−1.176
	(2.10)	(1.41)
Construction	−0.455	1.218
	(1.33)	(1.42)
Transport and public utilities	0.470	−2.53
	(2.32)	(2.39)
Trade	−0.175	1.844
	(1.79)	(2.74)
Finance, insurance, and real estate	−0.234	1.966
	(1.44)	(3.55)
Hotels and catering	−0.883	2.031
	(3.76)	(2.65)
Other services	−0.700	1.165
	(6.06)	(2.16)
Mining	0.281	−1.189
	(1.71)	(3.59)
R^2	0.731	0.432
R^2 sectoral dummies + trend	0.716	0.379
R^2 sectoral dummies	0.649	0.325

Notes: [a]Weighted least squares estimates. The reference sector is manufacturing. Units: all variables in percentage terms except the share of the population of 20–24 years old, union coverage, and firm-level coverage.

Source: Own calculations on Social Security data set (see Appendix).

sectoral hiring rate and, for small firms, with a higher share of the population with a university degree. The latter is again consistent with the potential importance of heterogeneity of college educated employees working in small firms.

1.7. CONCLUSIONS

In this paper, we provide a detailed account of the evolution of earnings and returns to skill and experience in Spain over the 1980s, using a new matched employer–employee database of Social Security records. We employ a sample of monthly earnings for more than 30,000 male employees for the period 1980–87.

We start with a description of the evolution of the quantiles of the earnings distribution and show that Spain conforms to the Continental European pattern, experiencing little changes in dispersion below the median, but behaves more like Anglo-Saxon countries in showing a significant increase in dispersion above the median. The more skilled workers benefited from earnings increases, mostly at the end of the period. Increases in the relative earnings of older workers are also evident over the period.

We pursue a two-stage empirical strategy. In the first stage, we estimate the common component of earnings—or basic earnings, returns to skill for college and junior college educated workers vis-à-vis unskilled workers, and returns to potential experience (age), all by sector and year. We estimate both conditional means and conditional variances, which are allowed to vary by firm size (except for returns to experience). We find that larger firms tend to pay higher wages and also a pro-cyclical evolution of earnings. Returns to skill are found to have increased over the sample period except for workers with a college degree working in small firms. We speculate that the latter finding may stem from higher heterogeneity among those workers within that size class, and find some support for this idea from our analysis of conditional variances. Returns to potential experience are found to have steadily increased over the period.

Our second stage estimation draws from a simple theoretical model of wage bargaining at firms employing skilled and unskilled labour, and operating in imperfectly competitive product markets. We assume unskilled labour bargains for its wage with the firm ex-ante, while skilled labour is supplied according to an upward-sloping curve. We find wages and returns to skill to depend on union bargaining power and reservation utility levels, technological change, the extent of product market competition, and the wage elasticity of skilled labour supply.

We then estimate the effects of empirical measures of these variables on the sector-period sets of estimates for basic earnings, returns to skill, and returns to experience. Our results suggest the following underlying forces affecting earnings inequality. Labour union activity tends to reduce inequality across skill groups, while firm-level bargaining and public employment (once sectoral coverage of collective bargaining is controlled for) tend to raise it. Long-term unemployment has an asymmetric effect, reducing unskilled workers' earnings but increasing returns to skill, thereby raising inequality. Investments in R&D tend to increase the earnings of most workers, with no clear effects on returns to skill, although we believe this variable provides a very poor measure of technical progress in our data. The expected tradeoff between earnings of different skill classes of workers and their respective unemployment rates is evident in the data. Probably due to the limited amount of variability across sectors and over time, economic variables do not seen to have a large amount of explanatory power; in particular, they explain slightly more than a simple specification with just sectoral dummies and a linear trend.

We also find increases in dispersion, in terms of conditional variances, within the group of college-educated workers. Such dispersion depends positively on the share of collective bargaining being carried out at the firm level, on the share of educated workers in the population, and on the state of the cycle.

Our estimates also indicate that returns to potential experience increased over the period. They are found to depend positively on the share of youth in the population and the share of employment in the public sector, and negatively on the state of the business cycle.

In sum, we find that Spain experienced a non-negligible increase in earnings inequality in the 1980s, mostly in the upper half of the earnings distribution and in the second half of the decade. As in other OECD countries, returns to skill and to potential experience increased, as well as inequality among college graduates. These evolutions are found to be related to labour supply forces but also to the features of the wage bargaining system in the Spanish economy once cyclical factors are controlled for. The effects of union activity turn out not to be very well determined, but the interpretation of this result is not straightforward. It may be that union activity is not a very important factor in the evolution of wage inequality. However, there may be other explanations. For instance, union activity or bargaining power may be poorly approximated by the empirical measure we use, namely the sectoral coverage of collective bargains. Or it may be that union coverage does not show enough variability in our sample. Lastly, lack of observability of certain potentially important characteristics, like the sectoral breakdown of the types of degrees attained by workers with college and junior college education or sectoral measures of market power, led us to include sectoral dummies in our estimation. If union power varies essentially by sector, then its specific effect is bound to be very hard to disentangle from the differences already captured by the sectoral dummies.

APPENDIX

Sources and Definitions

Individual Data

Source. Panel of data from the Social Security records from 1980:12 to 1987:12 (June and December observations only), provided by the Spanish Ministry of Labour and Social Security (Ministerio de Trabajo y Seguridad Social (MTSS)). The data set is extensively described in Toharia and Muro (1990).

Sample. From a sample of men of 20–64 years of age we exclude workers

- in agriculture, farming, forestry, and fisheries
- with earnings below the bottom coding level in his occupation
- whose earnings have doubled from one year to the next
- living in Ceuta or Melilla (Spanish provinces in the North of Africa)
- with a missing observation for age, occupation, region, or firm identifier (deleted only in the period when one of these four variables is missing).

Once we keep the December observations only, we extract a random sample of 140,545 observations, which correspond to 32,291 workers.

Earnings. The earnings measure is the monthly taxable earnings base declared by the firm for Social Security tax purposes.

Skill. Four groups are formed from the information on occupation (grupo de tarifa). The groups are as follows: (1) College (*ingenieros y licenciados*); (2) Junior college (*ingenieros técnicos, peritos, ayudantes titulados y asimilados*); (3) Medium skill (residual) (*jefes administrativos y de taller, ayudantes no titulados, oficiales administrativos, subalternos, auxiliares administrativos, oficiales de 1^a y 2^a, oficiales de 3^a y especiales*); and (4) Unskilled (*peones*).

Economic sector. Sectors are grouped in the following way: Mining (8); Construction (1); Manufacturing (2); Transport and public utilities (3); Wholesale and retail trade (4); Finance, insurance, and real estate (5); Hotels and Catering (6), and Other services (7).

Table 1.7 provides the frequencies of the individual variables for the sample used in the econometric estimation.

Aggregate and Sectoral variables

Aggregate variables. Long term unemployment. Unemployed for a year or more (share).

Unemployment rates by skill: Unskilled (no studies), *Analfabetos y sin estudios,* Junior college (three-year university degree), *Estudios de nivel anterior al superior,* College (five-year university degree), *Estudios superiores.*

Population aged 20–24 years old. Share in population aged 16–64.

Population with a university degree (includes college and junior college). Share in population aged 16–64.

Source: *Encuesta de Población Activa* (EPA) of the Instituto Nacional de Estadística (INE). Descriptive statistics are provided in Table 1.8.

Sectoral Variables. Coverage of collective agreements (see Tables 1.9 and 1.10). (a) Numerator: number of workers covered, by starting year of effectiveness of the agreement, broken down by the eight sectors listed above. It includes both firm-level and wider agreements. Period: (i) For 1980 the sectoral breakdown and the data for Cataluña and País Vasco are missing, and so this year is omitted. (ii) 1981 and 1982 figures have been corrected because data for Cataluña are missing. The original data are multiplied by the factor (1/0.9189), using the fact that Cataluña had, in 1983, 8.11 per cent of the total number of workers covered in Spain. (iii) The original 1983 observation for the sector of Finance, insurance, and real estate was artificially low, due to partial official recording of coverage of the main collective agreement, because it was signed originally by only one of the two main unions and many workers adhered to it with a lag. Thus, we use instead the average of the 1982 and 1984 values. Source: *Boletín de Estadísticas Laborales* (MTSS). (b) Denominator: Employees per sector. Source: EPA. Due to different sources for the numerator and the denominator, the ratio is above 1 for some sectors. This may also arise from double counting: for instance, if there are firm-level agreements in a sector with a sector-wide agreement, it might happen that

Table 1.7. *Frequencies of individual variables*

	Number	Percentage
Observations	140,545	100.00
Non-censored	112,828	80.28
Censored of which	27,717	19.72
Bottom coded	725	0.52
Top coded	26,992	19.21
Workers		
Total observed	32,291	100.00
1 year	6,159	19.07
2 years	4,143	12.83
3 years	3,103	9.61
4 years	2,553	7.91
5 years	2,447	7.58
6 years	2,858	8.85
7 years	11,028	34.15
Individual characteristics		
Cohort (avg. age = 37.9 yrs old)		
1916–29	11,346	8.07
1930–39	28,897	20.56
1940–49	37,647	26.79
1950–59	49,778	35.42
1960–67	12,877	9.16
Skill		
Unskilled	14,915	10.61
Medium-skilled	110,353	78.52
Junior college	4,623	3.29
College	10,654	7.58
Firm characteristics		
Sector		
Mining	11,285	8.03
Construction	17,217	12.25
Manufacturing	45,020	32.03
Transport and public utilities	12,739	9.06
Wholesale and retail trade	19,285	13.72
Finance, insurance, and real estate	13,322	9.48
Hotels and restaurants	5,304	3.77
Other services	16,373	11.65
Size (number of employees)		
Up to 100	75,175	53.49
Between 101 and 1000	41,285	29.37
More than 1000	24,085	17.14

Table 1.7. *(Continued)*

Year (no. of workers observed)	Number	Percentage
1981	19,424	13.82
1982	19,448	13.84
1983	19,488	13.87
1984	19,288	13.72
1985	19,610	13.95
1986	21,067	14.99
1987	22,220	15.81

Source: Own calculations on Social Security data set (see Appendix).

Table 1.8. *Sample statistics of aggregate economic variables (%)*[a]

	Mean	Standard deviation	Value in 1981	Value in 1987	Change 1981–87
Long-term unemployment	53.04	6.62	40.14	61.96	21.82
Unskilled unemployment rate $(t-1)$	15.64	3.93	10.70	20.78	10.08
Junior coll.–Unskilled unempl. $(t-1)$	−1.65	2.49	−0.44	−5.13	−4.69
College–Unskilled unempl. $(t-1)$	−1.56	2.63	−1.05	−5.33	−4.28
Population with university degree	8.35	0.91	7.25	9.72	2.47
Population aged 20–24 years old	13.00	0.30	12.60	13.50	0.84

Notes: [a]Population aged 20–24 years old is used as a ratio (as opposed to percentages) in the empirical estimation.

Source: Own calculations on Social Security data set (see Appendix).

those reporting the coverage of the latter do not subtract the number of workers covered by the former. Sectors: Other services excludes subsectors in which the vast majority of workers are tenured public employees (Spanish classification CNAE-1974 subsectors 91, 93, 94, and 99).

Coverage of firm-level collective agreements. As in union coverage, but using as the numerator only the number of workers covered by agreements signed at the firm level.

Hiring rate. Ratio of hires to employed workers (Colocaciones registradas divided by ocupados). Two sectors, Trade and Hotels, are considered jointly because the numerator cannot be disaggregated. Source: *Estadísticas de Empleo*, Boletín, Instituto Nacional de Empleo, for the numerator and EPA for the denominator.

Percentage of employees in the public sector. Broken down by the eight sectors listed above. Source: EPA.

Research and development expenditures. Expenditures divided by value added (Total gastos intramuros en I + D divided by valor añadido). Broken down by six sectors, e.g. considering Trade and Hotels together, and Finance, insurance and

Table 1.9. *Sample statistics of sectoral economic variables (%)*[a]

	Mean	Standard deviation	Value in 1981	Value in 1987	Change 1981–87
Hiring rate $(t-1)$					
1. Construction	56.2	16.8	43.5	84.0	40.5
2. Manufacturing	16.9	4.9	11.7	25.3	13.6
3. Transport and public utilities	7.7	2.4	5.4	11.7	6.4
4. Wholesale and retail trade	15.5	6.0	9.4	24.8	15.4
5. Finance, insurance and real estate	11.8	5.8	6.9	21.4	14.5
6. Hotels and catering	15.5	6.0	9.4	24.8	15.4
7. Other services	10.1	5.9	4.4	18.9	14.5
8. Mining	7.9	2.9	5.0	12.6	7.6
Union coverage					
1. Construction	74.3	18.9	33.4	82.8	49.4
2. Manufacturing	114.1	14.9	82.5	121.9	39.4
3. Transport and public utilities	78.5	6.7	64.9	83.8	18.9
4. Wholesale and retail trade	96.7	18.1	60.2	96.0	35.8
5. Finance, insurance and real estate	107.8	11.8	128.0	98.7	−29.3
6. Hotels and catering	89.3	14.2	65.7	86.8	21.1
7. Other services	40.3	11.0	22.5	44.8	22.3
8. Mining	103.4	6.5	95.6	104.4	8.8
Firm-level coverage					
1. Construction	1.3	0.7	2.7	1.2	−1.5
2. Manufacturing	21.0	1.4	18.4	20.0	1.6
3. Transport and public utilities	48.8	3.2	44.6	49.9	5.3
4. Wholesale and retail trade	4.9	0.5	5.3	4.1	−1.2
5. Finance, insurance and real estate	7.5	2.0	9.1	5.6	−3.5
6. Hotels and catering	3.3	0.5	3.3	2.7	−0.6
7. Other services	7.3	1.9	3.4	8.5	5.1
8. Mining	27.9	2.4	31.8	26.8	−5.0
R&D expenditure $(t-1)$[b]					
1. Construction	0.8	0.2	0.7	0.7	0.0
2. Manufacturing	8.1	2.2	6.2	11.4	5.3
3. Transport and public utilities	2.3	0.5	1.5	2.9	1.4
4. Wholesale and retail trade	0.0	0.0	0.0	0.0	−0.0
5. Finance, insurance and real estate	0.5	0.2	0.4	0.9	0.5
6. Hotels and catering	0.0	0.0	0.0	0.0	−0.0
7. Other services	0.5	0.2	0.4	0.9	0.5
8. Mining	10.8	1.5	9.5	13.4	3.9
Public employment share					
1. Construction	6.4	2.5	5.0	4.8	−0.1
2. Manufacturing	5.6	0.8	4.8	4.9	0.2
3. Transport and public utilities	49.7	2.7	45.4	47.4	2.0
4. Wholesale and retail trade	2.1	0.6	1.7	1.6	−0.1
5. Finance, insurance and real estate	3.6	0.8	3.0	3.6	0.6
6. Hotels and catering	2.1	0.6	1.6	1.7	0.1

Table 1.9. *(Continued)*

	Mean	Standard deviation	Value in 1981	Value in 1987	Change 1981–87
7. Other services	59.5	1.8	58.0	59.9	1.9
8. Mining	10.0	0.6	9.2	10.2	1.0

Notes: [a]The following variables are used as ratios (as opposed to percentages) in the empirical estimation: Union coverage, firm-level coverage.
[b]0.0 means lower than 0.05%.

Source: Own calculations on Social Security data set (see Appendix).

Table 1.10. *Second stage estimates with sectoral dummies and trend only*[a]

	Basic earnings			Returns to junior college		Returns to college		Returns to experience
	Small	Med.	Large	Small	Med–large	Small	Med–large	
Constant	10.261 (357.60)	10.481 (349.77)	10.501 (339.01)	0.658 (9.43)	0.546 (8.99)	0.691 (24.47)	0.945 (22.53)	0.008 (31.59)
Construction	0.595 (21.05)	0.440 (14.81)	0.540 (17.03)	−0.017 (0.38)	0.222 (7.07)	0.024 (0.83)	0.075 (1.30)	−0.006 (24.07)
Transpt. and p. util.	0.078 (1.79)	0.135 (3.04)	0.206 (4.55)	0.435 (1.72)	0.168 (2.91)	0.196 (3.40)	0.193 (2.01)	3×10^{-4} (0.83)
Trade	−0.007 (0.23)	−0.095 (2.78)	0.006 (0.17)	−0.159 (4.27)	0.331 (1.77)	−0.006 (0.22)	0.269 (2.72)	0.001 (3.46)
Finance, ins., etc.	−1.323 (20.02)	−1.426 (21.41)	−1.390 (20.68)	−0.150 (2.75)	−0.129 (3.64)	0.405 (8.42)	−0.080 (1.66)	0.016 (24.48)
Hotels and catering	0.342 (8.10)	0.257 (5.43)	0.207 (3.83)	−0.331 (5.03)	—	−0.070 (1.40)	−0.252 (2.79)	−0.003 (6.99)
Other services	0.039 (1.08)	−0.037 (1.01)	0.001 (0.03)	−0.257 (8.65)	−0.242 (12.97)	0.042 (1.68)	−0.362 (11.97)	−0.001 (3.16)
Mining	−0.115 (2.55)	−0.047 (1.01)	−0.125 (2.61)	0.137 (2.61)	−0.011 (0.34)	0.444 (9.65)	−0.070 (1.65)	9×10^{-7} (0.00)
Trend	−0.024 (4.29)	−0.029 (5.08)	−0.020 (3.35)	0.017 (1.04)	0.036 (2.49)	−0.015 (2.88)	0.040 (4.29)	0.001 (13.79)
R^2	0.962	0.941	0.935	0.627	0.814	0.832	0.772	0.937

Notes: [a]The reference sector is manufacturing.

Source: Own calculations on Social Security data set (see Appendix).

real estate and Other services together. Source: numerator from *Estadística sobre las actividades en investigación científica y desarrollo tecnológico*, INE, and denominator from Banco de España.

REFERENCES

Abadíe, A. (1998). Changes in Spanish labour income structure during the 1980s: A quantile regression approach, *Investigaciones Económicas*, 21, 253–72.

Abellán, C., F. Felgueroso, and J. Lorences (1995). La negociación colectiva en España: una reforma pendiente, *Papeles de Economía Española*, 72, 250–60.

Acemoglu, D., P. Aghion, and G. Violante (2000). Deunionization, technical change and inequality, mimeo, MIT.

Bentolila, S. and J. Dolado (1994). Labour flexibility and wages: Lessons from Spain, *Economic Policy*, 18, 53–99.

Blanchard, O. and L. Katz (1996). What we know and do not know about the natural rate of unemployment, *Journal of Economic Perspectives*, 1(1), 51–72.

Bover, O., P. García-Perea, and P. Portugal (2000). Labour market outliers: Lessons from Portugal and Spain, *Economic Policy* 31, 380–428.

Brown, C. and J. Medoff (1989). The employer size-wage effect, *Journal of Political Economy*, 97, 1027–59.

Card, D. (1992). The effect of unions on the distribution of wages: Redistribution or relabeling?, *NBER working paper*, 4195.

Dolado, J., F. Felgueroso, and J. F. Jimeno (1997). The effects of minimum bargained wages on earnings: Evidence from Spain, *European Economic Review*, 41, 713–21.

Escobar, M. (1995). Spain: works councils or unions?, in J. Rogers and W. Streeck (eds.), *Works Councils: Consultation, Representation, and Cooperation in Industrial Relations*, University of Chicago Press, Chicago.

Freeman, R. (1980). Unionism and the dispersion of wages, *Industrial and Labor Relations Review* 34, 3–23.

—— (1993). How much has de-unionisation contributed to the rise in male earnings inequality?, in S. Danziger and P. Gottschalk (eds.), *Uneven Tides: Rising Inequality in America*, Russell Sage Foundation, New York.

García Perea, P. (1991). Evolución de la estructura salarial española desde 1963, in S. Bentolila and L. Toharia (eds.), *Estudios de Economía del Trabajo en España. III. El problema del paro*, Ministerio de Trabajo y Seguridad Social, Madrid.

Idson, T. and W. Oi, (1999). Workers are more productive in large firms, *American Economic Review*, 89, 104–8.

Jimeno, J. (1992). Las implicaciones macroeconómicas de la negociación colectiva: el caso español, *Moneda y Crédito*, 195, 223–81.

—— and L. Toharia (1994). *Unemployment and Labour Market Flexibility: Spain*, International Labour Office, Geneva.

Juhn, C., K. Murphy, and B. Pierce (1993). Wage inequality and the rise in returns to skill, *Journal of Political Economy*, 101, 410–42.

Katz, L., G. Loveman, and D. Blanchflower (1995). A comparison of changes in the structure of wages in four OECD countries, in R. Freeman and L. Katz (eds.), *Differences and Changes in Wage Structures*, The University of Chicago Press, Chicago.

—— and K. Murphy (1992). Changes in relative wages, 1963–1987: Supply and demand factors, *Quarterly Journal of Economics*, 107, 35–78.

Krusell, P., L. Ohanian, J.-V. Rios-Rull, and G. Violante (1997). Capital-skill complementarity and inequality: a macroeconomic analysis, *Econometrica*, 68, 1029–1053.

Layard, R., S. Nickell, and R. Jackman (1991). *Unemployment. Macroeconomic Performance and the Labor Market*, Oxford University Press, Oxford.

Lemieux, T. (1998). Estimating the effects of unions on wage inequality in a panel data model with comparative advantage and nonrandom selection, *Journal of Labor Economics*, 16, 261–91.

Melis, F. and C. Díaz (1993). La distribución personal de salarios y pensiones en las fuentes tributarias, in, *I Simposio sobre igualdad y distribución de la renta y la riqueza*, vol. 2, Fundación Argentaria, Madrid.

Mincer, J. (1991). Human capital, technology, and the wage structure: What do time series show?, *NBER working paper*, 3581.

Oi, W. and T. Idson (1999). Firm size and wages, in O. Ashenfelter and D. Card (eds.), *Handbook of Labor Economics*, vol. 3, Elsevier, Amsterdam.

Oliver, J., J.-L. Raymond, J.-L. Roig, and F. Barceinas (1999). Returns to human capital in Spain: A survey of the evidence, in R. Asplund and P. Pereira (eds), *Returns to Human Capital in Europe. A Literature Review*, ETLA, Helsinki.

Organization for Economic Cooperation and Development (1993). *Economic Outlook 1993*, Paris.

Toharia, L. and J. Muro (1990). Obtención de indicadores salariales a partir de los datos de la Seguridad Social, mimeo, Ministerio de Trabajo y Seguridad Social.

Torres, X. (2002). Dispersión salarial y cambio tecnológico en la industria española, *Investigaciones Económica* (forthcoming).

Van Reenen, J. (1993). Getting a fair share of the plunder? Technological change and the wage structure, mimeo, Institute for Fiscal Studies.

2

Earnings Inequality in Portugal and Spain: Contrasts and Similarities

OLGA CANTÓ, ANA R. CARDOSO, AND JUAN F. JIMENO

2.1. INTRODUCTION

Earnings inequality was on the rise in most OECD countries during the 1980s (OECD, 1993). In the first half of the 1990s, earnings inequality continued rising in the US and the UK, but not in Continental Europe, where the tendency towards increased inequality appears to have slackened somewhat (OECD, 1996; Gottschalk and Smeeding, 1997). Several explanations have been proposed for increasing inequality. Some studies refer to widespread changes in labour market institutions which have led to higher decentralization of wage determination (in those countries where this process is mainly through collective bargaining) and the decline in unionization (in those countries where collective bargaining covers only a small fraction of the workforce, as the US, for instance).[1] Second, another plausible culprit for rising earnings inequality is the change in relative supply of skilled and non-skilled workers. However, if anything, the relative supply of skilled workers has increased over the last twenty years in most OECD countries, and there seems to be no significant correlation between immigration flows (which supposedly increase the supply of relatively unskilled workers) and changes in earnings inequality across countries. Third, there is the presumption that changes in demand, biased technological progress, and the globalization of international trade are changing the sectoral composition of the demand for labour and the relative demand for skilled and non-skilled workers in favour of the former. Although this is the most often cited explanation for rising earnings inequality, there seems to be little correlation across countries between changes in earnings inequality and changes in the sectoral composition of employment and between the former and openness to international trade. Furthermore, within-group inequality has also risen, suggesting that recent trends in earnings inequality are not only a matter of the relative supply and demand of skilled and non-skilled workers, but also of labour market institutions.

---

[1] See Soskice (1990) and Freeman (1993).

Thus, the conventional wisdom on the evolution of earnings inequality across countries is that it is an issue of changes in the relative supply of different types of workers with respect to changes in the relative demand of these types of workers combined with differently evolving labour market institutions. In those countries where 'institutions' are the main determinants of earnings, changes in the relative supply of different types of workers respect to changes in the relative demand do not translate into widening earnings structures. In countries where the wage determination process is more 'flexible' (meaning that is more responsive to supply and demand factors), earnings inequality is mostly driven by changes in the relative supply of different types of workers with respect to changes in the relative demand of these types of workers. This explanation seems to fit well with the contrasts between the US and the UK experience, on the one hand, and the (Continental) European experience, on the other hand.

The main objective of this chapter is to test this explanation for the determinants of earnings inequality on the Spanish and the Portuguese labour markets. Spain and Portugal are two neighbouring countries that have shared many developments in the past three decades. However, the Portuguese labour market is regarded as a very flexible market (see Luz and Pinheiro, 1994), while the Spanish labour market is regarded as a very rigid market (see Dolado and Jimeno, 1997).[2] During most of the 1980s and 1990s the Spanish unemployment rate was more than twice the Portuguese one. With regards to wage inequality and according with previous explanations, we should observe that, to the extent that supply and demand factors have evolved similarly in both countries, which seems to be the case, earnings inequality should be much higher in Portugal than in Spain.

We compare earnings inequality in both countries making use of data provided by similar Earnings Surveys in Portugal and Spain. We find that earnings inequality is higher in Portugal, but the difference is not as large as could have been expected *a priori*. Additionally, we investigate the sources of inequality in both countries by computing the relative contribution of workers' characteristics and employers' characteristics to wages. In a more flexible labour market, we will expect both employers' and workers' characteristics to play a role in shaping wage differentials. In contrast, in rigid labour markets employers' characteristics are less relevant factors in determining wages. In fact, we find that the wage structure in Spain is more compressed than in Portugal mainly because wage differentials between industries and occupations are lower.

The structure of the chapter is as follows. In Section 2.2 we highlight the main institutional peculiarities of the Portuguese and Spanish labour markets. In Section 2.3 we comment on the recent trends in the composition of labour supply by educational attainments and in the sectoral composition of employment. We

---

[2] The different degree of flexibility of both markets is also documented by Castillo, Dolado, and Jimeno (1998), who estimate, using structural VAR techniques, the response of labour market variables to different types of shocks, and find that the response of wages and unemployment to shocks is much more sluggish in Spain than in Portugal.

also analyse the shifts in employment composition that took place in both countries during the 1980s, disentangling the effects of changes in the relative demand of skilled versus unskilled labour within and between industries. From this analysis we conclude that the trend in the relative demand of skilled labour seems to be similar in both countries. In Section 2.4 we describe the level and patterns of earnings inequality in both countries. In Section 2.5 we decompose the variance of earnings in the contributions of workers' and employers' attributes and estimate earnings equations by regressing the (log of) earnings on a set of workers' and employers' characteristics, to measuring to what extent these characteristics are priced differently in both labour markets. Finally, Section 2.6 contains our conclusions.

2.2. THE INSTITUTIONAL FRAMEWORK: SPAIN VERSUS PORTUGAL

At first sight the Portuguese and the Spanish labour markets share common institutional features. Both countries are regarded as having very stringent job security legislation, the regulation and structure of collective bargaining seem to be similar in both countries, and, nowadays, the main parameters of the social protection system seem be of the same order of magnitude. In fact, this institutional resemblance and the similarity of political and economic developments during the 1970s and the 1980s has led some authors to pose the large difference in unemployment rates between the two countries as a test for theories of unemployment (see Blanchard and Jimeno, 1995).

However, this first sight of the institutional features of the Portuguese and Spanish labour markets can be misleading. Bover, García-Perea, and Portugal (2000) argue that, in practice, job security legislation is much more stringent, unemployment benefits are more generous, and collective bargaining compresses the wage structure more in Spain than in Portugal. They also relate the higher degree of wage flexibility in Portugal to the role that unemployment benefits and job protection legislation play as determinants of wage evolution. Regarding wage determination, the main institutional constraints in both countries are the following:

1. The coverage rate of collective bargaining (the proportion of employees whose employment conditions are determined by collective agreements or by extension of them) is around 80 per cent both in Portugal and in Spain. Also, in both countries, collective bargaining is mostly at the sectoral level: in Spain only around 20 per cent of employees have their employment conditions set by firm-level agreements, while in Portugal this proportion is around 7 per cent and firm-level collective bargaining is, to a great extent, restricted to public corporations. In both countries, collective agreements are extended to all workers in the corresponding sector, so that union affiliation status does not make a difference in earnings.

2. In both countries employers make use of different employment contracts. In particular, there are permanent employees who enjoy a high deal of employment protection and fixed-term employment employees whose contracts have a pre-determined duration and, therefore, have a much lower bargaining power. The incidence of fixed-term employment is, however, much larger in Spain (where about 33 per cent of the employees have fixed-term contracts) than in Portugal (only about 12 per cent of fixed-term employment). The wage differential between permanent and fixed-term employees is higher in Spain than in Portugal. The incidence of fixed-term employment among occupational groups is also very different in both countries (see Bover *et al.*, 2000).
3. There are two layers of minimum wages, one established annually by the government and applying to the whole economy, and, in practice, the bargained wages resulting from collective bargaining agreements. The statutory minimum wage as a proportion of the average wage is higher in Portugal (above 40 per cent) than in Spain (around 30 per cent). The incidence of the statutory minimum wage is also higher in Portugal, while in Spain a myriad of minimum bargained wages are binding, especially for low-skilled workers (see Dolado *et al.*, 1997).

2.3. LABOUR DEMAND AND LABOUR SUPPLY BY SKILLS

Both the relative supply and the relative demand for skilled labour seem to have followed similar trends in Portugal and in Spain. As for labour supply, there has been a noticeable increase in female labour participation: in Portugal, the share of women in the labour force went up from 30 per cent in the mid-1980s to about 40 per cent in 1992, while in Spain a similar rise occurred between 1985 and 1995. Also, in both countries, there has been an upgrading of the labour force by the entry into the labour market of younger, more educated cohorts, although Portugal and Spain are still among the OECD countries with the lowest levels of human capital. As seen in Table 2.1(a), only 31 per cent of the Portuguese aged 25–64 years and 43 per cent of the Spaniards of the same age have completed at

Table 2.1(a). *Educational attainments by age group, 1995*

	(A) Upper secondary education				(B) University degree			
	25–64 years	25–34/ 35–44	25–34/ 45–54	25–34/ 55–64	25–64 years	25–34/ 35–44	25–34/ 45–54	25–34/ 55–64
Portugal	20	1.3	1.9	3.4	11	1.0	1.4	2.3
Spain	28	1.5	2.6	4.7	16	1.5	2.5	4.5
OECD	60	1.1	1.3	1.7	22	1.0	1.3	1.9

Source: OECD (1997). Columns (2) and (6) give the percentage of the population aged 25–64 who have completed at least upper secondary and university education, respectively. The other columns give the ratios between proportions for those 25–34 years of age and those corresponding to the other age groups.

Table 2.1(b). *Educational attainments of new school leavers among the population aged 16–29 years, 1996*

	Men		Women		Gender gap
	(A) Lower secondary or less	(B) University level	(C) Lower secondary or less	(D) University level	(E)
Portugal	51	15	33	26	29
Spain	44	25	23	39	35
OECD	36	23	31	26	8

Source: OECD (1997). The gender gap is defined as $[(A)-(B)]-[(C)-(D)]$.

Table 2.2. *Sectoral composition of employment (as percentage of total employment), 1995*

		Portugal	Spain		
		Total	Total	Men	Women
Agriculture	1	11.29	9.19	10.20	7.28
Manufacturing	2–4	24.39	20.64	24.76	12.91
Building	5	8.08	9.43	13.93	0.98
Private services	6–8	28.96	34.15	33.01	36.30
Community, social, and personal services	9	31.88	26.60	18.10	42.53
Total employment (thousands)	1–9	3,350	12,050	7,861	4,190

Source: Labour Force Survey.

least upper secondary education. However, Table 2.1(a) also shows that the younger cohorts are much more educated than the older ones reflecting large changes in the educational composition of the labour force. Table 2.1(b) confirms this fact by showing the educational attainments of new school leavers among the population aged 16–29 years of age. Moreover, the gender difference in skill upgrading shows that it is the female population which has increased by most its educational level. On top of that, the participation rate of females has also increased notably in both countries (from 59.8 per cent in 1983 to 64.1 per cent in 1995, in Portugal, and from 34.7 to 47.4 per cent, during the same period, in Spain).

As for labour demand, the sectoral composition of employment has also changed in the same pattern (see Table 2.2) and has more or less converged in both countries. Traditionally, agricultural employment has been relatively higher in Portugal than in Spain. Also, Portugal has kept a larger fraction of employment in manufacturing, while the proportion of services in employment is roughly similar in both countries but with a higher participation of social and community services in Portugal.

An analysis of the shifts in relative demand and supply of skilled labour requires a closer look at the employment shares across industries (at a disaggregated level) and broad occupational groups. To measure the incidence of these shifts, we decompose changes in employment into its between and within-industry components for manual ('blue-collar' workers) and non-manual workers ('white-collar' workers). This decomposition is according to following formula:

$$\Delta P_n = \sum_i \Delta S_i \cdot \bar{P}_{ni} + \sum_i \Delta P_{ni} \cdot \bar{S}_{ni} \qquad (2.1)$$

where i refers to an industry, n stands for a category of workers (gender/schooling/manual, non-manual); P_{ni} is the share of employment category n in industry i, P_n is the share of employment category n in total employment, and S is the share of employment in industry i in total employment. The first term of the right-hand side of eqn (2.1) represents between-industry employment changes, i.e., those due to the sectoral reallocation of labour. The second term of the right-hand side of eqn (2.1) gives the within-industry component, i.e. the change in the relative demand of category n that is independent of sectoral shifts. We perform this decomposition for 20 industries, and workers are classified by gender, schooling years, and occupation (manual and non-manual).

Table 2.3 reports the results from this decomposition in Portugal and Spain for the 1983–92 period.[3] In columns (6) and (10) we report the within-industry component as a proportion of the total change in the corresponding employment share. As seen in the Table, both in Portugal and Spain the most relevant component of the change in the employment structure is the within-industry component, which accounts for more than 90 per cent of the changes in employment shares for most workers' groups considered. This confirms that changes in the composition of employment took place in all the economic sectors and that the underlying driving force is likely to be similar in both countries.

2.4. LEVELS AND PATTERNS OF EARNINGS INEQUALITY

We now turn to measure earnings inequality in Portugal and Spain using individual data from two similar surveys (*Quadros de Pessoal*, QP, from the Ministry of Employment and Social Security, 1996, in Portugal; and *Encuesta de Estructura Salarial*, EES, from the National Statistical Office, 1995, in Spain).[4] Our samples only cover establishments with over 10 employees in the non-agricultural sector, and do not include Public Administration employees. In these samples, Portugal presents a more traditional productive structure than Spain. In fact, small firms predominate in the Portuguese economy, where trade has a relatively high weight, while finance and manufacturing have a relatively high weight in Spain. Some contrasts can also be identified between both countries' labour

---

[3] During this period (1983–92), earnings inequality increased in Portugal (Cardoso, 1998) and also, to a lesser extent, in Spain (Bover *et al.*, 2000).

[4] For a brief description of these surveys see the Appendix.

Table 2.3(a). *Changes in the structure of employment. Portugal, 1983–92*

Schooling	Occupation	Men change in the employment share[a]				Women change in the employment share[a]			
		Total	Between-industry component[b]	Within-industry component[b]		Total	Between-industry component[b]	Within-industry component[b]	
(1)	(2)	(3)	(4)	(5)	(6)[c]	(7)	(8)	(9)	(10)[d]
less than 5 yrs	Non-manual	−2.82	−0.08	−2.74	97.2	−0.68	0.37	−1.05	154.2
	Manual	−11.82	−2.67	−9.15	77.4	−1.06	0.56	−1.62	153.3
6 yrs	Non-manual	−0.98	0.08	−1.06	107.8	0.04	0.29	−0.25	670.9
	Manual	3.09	−0.28	3.38	109.2	4.00	0.22	3.78	94.5
9 yrs	Non-manual	1.07	0.11	0.96	89.4	1.39	0.34	1.05	75.4
	Manual	1.50	0.02	1.49	99.0	1.05	0.08	0.97	92.3
11–12 yrs	Non-manual	0.02	0.12	−0.10	−459.5	1.65	0.38	1.28	77.2
	Manual	0.74	−0.01	0.75	100.9	0.74	0.08	0.66	89.0
University	Non-manual	0.32	0.07	0.25	79.0	0.51	0.22	0.29	56.5
	Manual	0.69	0.02	0.67	97.0	0.54	0.09	0.45	83.8

Source: Computations based on Portugal, MESS, DE (1983–92).

Table 2.3(b). *Changes in the structure of employment. Spain, 1983–92*

Schooling	Occupation	Men change in the employment share[a]				Women change in the employment share[a]			
		Total	Between-industry component[b]	Within-industry component[b]		Total	Between-industry component[b]	Within-industry component[b]	
(1)	(2)	(3)	(4)	(5)	(6)[c]	(7)	(8)	(9)	(10)[d]
less than 5 yrs	Manual	−2.87	−1.32	−1.549	54.1	−1.086	−0.811	−0.27	25.2
	Non-manual	0.05	0.06	−0.005	9.43	−0.012	0.050	−0.06	516.7
6 yrs	Manual	−12.19	−2.92	−9.275	76.01	−3.515	−1.429	−2.09	59.3
	Non-manual	−2.51	0.97	−3.475	138.7	−0.656	0.337	−0.99	151.2
9 yrs	Manual	6.20	0.03	6.165	99.5	1.475	−0.246	1.72	116.7
	Non-manual	0.43	0.65	−0.215	−50.0	0.953	0.426	0.53	55.3
11–12 yrs	Manual	3.79	0.15	3.642	96.1	0.724	0.015	0.71	97.8
	Non-manual	2.51	0.88	1.625	64.8	3.268	0.696	2.57	78.7
University	Manual	0.22	−0.01	0.220	104.7	0.085	0.013	0.07	83.5
	Non-manual	0.93	1.48	−0.551	−59.1	2.206	0.975	1.23	55.7

Notes: a: Difference between the employment share in 1992 and that in 1983 (both evaluated in percentage points). Note that, since the values refer to absolute changes in the employment shares, they should not be used to evaluate relative changes (as an example, the rise of about 2 percentage points in the share of university graduates means an extremely pronounced increase, from 2 to 4 per cent of the workforce). b: A two-digit disaggregation was considered, yielding 20 industries. c: (6) = (5)/(3). d: (10) = (9)/(7).

Source: Computations from the Labour Force Survey.

forces. In Portugal, the labour force is younger, less schooled and women take up a larger share of employment. Tenure is higher in Spain than in Portugal: mean tenure is 11 years and 8 years, in Spain and Portugal, respectively. The degree of centralization of wage bargaining is also significantly different in both countries: while 25.6 per cent of the Spanish labour force is covered by

O. Cantó, A. R. Cardoso, and J. F. Jimeno

Table 2.4. *Earnings inequality in Portugal and Spain, 1995*

	Q9010	Q9050	Q5010	CV	Gini coefficient
Portugal	4.09	2.59	1.58	0.96	0.36
Spain	3.62	2.18	1.66	1.14	0.32

Notes: Q9010, Q9050, and Q5010 are, respectively, the ratios of the percentile 90 to 10, 90 to 50, and 50 to 10. CV: Coefficient of variation.

Sources: Computations based on Portugal, MESS, DE (1995) and on Spain, INE, *Encuesta de Estructura Salarial* (1995).

Note: See the Appendix for definitions.

firm-level agreements, only 6 per cent of the workers in the Portuguese sample are covered.[5] It should nevertheless be noticed that the wage drift is higher in Portugal, which may contribute to the adjustments of wages set at a centralized level to the conditions prevailing at the firm level. As for our measure of earnings, we compute average hourly earnings as the ratio between total wage (the sum of the base-wage, tenure payments, and subsidies, but excluding overtime payments) and the normal hours of work.

Table 2.4 reports some indexes of earnings inequality. It shows a higher degree of wage inequality in Portugal than in Spain. This appreciation is confirmed by other indexes of earnings inequality as the Gini coefficient that has a value of 0.36 in Portugal and 0.32 in Spain.[6] The ratio of the 90th percentile to the 10th percentile is 4.1 for Portugal and 3.6 for Spain. Similarly, the ratio of the 90th percentile and the median is also higher in Portugal, 2.6 versus 2.2. However, the ratio of the 50th to the 10th is higher in Spain, 1.7, than in Portugal, 1.6. Thus, the wage distribution in Portugal has a more compressed bottom tail and a more stretched top tail than the Spanish wage distribution.

What explains these patterns of earnings inequality? Both Portugal and Spain display relatively high earnings dispersion for European standards (see Cardoso, 1998). In Portugal, a relatively high minimum wage (which is above 40 per cent of the average wage), unions weaker at collective bargaining, and high returns to education yield an earnings distribution with a fat lower tail but a stretched upper tail. In Spain, the minimum wage, in terms of average earnings, is lower (about 30 per cent), unions are stronger at collective bargaining and the returns to education are lower, so that the earnings distribution is less compressed at the bottom and less stretched at the upper tail. However, the high incidence of fixed-term employment (about one-third) increases the degree of earnings inequality. While the earnings distribution for full-time permanent employees shows a degree of dispersion roughly similar to that observed in the average Continental European

---

[5] In Portugal, agreements signed between one or several unions and one or several employers' associations, often covering an economic sector, are considered as national/industrial level bargaining agreements.

[6] A similar result arises when inequality indexes are computed using monthly earnings instead of hourly average earnings (see Bover *et al.*, 2000).

country, fixed-term employees earn lower wages on a much more disperse distribution.[7]

2.5. DETERMINANTS OF EARNINGS

In this section, we focus on the determinants of the wage structure by performing an analysis of the variance of earnings and estimating earnings regressions to measuring the contribution of given employers' and workers' characteristics to wages. The analysis of variance (ANOVA) provides a very intuitive framework to decompose the dispersion of earnings into different components. We will be interested in particular in quantifying the relative contribution of supply-side and demand-side variables to earnings inequality. The regression analysis is also useful to assess how different workers' characteristics and job positions are remunerated in the labour market.

As for the analysis of variance, we consider the following model:

$$W_{ijk} = \alpha + Y_j\beta + X_k\delta + e_{ijk} \tag{2.2}$$

where W_{ijk} stands for the (log) wage of worker i of type k, in employer j; Y_j is a vector of firm dummies; X_k is a (set of) dummy variable(s) representing the type of worker. Simpler versions of this version of the model which consider just employers' or workers' characteristics are

$$W_{ijk} = \chi + Y_j\eta + v_{ijk} \tag{2.3}$$

$$W_{ijk} = \zeta + X_k\gamma + \xi_{ijk}. \tag{2.4}$$

Model (3) gives the impact of employers' characteristics on the earnings distribution while model (4) gives the impact of workers' characteristics. The coefficient of determination of a regression of earnings on employers' characteristics (from model 3) can be interpreted as an upper bound on the contribution of employers' characteristics to earnings dispersion and to gross inequality. Adding workers' characteristics, i.e., considering model (2), and evaluating the change in the coefficient of determination, yields an approximation to the marginal impact of workers' attributes on inequality, controlling for employers' characteristics. Similarly, the marginal contribution of employers' characteristics can be assessed as the difference between the coefficients of determination between models (4) and (2).

Table 2.5 reports these decompositions of the variance of wages among employers' and workers' characteristics. The cross-firm variation of earnings is similar in both countries: a regression of earnings on a set of firm dummies explains a similar percentage of the variance of earnings in both countries (65 per cent).

---

[7] The wage premium for permanent employees is estimated at about 10 per cent after controlling for observable individual characteristics (see Jimeno and Toharia, 1993).

Table 2.5. *Analysis of variance of earnings, Portugal and Spain, 1995*

	Independent variables (sources of dispersion)	Explained sum of squares (% of total)	
		Spain	Portugal
(1)	Firm dummies	65	65
(2)	Workers' characteristics (gender, schooling, age, occupations) (1)	39	48
(3)	Employers' and workers' characteristics	78	78
(4) = (3)–(2)	Marginal impact of employers' characteristics (controlling for workers' characteristics)	39	30
(5) = (3)–(1)	Marginal impact of the workers' characteristics (controlling for employers' characteristics)	13	13
(6)	Employers' characteristics (2)	23	31
(7)	Number of observations	149,072	146,096

Notes: (1) Nine occupational groups were defined, according to the Portuguese and Spanish classification of occupations, which are consistent at that level of aggregation; schooling groups were defined according to the years of completed education; three age categories were considered (16–25, 26–39, 40–65 years). (2) The following employer attributes were considered: industry (ten categories), size (five categories), region (two categories), owner (four categories), type of bargaining contract (four categories).
Sources: Computations based on Portugal, MESS, DE (1995) and on Spain, EES–INE (1995).

Despite this fact, the results from ANOVA analysis show significant differences across the determinants of the earnings distribution. First, employers' characteristics explain a lower fraction of the variance of earnings in Spain, 23 per cent, than in Portugal, 31 per cent, which together with the similar variation of earnings across firms suggests that non-observable employers' characteristics (such as financial variables, for instance) are more relevant in Spain at shaping the earnings distribution. This is consistent with the higher decentralization of wage determination in Spain and can be rationalized as a higher insider weight in wage determination in this country. Second, in Portugal, workers' characteristics are more relevant at explaining the earnings distribution than in Spain: workers' characteristics explain 48 per cent of the variance of earnings in Portugal, only 39 per cent in Spain. Third, the marginal impact of employers' characteristics controlling for workers' characteristics is higher in Spain, 39 per cent, than in Portugal, 30 per cent, and the marginal impact of workers' characteristics, controlling for employers' characteristics, is roughly similar in both countries, 13 per cent. Finally, both workers' and employers' characteristics together account for a similar share of the earnings dispersion in both countries, 78 per cent.

Further insights on the determinants of earnings can be obtained by looking at the regression coefficients of each variable in these earnings regressions. The specification of our earnings equations is standard. We regress (log) hourly earnings on a set of workers' characteristics (tenure, schooling, gender, experience,

Table 2.6. *Earnings regressions. Dependent variable: (log) hourly wages, 1995*

Dependent variable: Log (hourly earnings)	Portugal	Spain
Workers' characteristics		
Tenure	.0046**	.0069
Sex × Tenure	.00009	.0038**
Sex	−.0065	−.155**
Dummy Tenure < 1 year	−.040**	−.034**
Sex × Dummy Tenure < 1 year	−.003	.047**
Schooling	.070**	.050**
Sex × Schooling	−.004**	−.0006
Experience	.036**	.030**
Sex × Experience	−.012**	−.0047**
Experience squared	−.00046**	−.00036**
Sex × Experience squared	.00018**	.00002*
Blue-collar	−.136**	−.167**
Sex × Blue-collar	−.046**	.0088
Firm Economic Activity		
Mining	.184**	.089**
Manufacturing	Reference	Reference
Electricity and Gas	.351**	.180**
Building	.065**	.013**
Trade	.019**	−.115**
Hotels and Restaurants	−.128**	−.107**
Transport, Communications	.183**	.002
Finance	.399**	.198**
Real Estate and Services to companies	.114**	−.101**
Firm Size		
10–19 workers	Reference	Reference
20–49 workers	.083**	.060**
50–99 workers	.133**	.114**
100–199 workers	.178**	.171**
> =200 workers	.162**	.209**
Sex × (10–19 workers)	Reference	Reference
Sex × (20–49 workers)	−.036**	−.015*
Sex × (50–99 workers)	−.054**	−.021**
Sex × (100–199 workers)	−.094	−.028**
Sex × (> =200 workers)	−.029	−.048**
Type of Collective Agreement *(a)*		
National	Reference	Reference
Over firm	.078**	.006**
Firm	.027**	.138**
Other	—	.019**
Firm Ownership Status		
Public	.067**	−.065**
Private	Reference	Reference
Mostly public	.220**	.111**

Table 2.6. *(Continued)*

Dependent variable: Log (hourly earnings)	Portugal	Spain
Other		.272**
Foreign	.225**	
Region		
Spain: Madrid, Basque Country and Catalonia		.131**
Portugal: Lisbon and Tagus Valley	.133**	
Spain: Sex × Madrid, PV and Catalonia		−.015**
Portugal: Sex × Lisbon and Tagus Valley	−.023**	
Constant	5.359**	6.031**
Number of observations	146,096	149,072
R squared	0.551	0.462

Sources: Computations based on Portugal, MESS, DE (1995) and on SPAIN, ESS – INE DE (1995).
Notes: (1) * = coefficient is significant at a 10% level., ** = coefficient is significant at a 5% level.
(2) When coding the variables for Portugal, agreements signed between one or several unions and one or several employers' *associations*, often covering an economic sector, were considered as national/industrial level bargaining agreements.

skill level) and a set of employers' characteristics (economic activity, firm's size, location, type of collective agreement, ownership structure). We search for comparable specifications in both countries.

Table 2.6 reports the results of this regression analysis. They show the following facts:

- The female wage gap is slightly lower in Spain than in Portugal. Precise estimates on the time evolution of the female wage gap in Spain are not available. Estimates from different cross-section samples at different years suggest that it has remained more or less stable. This is so despite the fact that there has been an intense skill upgrading of the new cohorts of women relative to men. This upgrading has resulted in increasing female employment rates but happened at the cost of a 'downgrading' of the women's entry jobs in which wages are lower and less disperse (see Dolado *et al.*, 1999). In contrast, in Portugal the gender wage gap has increased (see Jimeno *et al.*, 2000).
- Returns to tenure are still significantly higher in Spain than in Portugal, in particular, given the sharp decrease observed in Portugal in later years. Also, the wage penalty to newcomers into the firm (less than one-year tenure workers), which has declined in Portugal, is still high in Spain. This is related to the high incidence of fixed-term employment contracts in Spain, who receive lower wages and have shorter job tenure than employees with permanent contracts.
- In Spain, production workers' wages are 11 per cent lower than those of non-production workers, while in Portugal this gap is about 22 per cent. This lower gap between the wages of production and non-production workers in Spain

can be explained by the compressing effects of trade union intervention in wage determination, which results in binding bargained wages and higher unemployment for low-skill workers (see Dolado *et al.*, 1997).

- Inter-industry wage differences are lower in Spain than in Portugal. As in the latter country, workers in the finance sector receive a wage premium above 30 per cent. As for workers in transportation and communications, their relative wages are higher in Portugal. However, above all, the most interesting fact is the negative gap observed for Portuguese workers in the textiles industry and in hotels and restaurants, which is not observed in Spain. Thus, it seems that in Portugal there are some low-wage, labour intensive industries where low-skill workers can still be employed. This is contrast with Spain where relatively high wages in these types of industries have resulted in high unemployment among low-skill workers.
- Finally, the regional differences in wages are much larger in Spain than in Portugal: wages in Extremadura, Galicia and Murcia, for instance, are more than 20 per cent lower than in Madrid. Interestingly enough, Extremadura and Galicia are the two Spanish regions geographically closest to Portugal.

Overall, institutional factors like fixed-term employment in Spain and the effectiveness of trade unions at compressing the wage distribution are key for the understanding of wage inequality in both countries. The incidence of the minimum wage in Portugal is the main reason for a compressed wage structure at the bottom tail, but higher returns to education (mainly due to still low relative supply of educated workers) results in high wage inequality for European standards. In Spain, the main dimensions along which wage inequality is increased are returns to tenure (due to the incidence and characteristics of fixed-term employment) and the territory (due to large differences in wages among regions).

2.6. CONCLUSIONS

We have compared the Portuguese and the Spanish earnings distributions to gauge to what extent different degrees of labour market flexibility translate into inequality and how the contribution of workers' and employers' attributes to total inequality differs in both countries. We first have reported the level and patterns of earnings inequality in Portugal and Spain. Second, we have estimated earnings regressions in both countries with comparable large data sets (around 150,000 observations in Spain and over 200,000 observations in Portugal). Our results suggest that the difference in earnings inequality is not as large as could be expected beforehand. In Portugal the lower tail of the earnings distribution is tighter, skills differences contribute more to total inequality, the returns to schooling are higher, and there seem to be more earnings variations between firms. In Spain, regarding workers' attributes, within-group inequality and the returns to tenure are higher (which can be explained by the high incidence of fixed-term employment across all sectors and occupations), and there is less dispersion among different industries and collective bargaining agreements.

Our results raise further research questions. The first one is in relation to the evolution through time. There are some indications that biased technological progress is changing the remuneration of different characteristics in the labour market, and that the change may depend on institutional features of the labour market. Here, the comparison of the evolution of wage inequality in the last decade or so in Portugal and Spain could shed some insights, which we have explored in another paper (see Jimeno *et al.*, 2000). Secondly, there is the issue of the dynamics within the earnings distribution, in other words the degree of social mobility and individual changes within the distribution as time passes by. We plan to pursue these topics in further research.

APPENDIX

Databases on Wages in Portugal and in Spain

In Portugal, there is very detailed information on wage structure since 1982. An extensive data set is gathered annually by the Ministry of Employment and Solidarity *(Quadros de Pessoal—QP)*, based on a questionnaire that every establishment with wage earners is legally obliged to fill in. Reported data match the *establishment* (location, economic activity and employment), the *firm* (location, economic activity, employment, sales, legal setting) and each of the *workers* (gender, age, skill, occupation, schooling, tenure, earnings—split into basewage, tenure-related earnings, other regular paid subsidies, irregular subsidies and overtime pay, duration of work—normal and overtime), as well as the mechanism of wage bargaining. By design, public administration and domestic work are not covered by the database (though state-owned companies are) and in practice neither is agriculture. For the remaining sectors, *QP* is a very reliable source of information, being in fact a census of firms, establishments, and their employees.

In Spain reliable microeconomic data on wages are available only for 1988 (when EUROSTAT *Labour Costs Survey—LCS*, was first conducted in this country), 1992 (the second Spanish wave of the *LCS*) and 1995 (*Encuesta de Estructura Salarial—EES*, conducted by the Spanish National Statistical Office). The latter collects detailed information on individual earnings as well as employers (economic activity, size, legal setting, type of wage bargaining) and workers' (gender, education, skill, occupation, tenure and, most importantly, monthly earnings) characteristics, information which is missing in the *LCS*. The *EES* sample is selected from the population of establishments with more than 10 dependent workers in a two-stage sampling method. The economic activity, region, and size of the firm determine the first stage selection while the number of workers within each of the groups was chosen in a second stage. Our EES sample refers to 1995

Table 2.7. *Descriptive statistics, Portugal, 1995*

Firms' characteristics		Workers' characteristics	
Size (%)		*Gender (%)*	
10–19 workers	49.8	Male	63.3
20–49 workers	31.9	Female	36.7
50–99 workers	10.2	*Age*	
100–199 workers	4.9	16–25	20.3
≥ 200 workers	3.3	26–39	43.9
Firm Economic Activity (%)		40–65	35.8
Mining	1.0	*School (yrs)*[a]	
Manufacturing	46.7	0	3.0
Electricity and gas	0.1	4	43.4
Building	12.1	6	22.0
Trade	24.6	9	14.1
Hotels and restaurants	5.9	12	13.0
Transport, communications	3.5	15	1.4
Finance	1.4	17	3.1
Real estate, services to cos.	4.6	*Occupations (%)*[b]	
Region (%)		Industrial directors and executives	2.8
North	37.0	Professionals and scientists	2.3
Centre	22.1	Middle management and technicians	9.2
Lisbon and the Tagus Valley	35.6	Administrative and related workers	16.2
Alentejo	2.3	Service and sales workers	8.6
Algarve	3.0	Farmers and skilled agricultural and fish workers	0.2
Firm Ownership (%)		Skilled workers, craftsmen and similar	31.3
Public	0.3	Machine operators and assembly workers	15.4
Private	94.6	Unskilled workers	14.1
Mostly public	0.2	*Firm Size (%)*	
Foreign	4.9	10–19 workers	27.5
		20–49 workers	26.9
		50–99 workers	13.1
		100–199 workers	9.7
		≥ 200 workers	22.8
		Firm Economic Activity (%)	
		Mining	0.9
		Manufacturing	47.6
		Electricity and gas	0.9
		Building	10.6
		Trade	19.6
		Hotels and restaurants	4.9
		Transport, communications	6.6
		Finance	4.5
		Real estate, services to companies	4.4

Table 2.7. *(Continued)*

Firms' characteristics		Workers' characteristics	
		Region (%)	
		North	35.2
		Centre	19.9
		Lisbon and the Tagus Valley	40.7
		Alentejo	1.9
		Algarve	2.4
		Firm Ownership (%)	
		Public	4.5
		Private	86.2
		Mostly public	0.7
		Foreign	8.6
		Collective Agreement[c] *(%)*	
		National	90.7
		Over firm	3.7
		Firm	5.6
		Mean tenure in years	8.1
		Mean hourly wage	735.2
Number of observations	16,234	Number of observations	147,017

[a]Education below the primary level was coded as 0. [b]The Portuguese Classification of Occupations in 1985 and 1991 was not strictly comparable to this one. [c]Agreements signed between one or several unions and one or several employers' associations, often covering an economic sector, were coded as national/industrial level bargaining.

Source: MESS, DE (1995).

Table 2.8. *Descriptive Statistics, Spain 1995*

Firms' characteristics		Workers' characteristics	
Size (%)		*Gender (%)*	
10–19 workers	36.1	Male	78.6
20–199 workers	54.8	Female	21.4
≥ 200 workers	9.1	*Age (%)*	
Firm Economic Activity (%)		16–25	11.3
Mining	1.1	26–39	44.0
Manufacturing	62.0	40–65	44.6
Electricity and gas	1.4	*School (yrs)*	
Building	7.4	0	2.3
Trade	8.8	5	32.0
Hotels and restaurants	5.3	8	31.0
Transport, communications	4.2	10	4.9
Finance	5.2	11	5.0
Real estate, services to firms	4.5	12	12.9

Table 2.8. *(Continued)*

Firms' characteristics		Workers' characteristics	
Region (%)		14	1.0
Andalucía	8.3	15	4.7
Aragon	5.6	17	5.8
Asturias	4.0	*Occupations (%)*	
Baleares	3.4	Industrial directors and executives	4.1
Canarias	4.6	Professionals and scientists	4.7
Cantabria	2.8	Middle management and technicians	10.6
Castilla-La Mancha	5.5	Administrative and related workers	14.0
Castilla-León	6.3	Service and sales workers	6.2
Cataluña	12.3	Farmers and skilled agric. and fish. workers	0
Comunidad Valenciana	8.6	Skilled workers, craftsmen and similar	21.9
Extremadura	2.5	Machine operators and assembly workers	26.9
Galicia	6.5	Unskilled workers	11.4
Madrid	10.2	*Firm Size (%)*	
Murcia	4.7	10–19 workers	19.2
Navarra	4.1	20–199 workers	58.5
País Vasco	6.9	≥ 200 workers	22.3
Rioja	3.2	*Firm Economic Activity (%)*	
Ceuta y Melilla	0.2	Mining	0.8
Firm Ownership (%)		Manufacturing	62.7
Public	0.9	Electricity and gas	1.7
Private	99.1	Building	6.6
		Trade	8.5
		Hotels and restaurants	4.5
		Transport, Communications	4.0
		Finance	6.6
		Real estate, services to companies	4.2
		Region (%)	
		Andalucía	8.7
		Aragon	5.1
		Asturias	3.3
		Baleares	2.6
		Canarias	4.0
		Cantabria	2.2
		Castilla-La Mancha	5.0
		Castilla-León	6.4
		Cataluña	15.4
		Comunidad Valenciana	8.9
		Extremadura	1.8
		Galicia	6.3
		Madrid	13.0
		Murcia	3.6
		Navarra	3.6
		País Vasco	7.2

Table 2.8. *(Continued)*

Firms' characteristics		Workers' characteristics	
		Rioja	2.3
		Ceuta y Melilla	0.1
		Firm Ownership (%)	
		Public	1.4
		Private	98.5
		Collective Agreement (%)	
		National	34.3
		Over firm	41.6
		Firm	23.5
		Other	0.6
		Mean tenure in years	10.9
		Mean hourly wage	1,366
Number of observations	14,636	Number of observations	130,197

Source: ESS, INE (1995).

and includes 14,636 establishments and 130,197 full-time workers between 16 and 65 years. For our measures of inequality we only consider full-time employees. To guarantee comparability of the Portuguese data with the available Spanish data set, we draw a sample from the *QP* following similar procedures to those the Spanish National Statistical Office uses to choose the sample of the *EES*.[8] Tables 2.7 and 2.8 present the main descriptive statistics of our Portuguese and Spanish samples of employees.

REFERENCES

Blanchard, O. and J. F. Jimeno (1995). Structural unemployment. Spain versus Portugal, *American Economic Review, Papers and Proceedings*, 82, 2 May.

Bover, O., P. García-Perea, and P. Portugal (2000). Labour market outliers: Lessons from Spain and Portugal. *Economic Policy*, 31, 379–428.

Cardoso, A. R. (1997). Workers or employers. Who is shaping wage inequality?, *Oxford Bulletin of Economics and Statistics*, 59, 4.

—— (1998). Earnings inequality in Portugal. High and rising?, *Review of Income and Wealth*, 44, 325–43.

Castillo, S., J. J. Dolado, and J. F. Jimeno (1998). A tale of two neighbour economies. Labour market dynamics in Spain and Portugal, *CEPR working paper* 1954.

Dolado, J. J. and J. F. Jimeno (1997). The causes of Spanish unemployment. A structural VAR approach, *European Economic Review*, 41.

[8] The sampling process involved two steps: a 75 per cent random sample of firms was drawn, stratified according to industry (48 categories), region (five categories) and firm size (five categories); subsequently, workers within the firm were sampled. Five workers were selected from firms with 10–19 wage-earners; 25 per cent of the wage earners were kept from firms with 20–49 wage earners; 17 per cent, 13 per cent and 10 per cent of workers were drawn from firms with 50–99, 100–199, and over 200 wage-earners, respectively.

—— F. Felgueroso, and J. F. Jimeno (1997). The effects of minimum bargained wages on earnings. Evidence from Spain, *European Economic Review, Papers and Proceedings*, 41.

—— —— and —— (1999). The causes of youth labour market problems in Spain. Crowding-out, institutions, or technology shifts?, mimeo, FEDEA.

Freeman, R. (1993). How much has de-unionization contributed to the rise in male earnings inequality? in S. Danzinger and P. Gottschalk (eds.), *Uneven Tides. Rising Inequality in the 1980s*, Russell Stage Foundation. New York.

Gottschalk, P. and T. M. Smeeding (1997). Cross-national comparison of earnings and income inequality, *Journal of Economic Literature*, vol. XXXVF, June, 633–87.

INE (1995). Encuesta de Estructura Salarial (EES-INE), Madrid.

Jimeno, J. F., O. Cantó, A. R. Cardoso, M. Izquierdo, and C. F. Rodrigues (2000). Integration and inequality. Lessons from the accessions of Portugal and Spain to the EU, *FEDEA Working Paper*, 2000–10.

—— and L. Toharia (1993). The effects of fixed-term employment on wages. Theory and evidence from Spain, *Investigaciones Económicas*, XVII(3), 475–94.

Luz, S. and M. Pinheiro (1994). Wage rigidity and job mismatch in Europe: Some evidence, *Banco de Portugal Working Paper*, 2–94.

Ministry of Employment and Social Security (1995). Quadros de Pesioal (MESS-DE), data in magnetic medium.

OECD (1993). *Employment Perspectives*, Paris.

—— (1996). *Employment Perspectives*, Paris.

—— (1997). *Education at a glance*, Paris: OECD.

Soskice, D. (1990). Wage determination. The changing role of institutions in advanced industrialized countries, *Oxford Review of Economic Policy*, vol. 6, p. 4.

3

Changes in Unemployment and Wage Inequality: An Alternative Theory and Some Evidence

Between 1979 and 1987, the average weekly wages of college graduates with 1–5 years of experience increased by 30 per cent relative to the average weekly earnings of comparable high-school graduates (John Bound and George Johnson, 1992; Lawrence F. Katz and Kevin M. Murphy, 1992). Within-group (residual) wage inequality may have started increasing earlier: after controlling for education and experience, the differential between the 90th and the 10th percentile wages stood at 118 per cent in 1988 compared to 92 per cent in 1970 (Chinhui Juhn *et al.*, 1993). The rise in inequality over this period was not only due to wage increases for high-paid workers. Real wages of high-school graduates with 1–5 years of experience, for example, fell by 20 per cent from 1979 to 1987 (Katz and Murphy, 1992, Table I). Meanwhile, the unemployment rates of all education groups have also increased. In 1970, the unemployment rate for civilian males between the ages of 25 and 64 with less than 4 years of high school stood at 4 per cent. For those with high-school and college degrees, the same numbers were 2.4 and 1.1 per cent. Averaged between 1992 and 1994, the unemployment rates for these three groups were, respectively, 13.9, 6, and 3.2 per cent, approximately three times higher than the rates during the 1970s (*Statistical Abstracts of the United States*, 1995, Table 662).[1]

I am grateful to three anonymous referees, and to Joshua Angrist, Brian Bell, Peter Diamond, Michael Kremer, Frank Levy, Steve Pischke, Jim Robinson, Robert Shimer, Jaume Ventura, and various seminar participants for comments and useful suggestions. I also thank Matthew Barmack for help with the Panel Study of Income Dynamics data, Francesco Caselli for Figure 3, and David Autor for extracts from the decennial censuses. Maciej Dudek, Jonathan Dworak, John Johnson, and John Romalis provided excellent research assistance. Finally, I gratefully acknowledge financial support from National Science Foundation Grant No. SBR-9602116 and the World Economic Laboratory at MIT.
  Previously published in *The American Economic Review* 89 (1999), 1259–78, reproduced with the permission of the American Economic Association.

[1] See also Murphy and Robert H. Topel (1987) and Stephen Nickell and Brian Bell (1995). The unemployment rates have decreased recently due to sustained high growth of the US economy but are not at their 1970 levels.

This chapter offers a theory in which these labour-market developments may be caused by a *qualitative* change in the composition of jobs. Namely, in response to changes in the skill level of the labour force or technology, 'middling' jobs open both to skilled and unskilled workers may be replaced by high-quality (capital) jobs designed for the skilled and low-wage jobs targeted at the unskilled. This change in the composition of jobs leads to higher skilled wages, lower unskilled wages, and higher unemployment rates for both skilled and unskilled workers. To the extent that skills are positively but imperfectly correlated with education, these changes imply higher returns to education, increased residual inequality, and higher unemployment rates for all education groups.

The first possible driving force for the change in the composition of jobs is an increase in the proportion of skilled workers in the labour force. According to the standard approach, an increase in the relative supply of skills depresses the skill premium and reduces inequality. In contrast, in this model when the supply of skills reaches a critical threshold, it becomes more profitable to create jobs designed for skilled workers, and the composition of jobs undergoes a qualitative change, altering the structure of wages and unemployment.[2] In other words, an increase in the supply of skills can create more than its own demand and increase inequality. The second possible driving force is an exogenous increase in the relative demand for skilled workers, which may be due to skill-biased technical change or increased international trade. In this case, the change in the composition of jobs emphasized in this chapter is a novel economic mechanism for a familiar shock, enabling us to explain the fall in the wages of low-paid workers and the increase in unemployment for both skilled and unskilled workers, which are not features readily explained by existing theories.

There are two crucial ingredients in this chapter. The first is the presence of search frictions, which makes it costly for firms to find suitable workers. John M. Barron *et al.* (1985), among others, document the costs of recruiting workers. These problems appear to be more serious when firms attempt to select skilled workers, especially given the imperfect correlation between education and skills. Similarly, the evidence in Topel and Michael P. Ward (1992) indicates that it takes a long time for young workers to find suitable jobs. The second ingredient is that firms have to choose what type of job to open before meeting a worker. This also appears plausible, since in practice a firm which has opened a service job cannot easily change it to a manufacturing job, nor can a firm easily downgrade its technology.

These two ingredients imply that the skill composition of the labour force affects the types of jobs that firms want to create. When the supply of skills is limited, it is not profitable to create jobs specially designed for the skilled, because it is difficult to find skilled workers and these jobs would not be as productive

---

[2] Katz and Murphy (1992) show that in the short run a higher supply of skilled workers reduces the skill premium. The forces I emphasize instead operate over a longer time frame as capital and job composition adjust.

when employing unskilled workers. As a result, when there are few available skilled workers and there is a small gap between their productivity and that of the unskilled, the economy will be in a pooling equilibrium where firms create 'middling' jobs, do relatively little screening, and hire most applicants. Because in a pooling equilibrium, both skilled and unskilled workers are employed in the same jobs with the same amount of physical capital, unskilled workers are employed at *higher* physical to human capital ratios than the skilled, and wage differentials are compressed. Also, because firms recruit most applicants, unemployment is low.

The alternative to pooling is a separating equilibrium in which firms create separate jobs for skilled and unskilled workers, and search for the appropriate candidates. Jobs for skilled workers are of a higher quality in a separating than in a pooling equilibrium, while unskilled jobs are of higher quality in a pooling equilibrium. As a result, in a separating equilibrium skilled workers earn more, and the unskilled less, than in a pooling allocation. Furthermore, since skilled workers produce only with high-capital firms and the unskilled work only with low-capital firms, the unemployment rates for both types of workers are higher. Starting from a pooling equilibrium, an increase in the proportion of skilled workers and/or skill-biased technical change can push the economy to a separating equilibrium, changing the composition of jobs, reducing unskilled wages, and raising skilled wages and unemployment rates for both groups.

Both possible driving forces of this theory are empirically plausible. Many studies argue that the past two decades witnessed rapid skill-biased technical change (e.g., Eli Berman *et al.*, 1994; David H. Autor *et al.*, 1998). This period was also characterized by an unusually rapid increase in the supply of skills. For example, the ratio of college graduates to non-college graduates in the labour force increased by over 54 per cent between 1970 and 1980. Finally, there is some evidence suggesting that there was a change in the composition of jobs in the US between the 1970s and the 1990s, consistent with a shift from a pooling to a separating equilibrium. In particular, high-wage firms are more selective in their hiring than they were two decades ago, the distribution of physical capital to labour ratios across industries has become more unequal, workers appear to be better matched to their jobs, the distribution of on-the-job training across education groups has become more unequal, and some of the jobs in industries and occupations that typically pay close to the median of the wage distribution have been replaced by jobs from the more extreme parts of the quality distribution of jobs. These patterns are consistent with the theory outlined above and suggest that changes in the composition of jobs may be an important component of the changes in the structure of wages and unemployment.

This chapter builds on the search and matching models of Peter A. Diamond (1982), Dale T. Mortensen (1982), and Christopher A. Pissarides (1987). In contrast to those and as in Michael Sattinger (1995), Kenneth Burdett and Melvyn Coles (1997), and Robert J. Shimer and Lones A. Smith (1998), workers and firms are *ex ante* heterogeneous. The approach in this chapter, however, constitutes an improvement over these studies because the heterogeneity of firms is not assumed exogenous but is derived from their investment decisions. In this respect, the model has a similarity to Acemoglu (1996a), Steven J. Davis (1996), and Acemoglu and Shimer (1998), who also analyse models with *ex ante* investments. However, these articles do not discuss the changes in the composition of jobs, and do not allow for two-sided heterogeneity. My work is also related to the growing literature on the causes of wage inequality, including Michael Kremer and Eric Maskin (1997). They consider a model of assignment where workers of different skill levels form teams. If the distribution of skills is sufficiently disperse, a further increase in the variance of skills may induce high-skill workers to produce with other high-skill workers and increase inequality. Their approach is therefore complementary to, but different from, this chapter. In particular, in their model there are no firms (independent from workers), so there is no change in the composition of jobs and in the recruitment practices of firms, which are at the heart of my chapter. There is also no unemployment (hence no change in unemployment). Furthermore, in the data there is basically no increase in the variance of skills, which is the driving force in Kremer and Maskin's article, whereas there is a large increase in the supply of skills, which is one of the driving forces in this chapter. Finally, in more recent work (Acemoglu, 1998), I extend the approach in this chapter and point out another reason why an increase in the supply of skilled workers may increase inequality: when technical change is endogenous, an increase in the supply of skills increases the market size for skill-complementary technologies and may induce skill-bias technical change.

The plan of the chapter is as follows. Section 3.1 uses a static model to expose the main ideas. Section 3.2 considers a dynamic and more standard framework which confirms the main insights that follow from the static model, and generates a number of new results. Section 3.3 provides some evidence of a change in the composition of jobs in the US. Section 3.4 concludes.

3.1. A STATIC MODEL

In this section, I start with the simplest model of endogenous job composition. Firms choose what type of jobs to open and then search for workers. I show that there exist two types of equilibria with different structures of jobs and wages: pooling and separating. In the pooling equilibrium, firms open 'middling' jobs and recruit all workers. In the separating equilibrium, firms create jobs designed for high-skill workers. I show that changes in the relative supply of skills and/or in technology can switch the economy from a pooling to a separating equilibrium, transforming the structure of wages and unemployment.

3.1.1. Preferences, Technology, and the Walrasian Allocation

There is a mass 1 of risk-neutral workers and a mass 1 of risk-neutral and profit-maximizing firms. The economy lasts for one period, and contains workers in two education groups, high and low (e.g., high-school and college graduates). There is no perfect overlap between education and skills, however, so both groups contain skilled and unskilled workers. Naturally, high-education workers are more likely to be skilled. I denote the overall fraction of skilled workers by ϕ, and normalize the human capital of unskilled workers to $h = 1$ and the human capital of skilled workers to $h = \eta > 1$.

Production takes place in one firm–one worker pairs. A worker with human capital h and a firm with capacity k produce

$$y(h, k) = k^{1-\alpha} h^{\alpha}. \tag{3.1}$$

The timing of events is as follows. First, each firm has to choose its capacity ('physical capital'), k, irreversibly. This choice captures the type of job the firm has designed and the line of business it has chosen, and is assumed to be costless.[3] At this point, the firm does not know the type of the worker it will recruit. Next, the firm matches with a worker, finds out his type, and decides whether to shut down or continue. If it continues, it installs the required equipment and incurs a cost ck. Finally, wages are determined.

The Walrasian allocation of this economy corresponds to the case where at the wage determination stage, firms and workers can switch partners at no cost, and workers receive their full marginal product. In a Walrasian equilibrium, a fraction $1 - \phi$ of firms choose $k^L = ac^{-1/\alpha}$ and the remaining ϕ fraction choose $k^H = a\eta c^{-1/\alpha}$ where $a \equiv (1 - \alpha)^{1/\alpha}$. The Walrasian mechanism allocates skilled workers to high-capacity firms and maximizes output. Since workers receive their full marginal product, skilled wages are $w^H = y(\eta, k^H) - ck^H = \alpha a\eta/[(1 - \alpha)c^{(1-\alpha)/\alpha}]$, and unskilled wages are $w^L = y(1, k^L) - ck^L = \alpha a/[(1 - \alpha)c^{(1-\alpha)/\alpha}]$, so the skill premium is equal to $w^H/w^L = \eta$.

3.1.2. Equilibrium with Costly Search

Consider a trading environment with frictions and without the Walrasian auctioneer to mediate trade. Firms and workers come together randomly. Random matching implies that high- and low-capacity firms are equally likely to meet skilled workers.[4] I also assume that each firm meets one worker and vice versa. Once they meet, the worker–firm pair have to decide whether to produce together. In the dynamic version of the model, if the worker and the firm do not agree, they continue to search for a new partner, whereas here, because the economy lasts only for one period, the firm produces no output, and the worker receives zero

---

[3] An alternative interpretation is that there are many different types of firms, indexed by the variable k. In equilibrium, only the types that will make the highest profits will enter. Also, note that the main results hold if the firm incurs some cost $c_1 k$ when choosing its capacity, but also incurs the production costs ck, but the analysis becomes more complicated. If $c = 0$ so that all costs are incurred before matching, the static model would not work, but the dynamic model would give similar results.

[4] Random matching is plausible in this context. Since education and skills are imperfectly correlated, firms cannot easily target skilled workers, and targeting the highly educated workers will not be as profitable since many of those are unskilled.

income. Recall that at the wage-determination stage, the firm has already sunk the cost of capital, ck. Therefore, if the firm and the worker agree, they will share the total output $y(h, k)$. I assume that the worker obtains a fraction β of this amount, and the firm obtains the remainder. Hence, wages conditional on the capacity choice of the firm are: $w^H(k) = \beta k^{1-\alpha}\eta^\alpha$ and $w^L(k) = \beta k^{1-\alpha}$. To simplify the algebra, I also normalize $c \equiv (1 - \beta)$.

The expected value of a firm choosing capacity k can be written as

$$V(k, x^H, x^L) = \phi x^H(1 - \beta)[k^{1-\alpha}\eta^\alpha - k] + (1 - \phi)x^L(1 - \beta)[k^{1-\alpha} - k] \quad (3.2)$$

where x^j is the equilibrium probability that the firm produces with a worker of type $j = L$ or H, conditional on matching with this worker. Since a fraction ϕ of workers are skilled and there is random matching, the firm produces with a skilled worker with probability ϕx^H, and obtains $(1 - \beta) y(\eta, k) - ck = (1 - \beta)[k^{1-\alpha}\eta^\alpha - k]$. The second part of (3.2) is explained similarly. Note that when the firm decides not to produce with the worker, i.e., $x = 0$, it does not incur the cost of capital, ck.

In this static economy, workers are passive: they accept any match that comes along (since the alternative is to obtain zero). Therefore, an equilibrium is simply a distribution of capacity choices represented by the function $F(k)$ over some support $\mathcal{K}$, and two acceptance functions $x^H(k)$ and $x^L(k)$ such that for all $k' \in \mathcal{K}$, $(k', x^H(k'), x^L(k')) \in \arg\max_{k, x^H, x^L} V(K, x^H, x^L)$.

Proposition 1. *If*

$$\eta < \left(\frac{1 - \phi}{\phi^\alpha - \phi}\right)^{1/\alpha} \quad (3.3)$$

then, there is a unique equilibrium which is pooling. All firms choose

$$k^P = a[\phi\eta^\alpha + (1 - \phi)]^{1/\alpha},$$

i.e., $\mathcal{K} = \{k^P\}$, and $x^H(k^P) = x^L(k^P) = 1$. If $\eta > [(1 - \phi)/(\phi^\alpha - \phi)]^{1/\alpha}$, there is a unique equilibrium which is separating. All firms choose capacity $k^H = a\eta$, i.e., $\mathcal{K} = \{k^H\}$, $x^H(k) = 1$, and $x^L(k) = 0$.

Proof. An equilibrium $(k', x^H(k'), x^L(k'))$ maximizes (3.2). The first-order condition of (3.2) with respect to k for given x^L and x^H is: $(1 - \beta)[\phi x^H((1 - \alpha)k^{-\alpha}\eta^\alpha - 1) + (1 - \phi)x^L((1 - \alpha)k^{-\alpha} - 1)] = 0$. When $x^H = x^L = 1$, this solves for k^P in the text, and yields a maximal value of $V^P \equiv V(k^P, x^H = 1, x^L = 1) = (1 - \beta)\alpha a[\phi\eta^\alpha + (1 - \phi)]^{1/\alpha}/(1 - \alpha)$. Alternatively, for $x^H = 1$ and $x^L = 0$, the first-order condition solves for $k^H \equiv a\eta$ and yields $V^H \equiv V(k^H, x^H = 1, x^L = 0) = (1 - \beta)\alpha a\phi\eta/(1 - \alpha)$. Next note that $V(k, x^H < 1, x^L = 1) < V^P$, and $V(k, x^H < 1, x^L = 0) < V^H$. Now, comparing V^P and V^H gives condition (3.3). Finally, when (3.3) holds, $V(k, x^H \leq 1, x^L < 1) < V^P$ and when (3.3) does not hold, $V(k, x^H \leq 1, x^L < 1) < V^H$, so either the pooling or the separating allocation is the unique equilibrium.

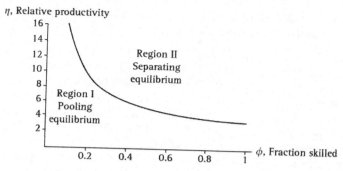

Figure 3.1. *Pooling and separating equilibria in the static model for*
$\alpha = 0.4$ *as a function of the fraction of skilled workers,* ϕ, *and the relative
productivity of skilled workers,* η.

The first type of equilibrium is called pooling because firms choose the same
amount of level of capacity (capital) and '*pool*' across the two types of workers. In
this equilibrium, unskilled workers have higher physical to human capital ratios
than skilled workers (k^P versus k^P/η). This differential in physical to human capital
ratios compresses the wage differential to $w^H/w^L = \beta y(\eta, k^P)/\beta y(1, k^P) = \eta^\alpha$, which
is lower than the wage differential in the Walrasian allocation, η. There is no
unemployment in the pooling equilibrium because each worker meets a firm and
they always agree. In the separating equilibrium, firms create *separate* jobs for
skilled workers and turn down the unskilled, and skilled workers earn more than
they did in the pooling equilibrium, because firms targeting the skilled choose a
larger capacity, i.e., $k^H > k^P$, and so $w^H_{pool} = \beta a[\phi\eta^\alpha + (1 - \phi)]^{(1-\alpha)/\alpha}\eta^\alpha/$
$(1 - \alpha) < w^H_{sep} = \beta a\eta/(1 - \alpha)$. In contrast, in a separating equilibrium, the
earnings and employment of the unskilled collapse.

Figure 3.1 draws eqn (3.3) in the space of the fraction of the skilled in the labour
force, ϕ, and the relative productivity of skilled workers, η. It is a downward-
sloping curve because a pooling equilibrium requires both ϕ and η to be relatively
small. Changes in these two variables give the main comparative static results of
the paper. An increase in the proportion of skilled workers, ϕ, may be driven by an
improvement in the educational attainment of the labour force, or by changes in
the curriculum of high schools and colleges increasing the fraction of skilled
workers in the two education groups. An increase in η is equivalent to skill-biased
technical change because it increases the productivity of capital when combined
with skilled workers but does not affect the productivity of capital used with
unskilled workers.[5] It can also be viewed as an increase in the relative price of
goods produced by skilled workers resulting from opening to international trade.

---

[5] To see this, consider the aggregate production function: $Y = K^{1-\alpha}[N_L^\rho + \zeta N_H^\rho]^{\alpha/\rho}$ where N_i is the
number of type i workers, and $\rho > 0$. An increase in ζ is skill-biased technical change. In the current
model, since each firm employs either a skilled or an unskilled worker, an increase in ζ is equivalent to
an increase in η.

To focus on the most interesting comparative statics, I consider an economy in the pooling equilibrium and analyse the impact of an increase in ϕ and η.

1. As long as we are inside Region I (pooling equilibrium) in Fig. 3.1, an increase in ϕ has no effect on wage inequality, which remains at $w^H/w^L = \eta^\alpha$. If ϕ continues to increase, eventually the economy switches from Region I to Region II, where the equilibrium is separating. The switch creates a qualitative change in the structure of the labour market: middling jobs open to both types of workers are replaced by high-capacity jobs designed for skilled workers, skilled wages increase, and unskilled employment and wages collapse.

2. An increase in η always increases wage inequality. As long as we stay in Region I, however, unskilled wages also increase with η. In contrast, when the change takes the economy from Region I to Region II, once again skilled wages jump up, amplifying the direct impact of η on w^H, and unskilled employment and wages collapse.

Increases in ϕ and η raise unskilled wages when the economy remains in Region I, because they increase k^P, the level of capital that the unskilled work with (Acemoglu, 1996a). Yet both changes hurt *unskilled* workers when the economy switches from pooling to separating equilibrium. Therefore, the impact of the supply of skills and technical change on unskilled workers is non-monotonic. In interpreting these results, it is also worth bearing in mind that in the dynamic model, similar results will be obtained, but the separating equilibrium will also involve low capital jobs designed for the unskilled. As a result, when the economy switches from a pooling to a separating equilibrium, the unemployment rates for both types of workers will increase. Finally, since there is no perfect overlap between education and skills and high-education workers are more likely to be skilled, when the economy switches from a pooling to a separating equilibrium, both residual wage inequality and returns to education increase as a result of the equilibrium switch.[6]

3.1.3. An Alternative Theory of US Labour-Market Changes

In the light of the comparative static results, the developments in the US labour markets during the late 1970s and the 1980s can be given a different interpretation. Recall that neither the existing skill-biased technical change stories nor others that have been advanced readily predict: (i) the fall in unskilled wages; (ii) the increase in the unemployment rates of all workers; (iii) a change in the

---

[6] There is another reason why residual inequality and returns to education may increase together in this setting. Consider an extension of the basic model with a more general matching technology where skilled workers are more likely to meet high-capital firms. A previous version of this chapter, Acemoglu (1996b), demonstrated that the main results of the paper continue to hold, but there is an equilibrium distribution of capital. Some workers will draw a high wage from the distribution of jobs open to them, and there will be a distribution of wages for workers of the same skill level due to pure luck. In a separating equilibrium, the distribution of capital choices is more disperse than in a pooling equilibrium, so there is more wage dispersion among identical workers and greater residual wage inequality.

composition of jobs. As pointed out in the introduction, the first two features have accompanied the recent increase in wage inequality, and Section 3.3 will provide detailed evidence that there has been a change in the composition of jobs.

First, suppose that, as many believe, the past 25 years have been characterized by skill-biased technical change, raising η. The increase in η can move the economy from a pooling to a separating equilibrium. This creates a *qualitative* change in the composition of jobs, reducing unskilled wages and increasing wage inequality and unemployment. As noted above, an increase in the prices of skill-intensive goods due to international trade would have the same effects.

A more novel explanation for the US labour-market trends also emerges from this simple model. The supply of skilled workers in the US labour market increased sharply during the 1970s.[7] A simple relative supply–demand approach would predict a decline in the relative wages of skilled workers in response to this increase. In the data, however, the large increase in the supply of skills during the 1970s is followed by a rise in the skill premium. In my model, when skilled workers become more abundant, firms find it profitable to design jobs for them rather than pool across the two skill groups. This transforms the structure of the labour market, increasing returns to education, residual inequality, and unemployment. Therefore, in contrast to the conventional approach, my theory predicts that even if technological possibilities remain unchanged, an increase in the proportion of skilled workers can switch the economy from a pooling to a separating equilibrium and increase inequality.

3.2. A DYNAMIC MODEL

I now describe a dynamic version of the environment of Section 3.1 which confirms the main insights obtained from the static model. When the economy switches from a pooling to a separating equilibrium, there will now be low-capital jobs targeted at the unskilled as well as the high-capital jobs designed for the skilled, and the unemployment rate of skilled workers will also increase.

3.2.1. Technology, Preferences, and the Walrasian Allocation

Consider a continuous time economy populated by a mass 1 of infinitely lived risk-neutral agents, discounting the future at the rate r. Once again, a fraction ϕ of these agents are skilled, with human capital $h = \eta > 1$, and the remaining $1 - \phi$ are unskilled with $h = 1$.

[7] See, for example, Autor *et al.* (1998), who show that while the employment share of college graduates grew by 6 percentage points between 1950 and 1970, it increased much faster, by 11.6 percentage points, from 1970 to 1990. This increase in skills was also at least partly exogenous, rather than a simple response to anticipated higher returns to skills in the future, driven by (i) the Vietnam-era draft laws which exempted males enrolled in college from military service and induced many more young males to stay in college in order to avoid the draft (see Lawrence M. Baskir and William Strauss, 1978); (ii) the increased government financial aid for colleges over this period (e.g., Michael S. McPherson and Morton Owen Schapiro, 1991). The large cohort sizes of the baby-boom generation interacted with these high college-enrolment rates and also contributed to the large increase in the supply of skills.

On the other side of the market, there is a larger mass of risk-neutral firms, also discounting the future at the same rate r. Each firm can employ at most one worker and is in one of three states: inactive, unfilled vacancy, and filled job. Inactive firms obtain a payoff of 0, and can rent a site to open a vacancy. There are $\theta \geq 1$ sites and the flow rental price of a site is $r\gamma$. The equilibrium rental price γ will be determined in equilibrium. Unfilled vacancies meet an unemployed worker at the instantaneous rate q, and unemployed workers meet a vacancy at the rate p; p and q are assumed exogenous, and p, $q < \infty$ so that decentralized trading takes time.

At every instant, some of the existing firms exit and new firms rent their sites. Immediately upon renting a site, and before meeting a worker, each firm has to design a job and choose its capacity (capital), k. As in the static model, this (irreversible) capacity choice captures the type of job created and its quality, and the firm incurs no costs until matching. New and old unfilled vacancies search for workers, and upon meeting a worker, they decide whether to employ the worker and whether to buy the necessary equipment at the cost Ck. This capital cost is incurred only once, but if the worker leaves the relation, the equipment becomes obsolete. Finally, the worker and the firm negotiate the wage rate. At the wage determination stage, the cost of capital is already sunk. If the firm and the worker reach an agreement, they produce flow rate of output given by (3.1) in the previous section; otherwise, they continue to search for new partners. The capital equipment of each firm breaks down at the instantaneous rate s, and in this event, the firm exits the market, the worker becomes unemployed, and the production site is rented to a new firm.

Before characterizing the equilibrium with costly search, it is instructive to look once again at the Walrasian allocation where trade takes place at full market-clearing prices announced by the auctioneer at time 0. In this allocation, a fraction $1 - \phi$ of active firms choose $k^L = a[(r+s)C]^{-1/\alpha}$ and produce with unskilled workers, while the remaining ϕ fraction choose $k^H = a\eta[(r+s)C]^{-1/\alpha}$ and produce with skilled workers, where $a \equiv (1-\alpha)^{1/\alpha}$. The equilibrium rental price of sites will be $\gamma = 0$, because there are more firms than workers. Workers, on the other hand, receive their full marginal product, which in this case is the flow rate of output, $y(h, k)$, minus the discounted cost of capital. That is, $w^H = (k^H)^{1-\alpha}\eta^\alpha - (r+s)Ck^H$, $w^L = (k^L)^{1-\alpha} - (r+s)Ck^L$. The wage differential between skilled and unskilled workers is therefore exactly equal to the skill differential: $w^H/w^L = \eta$. Notice also that there is a high degree of 'separation' as there are different jobs for skilled and unskilled workers, because high-capacity firms have a higher willingness to pay for skilled workers and employ them in equilibrium (see Sattinger, 1993).

3.2.2. Equilibrium with Costly Search

I now turn to the analysis of the search economy where matching is random, so that firms with different capacities have the same likelihood of meeting skilled workers. Throughout the chapter, I limit the analysis to steady states and only write the Bellman equations that apply in steady state. I also denote the fraction of workers in the unemployment pool who are skilled by λ. This will in general differ from ϕ because the two types of workers may have different job finding rates. Then

$$rV(k) = q[\lambda x^H(J^H(k) - Ck - V(k)) + (1 - \lambda)x^L(J^L(k) - Ck - V(k))]. \quad (3.4)$$

Intuitively, $V(k)$ is the asset value of a vacancy with capacity k (more formally, this should be $V(k, x^H, x^L)$ but I suppress the latter arguments to simplify the exposition). This vacancy receives no revenue in its current state but meets a worker at the flow rate q. Random matching implies that with probability λ, the worker is skilled, and the pair decide to produce together with probability x^H. In this case, the firm relinquishes the value of its current state, $V(k)$, incurs the cost of capital, Ck, and obtains $J^H(k)$, the value of a firm with capacity k, producing with a skilled worker. Alternatively, it meets an unskilled worker at the flow rate $q(1 - \lambda)$, agrees to produce with him with probability x^L, and obtains $J^L(k) - Ck - V(k)$.

With a similar logic, the asset values for a matched firm are

$$rJ^j(k) = k^{1-\alpha}h_j^\alpha - w^j(k) - s(J^j(k) - \gamma) \qquad (3.5)$$

where $j = H, L$. Recall that the capital equipment breaks down at the flow rate s, and in this case, the firm exits the market and stops paying the rental price of the site, hence the term γ in the last expression. I denote the distribution of capacity choices *among vacancies* by $F(k)$ and its support by $\mathscr{K}$. The asset values for unemployed workers are

$$rU^j = p \int_{\mathscr{K}} x^j(k)(W^j(k) - U^j)dF(k) \qquad (3.6)$$

for $j = H, L$, where $W^j(k)$ is the value of a worker of type j employed by a firm with capacity k, and $x^j(k)$ is the probability that a worker of type j and a firm with capacity k agree to produce together. Intuitively, a worker receives nothing when unemployed, but at the flow rate p, he meets a vacancy with capacity randomly drawn from the distribution $F(k)$. Also, the values for employed workers are

$$rW^j(k) = w^j(k) - s(W^j(k) - U^j). \qquad (3.7)$$

Because trading is a costly process, matched pairs have a quasi-rent to be shared. I assume that wages are determined by bargaining with alternating offers.[8] Namely,

---

[8] See Ariel Rubinstein (1982) and Avner Shaked and John Sutton (1984). The resulting sharing rule is different from Nash bargaining normally used in search models, but may be argued to have somewhat better microfoundations. The main reason why I use it here is that it simplifies the algebra, without affecting the main results. See Acemoglu (1996a) for a derivation of this wage rule in a search equilibrium.

if $r[U^j + V(k)] > k^{1-\alpha}h_j^\alpha$, then worker j and a firm with capacity k would break up the relation. Otherwise, the wage is

$$w^j(k) = \max\langle rU^j;$$
$$\min\{\beta k^{1-\alpha}h_j^\alpha; k^{1-\alpha}h_j^\alpha - rV(k)\}\rangle \tag{3.8}$$

where β is the bargaining power of the worker. In words, this wage rule states that the worker and the firm divide the flow return of the match, $k^{1-\alpha}h_j^\alpha$, with shares β and $1 - \beta$, unless the return to one of the parties is less than what they could obtain by not agreeing. The cost of capital investment does not feature in this wage rule because it is already sunk, and the outside option of the firm is $rV(k)$, because in case of a disagreement, it will look for a new worker, and its capital will become obsolete.

Finally, from steady-state accounting, we have

$$u^j = \frac{s}{s + p \int_K x^j(k)\, dF(k)} \tag{3.9}$$

and

$$\lambda = \frac{\phi u^H}{\phi u^H + (1 - \phi)u^L} \tag{3.10}$$

where $j = H, L$, u^j is the unemployment rate of workers of type j, and λ is the fraction of skilled workers in the unemployment pool.

A steady-state search equilibrium is a tuple $\langle F(k), \mathcal{K}, x^L(k), x^H(k), \lambda, u^H, u^L, \gamma\rangle$ such that $V(k)$, $J^j(k)$, U^j, and $W^j(k)$ satisfy (3.4), (3.5), (3.6), and (3.7) for $j = H, L$, wages are given by (3.8), and the following conditions hold:

(1) (Optimal capacity decision): for all $k \in \mathcal{K}$, $k \in \arg\max_{k'} V(k')$.
(2) (Free entry): for all $k \in \mathcal{K}$, $V(k) = \gamma$.
(3) (Optimal agreement): for all $k \in \mathcal{K}$, $(x^L(k), x^H(k)) \in \arg\max V(k)$.
(4) (Steady-state accounting): u^H, u^L, and λ satisfy (3.9) and (3.10).

In a steady-state equilibrium, firms make optimal capacity choices, the rental market for production sites clears (free-entry), and agreement decisions are optimal. The next proposition establishes that an equilibrium exists, and gives some details about capacity choices and acceptance decisions. To simplify the expressions, I normalize $C \equiv (1 - \beta)/(r + s)$.

Proposition 2. *A steady-state equilibrium exists. In any equilibrium, the support of the capacity distribution among vacancies, $\mathcal{K}$, has at most three elements, k^L, k^P, and $k^H = a\eta$, and we have: $x^L(k^L) = 1$, $x^H(k^L) = 0$, $x^L(k^P) = 1$, $x^H(k^P) = 1$, $x^L(k^H) = 0$, and $x^H(k^H) = 1$.*

The proof of this proposition is given in Appendix A, which is available upon request. In equilibrium, there are at most three different levels of capacity, and one of these, k^H, is equal to $a\eta$, and is chosen by firms which only produce with skilled workers. k^L maximizes (3.4) when $x^H = 0$ and $x^L = 1$, and is chosen by firms which only produce with unskilled workers. Finally, k^P, the capacity choice of firms producing with both types of workers, maximizes (3.4) at $x^H = x^L = 1$.

3.2.3. Pooling and Separating Equilibria

I denote the fraction of vacancies with capacities k^L, k^P, and k^H by μ^L, μ^P, and μ^H. A pooling steady-state equilibrium is an allocation where $\mu^P = 1$, so that all firms create middling jobs with capacity k^P and recruit all workers they meet. In this equilibrium, $u^H = u^L$ and $\lambda = \phi$. Because all jobs have the same capacity, workers' outside options do not bind (firms' outside options never bind—see Appendix A, which is available upon request), so the wage rule (3.8) becomes $w(h, k) = \beta k^{1-\alpha} h^\alpha$. The maximization of (3.4) yields $k^P = a[(1 - \phi) + \phi \eta^\alpha]^{1/\alpha}/[(1 - \alpha)r(r + s + q)] = \gamma$. The condition for the steady-state equilibrium to take this form is that there should be no profitable deviation, especially by a firm choosing k^H and employing only skilled workers. Therefore, we need $V(k^H) < \gamma$ (and also $V(k^L) < \gamma$ which is automatically satisfied). Substituting $x^H = 1$, $x^L = 0$, $\lambda = \phi$, and $k^H = a\eta$ in (3.4) and (3.5), we obtain $V(k^H) = q\phi(1 - \beta)\alpha a\eta/[(1 - \alpha)(r + s)(r + q\phi)] + q\phi s\gamma/[(r + s)(r + q\phi)]$. Simple algebra gives the condition for a pooling equilibrium as

$$\eta \le \left[\frac{(1 - \phi)(r + s + q\phi)^\alpha}{(r + s + q)^\alpha \phi^\alpha - (r + s + q\phi)^\alpha \phi} \right]^{1/\alpha}. \tag{3.11}$$

This parallels (3.3) from the previous section and is drawn in Fig. 3.2. Intuitively, a pooling equilibrium requires that firms find it profitable to employ skilled and unskilled workers in the same type of job, a strategy which will be profitable when the productivity differential between the two types of labour, η, is small. Also, the strategy of choosing a higher capacity and searching for skilled workers, the main alternative to pooling, will be less profitable when the fraction of skilled workers, ϕ, is small. Hence (3.11) traces a downward-sloping curve.

Three important features of the pooling equilibrium are: (i) there is only one type of job with capacity, k^P, which employs both skilled and unskilled workers. Therefore, as noted in Section 3.1, skilled workers are employed at a lower capacity to human capital ratio than unskilled workers (k^P/η versus k^P); (ii) as a result of the first observation, wage differentials are *compressed*—$w^H/w^L = \beta(k^P)^{1-\alpha}\eta^\alpha/\beta(k^P)^{1-\alpha} = \eta^\alpha$ is less than η, the wage differential in the frictionless model; (iii) since all firms are the same and accept all workers, both groups have the same unemployment rate, $u^H = u^L = u_{\text{pool}} \equiv s/(p + s) > 0$.

As in the static model, another possibility is a separating equilibrium. Firms create jobs with capacity k^H for skilled workers and k^L for the unskilled. In this equilibrium, $\mu^P = 0$, and λ is no longer equal to ϕ. Also, observe that since there is only one type of job open to each worker, outside options are once again non-binding along the equilibrium path, so (3.8) becomes $w^j(k) = \beta k^{1-\alpha} h_j^\alpha$. For $\mu^L > 0$

D. Acemoglu

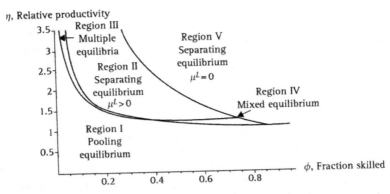

Figure 3.2. *Pooling and separating equilibria in the dynamic model for $\alpha = 0.4$, $p = 5$, $q = 5$, $r = 0.05$, and $\beta = 0.5$ as a function of the fraction of skilled workers, ϕ, and the relative productivity of skilled workers, η.*

to be equilibrium, the expected values of opening vacancies with capacity k^H and with capacity k^L have to be equal, that is, $V(k^H) = V(k^L) = \gamma$. Using eqns (3.4) and (3.5) for $j = H$, L, this implies $\lambda \eta / (r + s + q\lambda) = (1 - \lambda)/(r + s + q(1 - \lambda))$, which solves uniquely for $\lambda^*(\eta)$, and together with (3.10), determines μ^H. Now we can see that a separating equilibrium with $\mu^L > 0$ will exist if $V(k^P) \leq \gamma = q\lambda^*(\eta)(1 - \beta)\alpha a \eta / [(1 - \alpha)r(r + s + q\lambda^*(\eta))]$, where $V(k^P)$ is the maximized value of (3.4) when $x^L = x^H = 1$. This inequality is likely to hold when both η and ϕ are relatively low, thus defining another downward-sloping curve in Fig. 3.2. Finally, for ϕ and η sufficiently high, in Region V, there exist separating equilibria in which $\mu^L = 0$, so that no jobs are opened for unskilled workers.

In the separating equilibrium: (i) skilled workers work with higher capital, but physical to human capital ratios are equalized; (ii) there is no wage compression: $w^H/w^L = \beta(k^H)^{1-\alpha}\eta^\alpha / \beta(k^L)^{1-\alpha} = \eta$, and so there is more wage inequality in the separating equilibrium than in the pooling equilibrium. While skilled workers obtain higher wages in the separating equilibrium, i.e., $w_{\text{sep}}^H > w_{\text{pool}}^H$ the unskilled receive less, i.e., $w_{\text{sep}}^L < w_{\text{pool}}^L$. This is because in the separating equilibrium, firms targeting the unskilled choose $k^L < k^P$, so the unskilled work at lower capital firms and earn less; (iii) the unemployment rates for both groups are higher than in the pooling equilibrium, because high-capital firms do not accept unskilled workers, and the skilled prefer to wait for jobs designed for them.

Separating and pooling equilibria are not the only possibilities. There can also be 'mixed equilibria' with μ^P, $\mu^H > 0$, where some firms choose k^P and pool, while others choose k^H and only accept skilled workers. In this equilibrium, there is higher unskilled unemployment than u_{pool}, but since all firms accept skilled workers, skilled unemployment is still equal to u_{pool}. Unskilled wages are lower in the mixed equilibrium than in the pooling equilibrium because $\lambda < \phi$, so k^P is now less than $a[(1 - \phi) + \phi\eta^\alpha]^{1/\alpha}$, and wage inequality is higher because some of the high-skill workers are employed in high-capital jobs designed for them, earning $w_{sep}^H = \beta a \eta /(1 - \alpha)$. Finally, there are multiple equilibria in the part of the parameter space denoted as Region III in Fig. 3.2. The intuition for the multiplicity is that when there are separate jobs for skilled workers, their outside option may be high enough that a firm which deviates to a lower capital, k^P, will have to pay the outside option of skilled workers. This reduces profits from deviation and ensures a separating equilibrium. In contrast, when other firms also choose k^P, the outside options of skilled workers do not bind, and choosing k^P is more profitable than targeting only the skilled, and this makes the pooling allocation an equilibrium.

The main comparative static results from Fig. 3.2 are similar to those from Fig. 3.1. An increase in η always raises wage inequality, and may take us from a pooling to a separating equilibrium. An increase in the supply of skills as captured by a rise in ϕ can also switch the economy to a separating equilibrium, perhaps via Regions III and IV, reducing unskilled wages, and increasing skilled wages and unemployment for both groups. The main differences from Section 3.1 are that unskilled employment and wages do not collapse completely and the unemployment rate for skilled workers also increases.

3.3. SOME EVIDENCE

The theoretical analysis established that a change in the composition of jobs could be responsible for the US labour-market trends taking place since the late 1970s. I now offer a variety of evidence suggesting that there was a change in the composition of jobs. Most individual pieces of evidence are open to alternative interpretations, and the changes may have been caused by technology, the increase in the supply of skills, or other factors. Nevertheless, together this evidence paints a picture consistent with the approach in this chapter, and suggests that the changing composition of jobs may be an important component of the changes in the structure of wages.

3.3.1. Changing Recruitment Practices of Firms

The first piece of evidence is that there has been a change in the recruitment practices of firms. In my model, the pooling equilibrium is a situation where firms recruit all applicants. In contrast, in the separating equilibrium, firms with high capacity only accept the skilled. Therefore, we should observe more screening and 'selectiveness' on the part of firms. Although human resource practitioners whom I talked with agree that there is more screening now than 20 years ago, there are relatively little data to back this up. The increased spending by companies on their own human resource departments and human resource consulting firms is consistent with this view, but does not prove it.

The most suggestive evidence comes from case studies. Richard J. Murnane and Frank Levy (1996) report their interviews with human resource personnel at a number of companies. A manager at Ford Motor company in 1967 describes their hiring strategy as follows: 'If we had a vacancy, we would look outside in the plant waiting room to see if there were any warm bodies standing there. If someone was there and they looked physically OK and weren't an obvious alcoholic, they were hired' (p.19). Ford at the time was a high-wage employer, and its lack of screening can be interpreted as a pooling strategy: it realized that some of the workers would be less productive, but it still chose to recruit them because it was not profitable to search and wait for more skilled workers. In contrast, similar companies in the late 1980s appear to use a very different recruitment strategy. Murnane and Levy discuss the cases of Honda of America, Diamond Star Motors, and Northwestern Mutual Life. These are high-wage employers, with somewhat higher real wages than Ford in the 1960s, and the first two are in the same industry as Ford. All three companies spend substantial resources on recruitment and hire only a fraction of those who apply. The first two use formal cognitive tests, including mathematics, aptitude, and English tests, as well as a series of lengthy interviews. The third company employs more intensive interviews but no formal tests. The interview process in all three companies is quite costly as it involves a large number of fellow employees and managers, but they view this as a worthwhile activity. Although there may be different interpretations for these trends (e.g., the increased importance of team production), a plausible interpretation is that firms are no longer happy to 'pool' across different skills, and they want to hire only high-skill workers for their relatively high-quality jobs. Moreover, in line with the theory in this chapter, not all employers are following this hiring strategy. Murnane and Levy discuss the case of another company, Sports Plus, which employs assemblers. It pays between $5.50 and $7.00 per hour, offers little training, and basically hires every applicant without any screening.

The results of Peter Cappelli and Steffanie Wilk (1997) are also of interest in this context. They employ a new data set of 2945 establishments to analyse the determinants of hiring practices and intensity of screening of production workers. Of most interest for this chapter's focus, they look at how average wages of production workers, average education of production workers, the reported level of skill requirements of jobs, and the fraction of workers using computers covary with hiring practices. They find that each of these four variables has a statistically significant and robust positive effect on selection intensity, and the component of screening that increases most in response to these variables is selection on education and ability (as opposed to experience or recommendation). Therefore, firms using more computers and more skills, which are also the ones offering higher-wage jobs, spend more resources on screening in order to find workers that have the required level of education and are generally 'skilled'. These results are cross-sectional and cannot be directly extrapolated to changes from the 1970s to the 1990s. Nonetheless, combined with the case study evidence, they suggest that the widespread increase in computer use (Autor et al., 1998) and rising skill requirements (Cappelli, 1996; Murnane and Levy, 1996) are likely to have been associated with increased screening.

3.3.2. Changes in Mismatch between Jobs and Workers

In a pooling equilibrium high- and low-skill workers are employed in the same jobs using the same quality equipment. Therefore, skilled workers, employed at the physical to human capital ratio k^P/η, are 'overskilled' for their job, while the unskilled, working at the physical to human capital ratio k^P, are 'underskilled'. In contrast, in a separating equilibrium, both types of workers are employed at the physical to human capital ratio a where $k^P > a > k^P/\eta$. So, workers are better matched to their jobs in separating equilibrium than in pooling equilibrium. The forces I discuss may be less important for education than for other dimensions of skills, because schooling is observable, making the search for educated workers relatively easy. Nevertheless, in a world of costly search and imperfect correlation between skills and education, there will be educational mismatch in the labour market, and more so in a pooling equilibrium. Therefore the approach in this paper predicts less over- and undereducation during the 1980s than in the 1970s.

There is a large literature on overeducation in the labour market. The most interesting and careful paper in this literature is by Nachum Sicherman (1991), who studies data from the Panel Study of Income Dynamics (PSID) in response to the question: 'how much formal education is required to get a job like yours?' He constructs over- and undereducation variables by subtracting the response to this question from actual education. He finds that workers who report to be over-educated for their job earn less than others with the same amount of education, but more than workers with less education doing the same job. This is reversed for undereducated workers. Moreover, overeducated workers switch to higher-wage jobs more quickly than others, suggesting that they are truly overeducated for their jobs, rather than less skilled in some other dimension unobserved to the econo-metrican. These findings are consistent with this chapter's predictions: on an average, overeducated workers are those working with lower physical to human capital ratios; they earn less than workers with the same education, but more than others with lower education working with the same amount of physical capital.

The question on required education in the PSID is asked in 1976, 1978, and 1985. Sicherman pools the three years. Here I repeat this exercise separately for each year to see whether the amount of over- and undereducation (mismatch) has changed from mid-1970s to 1980s.[9] First, results not reported here confirm that Sicherman's findings hold in each year, and the coefficients in these

---

[9] The required education variable is bracketed, with the following brackets: 0–5, 6–8, 9–11, 12, 13–15, 16, 17. The actual schooling variable is last grade completed. Because in 1985, actual schooling was only available in the individual files, for consistency, the education variable from the individual files has been used for 1976 and 1978 as well. Using the education variable from the family files for 1976 and 1978 does not change any of the results for these years. In all the calculations, the following values were substituted for the required education variable: 4 when the bracket was 0–5, 8 for the bracket 6–8, 10 when the bracket was 9–11, and 14 when the bracket was 13–15. These are the values used by Sicherman (1991) and using the means of the relevant brackets (e.g. 2.5 instead of 4) increases the magnitude of the changes from 1976 to 1985.

D. Acemoglu

Table 3.1. *Changes in mismatch from 1976–85*

Year	Panel A			Panel B		
	Number of observations			Average overeducation		
	(1) 1976	(2) 1978	(3) 1985	(4) 1976	(5) 1978	(6) 1985
Overeducated	978 [0.40]	1028 [0.38]	1149 [0.39]	4.78 (2.81)	4.83 (2.83)	3.50 (3.13)
Exact	1045 [0.43]	1174 [0.43]	1350 [0.46]	−0.05 (0.42)	−0.03 (0.37)	0.00 (0.27)
Undereducated	426 [0.18]	517 [0.19]	438 [0.15]	−2.38 (1.58)	−2.42 (1.63)	−2.71 (1.51)
Total	2447	2719	2937	1.47 (3.40)	1.35 (3.42)	0.966 (3.02)
Variance of overeducation	11.6	11.7	9.1			
Absolute deviation of overeducation	2.3	2.3	1.8			

Notes: All data from PSID. Sample includes male heads of households in employment, between the ages of 18 and 60. Overeducation is defined as actual education minus required education. The last two rows give the variance and average absolute deviation of overeducation in each of the three types. Proportion of the total is given in square brackets in the first three columns and standard deviations in parentheses in the last three columns.

cross-sectional regressions, except the return to schooling, are quite similar, suggesting that there has not been a major change in the interpretation of these questions by the respondents. The key results for my hypothesis are reported in Table 3.1. The sample includes male heads of households between the ages 18 and 60, who are currently in employment or temporarily laid off, excluding the self-employed. No other sample restrictions are applied. The first part of Table 3.1 reports the number and fraction of workers who have their last grade completed within the bracket of required education (*exact*), those who have more education than required for their jobs (*overeducated*), and those with less education than required (*undereducated*) for each year. The columns (4) to (6) give the mean years of overeducation for each group, with standard deviations in parentheses. Recall that overeducation is defined as actual minus required education, so a negative number means that required education for that group exceeds actual education. Finally, the last two rows give the variance and average absolute deviation of the overeducation variable.

The results in Table 3.1 show that both the amount and variance of over-education have decreased. The proportion of workers who have exactly the required education for their job has increased from less than 43 per cent in 1976 to over 46 per cent in 1985. This increase is significant at 1 per cent. Also, the average number of years of schooling that an overeducated worker has beyond what is required for his job has declined from 1976 to 1985, which also suggests that workers are better matched to their jobs in 1985 than during the 1970s. The changes from 1976 to 1978 are insignificant at 10 per cent whereas all the changes from either 1976 or 1978 to 1985 are once again significant at 1 per cent. Also corroborating this picture, the cross-sectional variance of overeducation fell from 11.6 in 1976 to 9.1 in 1985 and the average absolute deviation fell from 2.4 to 1.8. In both cases, this drop of over 20 per cent is statistically significant at 1 per cent. Therefore, these numbers suggest that there is less mismatch in the 1980s than during the 1970s.

An alternative explanation for this finding is that firms hire through 'ports-of-entry', and as a result, young workers are overeducated for their jobs. If there are fewer young workers in 1985, overeducation will have declined. To investigate this, I restricted the sample to either young workers or to those with short tenure. The results were very similar and, in fact, stronger. In particular, restricting the sample to those between the ages of 18 and 45, I found that in 1976, 43 per cent of workers had exactly the required education. This number increased to 47 per cent in 1985. Restricting the sample to those with less than 35 months of tenure, 39 per cent of workers had exactly the required years of education in 1976, and this fraction had risen to 45 per cent by 1985. Therefore, it appears that there is a significant decline in educational mismatch between 1976 and 1985, which is consistent with a switch from a pooling to a separating equilibrium, and more generally, with increased screening and selection by employers.

3.3.3. Changes in the Distribution of Jobs

In this subsection, I provide some evidence that 'middling' jobs have been replaced by jobs from more extreme parts of the quality distribution. The difficulty with this exercise is to define and rank jobs. A reasonable first pass is to use industry-occupation cells to represent job categories, and rank them according to average wages (or average residual wages after controlling for worker characteristics). Middling jobs would correspond to industry-occupation cells that pay close to the median of the wage distribution. Having ranked job categories, changes in the distribution of employment across the cells can be analysed to see whether in the late 1980s there is more weight in the cells at the tails of the quality distribution of jobs than earlier. This approach may underestimate the change in the distribution of jobs if a substantial fraction of the shift from middling to high-and low-quality jobs took place within narrow industry-occupation cells, but there is no easy way of analysing changes in job composition within these cells.

I use the Annual Earnings File of the Current Population Survey (CPS), Outgoing Rotation Group files uniform extract of the National Bureau of Economic Research, from 1983 to 1993 to study the changes in the distribution of jobs (the information refers to the previous year). I limited the sample to those who are employed or temporarily out of work and between the ages of 18 and 60. I also excluded everyone who reported less than $1 or more than $100 per hour wage and all those who are in the agriculture, forestry, fishing, armed forces, and public administration industries. The years before 1983 cannot be used because industry and especially occupation classifications are non-comparable.

I constructed cells using 19 major industries (excluding public administration, armed forces, forestry and agriculture) and 12 one-digit occupation categories. I excluded the cells that contained less than 200 workers between 1983 and 1993. This gave a total of 174 cells, containing over 72 per cent of total employment in the CPS. Although it is possible that workers in a given cell are performing very different jobs in 1993 than they were in 1983, this seems unlikely to be true for a large fraction of the 174 cells. In fact, average cell wages are very highly correlated across years. Therefore, in terms of the model one can consider each cell as a separate job category corresponding to a different level of k. In the model, a worker with given characteristics obtains a higher wage in a job with higher k. This suggests that we can rank cells according to residual wages from 1983 to 1993, and interpret the higher-ranked cells as containing higher-quality jobs. More precisely, consider the regression of real wages on four education dummies, sex, race, a quartic in experience, and a dummy for those living in a metropolitan area, and let ω_{it} be the average residual in cell i and year t. Then, I calculate $\bar{\omega}_i = \Sigma_t \, \omega_{it}$, and rank cells in ascending order according to $\bar{\omega}_i$ (so cell ranks are the same in all years). The average correlation of $\bar{\omega}_i$ with ω_{it} is 0.95, suggesting that there are no major changes in the distribution of residual wages across cells. Observe also that the increase in wage inequality from 1983 to 1993 does not imply anything about how the distribution of employment across cells should have changed. For example, the changes in inequality could have taken place within cells, and the distribution of employment across cells may have remained unchanged.

Table 3.2 reports the cumulative percentage of employment in the corresponding year at the cells with 10th, 25th, 50th, 75th, and 90th percentile ranks. Formally, let e_{it} be the percentage of the (restricted) sample employment in year t and cell i. Then, for all t, $\Sigma_{i=1}^{N} \, e_{it} = 100$ where N is the number of cells (in this case $N = 174$). Also recall that if $i > i'$, then average residual wage in cell i is higher than in i', i.e., $\bar{\omega}_i > \bar{\omega}_{i'}$. The cumulative percentage at the 25th percentile in year t is then equal to $\Sigma_{i=1}^{N/4} \, e_{it}$, and the 75th percentile is equal to $\Sigma_{i=1}^{3N/4} \, e_{it}$. The number 79.5 at the 75th percentile in 1993, for example, implies that in this year, 20.5 per cent of employment is in the quarter of the job categories with the highest average residual wages. The last column of Table 3.2 reports 'weight at the tails', WT, defined as the cumulative percentage at the 25th percentile plus one minus the cumulative percentage at the 75th percentile.[10] That is,

---

[10] The cells above the 75th percentile include, among others, transport, mining, and communication technicians; speciality occupations in transport, business and repair services, construction, finance, communications, hospital, and mining, durable manufacturing sales occupations, and a variety of executive, administrative, and managerial occupations. The cells below the 25th percentile include handlers, labourers, and a variety of service occupations in a variety of industries, including retail trade (which includes, among others, department and food stores, eating and drinking places), business and repair, and social services.

Table 3.2. *Changes in the composition of employment, 1983–93*

Year	Percentiles					*WT*: weight at the tails 25th + (1–75th)
	10th	25th	50th	75th	90th	
1983	7.4	16.0	47.0	80.8	92.2	35.2
1984	7.3	15.7	46.3	80.5	91.9	35.2
1985	7.4	15.8	46.0	80.2	91.8	35.6
1986	7.3	15.9	45.8	80.1	91.7	35.8
1987	7.2	15.8	45.8	79.9	91.6	35.8
1988	7.1	15.8	45.6	79.6	91.5	36.2
1989	7.3	16.0	45.9	79.6	91.3	36.4
1990	7.2	16.2	46.2	79.5	91.4	36.7
1991	7.5	16.5	46.5	79.2	91.2	37.3
1992	7.7	17.0	46.9	79.7	91.9	37.3
1993	7.8	17.1	47.0	79.5	91.8	37.6

Notes: The numbers are the cumulative percentage of workers employed in the one-digit industry, one-digit occupation cell at the indicated percentile of the job distribution. The cells are ranked according to average residual wages between 1983 and 1993. Residual wages are obtained from a regression of real wages on four education dummies, a quartic in experience, sex, race, and a dummy for those living in a metropolitan area. The total number of cells is 174, which excludes those with less than 200 observations between 1983 and 1993. The last column gives a measure of the weight at the tails of the employment distribution, *WT*. *WT* is defined as the sum of the fraction of people employed at the bottom 25 per cent and top 25 per cent cells. All calculations are from the Outgoing Rotation Group Files of the Current Population Survey, and use CPS weights.

$WT_t \equiv \Sigma_{i=1}^{N/4}\ e_{it} + \Sigma_{i=3N/4}^{N}\ e_{it}$. This measure therefore gives the total percentage of workers employed in the top 25 per cent and bottom 25 per cent cells. An increase in *WT* implies that middling jobs have been replaced by jobs that are typically either higher or lower quality.

Table 3.2 shows that 35 per cent of employment was in the top and bottom 25 per cent job categories. By 1993, this number had risen to just under 38 per cent. So, approximately 2.5 per cent more workers now have either higher- or lower-quality jobs rather than middling jobs. In other words, the fraction of employment in highest- and lowest-quality job categories has increased approximately by 7 per cent of its 1983 value. These changes are not due to business-cycle variations: the years 1983–84 were at a similar stage of the business cycle to 1992–93. It is possible that even more major changes in job composition took place before 1983, but due to changes in the occupation and industry codes, this is much harder to study.

To investigate the sources of this finding, I looked at the changes for men and women separately, and also analysed the changes by education group (in all cases maintaining the same ranking of cells as above). For men, there is an increase of 1.5 percentage points in *WT* from 36.3 per cent to 37.7 per cent between 1983 and 1993. For women, the increase is approximately 4 percentage points, from 33.7 per cent to 37.5 per cent. Among education groups, the largest changes are for those with high school or less. WT for this group increases by 3 percentage points, and most of this increase is at the lower tail. WT for college graduates increased by over 1 percentage point, mostly at the upper tail. Interestingly, there is no increase in WT for those with some college.

To check the robustness of the results, I repeated the exercise by ranking cells according to average wages (rather than average residual wages). The results are unchanged; WT increases from 52.2 per cent in 1983 to 54.1 per cent in 1993. When I exclude cells that have less than 20 observations in any year (rather than only those with less than 200 in total), the number of cells is reduced to 161, and WT increases from 34.5 per cent in 1983 to 36.9 per cent in 1993. I also performed the same calculations using different levels of aggregation (and once again ranking the cells according to residual wages). Using one-digit industry as above but 72 occupation categories,[11] I obtain 576 cells with over 67 per cent of the total CPS employment. In this case, WT increases from 40.3 per cent in 1983 to 42.7 per cent in 1993. This increase in WT from 1983 to 1993 is approximately 2 percentage points for men, 4 percentage points for women, 3 percentage points for workers with high school or less, and 2 percentage points for college graduates. When I use two-digit occupation and two-digit industry, there are 865 cells containing over 65 per cent of CPS employment, and WT in this case shows an increase from 53.2 per cent in 1983 to 55.3 per cent in 1993.

Finally, to investigate longer-term changes, I looked at census data on 138 industries from 1970 to 1990.[12] I do not know of any consistent occupation codes for these years, so I only analysed the changes in the industrial composition of employment. Ranking these 138 industries according to average wages between 1970 and 1990, WT was 43.2 per cent in 1970, 42.4 per cent in 1980, and increased to 43.9 per cent in 1990. To compare this increase to the results from the CPS data, I created cells using only three-digit industries, which gave 189 cells, containing 70 per cent of total CPS employment. In this case, WT increases from 50.5 per cent in 1983 to 51.8 per cent in 1993. Therefore, the census and CPS results using industries only are similar, which is reassuring. But the changes are also somewhat smaller than the other CPS results, suggesting that a significant fraction of the change in job composition is within industries and that these latter measures may significantly underestimate the change in the distribution of jobs.

Overall, these results suggest that the composition of employment underwent a number of changes during the 1980s and the early 1990s. In particular, part of the employment in job categories that typically pay close to the median of the wage distribution appears to have been replaced by employment in higher- and lower-quality jobs, which is the pattern predicted by a switch from a pooling to a separating equilibrium.

---

[11] These are an extended version of the two-digit occupations created by splitting some of the larger occupations along the three-digit lines (see Acemoglu, 1997).

[12] Agriculture, forestry, fishing, and public administration are excluded. These are industries aggregated consistently across the censuses and used in Autor et al. (1998). I thank David Autor for providing me with these data.

3.3.4. Changes in the Distribution of On-the-Job-Training

To study another dimension of the change in the quality distribution of jobs, one can look at how on-the-job-training has changed. Workers who obtain training receive higher wages, and more advanced and expensive equipments generally require more training. If unskilled workers are now working with less capital and the skilled with more, we might expect such a change to be reflected in the distribution of on-the-job-training. Since skills are unobserved, I looked at the distribution of training across education categories.

Jill M. Constantine and David Neumark (1994) analyse data from the CPS Supplements of 1983 and 1991, and report the following figures for 'training to improve skills on the current job'. In 1983, 18 per cent of those with less than high school received any type of 'training to improve skills on the current job'. The same proportion was 33 per cent for high-school graduates, 43 per cent for those with some college, and 55 per cent for the college graduates. These numbers indicate that the distribution of training was very unequal across the education groups in 1983. But in the next eight years, it became even more unequal: in 1991, 17 per cent of those without high school, 35 per cent of high-school graduates, 45 per cent of those with some college, and 63 per cent of college graduates received such training. Although Constantine and Neumark show that the changes in training only account for a small fraction of the changes in wage inequality, this process is indicative of changes in the composition of jobs. In fact, this pattern is consistent with the view that the composition of jobs has been changing, and the more skilled (educated) workers have been the winners in this process.

3.3.5. Changes in Physical Capital and Labour Ratios

Another implication of my model is that the amount of physical capital workers produce with should become more heterogeneous as we move from a pooling to a separating equilibrium. Recall that the dispersion of physical to human capital ratios falls (for the same reason that mismatch falls). But when instead of looking at human capital, we look at capital per employee, we see that in a pooling equilibrium all workers are employed at capital k^P, while in a separating equilibrium, some use k^H while others use $k^L < k^H$. Therefore, the dispersion of capital to labour (as opposed to human capital) ratios should increase around the same time as the switch from pooling to separating equilibrium. Francesco Caselli (1999) also constructs a theory which predicts the same outcome (though not the other predictions discussed here). To provide evidence in favour of this pattern, Caselli calculates measures of dispersion of the ratio of dollar value of equipment divided by total employment for 450 four-digit manufacturing industries. Caselli's Fig. 3.3 reports the log difference between the 90th and 10th percentiles of the distribution of the ratio of dollar value of equipment capital to employment across these 450 industries, which is reproduced here as Fig. 3.3. It shows that the dispersion of equipment capital to labour is fairly constant until the 1980s, and

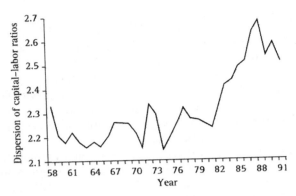

Figure 3.3. *Log difference of the 90th and 10th percentiles of the distribution of the dollar value of equipment capital to employment across 450 4-digit manufacturing industries.*

Note: The change from 1975 to 1995 is 17.5 per cent.

Source: This figure is taken from Caselli (1999).

then starts increasing rapidly. The capital–labour ratio difference between the 90th and 10th most capital-intensive industries has increased by 17.5 per cent between 1975 and 1990.[13] Caselli (1999) also shows that industries which increased their capital–labour ratio were the ones paying higher wages during the 1970s, and they were also more likely to increase their average wages further and hire more skilled workers (non-production workers). These findings are consistent with the view that beginning in the late 1970s, some jobs targeted skilled workers and became more capital intensive, while industries that already employed less skilled workers reduced capital per employee as implied by a switch from a pooling to a separating equilibrium.

3.4. CONCLUSIONS

This chapter has offered a model of endogenous job composition. In the model economy, firms decide what types of jobs to create and then search for workers. When there are relatively few skilled workers and the productivity gap between the skilled and the unskilled is limited, the equilibrium is pooling: firms create one type of—middling—job and pool across different skill levels. When the productivity gap between the skilled and the unskilled increases or when the

---

[13] The numbers reported in Fig. 3.3 do not weight industries. Caselli obtains very similar results when he weights each industry with the time-average of its employment, and when he uses other measures of dispersion, such as the log variance. When he uses current employment as weights, the 90th and 10th differential still increases by 8.4 per cent between 1975 and 1990, but the log variance shows a slight decline over this period. Changes in the fraction of high-skill workers over this period, however, make the log variance with current weights harder to interpret. For example, even when the amounts of physical capital that skilled and unskilled workers use remain constant, a change in the fraction of skilled employees in the work force will have a first-order effect on this measure.

proportion of skilled workers in the labour force rises, the economy may switch to a separating equilibrium with higher-quality jobs designed for the skilled and low-capital jobs targeted at the unskilled. This qualitative change in the composition of jobs reduces unskilled wages, increases the earnings of the skilled, and increases the unemployment rates for both types of workers.

Either one of two developments may have triggered a switch from a pooling to a separating equilibrium: (i) the proportion of college graduates in the US labour force increased substantially over the past 25 years; (ii) as many economists believe, new technologies or increased international trade may have increased the marginal product of skilled workers more than that of the unskilled during this period. The resulting transformation of the composition of jobs leads to higher returns to education, greater residual wage inequality, lower wages for unskilled workers, and higher unemployment for all education groups, and may therefore be an important component of the changes in unemployment and wage inequality in the US. The chapter also provided a variety of evidence consistent with the notion that there have been changes in the composition of jobs since the 1970s.

A number of important issues are not covered in this chapter:

1. The evidence presented in Section 3.3 suggests that there was a change in the composition of jobs, but does not distinguish between different driving forces. Since the mechanism offered in the chapter should apply in local labour markets, analysing the changes in the composition of jobs in different US states and how they vary with the supply of skilled workers may be a fruitful area for further work.

2. Endogenizing education choices is also an obvious next step. Since the presence of more skilled workers may increase the skill premium, the model can easily generate multiple equilibria. Further, in this case, relatively small shocks to the cost of education may have large effects on the supply of skills (see Acemoglu, 1998).

3. An important area of research is to explain the different experiences of the United States and Continental Europe. Germany, for example, has experienced very little increase in wage inequality and until the unification, no significant change in unemployment (see Nickell and Bell, 1995). The theory in this chapter suggests that the training system in Germany may be an important factor. Because training increases the human capital of less skilled (educated) workers, a developed training system may make the strategy of creating separate jobs for the skilled less profitable and a pooling equilibrium more likely. More generally, the impact of labour-market institutions on job composition is another area for further research.

REFERENCES

Acemoglu, Daron. (1996*a*). A microfoundation for increasing returns in human capital accumulation, *Quarterly Journal of Economics*, 111 (3), 779–804.

Acemoglu, Daron. (1996b). Changes in unemployment and wage inequality: An alternative theory and some evidence. Centre for Economic Policy Research Discussion Paper 1459.
——. (1997). Good jobs versus bad jobs: Theory and some evidence. Working paper, Massachusetts Institute of Technology.
——. (1998). Why do new technologies complement skills? Directed technical change and wage inequality, *Quarterly Journal of Economics*, 113 (4), 1055–90.
—— and Shimer, Robert. (1998). Wage and technology dispersion. Working paper, Massachusetts Institute of Technology and Princeton University.
Autor, David H., Katz, Lawrence F. and Krueger, Alan B. (1998). Computing inequality: Have computers changed the labour market? *Quarterly Journal of Economics*, 113 (4), 1169–215.
Barron, John M., Bishop, John, and Dunkelberg, William C. (1985). Employer search: The interviewing and hiring of new employees, *Review of Economics and Statistics*, 67 (1), 43–52.
Baskir, Lawrence M. and Strauss, William. (1978). *Chance and Circumstances: The Draft, The War and The Vietnam Generation*. New York: Knopf.
Berman, Eli, Bound, John, and Griliches, Zvi. (1994). Changes in the demand for skilled labour within US manufacturing industries: Evidence from the annual survey of manufacturing, *Quarterly Journal of Economics*, 109 (2), 367–98.
Bound, John, and Johnson, George. (1992). Changes in the structure of wages in the 1980s: An evaluation of alternative explanations, *American Economic Review*, 82 (3), 371–92.
Burdett, Kenneth, and Coles, Melvyn. (1997). Marriage and class, *Quarterly Journal of Economics*, 102 (1), 115–40.
Cappelli, Peter. (1996). Technology and skill requirements: Implications for establishment wage structures, *New England Economic Review*, 139–54.
—— and Wilk, Steffanie. (1997). Understanding selection processes: Organization determinants and performance outcomes. Mimeo, The Wharton School.
Caselli, Francesco. (1999). Technological revolutions, *American Economic Review*, 89 (1), 78–102.
Constantine, Jill M. and Neumark, David. (1994). Training and the growth of wage inequality, *National Bureau of Economic Research* (Cambridge, MA) *working paper* 4729.
Davis, Steven J. (1996). The quality distribution of jobs in search equilibrium. Mimeo, University of Chicago.
Diamond, Peter A. (1982). Aggregate demand management in a search equilibrium, *Journal of Political Economy*, 90 (5), 881–94.
Juhn, Chinhui, Murphy, Kevin M., and Pierce, Brook. (1993). Wage inequality and the rise in returns to skill, *Journal of Political Economy*, 101 (3), 410–42.
Katz, Lawrence F. and Murphy, Kevin M. (1992). Changes in relative wages: Supply and demand factors, *Quarterly Journal of Economics*, 107 (1), 35–78.
Kremer, Michael, and Maskin, Eric. (1997). Segregation by skill and the rise in inequality. Mimeo, Massachusetts Institute of Technology and Harvard University.
McPherson, Michael S. and Schapiro, Morton Owen. (1991). *Keeping College Affordable: Government and Educational Opportunity*. Washington, DC: Brookings Institution.
Mortensen, Dale T. (1982). Property rights and efficiency in mating, racing, and related games, *American Economic Review*, 72 (5), 968–79.

Murnane, Richard J. and Levy, Frank. (1996). *Teaching the Basic New Skills.* New York: Free Press.

Murphy, Kevin M. and Topel, Robert H. (1987). The evolution of unemployment in the United States: 1968–1985, in Stanley Fischer, ed., *NBER Macroeconomics Annual: 1987.* Cambridge, MA: MIT Press, 11–58.

Nickell, Stephen, and Bell, Brian. (1995). The collapse in the demand for the unskilled and unemployment across OECD countries, *Oxford Review of Economic Policy,* 11 (1), 40–62.

Pissarides, Christopher A. (1987). *Equilibrium Unemployment Theory.* Oxford: Blackwell.

Rubinstein, Ariel. (1982). Perfect equilibrium in a bargaining model, *Econometrica,* 50 (1), 97–109.

Sattinger, Michael. (1993). Assignment models of distribution of earnings, *Journal of Economic Literature,* 31 (2), 831–80.

—. (1995). Search and the efficient assignment of workers to jobs, *International Economic Review,* 36 (2), 283–330.

Shaked, Avner and Sutton, John. (1984). Involuntary unemployment as a perfect equilibrium in a bargaining model. *Econometrica,* 52 (6), 1341–64.

Shimer, Robert J. and Smith, Lones A. (1998). Search and assortative matching. Mimeo, Massachusetts Institute of Technology, *Econometrica,* 2000 (forthcoming).

Sicherman, Nachum. (1991). Overeducation in the labour market, *Journal of Labour Economics,* 9 (2), 101–22.

Topel, Robert H. and Ward, Michael P. (1992). Job mobility and the careers of young men, *Quarterly Journal of Economics,* 107 (2), 439–80.

4

Does Competition at School Matter? A View Based upon the Italian and Japanese Experiences

GIORGIO BRUNELLO AND TSUNEO ISHIKAWA

4.1. INTRODUCTION

Education and human capital accumulation are often viewed as key to economic performance and growth. This chapter looks at a closely related but often overlooked question: do selectivity and competition at school affect economic performance and welfare? By inducing individuals to invest in the competition for access to the best schools, a selective schooling system increases the stock of *common basic academic skills*. Examples of these skills include the basics of reading, mathematics and science and problem-solving skills. If the accumulation of these skills and training are complements, selective education reduces training costs and increases the relative advantage of adopting complex and highly productive technologies.

When competition is excessive, however, it could hamper the development of *individual skills*, because of the strong incentives it places on the development of common basic skills. Examples of individual skills are self-expression, creative thinking, and idiosyncratic competencies. If individual skills are also important for industrial performance, too much competition in the schooling system could have negative spillovers on net national output and average per capita productivity.

This chapter is based upon the view that a satisfactory answer to this question requires that we focus not only on the schooling system but also on its interactions with the industrial structure and the labour market.

Consider first an environment with a single type of skills, common basic academic skills. Depending on the underlying parameters, we show that these interactions can produce multiple locally stable equilibria.[1] In one equilibrium (*P-equilibrium*), the schooling system induces individuals to invest in the

Tsuneo Ishikawa sadly passed away before the publication of this chapter.

[1] See Brunello and Ishikawa (1999a).

accumulation of common academic skills. The availability of these skills in the market and the complementarity between education and training facilitates the adoption of complex technologies that require substantial training costs. Firms that use these technologies pay relatively high wages and attract graduates from the best schools. Other firms, which operate in a secondary labour market, use relatively simple technologies and pay the reservation wage. The high expected gain from access into a good school stimulates investment in academic skills. If the economy is initially located in such an equilibrium, we show that an increase in competition at school leads to higher average productivity, higher average wages and higher economic welfare.

In another equilibrium (*M-equilibrium*), schooling does not induce individuals to accumulate more than the minimum stock of basic academic skills. The limited accumulation of these skills makes the adoption of complex technologies relatively less profitable. Labour turnover is important and labour market experience matters more than school quality in the reduction of training costs faced by firms. The relative scarcity of firms paying relatively high wages and the significant turnover rate further reduces the incentive to accumulate common academic skills, because of the relatively low expected returns. If the economy is initially located in this equilibrium, we show that an increase in the degree of competition at school has no consequences on the accumulation of average productivity or average wages, but reduces economic welfare, unless this increase can be matched by a coordinated change in the hiring policies of firms.

In the presence of multiple equilibria, government policy, which regulates the selectivity of the schooling system, can shift the economy from one equilibrium to the other. Suppose that the economy is initially located in a *P*-equilibrium. A substantial reduction in the competition of the schooling system could shift the economy to the *M*-equilibrium if the induced reduction in the accumulation of basic academic skills generates a change in the hiring patterns of firms in favour of workers with previous labour market experience. Once the economy has moved to the *M*-equilibrium, however, we show that a reversal in the original policy is not sufficient to re-establish the original equilibrium. Hence, the *M*-equilibrium is characterized by hysteresis.

Next, consider an environment with two types of skill, basic academic and individual skills. We argue that the relationship between individual and basic academic skills is likely to be hump-shaped: creative skills require basic academic skills to be effective.[2] Excessive accumulation of basic skills, however, damages the accumulation of individual skills. The basic idea is familiar in the theory of incentives: focusing incentives on a single dimension of individual behaviour can have undesirable side effects when other dimensions are important.[3]

In the new environment, our previous results change in a qualitative way only when the relationship between the two types of skill is negative. In particular, we

---

[2] See Brunello and Giannini (1999) for a more detailed discussion of this point.
[3] See Holmstrom and Milgrom (1991).

show that, if the economy is initially located in the *P*-equilibrium, an increase in the competition of the schooling system does not necessarily increase economic welfare. The reason is that an increase in the accumulation of basic academic skills reduces the accumulation of individual skills and has negative spillovers on the technologies that use these skills intensively. The presence of negative spillovers means that we cannot any longer Pareto rank equilibria that differ in the stock of accumulated basic academic skills.

We conclude our exploration of the interaction among schooling, industrial structure, and the labour market by arguing that the key features of the *M*- and *P*-equilibria are broadly consistent with a stylized characterization of the Italian and the Japanese economies.

The material of the chapter is organized as follows. In Section 3.2 we present the model with a single skill, drawing from our previous work (Brunello and Ishikawa (1999*a*)).[4] In the next section, we extend this model to the case of two skills. Finally, the concluding remarks are devoted to a stylized characterization of education, industrial structure, and labour market performance in Italy and in Japan. We argue there that most of the key differences can be interpreted as the outcomes of two locally stable equilibria.

4.2. THE MODEL WITH A SINGLE SKILL

Consider an economy populated by a given large number of individuals and firms. Each firm employs a single worker. In each period of time, a fraction *s* of employed workers quits the labour market forever and is replaced by an equal inflow of new workers. If the total number of firms is normalized to 1, total outflows and total inflows are both equal to *s*. For a single firm, new hires can be either new entrants or workers who quit other firms. For the economy as a whole, however, new hires must necessarily come from new entrants.

New entrants differ only in the level of education acquired before entering the labour market. While education is provided free of charge by schools run by the government, schooling systems can vary in the degree of selectivity and competitiveness. A very selective schooling system allocates individuals in upper- and lower-layer schools by adopting tough entry standards. Because of these standards, only a fraction of individuals investing in education can enter upper-layer schools.[5]

Competition for entry into upper-layer schools requires costly effort. Individuals have the same innate ability and the same disutility of effort spent in the education system. A competitive schooling system requires that individuals spend substantial effort in the development of common basic academic skills (such as

---

[4] Compared to Brunello and Ishikawa (1999*a*), the model with a single skill presented below has two important differences. First, wages are determined by an efficiency wage mechanism rather than by bargaining. Second, the structure of training costs faced by firms is more general.

[5] Examples of upper and lower-layer schools are high-ranked versus low-ranked universities or secondary schools, or universities versus secondary schools.

the ability to solve mathematical problems and language skills). We capture the key aspects of competition in the schooling system by modelling it as a tournament over an entry standard. The stricter the standard, the lower the fraction of individuals who gain access to upper-layer schools.

Let $\mu \in [\mu_0, 1]$ denote the effort spent by an individual to develop basic academic skills, which are used in the competition to enter upper-layer schools. There is a one-to-one relationship between effort spent and accumulated skills. Hence, μ denotes also the stock of basic academic skills. Maximum feasible effort is normalized to one and minimum effort, μ_0, can be produced without cost. A higher μ increases the probability of getting into upper-layer schools.

Firms can choose between two technologies, L and S. The L-technology has the following features: first, monitoring of individual effort spent by employees on the job is imperfect and costly.[6] In particular, the probability of detecting a worker who is shirking on the job is δ, with δ less than one. Second, output per head is equal to ϕy, with $\phi > 1$. Third, jobs require that new hires be trained at a cost. Skills are firm-specific and training is fully paid by firms. Let τ_l be the cost borne by the standard firm.[7] If the hired employee is a new labour market entrant who has just graduated from an upper-layer school, the employee's formal education and investment in the development of basic academic skills interact well with the requirements of this technology, thereby enhancing trainability. Hence, the training cost is reduced at the rate $1 - \beta_g \mu$ with $\beta_g > 0$.[8] On the other hand, if the hired employee is from a lower-layer school, the training cost is simply τ_l (for the standard firm).[9]

An alternative to hiring new school graduates is to hire experienced workers, who have already undertaken some training with the S-technology. While skills are firm-specific and cannot be fully transferred from firm to firm, labour market experience is useful in that it reduces training costs in the L-technology at the rate λ, with $\lambda \in [0, 1]$.[10] Thus, both education in upper-layer schools and labour market experience are productive in this model because they reduce the training costs borne by firms choosing the L-technology.[11]

---

[6] Individuals spend effort both in the education system and on the job.

[7] The meaning of 'standard' is explained later.

[8] It is useful to think of the relationship between formal education in upper-layer schools and basic academic skills as multiplicative and given by $\beta_g \mu$.

[9] This is a useful normalization with no significant consequences. The important assumption is that formal education in lower-layer schools is less efficient in the development of basic academic skills.

[10] In a broad sense, skills developed in firms using the S-technology are partially transferrable to the L-technology. See Stevens (1995) for a discussion of transferrable skills. In this chapter, we assume that labour market experience reduces training costs equally for all movers, independently of their education. This is equivalent to assuming that the relative advantage of being a new graduate from an upper-layer school rapidly decays with labour market experience.

[11] See Rosen (1976) and Brunello and Medio (2000) and the references therein for a similar interpretation of the economic role of education. In this paper, we assume that the cost of on-the-job training is fully borne by firms. More in general, and following Becker, costs and returns are shared by individuals and firms.

The obvious implication of these assumptions is that a firm choosing the L-technology will never hire new graduates from lower-layer schools, who are more costly to train.

The S-technology is characterized by perfect and costless monitoring of workers. Moreover, output per head and training costs for new hires are both lower than in the L-technology and equal, respectively, to y and τ_s (again, in the standard firm). Compared to the L-technology, schooling and investment μ are assumed to be ineffective in the reduction of training costs in this type of technology. Hence, firms choosing the S-technology are simply indifferent among graduates coming from different types of school.

Intuitively, it is useful to think of the L-technology as a complex environment that yields higher output but is more difficult to manage. Higher complexity requires adequate skills. These skills are provided to employees by firms and are more easily acquired by individuals with better (and more) education, prior to that being dissipated in work life. Hence, better education reduces training costs burdened by firms adopting this technology. On the other hand, firms adopting the S-technology have a simpler and less productive environment that requires simpler skills. The cost of acquiring these skills, also provided by the hiring firm, depends neither on the quality nor on the quantity of education.[12]

We assume that the training costs associated to the different technologies are related as follows

$$\tau_s < \tau_l(1 - \beta_g) \tag{4.1}$$

and

$$\tau_s < \tau_l \lambda. \tag{4.2}$$

Hence, either basic academic skills accumulated in the education process or experience in the labour market can reduce training costs faced by L-technology firms but cannot make training in that technology cheaper than training in the S-technologies.[13]

While individuals do not differ in their innate ability, firms differ in their underlying *managerial ability*. Abler managers are more likely to attract hires from upper-layer schools and to manage and properly organize the complexity of the L-technology, which requires higher training costs. On the other hand, the simpler S-technology is more likely to be chosen by less able managers. Managerial ability, α, is assumed to be distributed uniformly in the population of firms as

$$\int_{\alpha_{min}}^{\alpha_{max}} \frac{1}{\alpha_{max} - \alpha_{min}} \, d\alpha \equiv \int_{\alpha_{min}}^{\alpha_{max}} f(\alpha) \, d\alpha = 1 \tag{4.3}$$

[12] We assume hereafter that $(\phi - 1)y > (r + s)/\delta$, where r is the real rate of interest.
[13] Notice that these inequalities hold for any value of μ.

and affects on-the-job training costs as follows:

$$\frac{\tau_z}{\alpha_i} < \frac{\tau_z}{\alpha_j} \quad \text{iff } \alpha_i > \alpha_j$$

where $z = l, s$. Hence, firms endowed with higher managerial ability face lower training costs (and the 'standard' firm referred to earlier on is the firm with managerial ability equal to unity).

In this model, individuals invest in education and firms select the appropriate technology. Each agent is assumed to play a Nash non-cooperative game and select the optimal action by taking the action of all other agents as given. Thus, each individual chooses μ by taking both the action of other individuals and the allocation of firms to technologies as given. This is equivalent to assuming that individuals are too small compared to the size of the market to internalize the effect of their individual choice of μ on the allocation of firms. On the other hand, each firm chooses the most suitable technology by taking both the choice of other firms and the decision of individuals as given. Hence, each firm is also too small relative to the size of the market to explicitly take into account the impact of its choice of the appropriate technology on the educational choice of individuals. These features of the game played by each agent imply the presence both of spillovers and of strategic complementarities. As a consequence, there could be multiple equilibria.[14]

To solve for the steady-state decentralized Nash equilibrium, we start from the optimal allocation of firms to technologies when the individual choice of μ is given.[15] Firms in this frictionless economy live forever and fill immediately vacant jobs created by separations with new hires. Product prices are constant and equal to 1. Define with J the asset value of lifetime profits from a filled job and with R the asset value from a vacant job. In the steady state, the following relation must hold:

$$J_i = \frac{\xi_i + sR_i + (1 - s) J_i}{1 + r} \tag{4.4}$$

where i indicates the firm and ξ are current operating profits gross of training costs. Since vacant jobs are immediately filled and training costs are fully borne by firms, it must be that

$$R_i = J_i - \tau_i.$$

Substituting this relationship into eqn (4.4) we get that $rJ_i = \xi_i - s\tau_i \equiv \pi_i$ and we can simply focus hereafter on current operating profits net of expected training costs, π_i.

---

[14] See the discussion in Cooper and John (1988).
[15] By optimal allocation we mean that each firm in the market selects the technology that yields the highest profit for a given value of μ.

In the steady state, profits depend on the selection of the technology. In particular, for a firm choosing the L-technology, the current operating profit net of training costs (hereafter, simply 'profit') is defined as

$$\pi_{pi} = \phi y - w_p - \frac{s\tau_l(1 - \beta_g \mu)}{\alpha_i} \tag{4.5}$$

if it chooses to hire a new school graduate in case of a vacancy, and

$$\pi_{mi} = \phi y - w_m - \frac{s\lambda\tau_l}{\alpha_i} \tag{4.6}$$

if it chooses to hire an experienced worker from the labour market. Notice that w_p and w_m are (real) wages when firms hire either from schools or from the market of experienced workers and that the profit π_{pi} is a positive function of μ, the investment in basic academic skills. This is the source of positive spillovers in the L-technology.

Let F be the number of firms that choose the L-technology, with P firms hiring new graduates and $M = F - P$ firms hiring experienced workers from other firms. In what follows, we shall adopt the convention of identifying a firm adopting the L-technology and hiring new school graduates as a P-firm, and a firm hiring an experienced worker and using the same technology as an M-firm.

Let S be the number of firms using the S-technology. Clearly, $S = 1 - F$. Let Q be the total number of quits. Since only M-firms hire experienced workers from the market to replace sM separations, in the steady state equilibrium it must be that $Q = sM$. It is shown below that P- and M-firms pay the same wage to their workers and that S-firms pay a wage w_s strictly lower than the wage paid by the L-technology firms. Consequently, quits can only occur profitably from S-firms to M-firms, and the endogenous quit rate q is given by

$$q = \frac{sM}{1 - F}. \tag{4.7}$$

With endogenous quits, the profit for a firm i choosing the S-technology is

$$\pi_{si} = y - w_s - \frac{(s + q)\tau_s}{\alpha_i}. \tag{4.8}$$

The choice of the most profitable technology depends both on managerial ability and on the level of wages paid to workers. Notice first that the S-technology implies perfect and costless monitoring of workers. With no unemployment, competition among workers joining these firms drives the real wage down to b, the exogenous reservation level. Hence

$$w_s = b. \tag{4.9}$$

On the other hand, costly monitoring and limited information on worker effort force firms choosing the L-technology to pay efficiency wages in order to motivate workers and to achieve efficient production levels. Consider an M-firm. If a worker employed in such a firm is detected shirking, she is fired and moves to an S-firm, where wages are lower.[16] If she is not detected, she stays on. With risk neutrality, individual utility is given by

$$U = w - e \qquad (4.10)$$

where e is individual effort on the job, which can either be equal to zero or to one. In the steady state, the returns from not shirking are

$$rE_m = w_m - 1 - sE_m \qquad (4.11)$$

where E_m is the asset value from employment in an M-firm in the absence of shirking. Alternatively, the returns from shirking are

$$rE_m^S = w_m + \delta[E_c - E_m^S] - sE_m^S \qquad (4.12)$$

where E_m^S is the asset value from employment in the presence of shirking and E_c is the asset value from employment in the competitive sector of the labour market, composed of the firms adopting the S-technology. Hence, a worker who shirks on the job gains utility because her effort is equal to zero but faces the non-zero probability of being dismissed and forced to take a job in the competitive sector, where wages are lower.[17] Finally, define the returns from employment in the competitive sector as

$$rE_c = b - 1 + q[E_m - E_c] - sE_c. \qquad (4.13)$$

With endogenous quits, workers dismissed by M-firms can find their way back into the high wage sector by transiting in the sector of S-firms and by moving into another M-firm with probability q. Using the no-shirking condition $rE_m = rE_m^S$ and eqns (4.11)–(4.13), we obtain

$$w_m = b + \frac{(r+s)}{\delta} + \frac{q}{\delta} > w_s = b. \qquad (4.14)$$

As expected, M-firms pay a premium over the reservation wage in order to motivate workers to spend the efficient level of effort. Next, consider P-firms. These firms share with M-firms the L-technology and imperfect monitoring. For a given quit rate q, it is easy to check that the efficiency wage paid by P-firms is

---

[16] See Jones (1987) for an efficiency wage model in a dual labour market set-up. In Brunello and Ishikawa (1999a) wage determination is the outcome of bargaining between the worker and the firm.

[17] We are ruling out the possibility that M-firms hire straight from P-firms or other M-firms. With a positive wage differential, M-firms recognize that workers coming from P- or M-firms must be shirkers and avoid hiring them. Identification of workers as previous shirkers is difficult, however, if they are hired from S-firms.

also given by eqn (4.14), so that[18]

$$w_m = w_p.$$

$$(4.15)$$

Turning to the allocation of firms to the alternative technologies, we can use eqns (4.7), (4.14), and (4.15) into the definitions of current profits for firms choosing the L-technology to get

$$\pi_{pi} = \phi y - b - \frac{(r+s)}{\delta} - \frac{sM}{\delta(1-F)} - \frac{s\tau_l(1-\beta_g\mu)}{\alpha_i} \qquad (4.16)$$

and

$$\pi_{mi} = \phi y - b - \frac{(r+s)}{\delta} - \frac{sM}{\delta(1-F)} - \frac{s\tau_l\lambda}{\alpha_i}. \qquad (4.17)$$

Recalling that each firm chooses the most adequate technology by taking the decision of other firms as given, eqns (4.16) and (4.17) clearly suggest that, independently of the value of α, firms using the L-technology will prefer to hire new graduates rather than experienced workers if

$$\mu \geq \frac{1-\lambda}{\beta_g} \equiv \underline{\mu}, \qquad (4.18)$$

that is, if, for a given μ, the degree of positive interaction between basic academic skills and the L-technology, which depends on the quality of upper-layer schools, is high (β_g is high), and/or if previous labour market experience is of little use for training in the L-technology (λ is high). To put it differently, firms will adopt the P-hiring policy when investment μ exceeds a certain critical level, $\underline{\mu}$.[19]

If condition (4.18) holds, then *all* firms choosing the L-technology hire exclusively from schools. With no hirings of experienced workers, there can be neither endogenous quits nor M-firms in the optimal allocation. We call this situation the *P-regime*, where $P = F$. On the other hand, if condition (4.18) does not hold, then *all* firms using the L-technology hire experienced workers from the market. Endogenous quits are non-zero and there are only M-firms. This is called the *M-regime*, where $M = F$. We shall consider both regimes in turn.

4.2.1. The P-regime

In this regime, firms using the L-technology hire only from school and the endogenous quit rate q is equal to zero. Hence, the separation rate in this regime is

---

[18] This is only true *ex ante*, under the assumption that each firm, independently of the type, chooses the (real) wage by taking the quit rate q as given. We shall show below that $w_m \neq w_p$ in an *ex post* sense, because the endogenous quit rate varies between the two possible regimes.

[19] Notice that each firm takes M as given when choosing between hiring new graduates and hiring experienced workers in the L-technology. If every firm chooses P then $M = 0$ in the *ex post* equilibrium and profits π_p are higher *ex post* than *ex ante*.

given by s for each type of firm. The allocation of firms to technologies L and S can be characterized as follows. Assumptions (4.1) and (4.2) ensure that

$$\frac{\partial}{\partial \alpha} \pi_p > \frac{\partial}{\partial \alpha} \pi_s. \tag{4.19}$$

Thus, the profit function in the L-technology is steeper than in the S-technology. It is also reasonable to assume that

$$[\pi_p - \pi_s] < 0 \quad \text{when } \alpha = \alpha_{\min} \tag{4.20}$$

so that the marginal firm, which is endowed with the lowest level of managerial ability, prefers the S- to the L-technology. The allocation of firms between the two technologies depends on the condition

$$[\pi_p - \pi_s] \gtrless 0,$$

that is, the L-technology is chosen if

$$\alpha_i \geq \frac{s[\tau_l(1 - \beta_g \mu) - \tau_s]}{y(\phi - 1) - (r + s)/\delta} = \alpha_P. \tag{4.21}$$

In this case, the equilibrium share of firms that choose the S-technology is

$$\int_{\alpha_{\min}}^{\alpha_P} f(\alpha) \, d\alpha = S \tag{4.22}$$

and the share of firms choosing the L-technology is $F = 1 - S$.

Using definition (4.3), F is seen to be related to α_P by

$$\alpha_P = \alpha_{\max} - F(\alpha_{\max} - \alpha_{\min}). \tag{4.23}$$

Using equations (4.21) and (4.23) it is straightforward to show that

$$\frac{\partial F}{\partial \mu} > 0, \quad \frac{\partial^2 F}{\partial \mu^2} = 0 \tag{4.24}$$

so that the optimal number of firms selecting the L-technology in the P-regime is a linear and increasing function of the investment in basic academic skills μ.

Now consider the educational investment of individuals. The optimal allocation of firms to technologies implies that new school graduates can be hired either by firms with the L-technology at the wage w_p or by firms with the S-technology at the wage b. In a steady-state equilibrium, individuals going through the schooling system take these possible outcomes into account in their selection of investment in basic academic skills, μ.

With a constant population, the steady-state equilibrium requires that in each period of time there are s individuals graduating from school and entering the labour market. As discussed above, schooling systems can vary in their degree of selectivity. We measure selectivity by the exogenous parameter Φ, the number of slots available in upper-layer schools, with $\Phi < s$. The lower the Φ, the more selective is the schooling system. Among individuals graduating from school and entering the labour market, $\Phi = s\Theta$ are graduates from upper-layer schools and $s - \Phi = s(1 - \Theta)$ are graduates from lower-layer schools, where Θ is the proportion of new graduates coming from upper-layer schools. In the P-regime, only graduates from upper-layer schools can be hired with probability F/Θ by firms adopting the L-technology and paying the higher wage w_p. In what follows, we assume that the government chooses exogenously the selectivity parameter Θ to ensure that[20]

$$\Theta \geq F. \tag{4.25}$$

Hence, the net return that individual j can expect from access to an upper-layer school is

$$EU_{Gj} = \frac{F}{\Theta} E_{mj} + \left(1 - \frac{F}{\Theta}\right) E_{cj} - \Omega(\mu - \mu_0) \tag{4.26}$$

where $\Omega(\mu - \mu_0)$ is the cost of investment in education with the following properties

$$\Omega(0) = 0, \quad \Omega' \lessgtr 0 \text{ as } \mu \lessgtr \mu_0, \quad \Omega'' => 0, \tag{4.27}$$

$(1 - F/\Theta)$ is the probability of finding a job in an S-firm and μ_0 is the minimum level of investment in basic academic skills that yields zero investment costs. Moreover, E_{mj} is defined by eqn (4.11) and is equal to E_{pj} under the no-shirking condition, and E_{cj} is defined by eqn (4.13) with q set to zero under the P-regime.

On the other hand, the expected net return from entry into a lower-layer school is

$$EU_{Bj} = E_{cj} - \Omega(\mu - \mu_0). \tag{4.28}$$

With homogeneous individuals, entry into upper-layer schools is restricted by the selectivity parameter Θ and is modelled in this chapter as a tournament against an entry standard. Given a standard of performance σ^*, individuals who perform at least up to the standard get into upper-layer schools, while those who perform less than the standard remain in lower-layer schools. Since participants are homogeneous, they end up investing the same amount μ.[21]

---

[20] This strong assumption drastically simplifies the analysis. See Brunello and Ishikawa (1999a) for a detailed discussion of the case $\Theta < F$.
[21] See Malcomson (1984) for a detailed discussion of similar tournaments.

More in detail, define the probability of passing the standard as $Prob\{\sigma \geq \sigma^*\}$ and let individual performance in the schooling race be measured as

$$\sigma = \mu + \varepsilon \tag{4.29}$$

where ε is luck, which varies according to a standard normal distribution G. Individuals choose μ to maximize

$$Prob\{\sigma \geq \sigma^*\} \, EU_{Gj} + Prob\{\sigma < \sigma^*\} \, EU_{Bj}. \tag{4.30}$$

By substituting eqns (4.26) and (4.28) into (4.30), the first-order condition of this maximization problem is

$$g(\sigma^* - \mu)\left[\frac{F}{\Theta\delta}\right] = \Omega'(\mu - \mu_0) \tag{4.31}$$

where g is the normal density function and each individual sets μ by taking both F and Θ as given. Ex post, the probability of entering an upper-layer school must equal the proportion of available seats. Hence,

$$1 - G(\sigma^* - \mu) = \Theta \tag{4.32}$$

where G is the distribution function and we have used the fact that homogeneous individuals set the same value of μ.[22]

The comparative static properties of the choice of μ by each individual is summarized by the following lemma.

Lemma 1. *In the P-regime, individual investment in basic academic skills increases either (i) as the number of L-technology firms increases, or (ii) as the selectivity of upper-layer schools tightens.*

Proof. See Brunello and Ishikawa (1999).

We shall hereafter write the optimal level of investment μ in the P-regime as

$$\mu = \mu_P(F, \Theta). \tag{4.33}$$

Notice that, for a given Θ, the difference $\sigma^* - \mu$ stays constant and so does g, at the optimum. Hence we have the following.

Corollary 2. *If the cost of investing in homogeneous skills is quadratic, i.e.,*

$$\Omega(\mu - \mu_0) = \frac{\psi}{2} (\mu - \mu_0)^2, \tag{4.34}$$

then the optimal choice of education is a linear function of F, given Θ.

---

[22] We are supposing here that the government sets the standard σ^* passively given the decision of individuals. Alternatively, we could assume that the government sets σ^* by acting as a Stackelberg leader. The qualitative features of the comparative static properties discussed below, however, are not affected.

We can also show the following:

Proposition 3. *An interior locally stable steady-state equilibrium in the P-regime exists under a quadratic investment cost function for a given selectivity parameter* Θ, *if there exists a pair* (μ^*, F^*) *such that*

(i) $\underline{\mu} < \mu^* \leqq 1, \quad 0 < F^* \leqq \Theta$

(ii)

$$F^* = \frac{\alpha_{\max} - \widetilde{\alpha_P}(\mu^*)}{\alpha_{\max} - \alpha_{\min}}$$

and

$$\mu^* = \mu_P(F^*, \Theta)$$

(iii)

$$\frac{\psi\delta\Theta(a_{\max} - a_{\min})}{g(\sigma^* - \mu^*)} > -\frac{d\alpha_P(\mu^*)}{d\mu}.$$

There is at most one locally stable steady-state equilibrium in the P-regime.

In the P-regime, separations are exogenous and firms fill their vacant positions by hiring new school graduates. While firms adopting the L-technology strictly prefer to hire graduates from upper-layer schools, S-firms hire indifferently graduates from either type of school. There is no unemployment and P-firms pay higher wages to their employees in order to motivate them to produce the desired level of effort. On the other hand, S-firms pay the reservation wage. There is no inter-firm mobility from the S-sector to the L-sector. If we interpret high managerial ability as the ability to attract and organize not only trainable workers from upper-layer schools but also large capital stock, we can characterize the equilibrium in terms of firm size, measured by the capital–labour ratio. While large firms typically choose the L-technology, small and medium firms choose the S-technology.

4.2.2. The *M*-regime

Compared to the P-regime, non-zero quits are possible in the steady-state equilibrium of this regime. These quits occur because firms using the L-technology pay efficiency wages that are strictly higher than the reservation wage and prefer to fill their vacancies with experienced workers. These workers must come from S-firms, where wages are lower.[23] Since workers are homogeneous, the endogenous quit rate is defined, in equilibrium, by eqn (4.7), with $M = F$. Notice that

---

[23] Exogenous separations are flows out of the labour force. Moreover, the no-shirking condition ensures that no worker is fired from firms using the L-technology.

endogenous quits are costly to firms choosing the S-technology because they increase training expenses by raising separations.[24]

The comparison of profits in the L-technology and in the S-technology is also conditioned by the presence of quits. In particular, the choice between the L- and the S-technology depends on the following condition:

$$\alpha_i \geq \frac{s[\tau_l \lambda - \tau_s/(1-F)]}{y(\phi-1) - (r+s)/\delta - sF/\delta(1-F)} = \alpha_M \tag{4.35}$$

so that all firms with managerial ability higher than α_M will choose the L-technology. The shares of firms selecting the L- and S-technologies are again determined by eqn (4.22), except that α_M replaces α_P. Notice that α_M does not depend on μ. Hence, in this regime the share of L-technology firms, F, is independent of the level of individual investment in basic academic skills, μ. The following lemma characterizes the key property of the function α_M (the proof is relegated to the Appendix).

Lemma 4. *Given the boundary level of educational investment $\underline{\mu} = (1-\lambda)/\beta_g$, if the condition*

$$\alpha_P(\underline{\mu}) > \delta\tau_s \tag{4.36}$$

holds, then the function α_M in eqn (4.35) has the following property:

$$\alpha_M > \alpha_P(\underline{\mu}).$$

We shall hereafter assume that condition (4.36) is satisfied.

Turning to the choice of education by individuals, notice that firms choosing the L-technology in this regime prefer to hire experienced workers rather than new school graduates. On the other hand, firms choosing the S-technology are indifferent to the type of schools each new hire has graduated from. Therefore, the individual incentive to participate in the competition to enter upper-layer schools and to accumulate basic academic skills, that is to choose μ such that $\mu > \mu_0$, is simply zero.

The privately optimal level of educational effort in the M-regime is equal to μ_0, the minimum level of μ in terms of cost, quite independently of the distribution of firms among available technologies. More formally, we have

Proposition 5. *Under the conditions established in Lemma 4, a steady state equilibrium exists in the M-regime if*

$$\alpha_M < \alpha_{max}.$$

There is at most one such an equilibrium, and, if it exists, it is locally stable.

---

[24] With an exogenous reservation wage and a given number of firms, the marginal firm must be profitable even with higher separations. This we assume hereafter. Alternatively, we can endogenize the level of the reservation wage by introducing a zero profit condition for the firm run by the least able manager.

Given assumption (4.36), the equilibrium share of L-technology firms is smaller in the *M*-regime than that in the *P*-regime. By default, the share of *S*-firms is higher in the *M*-regime. If we characterize the equilibrium in terms of firm size, with large firms typically choosing the L-technology and small and medium firms choosing the S-technology, the *M*-regime features both significant labour market flows from small to large firms, with the small firms taking care of initial training in the labour market, and the limited role played by the schooling system in the matching of new entrants with private industry, which prefers experienced workers to new graduates of relatively low average quality.

4.2.3. The Possibility of Multiple Regime Equilibria

We have seen that there is at most one locally stable interior equilibrium in the *P*-regime (with $\mu > \mu_0$) and that there is also at most one locally stable equilibrium in the *M*-regime. While an equilibrium could also occur at the boundary of the two regimes, that is where the $E_P E_P$ curve intersects the vertical line at $\mu = \underline{\mu}$, such a point cannot be a (locally) stable equilibrium. Hence, we have

Proposition 6. *Depending on the parameters of the model, the economy can be characterized by (i) a single P-regime equilibrium, (ii) a single M-regime equilibrium, (iii) multiple regime equilibria, or (iv) no equilibrium.*

In the case of multiple regime equilibria, that is an equilibrium in the *P*-regime (*P-equilibrium*) and an equilibrium in the *M*-regime (*M-equilibrium*), historical accident decides which equilibrium the economy actually falls in. In the *P-equilibrium*, investment μ tends to be high because expected returns are high and large firms hire graduates from upper-layer schools. On the other hand, in the *M-equilibrium*, investment μ is low and labour market turnover is relatively high. As we shall see below, exogenous shocks such as a reduction in the selectivity of schooling can shift the economy from one equilibrium to the other.

4.2.4. Discussion

Interesting features of the model presented above are both the presence of multiple regime equilibria and the possibility that an economy shifts from an equilibrium to the other as a result of exogenous shifts in the parameters.

Suppose that initially the economy is in the *P-equilibrium* and that this steady-state equilibrium is perturbed by an exogenous change in the selectivity of the schooling system in the direction of keener competition, that is, lower Θ. In the new equilibrium, both accumulated basic academic skills μ and the share of L-firm F are higher. Since L-firms are more productive, average productivity increases. Thus, more competition at school increases average productivity and average wages. We shall show below that the presence of positive spillovers and strategic complementarities also implies that, in the *P*-regime, the equilibrium with higher μ can be ranked as Pareto superior to the equilibrium with lower μ. Hence, a policy that increases competition at school increases net national output and economic welfare.

Next, suppose that the exogenous change goes in the opposite direction, that is, schooling becomes less selective and Θ increases. If the change in Θ is sufficiently large, individual investment in basic academic skills falls to the point that large firms find it convenient to hire experienced workers from the market. The P-equilibrium disappears and the only equilibrium left in the economy is the M-equilibrium, which is unaffected by the change in Θ, no matter how large. In the new equilibrium, workers are willing to quit since large firms pay higher wages because of internal efficiency reasons. As the decentralized Nash equilibrium switches from the P-regime to the M-regime, the share of S-firms increases and the share of L-firms decreases.

Importantly, a reversal of the original shock, which increases the selectivity of the schooling system back to its original level, is unlikely to produce a return of the system to the original P-equilibrium in the P-regime. With no firms hiring from upper-layer schools, individuals gain nothing from increased competition and have no incentive to increase their effort over its minimum value, μ_0. The economy is stuck in the M-regime. In this particular sense, the M-equilibrium in the M-regime is characterized by hysteresis. If the economy is located in this equilibrium, improving the selectivity of the schooling system will not necessarily increase the effort put in acquiring basic skills if firms do not change their hiring policies and their choice of technology. Notice also that in this regime more competition at school does not affect net national output and economic welfare.

A key feature of the decentralized Nash equilibrium described in our model is the assumption that each agent (individual or firm) is too small to take into explicit account the effect of her own action on the optimal decision of other agents. This has implications both on the equilibrium level of educational investment μ and on the optimal number of firms using the L-technology, F. To see why, consider first the P-regime and notice that F is an increasing function of μ. While an increase in effort by a single individual has little effect on F, a coordinated and symmetric increase in μ increases the number of P-firms hiring from upper-layer schools. This in turn makes individual investment more attractive. In a symmetric cooperative equilibrium, positive spillovers and strategic complementarities are internalized and equilibrium investment μ is higher. As shown by Cooper and John (1988), the presence of positive spillovers and strategic complementarities implies that equilibria can be ranked in a Pareto sense, with the high μ equilibrium being Pareto superior to the low μ equilibrium.

Turning to the M-regime, individual investment is at its minimum level, μ_0, and the number of L-firms, F, is constant. The absence of a positive relationship between F and μ implies that a coordinated increase of μ over μ_0 cannot increase national output. Since effort increases, net national output falls. Hence, high μ equilibria in this regime are Pareto inferior to low μ equilibria.

Going back to the question whether more competition at school improves economic welfare, our answer is positive only when the economy is initially located in a P-equilibrium. In such an equilibrium, individuals accumulate basic academic skills in the schooling system and an important share of firms value these skills because they significantly reduce training costs. In these circumstances, we have shown that an increase in the competition of the schooling system increases economic welfare. If the economy, however, is initially located in a M-equilibrium, the accumulation of basic academic skills is at its minimum and firms prefer to hire experienced workers to new school graduates. In this case, increasing the competition of the schooling system reduces economic welfare, unless this increase can be coordinated with a substantial change in the hiring patterns of firms in favour of new school graduates.

4.3. THE MODEL WITH TWO SKILLS

The model in the previous section is based on the assumption that individuals accumulate a single type of skills, the basic academic competencies. In this section, we extend the model to include two skills, basic academic skills and *individual* skills. As mentioned in the Introduction, the former type can be exemplified with maths and science skills and the latter type with creative thinking. It is reasonable to expect that both types of skills are useful to firms that face a menu of available technologies. It is also reasonable to imagine a degree of complementarity between these skills: for instance, creative thinking and innovative skills require a reasonable degree of common academic skills to be effective. At the same time, however, excessive specialization in one type of skill is likely to hamper the development of the other type.

In short, we view the relationship between individual and academic skills as hump shaped, with individual skills first increasing and then decreasing in the amount of time and effort spent in the accumulation of basic academic skills. Consider first the case where individual skills increase with basic academic skills. Since the total stock of skills is increasing in the stock of basic academic skills, we expect that introducing individual skills will not affect in a qualitative way the results discussed in the previous section.

Things are rather different, however, when we focus on the negative portion of the hump-shaped relationship, that is, when we assume that the two skills are substitutes rather than complements. This is the relevant portion when we are interested in the consequences of excessive competition at school, which leads to a substantial accumulation of one type of skill at the cost of the other.

We analyse this case by introducing the following variations in the model discussed in the previous section. First, we assume that the total stock of skills accumulated by each individual during the schooling period is equal to 1, but allow the composition of basic and individual skills to vary. Hence, if an individual accumulates a stock $\mu \in [\mu_0, 1]$ of academic skills, this implies that she accumulates a stock $1 - \mu$ of individual skills.[25]

---

[25] Treating basic academic skills and individual skills as perfect substitutes is clearly a strong assumption, that is useful to sharpen our results.

Second, we add to the menu of available technologies a third option, the V-technology. This technology shares with the S-technology both the perfect and costless monitoring of workers and the training costs τ_s. To help intuition, it is useful to think of the V-technology as venture business or as a trial-and-error self-employment sector that relies on the flexibility, the creativity and the specialization provided by individual skills. Output per head in this technology, vy, is higher than in the S-technology, but lower than in the L-technology. Hence, $\phi > v > 1$.[26] Compared to the L-technology, training costs in the V-technology are lower the higher the level of individual skills held by the hired employee. Since individual skills reduce training costs in this technology by $\tau_s[1 - \beta_v(1 - \mu)]$, where $(1 - \mu)$ is the level of individual skills, training costs burdened by firms adopting the V-technology (V-firms) are an increasing function of μ. We capture this relationship by a convenient reparametrization of training costs in the standard firm as $\tau_s(1 + \beta_c\mu)$.[27]

Furthermore, we extend assumptions (4.1) and (4.2) as follows:

$$\tau_s < \tau_s(1 + \beta_c) < \tau_l(1 - \beta_g) \tag{4.37}$$

and

$$\tau_s < \tau_s(1 + \beta_c) < \tau_l\lambda. \tag{4.38}$$

With costless monitoring, V-firms pay the reservation wage, as S-firms do. Moreover, firm-to-firm quits involve also workers employed by V-firms. If V is the number of firms using the V-technology, we have that $S + V = 1 - F$, and the net real profit of a firm using the V-technology is given by

$$\pi_{vi} = vy - b - \frac{(s + q)\tau_s(1 + \beta_c\mu)}{\alpha_i}. \tag{4.39}$$

Importantly, profits in the V-technology are a negative function of μ. Hence, the degree of competition of the schooling system has negative spillovers on the selection of this technology.

One can check that the economy described in this section is also characterized by two regimes, which are briefly discussed below.

4.3.1. The P-regime

Compared to the model with only two technologies, the introduction of a third technology somewhat complicates the allocation of firms to technologies. It can be shown that the choice between the V- and the S-technology is regulated by the following condition:

$$\alpha_i \geq \frac{s\mu\tau_s\beta_c}{y(v - 1)} \equiv \alpha_V \tag{4.40}$$

so that firms with a level of managerial ability higher than α_V will find the V-technology more profitable than the S-technology.

---

[26] We assume hereafter that $(\phi - v)y > (r + s)/\delta$.

[27] In practice, the two types of skill are likely to be useful, to a different extent, in both the L- and the V-technology. The case illustrated in the text brings this to the extreme for the sake of clarity.

Notice that the π_p curve, expressed as a function of α, could intersect the π_v curve either to the left or to the right of α_V. If the π_p curve intersects the π_v curve to the left of α_V, there are no V-firms and we are back to condition (4.21) in the previous section. On the other hand, if the π_p curve intersects the π_v curve to the right of α_V, there is another critical point, $\alpha_{P'}$, defined by

$$\alpha_i \geq \frac{s[\tau_l(1 - \beta_g \mu) - \tau_s(1 + \beta_c \mu)]}{y(\phi - v) - (r + s)/\delta} \equiv \alpha_{P'} \tag{4.41}$$

such that all firms with managerial ability higher than $\alpha_{P'}$ will choose the L-technology. In this case, the number of firms selecting the V-, L-, and S-technologies are, respectively,

$$\int_{\alpha_V}^{\alpha_{P'}} f(\alpha)\,d\alpha = V$$

$$\int_{\alpha_{P'}}^{\alpha_{\max}} f(\alpha)\,d\alpha = P = F$$

and $S = 1 - F - V$.

The following lemma characterizes the allocation of firms to technologies in the P-regime.

Lemma 7. *There is a critical value of μ, such that allocations with no firms adopting the V-technology exist if $\mu \geq \bar{\mu}$. This critical value does not necessarily lie in the domain $\mu \in [0, 1]$.*

Proof. See the Appendix.

Using eqns (4.23) and (4.41) it is straightforward to show that $\partial F / \partial \mu > 0$, and $\partial^2 F / \partial \mu^2 = 0$, so that the optimal number of firms selecting the L-technology in the P-regime is a linear and increasing function of the investment in basic academic skills μ.

Turning to the individual choice of μ, one can verify that this decision is still characterized by eqns (4.31) and (4.32), by Lemma 1 and Corollary 2, provided that we interpret the cost of effort function Ω as measuring the cost of investing in basic academic skills rather than in individual skills. The P-equilibrium can then be characterized as follows.

Proposition 8. *An interior locally stable steady-state equilibrium in the P-regime exists under a quadratic investment cost function for a given selectivity parameter Θ, if there exists a pair (μ^*, F^*) such that*

(i)

$$\underline{\mu} < \mu^* \leq 1, \quad 0 < F^* \leq \Theta$$

(ii)

$$F^* = \frac{\alpha_{\max} - \widetilde{\alpha_P}(\mu^*)}{\alpha_{\max} - \alpha_{\min}}$$

where

$$\frac{d\widetilde{\alpha}_P(\mu)}{d\mu} = \begin{cases} -\dfrac{s(\tau_l\beta_g + \tau_s\beta_c)}{(\phi - v)y - \frac{(r+s)}{\delta}} & \text{if } \mu \leq \overline{\mu} \\[2ex] -\dfrac{s\tau_l\beta_g}{(\phi - 1)y - \frac{(r+s)}{\delta}} & \text{if } \mu > \overline{\mu} \end{cases},$$

and

$$\mu^* = \mu_P(F^*, \Theta).$$

(iii)

$$\frac{\psi\delta\Theta(a_{\max} - a_{\min})}{g(\sigma^* - \mu^*)} > -\frac{d\widetilde{\alpha}_P(\mu^*)}{d\mu}.$$

There is at most one locally stable steady-state equilibrium in the P-regime.

4.3.2. The M-regime

In this regime, firms prefer the V- to the S-technology if

$$\alpha_i \geq \frac{(s/(1 - F))\mu\tau_s\beta_c}{y(v - 1)} = \alpha_V \tag{4.42}$$

and the choice between the L- and the V-technology depends on the following condition

$$\alpha_i \geq \frac{s[\tau_l\lambda - \tau_s/(1 - F)(1 + \beta_c\mu)]}{y(\phi - v) - (r + s)/\delta - sF/(\delta(1 - F))} = \alpha_{M'}. \tag{4.43}$$

Total differentiation of (4.43) shows that the share of L-technology firms, F, is increasing in the level of individual investment in basic academic skills, μ. The following lemma characterizes the main properties of the function $\alpha_{M'}(\mu)$ (the proof is relegated to the Appendix).

Lemma 9. *Given the boundary level of educational investment* $\underline{\mu} = (1 - \lambda)/\beta_g$, *if the condition*

$$\alpha_P(\mu) > \delta\tau_s(1 + \beta_c\mu)$$

holds, then the function $\alpha_{M'} = \alpha_{M'}(\mu)$ *is well-defined for all* $\mu \in [0, \underline{\mu}]$. *Moreover, it has the following properties: (i)*$\alpha_{M'}(\mu) > \alpha_P(\mu)$, *(ii)*$\alpha_{M'}(\mu)$*is monotonically decreasing in the domain* $\mu \in [0, \underline{\mu}]$.[28]

---

[28] We can show that if $\alpha_P(\mu) < \delta\tau_s(1 + \beta_c\mu)$, $\alpha_M(\mu)$ is not well-defined in the neighbourhood of $\mu = \underline{\mu}$. However, we can still show that under the following regularity condition

$$\frac{s(\lambda\tau_l - \tau_s)}{(\phi - v)y - (r + s)/\delta} > \delta\tau_s$$

there exists a certain $\mu' < \underline{\mu}$ such that $\alpha_M(\mu)$ is well-defined for $\mu \in [0, \mu']$ with the property that $\alpha'_M(\mu) < 0$.

As in the *P*-regime, the choice of μ is unchanged with respect to the model with one skill discussed in Section 4.2. Hence, $\mu = \mu_0$.[29] More formally, we have

Proposition 10. *Under the conditions established in Lemma 9, a steady-state equilibrium exists in the M-regime if*

$$\alpha_{M'}(\mu_0) < \alpha_{max}.$$

There is at most one such an equilibrium, and, if it exists, it is locally stable.

The introduction of individual skills and of the V-technology does not change the result contained in Proposition 5 that there can be either a *P*-equilibrium, an *M*-equilibrium, multiple regime equilibria and no equilibrium at all. As for the model with a single skill, historical accident decides which equilibrium the economy actually falls in.

4.3.3. Discussion

The basic properties of the model with two skills are similar to the properties discussed for the model with a single skill. Because of this, we shall only stress here the relevant differences between the two models.

First of all, consider the *P*-regime. Individual investment in basic academic skills has both positive and negative spillovers on the selection of technologies. By increasing their investment in μ, individuals reduce the training costs faced by *L*-firms but increase the costs faced by *V*-firms, which use intensively individual skills. The share of *L*- and *S*-firms increases but the share of *V*-firms falls. Since *V*-firms are more productive than *S*-firms, we cannot say *a priori* whether average productivity has increased, nor can we Pareto-rank equilibria with different values of μ. As discussed by Cooper and John (1988), this ranking is precluded by the presence of negative spillovers. Thus, when competition at school is already high, so that basic academic skills and individual skills are substitutes rather than complements, an increase in the selectivity of schools does not necessarily improve net national output and economic welfare.

Next, let us turn to the *M*-regime, where investment in basic skills is at its minimum level, μ_0. Since the asset value from employment in the S- or V-sectors, E_c, is a function of the endogenous quit rate, q, that depends on F, the positive relationship between F and μ that exists in this version of the model implies that a

---

[29] Notice also that there is no incentive for individuals to set $\mu < \mu_0$. This is because the model in this paper assumes that workers are paid only their reservation wage in spite of the improved productivity effect of their investment in individual skills (that is, their small investment in μ). This feature is justified by the underlying assumption that increases in productivity can only be triggered by firm-specific training fully paid by firms. If these training costs were shared between V-firms and hired workers, individuals would have an incentive to decrease μ even at a cost. While this possibility is ruled out in the current paper, we do not expect it to change our results in a qualitative way.

coordinated increase of μ over μ_0 increases individual (expected) utility. The reason is that, by so doing, agents can increase both the endogenous quit rate and their chances of landing a job in the high wage sector composed of M-firms.

The argument above suggests that a decentralized Nash equilibrium leads to under-investment in basic academic skills μ in either regime. If individuals could coordinate their action, they would achieve an equilibrium with higher values of μ. Notice, again, that the presence of negative spillovers for firms that choose the V-technology makes it difficult to rank equilibria in a Pareto sense. More in detail, an equilibrium with higher values of F and μ is not Pareto superior to an equilibrium with lower values of both variables in the following sense: while individuals investing in education are always better off in the former equilibrium, a sub-set of firms is worse off. If the equilibrium is in the P-regime, only firms choosing the V-technology are worse off. On the other hand, if the equilibrium is in the M-regime, the increase in the endogenous quit rate reduces profits both in M- and in V-firms.

The bottom line of this discussion is that the presence of two skills and of the V-technology imply that the *M-equilibrium*, which has both a lower μ and a lower F, cannot be generally ranked as Pareto inferior to the *P-equilibrium* and *vice versa*. A simple way to compare the relative efficiency of the two equilibria is to compute total net output in each equilibrium. If lump-sum transfers are possible, the equilibrium with higher net output should be preferred on efficiency grounds. Total net output Y is equal to

$$Y = V(\mu)[vy - 1] - \int_{V(\mu)} \frac{s\tau_s(1 - \beta_c\mu)}{\alpha} f(\alpha)\, da + S(\mu)[y - 1]$$

$$- \int_{S(\mu)} \frac{s\tau_s}{\alpha} f(\alpha)\, d\alpha + F(\mu)[\phi y - 1]$$

$$- \int_{F(\mu)} \frac{s\tau_l(1 - \beta_g\mu)}{\alpha} f(\alpha)\, da - s\Omega(\mu - \mu_0)$$

in the *P-equilibrium*, and to

$$Y = V(\mu)[vy - 1] - \int_{V(\mu)} \frac{(s + q)\tau_s(1 + \beta_c\mu)}{\alpha} f(\alpha)\, da + S(\mu)[y - 1]$$

$$- \int_{S(\mu)} \frac{(s + q)\tau_s}{\alpha} f(\alpha)\, d\alpha + F(\mu)[\phi y - 1] - \int_{F(\mu)} \frac{s\tau_l\lambda}{\alpha} f(\alpha)\, d\alpha$$

in the *M-equilibrium*. The *P-equilibrium* yields a higher investment in μ and a higher value of F. This investment reduces the training costs in the highly productive sector of large firms but makes the venture business sector less efficient. While net output is higher in the sector of large firms, it is lower in the sector of small venture business firms. On the other hand, the *M-equilibrium* yields minimum investment in μ, μ_0, and a lower value of F. Contrary to the previous case, this leads to higher net output in the sector of small venture business and to lower net output in the sector of large firms. Whether total net output is higher in the former or in the latter case cannot be established *a priori* and depends on the parameters of the model.

To summarize, the model presented in this section is useful to qualify some of the results discussed in the previous section. One result obtained in the previous section that is worth emphasizing is that, when the economy starts from a *P*-equilibrium, more competition at school leads to higher output per head and to higher welfare. It turns out that this result is based on the assumption that the accumulation of basic academic skills does not damage the accumulation of other skills that are also relevant for the economy. The contribution of this section is to show that excessive competition in the schooling system, by reducing the stock of individual skills that are key to the V-technology, does not necessarily improve average productivity and net national output.

4.4. CONCLUSIONS

Rather than simply summarizing our results, we devote the concluding remarks to argue that the key properties of the multiple regime equilibria discussed in the chapter fit well important stylized features of the relationship between schooling, industrial structure and labour turnover of countries as different as (Northern and Central) Italy and Japan.[30] These features can be briefly summarized as follows:[31]

1. While the Japanese schooling system emphasizes uniformity, competition and the accumulation of basic skills in mathematics and sciences, the Italian system is both less competitive and less successful, on an average, in the provision of these skills to younger cohorts. By Western standards, the Japanese schooling system provides limited flexibility in the selection of curricula and little choice to individuals. Historically '... teaching has been characterized by carefully developed, tightly executed instructions standardized for the entire nation....The system, especially from middle school on, has always been very competitive. Because universities (particularly elite ones) serve as powerful signaling devices in the labour market, competition to enter them is severe.' (Rohlen, 1992). Stern

---

[30] These two countries are the countries of residence of the two authors. Their choice has only an illustrative purpose. We exclude Southern Italy because of the structural problems of Italian Mezzogiorno, which makes it different in economic terms from the rest of the country. From now on we shall refer to Northern and Central Italy simply as 'Italy'.

[31] A more extended discussion of these differences can be found in Brunello and Ishikawa (1999*b*).

and excessive competition is emphasized also by Porter in his comparative study of competitive advantage. While excessive competition stifles individual creativity, '... the system succeeds in providing the vast majority of students in the whole country with a solid base for further education and training. A graduate of a Japanese high school knows as much mathematics as most American college graduates...' (Porter, 1989).

Compared to Japan, the Italian system offers more flexible curricula and substantial freedom of access to all levels of education in exchange for a poorer quality of education. Competition and signalling are less important, as suggested by the virtual absence of cram schools specialized in preparing students for entry examinations, a key feature of the Japanese education system. Michael Porter, in his well known analysis of the competitive advantage of nations, emphasizes the relatively poor quality of the Italian schooling system and argues that '... in order to sustain growth and to acquire professional competencies, Italians need to improve their basic knowledge of mathematics, computers and other key disciplines...' (Porter, 1989).

2. In Japan, large private firms tend to hire new school graduates and schools are very active in the placement of new graduates. In Italy, there is a widely perceived mismatch between the supply of educated labour and the demand by firms operating in the private sector. Italian private industry has historically relied more upon internal and informal training than on formal education. A distinctive feature of the Japanese labour market is the willingness, and even the preference, that many firms show for hiring untrained and yet untainted youth just after graduation from school and training them according to their needs. Every year, well over a third of new hires by firms with more than 1000 employees consist of new school graduates, whereas only one in eight new hires of firms with less than 100 employees is a new school graduate. Another key feature in the transition from school to work in Japan is the active role played by schools in the placement of school graduates in the labour market. Schools in Japan often act at least in part as employment agencies. This role is noticeable in upper-secondary schools and above, particularly in junior colleges, science and engineering colleges, and in vocational schools.

In Italy, private industry has traditionally been characterized by 'low intensity of education' and by reliance on internal training rather than on formal education. As remarked by Michael Porter (1989) and by Piore and Sabel (1984), the success of Italian *industrial districts* has been based more on informal training, often provided by the extended family, that operates small artisan shops and small and medium firms, than on formal education. The geographical concentration of these districts has also helped in the diffusion of the relevant knowledge and skills. While Japanese private firms are closely involved in networking with schools of different levels and quality, Italian private firms have traditionally exhibited little interest in the national schooling system.[32]

---

[32] See Jannaccone Pazzi and Ribolzi (1992).

3. The industrial structure of both countries is characterized by the important presence of small and medium firms. While in the US and Germany only 34.8 per cent and 45.9 per cent of total employment is in firms with less than 100 employees, this percentage rises to 55.6 per cent in Japan and reaches 71.4 per cent in Italy.

4. Job turnover is higher in Italy than in Japan, both in small and in large firms. According to Contini and Rapiti (1994) '...in the sector of small firms there is a high share of young workers...who exhibit substantial turnover...young workers who have been through on the job training in a small firm make up the large majority of job-to-job changes occurring in the Italian economy' (p. 13). In this view, small and medium firms in Italy provide substantial internal training to workers, who often use accumulated skills either to move to larger firms, where wages are higher and labour conditions better, or to set up their own shop.

Although available figures are not exactly comparable between the two countries because of the differences in the coverage of data, they suggest that job turnover is larger in Italy than in Japan. Focusing only on the expansion and contraction of existing firms, job turnover in firms with less than twenty employees is estimated to be about 23 per cent in Italy and about 10 per cent in Japan. Considering firms with more than 100 employees, the corresponding values are, respectively, about 9 and 7 per cent.[33]

5. Hourly earnings in both countries vary significantly with firm size. In particular, earnings in firms with less than 100 employees are, respectively, 65 and 60 per cent of earnings in firms with more than 1000 employees in Italy and in Japan.[34] On the other hand, earnings in firms with 100 to 999 employees in the two countries are, respectively, 80 and 72 per cent of the earnings of firms with more than 1000 employees.

6. Both earnings and productivity differentials by firm size are wider in Japan than in Italy. Earnings differentials are partially matched by productivity differentials. Using data on Italian and Japanese real gross value added per worker for different industries within the manufacturing sector and for different firm sizes in 1989, we find that, while firm-size productivity differentials are quite small in Italy (except for small firms in the clothing industry), they are rather large in Japan, especially for Foodstuffs and for Electrical machinery and Motor vehicles, the two key exporting industries.[35] These patterns are likely to reflect, among other things, both the relative importance of highly productive industrial

---

[33] *Source:* Contini *et al.* (1995).

[34] *Sources:* For Italy, INPS (Social Security National Institute) administrative archives (1990). For Japan, Ishikawa and Dejima (1994). Differentials are based on hourly earnings for Japan and on annual earnings for Italy. Only regular workers for Japan, all workers with a social security account in Italy.

[35] The original values in national currencies are converted into US dollars by using the 1990 based PPP exchange rates computed by the OECD. Focusing on Electrical engineering, labour productivity in small Italian firms is 1.64 times labour productivity in small Japanese firms. This ratio falls to 0.53 when large firms are compared. Similar results apply to Textiles, Foodstuffs and General engineering.

districts in the Italian economy and the relative abundance of low productivity subcontractors in the Japanese economy.

These differences can be interpreted as features of two distinct locally stable equilibria, similar to those produced by the models discussed in the chapter. In one equilibrium (*the Japanese or P-equilibrium*), schooling is very competitive and individuals invest substantially in the accumulation of common academic skills. The availability of these skills in the market and the complementarity between education and training facilitates the adoption of complex technologies, which require substantial training costs. Large firms that use these technologies pay relatively high wages and attract graduates from the best schools. Small firms, which operate in a secondary labour market, use relatively simple technologies and pay the reservation wage. The high expected gain from access into a good school stimulates investment in academic skills.

In another equilibrium (*the Italian or M-equilibrium*), schooling is not as selective and more time is spent for individual development in flexible curricula, both formally at school and informally on the job. Lower accumulation of common academic skills makes the adoption of complex technologies relatively less profitable. At the same time, however, the higher stock of individual skills stimulates the adoption of technologies that are intensive in these skills. Labour turnover is higher and labour market experience matters more than school quality in the reduction of training costs faced by firms. The relative scarcity of large firms, which pay higher wages, and the higher turnover rate further reduces the incentive to accumulate common academic skills, because of the relatively low expected returns.

APPENDIX

Proof of Lemma 4

Define the function

$$H(F) \equiv \frac{s[\lambda \tau_l - \tau_s/(1 - F)]}{(\phi - 1)y - (r + s)/\delta - sF/\delta(1 - F)}$$

in the domain $F \in [0, 1]$ and notice that when $F = 0$ and $\mu = \underline{\mu}$, $H(0) = \alpha_P(\underline{\mu})$.

First, we examine the gradient of H with respect to F. By multiplying both the numerator and the denominator by $(1 - F)$ and partially differentiating with respect to F, and after rearrangement, we obtain

$$\{H_F(F)\Big\{ = \frac{s}{\delta}\{(\phi - 1)y - (r + s)/\delta\}\Big\{ \frac{s[\lambda \tau_l - \tau_s]}{(\phi - 1)y - (r + s)/\delta} - \delta \tau_s\Big\}\Big\} \Big/$$
$$[(1 - F)\{(\phi - 1)y - (r + s)/\delta\} - \frac{s}{\delta}F]^2.$$

Since the denominator and the first term in the numerator are positive,

$$\text{sign } H_F(F) = \text{sign } \left\{ \frac{s\{\lambda\tau_l - \tau_s\}}{(\phi - 1)y - (r + s)/\delta} - \delta\tau_s \right\}.$$

Let the inside of the bracket and its first term be denoted as ψ and γ, respectively. Notice that $\gamma = \alpha_P(\underline{\mu})$. Thus, by our assumption, $\psi > 0$ and $H_F(F) > 0$.

Second, the equilibrium value of α_M is defined by the following relationship

$$H(F) = \alpha_{\max} - F(\alpha_{\max} - \alpha_{\min}).$$

The RHS of the above equation is a downward sloping straight line connecting $(0, \alpha_{\max})$ and $(1, \alpha_{\min})$, while the graph of the LHS has been shown to be an upward sloping curve, with $H(0) = \alpha_P(\underline{\mu})$. Clearly, the two curves have a single intersection, that lies above $\alpha_P(\underline{\mu})$. Thus $\alpha_M(\underline{\mu}) > \alpha_P(\underline{\mu})$, which proves the lemma. QED

Proof of Lemma 7

Notice that $\alpha_V(\mu)$ is increasing and $\alpha_P(\mu)$ is decreasing in μ. Moreover, α_V goes to zero and α_P goes to a positive number as μ tends to zero. Hence, the two curves must have a unique intersection point, say, at $\mu = \bar{\mu}$. This intersection is given by

$$\frac{\tau_l - \tau_s}{\tau_s\beta_c} = \frac{\mu}{(v - 1)y}\left[(\phi - v)y - \frac{(r + s)}{\delta}\right] + \frac{(\tau_l\beta_g + \tau_s\beta_c)\mu}{\tau_s\beta_c} \equiv k(\mu).$$

It is easy to see that $k(\mu)$ is an increasing and linear function of μ, with $k(0) = 0$ and $\lim_{\mu \to 1} k(\mu) \to k_1$, a positive constant. A sufficient condition for $\bar{\mu}$ to be less than 1 is that k_1 be larger than the LHS of the equation above.

Proof of Lemma 9

Define a function

$$H(F, \mu) \equiv \frac{s[\lambda\tau_l - \tau_s/(1 - F)(1 + \beta_c\mu)]}{(\phi - v)y - (r + s)/\delta - sF/(\delta(1 - F))}$$

in the domain $F \in [0, 1]$ and $\mu \in [0, \underline{\mu}]$, and denote its numerator and the denominator by $N(F, \mu)$ and $D(F, \mu)$, respectively. Define also the value of F for each value of μ for which the numerator and the denominator becomes zero as $F_N(\mu)$ and $F_D(\mu)$, respectively. Note that $F_N(\mu)$ and $F_D(\mu)$ are well-defined for all $\mu \in [0, \underline{\mu}]$. We observe that

$$F_N(\mu) = 1 - \frac{\tau_s(1 + \beta_c\mu)}{\lambda\tau_l} < 1$$

$$F_N'(\mu) = -\frac{\tau_s\beta_c}{\lambda\tau_l} < 0$$

$$F_D(\mu) = \frac{\delta\{(\phi - v)y - (r + s)/\delta\}}{s + \delta\{(\phi - v)y - (r + s)/\delta\}} < 1$$

$$F_D'(\mu) = 0.$$

First we show the following subsidiary lemma.

Subsidiary Lemma

For all $\mu \in [0, \underline{\mu}]$, $F_N(\mu) \geqq F_D(\mu)$ if and only if $\alpha_P(\mu) \geqq \delta\tau_s(1 + \beta_c\mu)$. The equality $F_N(\mu) = F_D(\mu)$ occurs only when $\mu = \underline{\mu}$ and $\alpha_P(\underline{\mu}) = \delta\tau_s(1 + \beta_c\underline{\mu})$.

(*Proof*) *Because* $F_D'(\mu) > 0$ and $F_N'(\mu) < 0$, it is enough to show that $F_N(\underline{\mu}) \geqq F_D(\underline{\mu})$ if and only if $\alpha_P(\underline{\mu}) \geqq \delta\tau_s(1 + \beta_c\underline{\mu})$. By substituting the expressions above for $F_N(\mu)$ and $F_D(\mu)$ and setting $\mu = \underline{\mu}$, the inequality $F_N(\underline{\mu}) \geqq F_D(\underline{\mu})$ can be rewritten as

$$\frac{\lambda\tau_l - \tau_s(1 + \beta_c\underline{\mu})}{\lambda\tau_l} \geqq \frac{\delta\{(\phi - v)y - (r + s)/\delta\}}{s + \delta\{(\phi - v)y - (r + s)/\delta\}}$$

which, after rearrangement of terms, becomes

$$\frac{s\{\lambda\tau_l - \tau_s(1 + \beta_c\underline{\mu})\}}{(\phi - v)y - (r + s)/\delta} \geqq \delta\tau_s(1 + \beta_c\underline{\mu}).$$

But since $\lambda\tau_l = (1 - \underline{\mu}\beta_g)\tau_l$, the left hand side of this inequality is nothing but $\alpha_P(\underline{\mu})$. QED

We also notice that

$$\alpha_P(\underline{\mu}) = H(0, \underline{\mu}).$$

Second, we examine the gradient of H with respect to F for each $\mu \in [0, \underline{\mu}]$. By multiplying both the numerator and the denominator by $(1 - F)$ and partially differentiating with respect to F, and after rearrangement, we obtain

$$H_F(F, \mu) = \frac{\frac{s}{\delta}\{(\phi - v)y -)r + s)/\delta\}\left\{\frac{s\lambda\tau_l - \tau_s(1 + \beta_c\mu)}{(\phi - v)y - \frac{r + s}{\delta}} - \delta\tau_s(1 + \beta_c\mu)\right\}}{[(1 - F)\{(\phi - v)y - (r + s)/\delta\} - \frac{s}{\delta}F]^2}.$$

Since the denominator and the first term on the numerator are positive,

$$\text{sign } H_F(F, \mu) = \text{sign}\left\{\frac{s\{\lambda\tau_l - \tau_s(1 + \beta_c\mu)\}}{(\phi - v)y - (r + s)/\delta} - \delta\tau_s(1 + \beta_c\mu)\right\}.$$

Let the inside of the bracket and its first term be denoted as $\psi(\mu)$ and $\gamma(\mu)$, respectively. Clearly, $\gamma'(\mu) < 0$ and $\psi'(\mu) < 0$ for all $\mu \in [0, \underline{\mu}]$. Moreover, $\gamma(\underline{\mu}) = \alpha_P(\underline{\mu})$. Thus, by our assumption, $\psi(\underline{\mu}) > 0$ and since $\psi(\mu)$ is decreasing, $\psi(\mu) > 0$ for all $\mu \in [0, \underline{\mu}]$. We have thus shown that

$$H_F(F, \mu) > 0 \quad \text{for all } \mu \in [0, \underline{\mu}].$$

Third, we examine the existence of the schedule $\alpha_{M'}(\mu)$ and its properties. Note that $\alpha_{M'}(\mu)$ is defined by the value of $H(F, \mu)$ with the value of F solved as a solution to the equation

$$H(F, \mu) = \alpha_{max} - F(\alpha_{max} - \alpha_{min}).$$

The RHS of the above equation is a downward sloping straight line connecting $(0, \alpha_{max})$ and $(1, \alpha_{min})$, while the LHS for a given level of μ has been shown to be upward sloping. Because of *Subsidiary Lemma* $F_D(\mu) < F_N(\mu)$, so that we only need to consider the domain $F \in [0, F_D(\mu)]$. In fact, as F tends towards $F_D(\mu)$, $H(F, \mu)$ becomes asymptotic to the vertical line $F = F_D(\mu)$. Clearly, there is a unique intersection point with the downward sloping line, which yields the value of $\alpha_{M'}$ for $\mu = \underline{\mu}$. Thus $\alpha_{M'}(\underline{\mu})$ is well defined, and

$$\alpha_{M'}(\underline{\mu}) > \alpha_P(\underline{\mu}).$$

This shows part (i) of the lemma. Furthermore, since it is easily seen that

$$H_\mu(F, \underline{\mu}) < 0,$$

$\alpha_{M'}$ is also well-defined for any $\mu < \underline{\mu}$, with the property that

$$\alpha_{M'}(\underline{\mu}) < 0 \quad \text{for all } \mu \leqq \underline{\mu}.$$

This proves part (ii). QED

REFERENCES

Brunello, G. and Ishikawa, T. (1999*a*). Elite schools, high tech jobs and economic welfare, *Journal of Public Economics*, 72, 395–417.

—— and —— (1999*b*). Education, training and labor market structure: Italy and Japan in comparative perspective, *Economic Systems*, 23, 61–84.

—— and Giannini, M. (1999). Selective Schools, *FEEM Working Paper* 99–75.

—— and Medio, A. (2000). An explanation of international differences in education and workplace training, *The European Economic Review* (forthcoming).

Contini, B. and Rapiti, F. (1994). Young in old out: nuovi pattern di mobilita' nell'economia italiana, *Lavoro e Relazioni Industriali*, 3.

—— et al. (1995). A study on job creation and job destruction in Europe, mimeo, *Ricerche e Progetti*, Turin.

Cooper, R. and John, A. (1988). Coordinating coordination failures in Keynesian models, *The Quarterly Journal of Economics*, 3, 103, 441–63.

Dore, R. and Sako, M. (1991). *How the Japanese Learn to Work*, Routledge.

Holmstrom, B. and Milgrom, P. (1991). *Economics, Organization and Management*, Prentice-Hall International.

Ishikawa, T. and Dejima, K. (1994). Rodo Shijo no Niju Kozo, in Ishikawa, T., *Nihon no Shotoku to Tomi no Bumpai*, Tokyo University Press.

Jannaccone Pazzi, R. and Ribolzi, L. (1992). *Università Flessibile*, IBM Italia.

Jones, S. R. (1987). Minimum wage legislation in a dual labour market, *The European Economic Review*, 31, 1229–46.

Malcomson, J. (1984). Work incentives, hierarchy and internal labor markets, *Journal of Political Economy*, 92, 486–507.

Piore, M. and Sabel, C. (1984). *The Second Industrial Divide*, Basic Books.

Porter, M. (1989). *The Competitive Advantage of Nations*, Harvard University Press.

Rohlen, T. (1992). Learning: The mobilization of knowledge in the Japanese political economy, in Kumon, S. and H. Rosovsky (eds.) *The Political Economy of Japan*, vol. 3, Stanford University Press.

Rosen, S. (1976). A theory of life earnings, *Journal of Political Economy*, 84(4), S44–S67.

Stevens, M. (1995). Transferrable training and poaching externalities, in Booth, A. and D. Snower (eds.) *Acquiring Skills: Market Failures, their Symptoms and Policy Responses*, Cambridge University Press.

5

The Causes of the 'Youth Employment Problem': A (Labour) Supply Side View

ETIENNE WASMER

5.1. INTRODUCTION

In all OECD countries, young workers are the demographic category which has suffered most in the labour market over the past decades, either in terms of high unemployment, low wages or reduced participation. In 1990 in Europe, the unemployment rate of workers aged 25 and less reached 31.5 per cent in Italy, 19.3 per cent in France, 32.3 per cent in Spain, 6.1 per cent in Sweden (in 1991), and 6.4 per cent in Germany (in 1989), whereas the rates of unemployment of workers aged 26 and older was, respectively, in these countries, 7.0, 7.8, 12.2, 2.0, and 6.9 per cent. Between 1963 and 1987 in the US, the relative wage of the male workers with 1–10 years of potential experience declined by 70 per cent with respect to the 26–35 years of experience, controlling for education and other characteristics (Juhn *et al.*, 1993). In the UK, young male workers withdrew massively from the labour force. This evidence points out the fact that the youth problem in the labour market is two-fold, both in terms of low employment and in terms of low wages. Hereafter, by the denomination 'youth employment problem', I will refer to both aspects, which, combined, imply a downward trend to labour income of the young labour market participants.

It is somehow disappointing to note that more attempts were undertaken to document this impressive regularity than to understand its causes and to propose a rigorous explanation. A good example of this paradox can be illustrated by the 1996 NBER conference 'Youth Employment and Joblessness in Advanced Countries'. Most of the twelve papers, including the introduction by Blanchflower and Freeman, ignore potential causes of the deterioration of the position of young workers. The only one attempting to explain the trend by supply effects, by Korenman and Neumark (1997), argues that the 1980s–1990s should have seen an improvement in the position of youngsters, given their relative scarcity. In the text, this is referred to as the 1980s–1990s puzzle.

The whole literature faces this difficulty and usually has to invoke declining demand for young workers due to business cycles or technical change (Korenman and Neumark, 1997). It must be acknowledged that still, very little is known about the underlying mechanisms at work. This is certainly because it is difficult to be comfortable with the two usual mechanisms which are involved in the more general problem of rising labour income inequality in the OECD countries. The first of these two mechanisms is biased technical change, the second one is increased openness to international trade. In this chapter, I will discuss these two explanations and argue that none of them does really fit with the low wage/low employment problem of younger workers. Accordingly, finding alternative explanations is a valuable contribution, and this chapter attempts to do so.

The biased technological change hypothesis states that the introduction of new technologies, new capital goods like computers, software, communication techniques, will make some workers obsolete, and will increase the demand for the most skilled workers, usually the most educated. The question is: should younger workers suffer from such a trend? The answer to this question is not so clear; it might be argued, reasoning along the lines of human capital models, such as Ben Porath (1967), that in response to technical changes, the cohorts with the longer time horizon (the young workers especially, but perhaps also men with respect to women) should invest more to adapt their skills to the technology.[1] The simple and consensual human capital investment model casts many doubts about the idea of a lower relative propensity of young generations to use computer technologies. Only sophisticated theories of biased technical change can explain the adverse trend faced by the young workers.

The second suspect is international trade. However, there is no evidence that sectors exposed to international trade are more intensive in young workers. If one thinks of the manufacturing sector, the car industry, and the textile industry, the average age is higher than in the other sectors. To illustrate these points, I computed from the March CPS 1997 the average age of the 16–64 US active population (excluding those having never worked or with a previous job in armed forces). In all sectors including Public Administration, the average age is 38.2 years. Excluding Administration, the average is 38.1 years. In the Manufacturing sector for durable goods, the average age is 39.5 with 25th, median and 75th percentiles of 31, 39, and 48. In the Manufacturing sector for non-durable, the average is 39.4 and the percentiles are the same.[2] By contrast, in the service sectors,[3] the average age is lower than economy-wide, and two years below the Manufacturing sector, i.e., 37.6 years on average, with the 25th, median and

---

[1] A 'cheap' illustration of this differential in human capital investments can be observed within households: 12-year-old kids explain to their father how to access the Internet and repair their laserjet printer, while their 5-year-old sister programs the video recorder for her mother. At the other tail of the age distribution, the directors of most research institutions in 1988 did not use a computer (although things have slowly changed since then).

[2] At a higher level of disaggregation, the average age is the same in sectors such as Motor vehicles and equipment or Textile mill products, respectively, 39.5 and 39.6 years.

[3] Utilities and sanitary service, Wholesale trade, Retail trade, Banking and other finance, Insurance and real estate, Private household service, Business services, Repair services, Personal services excluding Household services, Entertainment and Recreation services, Hospitals, Health services

75th percentile at 28, 37, and 47. The worker of median age in services corresponds to the 42nd (respectively, 43rd) centile of the manufacturing sector for durable (respectively, non-durable). This is actually not surprising: the advantage of young workers over their elders is that they do not have as much sector-specific human capital and thus they can more easily choose their activity. It seems natural to expect young workers to be more willing to work, *ceteris paribus*, in the service sectors, less exposed to international competition.

Accordingly, the two ITs, international trade and information technology, are not the most obvious causes of the youth employment problem.[4] The goal of this chapter is to provide instead a simple labour supply explanation to the deterioration of the condition of the young workers market, and to illustrate it with both micro- and macroeconomic data. Indeed, the share of young workers in the labour force has increased in most countries. Moreover, the share of women has been and is still increasing quite fast. From these observations, one can develop two sides of the story, corresponding to the micro and macro view.

On the *micro side*, one can argue that women and young people share at least one characteristic: they supply on average a low efficient quantity of experience (young workers, mostly because of their age, and women, both because of periods of inactivity and because of low returns to experience). One should thus not be surprised to see the market return to experience to increase over time in the US. Moreover, it will be shown that, using the proper stock measure of the 'experience composition' (rather than flows, the size of the cohort), can solve a part of the puzzle of the 1980s discussed in Korenman and Neumark (1997) and more generally in all this literature. On the *macro side*, estimates of production function, also in the US, recurrently show that young people and women are substitutes for each other,[5] which implies that any increase in the relative size of a group should adversely affect the other group. Given wage rigidities, unemployment in the segment of young/women should rise.[6]

These points will be illustrated in this chapter: first, I will briefly detail the labour supply changes. Then, I run some regressions of the unemployment rate across countries showing the impact of labour supply; finally I look at microdata to illustrate the rising returns to experience as caused by labour supply in the US.

---

excluding Hospitals, Educational services, Social services and Other professional services, i.e., clearly non-tradable goods and services.

[4] These two conclusions are also reached by Blanchflower and Freeman (introduction of the NBER 1996 conference) who argue in the revised version of their introduction (dated 13 April 1999, available at http://www.nber.org/books/youth-employment/index.html) that the two IT factors should actually raise the relative demand for young workers.

[5] See Berger (1983), Hamermesh and Grant (1979), and Grant and Hamermesh (1982), Topel (1994).

[6] Women's improvement in relative wages can be seen as their own investment in on-the-job skills, careers, a decrease in discrimination, or alternatively a rise in demand for women.

5.2. RELATIVE LABOUR SHARES

Table 5.1 illustrates the cross-country differences and resemblances in the evolution of the age structure. The first country rows ($age \le 24$) provide an indicator of the cohort size of labour market participants, which is a flow measure interacting with enrolment in higher education. This indicator has some variability due to this education effect and due to its flow nature. A slightly better measure is the flow net of the higher education effect: $25 \le age \le 29$. Finally, one may prefer the measures of the stock of young workers, as in the last two rows. One can see first that the share of young workers as measured by the flow indicators increased over the period 1960–80 in countries such as the US, France and Spain, and over the period 1970–90 for Italy, the share remaining stable in Germany. Second, the levels of the stock of young workers are higher in the US, followed by France, Spain and Italy, and are lower in Germany. This table illustrates both the supply shock faced by those OECD countries, and the cross-country variation in its amplitude. Note that Germany, where the shock is almost non-existent, is also the only of these countries for which young unemployment is lower than adult unemployment (see the first lines of the introduction of this

Table 5.1. *Share of age groups in the active population, source ILO, 1990 values are projections*

		1960	1970	1980	1990
US	$age \le 24$	0.18	0.24	0.24	0.18
	$25 \le age \le 29$	0.10	0.11	0.14	0.14
	$age \le 29$	0.28	0.35	0.39	0.33
	$age \le 34$	0.39	0.44	0.52	0.47
France	$age \le 24$	0.19	0.23	0.20	0.18
	$25 \le age \le 29$	0.11	0.11	0.15	0.14
	$age \le 29$	0.31	0.34	0.35	0.32
	$age \le 34$	0.42	0.44	0.49	0.46
Italy	$age \le 24$	0.26	0.24	0.22	0.22
	$25 \le age \le 29$	0.12	0.12	0.13	0.14
	$age \le 29$	0.38	0.35	0.35	0.36
	$age \le 34$	0.50	0.48	0.48	0.49
Spain	$age \le 24$	0.24	0.27	0.24	0.24
	$25 \le age \le 29$	0.12	0.11	0.13	0.15
	$age \le 29$	0.35	0.37	0.37	0.39
	$age \le 34$	0.47	0.46	0.49	0.51
W. Germany	$age \le 24$	0.27	0.21	0.23	0.19
	$25 \le age \le 29$	0.10	0.12	0.12	0.14
	$age \le 29$	0.38	0.33	0.34	0.33
	$age \le 34$	0.48	0.46	0.45	0.45

Table 5.2. *Share of women in active population, source OECD*

	USA	Europe (12)	Europe (11)	France
1962	0.327	—	—	—
1968	0.355	—	—	
1975	0.391	—	—	0.345
1982	0.427	0.373	0.350	0.374
1992	0.451	0.401	0.374	0.405
			0.410	0.440

chapter: unemployment was 6.4 per cent for young workers, and 6.9 per cent for adults in 1989).

The other important supply shock is the rising supply of women, whose relative share increased in the labour force, from 30 to 45 per cent in almost all OECD countries between the 1960s and the 1990s (see Table 5.2). It is important to notice that the share is a relative measure, i.e., the relevant variable in a constant return to scale world, as opposed to absolute measures, such as participation levels or employment to population ratios.[7]

5.3. CROSS-COUNTRY UNEMPLOYMENT

What are the consequences of these supply trends? In theory, given the patterns of substitutability between young people and women surveyed in the Introduction, young workers' employment prospects should be adversely affected by both the share of women in the labour force, and their own share in the labour force, controlling for country-specific wage determination factors. The goal of this section is to provide some evidence of this by estimating cross-country unemployment regressions. Young workers are those less than 29 years old (though similar results come with those less than 34 years). A crucial problem to address here is the existence of endogeneity of female participation to unemployment, as well as young workers' participation to unemployment. Let u_y, u_f, s_y, s_f, be in order the youth, female unemployment rates, the share of youth and females in the labour force. The unemployment rates are averaged over the 1980s and 1990s, as well as the explanatory variables.

The system to be estimated can be written as

$$u_y = \alpha s_f + \beta s_y + \gamma X + \epsilon = \alpha s_f + \gamma' X' + \varepsilon \tag{5.1}$$
$$s_f = -\delta u_f + \phi Z + \eta \tag{5.2}$$
$$u_f = \alpha_0 s_f + \beta_0 s_y + \gamma_0 X + \phi_0 Z + \theta = \alpha_0 s_f + \gamma_0' X' + \phi_0 Z + \theta \tag{5.3}$$

---

[7] The latter indicators actually show fewer clear patterns of increase over the period, in contrast with relative indicators. There is of course no contradiction here: countries with fast rising female participation have had little decline in male participation, whereas countries with slowly rising female participation faced a decline in male participation (concentrated among the very young, the very old and the very unable workers).

with X being a set of control variables for unemployment, $X' = [X, s_y]$ for convenience of notations. Disturbances ε, θ and η have 0 mean and are not correlated between them. Finally, Z is a vector of instruments for s_f. The shares of young workers are the average of the 1980 *actual* value and the 1990 *predicted* value, by the UN department in 1980. Since the prediction is purely based on demographic trends but not on unemployment trends, this variable is treated as exogenous (an assumption not rejected by exogeneity tests). The identification of the system (notably, α, β and δ) is derived in the Appendix. The instruments for the share of women in the labour force are four variables proxying the attitude of societies with respect to female participation: enrolment of women in higher education (share of women in total), divorce rates, fraction of women in parliaments, and birth rates. The set of control variables is based on Calmfors and Driffill (1988): the index of centralization in wage bargaining and its square aim at controlling for aggregate wage pressures. Note that (5.1) and (5.3) reflect a relative demand for young and female workers, whereas (5.2) represents a female labour supply function.

The Tables 5.3 and 5.4 first ignore s_f. Table 5.3 shows that across countries, youth unemployment is significantly correlated with youth labour supply. The coefficients are always positive and significant at the 10 per cent (*) or the 5 per cent (**) level, and imply that an increase in their share in the labour force from 25 to 30 per cent increases unemployment between 3 and 4 per cent of the labour force. The pure supply side effect (independently of the effects of institutions) on

Table 5.3. *Cross-country youth unemployment, supply variables*

Estimator	u_{y80-95} GLS	u_{y80-95} GLS	u_{y80-95} GLS	u_{y80-95} GLS	u_{y80-95} GLS
Centr	—	2.23 (2.34)**	—	1.97 (1.86)*	—
Centr^2	—	−0.09 (2.12)*	—	−0.08 (1.85)*	—
$s_{y<29,8090}$	0.71 (3.32)**	0.58 (3.01)**	—	—	0.011 (0.46)
$s_{y<34,8090}$	—	—	0.84 (2.64)**	0.69 (1.86)*	—
$s_{y<29,8090} \times Centr$	—	—	—	—	0.077 (2.32)**
$s_{y<29,8090} \times Centr^2$	—	—	—	—	−0.0029 (2.13)**
R^2	0.24	0.40	0.22	0.36	0.42
Adj. R^2	0.20	0.28	0.17	0.23	0.30
# obs.	20	19	20	19	19

t-stat in parentheses.

Source: author's calculations.

Table 5.4. *Cross-country youth unemployment, institutional variables*

Estimator	u_{y80-95} GLS	u_{y80-95} GLS	u_{y80-95} GLS
$S_{y<29,8090}$	0.48 (3.49)**	0.58 (5.54)**	0.54 (3.72)**
$S_{y<29,8090}$*employees' coordination	0.25 (1.79)*	0.24 (1.89)*	0.24 (1.70)*
$S_{y<29,8090}$*employers' coordination	−0.31 (2.34)**	−0.28 (2.36)**	−0.31 (2.14)
$S_{y<29,8090}$*duration of unemployment benefits	0.014 (0.55)	—	—
$S_{y<29,8090}$*replacement ratio of benefits	0.001 (0.31)	—	—
Duration of unemployment benefits	—	—	0.01 (0.67)
Replacement ratio of benefits	—	—	0.001 (0.23)
R^2	0.66	0.65	0.67
Adj. R^2	0.55	0.57	0.53
# obs.	18	18	18

t-stat in parentheses.

Source: author's calculations.

unemployment are uncontroversial and have been observed by other researchers (Bloom *et al.*, 1987; Korenman and Neumark, 1997).

Our specification has however two advantages: first, it exclusively concerns the 1980s–mid 1990s, a time period which is not believed to be favourable to supply effects according to the earlier literature, as noted above. Second, it is a cross-section of countries averaged over time (two or more economic cycles), which allows us to avoid the confusion with cyclical effects (whereas country-specific institutional factors are captured by the Calmfors–Driffill indicator).

In addition, our last specification (column 5) shows evidence of an inverted U-shaped relation between relative supply and unemployment along the dimension of centralization of wage bargaining. This last point suggests, as a confirmation of Calmfors and Driffill (1988), that either a flexible wage determination or a high degree of centralization ensure high employment of young people. In contrast, intermediately centralized institutions tend to protect insiders (the older workers) against outsiders (young workers). These institutional results are intuitive, though rarely formalized in the context of age differences in unemployment.

To check the robustness of the results, I report another specification for the country-specific institutional variables, including the centralization of employer union, of employee union, the duration of unemployment benefits and the replacement ratio of these benefits, as presented in Table 5.4. The interaction between

E. Wasmer

Table 5.5. *Cross-country youth unemployment,*
female labour supply

Estimator	u_{y80-95} W2SLS	u_{y80-95} GMM
Centr	2.37	2.37
	(1.64)	(2.67)**
Centr^2	−0.10	−0.10
	(1.67)	(2.34)**
$s_{y < 29,8090}$	0.466	0.466
	(1.42)	(3.40)**
s_f	0.854	0.854
	(1.70)*	(2.67)**
R^2	0.08	0.08
Adj. R^2	−0.20	−0.20
# obs.	18	18

t-stat in parentheses.

Source: author's calculations.

unemployment benefits and labour supply is not significant. This could have been expected from the fact that young workers are generally uncovered by unemployment benefits, having low seniority if any.[8] In contrast, centralization of employer unions is negatively significant and centralization of employee unions is positively significant: the supply shocks of young workers are better absorbed when employers are more unified and employee unions are dispersed.

The unemployment effect of another important supply factor, female workers' share in the labour force, is investigated in Table 5.5. Using the instruments described above, both the two-stage least square and the GMM method (in which the moment condition is the exogeneity of instruments), provide the same result: a positive and significant impact of the female labour supply indicator on youth unemployment, similar to those found on aggregate unemployment and female unemployment in Wasmer (1997). For tests of endogeneity of this variable and tests of the validity of the instruments, one can refer to this article.

In conclusion, there is strong evidence that the supply of young workers is a key cause of their high unemployment across country. Additional adverse effects seem to come from higher female participation, higher centralization of unions, lower centralization of employers, whereas unemployment benefits play no strong role.

---

[8] The non-significance of the unemployment benefit variables on youth unemployment is an interesting feature which appears to be still true when the variables themselves (instead of the interactions) are in the econometric specification. The results with this specification are not reported here.

5.4. RETURNS TO EXPERIENCE

Another view of the youth problem and its causes can be addressed under a more microeconomic perspective. I investigated in Wasmer (1999) the differences in the (hourly) wage return to true experience of men and women, using a representative cross-section of the French labour force, in which individuals were asked the number of years in part-time and full-time experience. It appeared that the wage return for men for an additional year of true experience is about 30 to 45 per cent higher than for women in the first 30 years of employment; the difference falls to 15 per cent in the last years of active life. The conclusion one should draw from these figures is that the number of efficient units of experience supplied by female workers is likely to be much lower than the corresponding number for men. Since young workers also have obviously lower efficient units of experience, it follows that the supply trends detailed in Section 5.2 (i.e., young workers and women) should significantly reduce the average number of efficient units of experience supplied by the labour force. If one believes in decreasing returns to scale in this type of skills, a natural consequence is a rise in the return to experience.

As a matter of fact, a strong rise in the return to experience was actually observed in the US by Juhn *et al.* (1993). If the supply forces explain it well until the late 70s, no clear explanation of this fact has been given for the 80s, as is acknowledged by Katz and Murphy (1992).

The numbers displayed in Table 5.6 are an attempt to measure the number of efficient units of experience of the labour force: in using the predicted wage of workers (from a Mincer's type wage equation, with additional variables such as education, race, region and industries), one can use the part linked to experience (a linear and a quadratic term), and estimate in each year, what is the contribution of experience in wages, as a first-order proxy for productivity. In the equation

$$w_i = \alpha \, Education_i + \beta_1 \, Exp_i + \beta_2 \, Exp_i^2 + \gamma X_i + \varepsilon_i,$$

w_i and X_i represent the log hourly wage and other personal characteristics of an individual i. Education is a set of dummy variables for different schooling levels. The efficient units of supply of experience are then calculated as $\sum_i (\beta_1 \, Exp_i + \beta_2 \, Exp_i^2)/N$ where N is the number of labour force participants. Coefficient α and β are estimated in a given year, here 1964 in column 1, 1980 in column 2 and 1991 in column 3. One can see (for instance from column 2) that the contribution of experience declines continuously from 50 per cent in 1964 to 1985 where it reached 42 per cent, and then it recovers in 1997 to 46 per cent.[9] The first three columns representing the efficient supply of experience can be

---

[9] An interpretation of these figures is that it is the contribution of average experience of labour market participants to the average wage, i.e., an increase by 50 per cent, etc. The higher the figure, the higher the supply of experience.

E. Wasmer

Table 5.6. *US, efficient units of experience (X) (SD across the active population in parentheses)*

Efficient units of experience	β_T estimated in			β_T after 20 years, men
	$T=1964$	$T=1980$	$T=1991$	
1964	0.480 (0.24)	0.500 (0.28)	0.507 (0.26)	0.0250
1970	0.451 (0.25)	0.462 (0.29)	0.478 (0.26)	0.0232
1977	0.413 (0.25)	0.420 (0.28)	0.439 (0.26)	0.0278
1985	0.414 (0.24)	0.419 (0.27)	0.441 (0.25)	0.0290
1991	0.426 (0.23)	0.447 (0.27)	0.455 (0.24)	0.0270
1997	0.443 (0.23)	0.464 (0.26)	0.472 (0.23)	0.0265

Source: author's calculations.

contrasted with the evolution of the returns to experience at 20 years of experience (last column). The correlation is quite clearly negative. For instance, when calculated over the full 33 year sample (i.e., between 1964 and 1997), the correlation is equal to −0.64. The negative sign suggests that the changes over time of the returns to experience are primarily due to labour supply: the higher the supply of experience, the lower the return, and *vice versa*.

Note that these results are based on two wage equations, one for men and one for women. Since we argued previously that the returns to experience differed significantly by gender, part of the decline over time of experience is driven by rising female participation. Results in Table 5.7 indicate what would have been the changes in the supply of experience if women had in reality the return to experience β_f defined as: $\beta_f = \beta_f^{\text{measured}} + \lambda(\beta_m^{\text{measured}} - \beta_m^{\text{measured}})$. Here, λ characterizes the degree of gender discrimination in the return to experience. For instance, $\lambda = 0$ indicates no discrimination (or alternatively, no error in the measurement of β_f); whereas $\lambda = 1$ indicates that the true price of experience for women is the one measured for men, i.e., a 'full' discrimination case.

One can observe from this table the same swing in the level of experience as in Table 5.6, even with high values of λ.[10] In this table, the results in the column $\lambda = 1$ indicates, either what is the true experience of the labour force if one believes that all the gender difference in the returns is due to discrimination, or what would have been the experience level of the labour force if women had not increased their relative share: under both interpretations, the 1997 level of experience would have gone back to the 1964 level. A more systematic discussion of the quality of this measure of experience, the sources of bias and the interactions with education can be found in Wasmer (1999).

The first lesson of this exercise is that rising wage inequality along the dimension of age is very probably a supply side phenomenon, caused by the cohorts of

---

[10] The prices β_f and β_m are estimated in 1964 in the table, but the same qualitative results hold if the price was estimated in 1980 or in any other year.

Table 5.7. *US, decomposition of wages on experience and education accounting for gender discrimination (SD in parentheses)*

Efficient units of experience average in the labour force	β_T estimated at $T=$ 1964				
	$\lambda = 0$	$\lambda = 0.25$	$\lambda = 0.50$	$\lambda = 0.75$	$\lambda = 1$
1964 :$\beta_T . <X_i>$	0.480 (0.24)	0.506 (0.24)	0.532 (0.23)	0.557 (0.23)	0.583 (0.24)
1970 :$\beta_T . <X_i>$	0.451 (0.25)	0.478 (0.24)	0.504 (0.24)	0.530 (0.25)	0.557 (0.26)
1977 :$\beta_T . <X_i>$	0.413 (0.25)	0.439 (0.24)	0.465 (0.25)	0.491 (0.25)	0.517 (0.26)
1985 :$\beta_T . <X_i>$	0.414 (0.24)	0.442 (0.23)	0.471 (0.23)	0.500 (0.23)	0.529 (0.24)
1991 :$\beta_T . <X_i>$	0.426 (0.23)	0.457 (0.22)	0.488 (0.22)	0.520 (0.23)	0.551 (0.24)
1997 :$\beta_T . <X_i>$	0.443 (0.23)	0.476 (0.22)	0.510 (0.22)	0.544 (0.23)	0.579 (0.24)

Source: author's calculations.

the baby-boom and the interaction with rising female participation. If the US labour market did well in terms of employment to absorb those supply trends, it seems to have done much less in terms of wage dispersion.

The second lesson is that our measure of experience is a true 'stock' measure, which performs quite well in that it is negatively correlated to the price of experience. Although this is a conjecture, we believe that a part of the 1980s–1990s puzzle noted by the literature comes from the lag between the stock and the flows measure, even if this is not the whole story.

5.5. CONCLUSIONS

According to the views taken in this chapter, namely that young workers and women compete to some extent in the labour market, there are some reasons to be optimistic about the future: in the next few years, the share of young workers in the labour force will follow the US trend, that is, will decrease. The congestion of the youth labour markets will thus be less marked. At constant female participation, applying the projections reported in Table 5.1 for years 2010 and 2020 for the share of those under 34 years old, French and Spanish youth unemployment should decrease by 5–7 per cent of the labour force and Italian youth unemployment should decrease by 6–8 per cent. Another reason for being optimistic is that female participation will be of higher quality. By quality we mean, good jobs providing valuable experience, and high education, so that competition with young workers should decrease.

Unfortunately, there are also two reasons for being more pessimistic. First, the trends to higher demand for education, which I have not detailed here, will adversely affect the young workers who are unable to reach the level of education demanded by the market (for ability reasons or because of credit constraints). This will increase within-cohorts inequality. Second, the transition from low to high female labour market participation has been quite slow for some European countries, such as Spain or France, which may reflect the existence of important gender discrimination. If it is the case that these labour markets face high gender inequality, this must produce supplementary adverse effects: women are discouraged to participate in the 'high quality occupations', which tends to increase their relative supply in the low skill/low wage segments where they compete with the young (static adverse effect) and tends to discourage human capital accumulation (dynamic adverse effect).[11]

Accordingly, macroeconomists should realize the importance of both labour supply forces and determinants of these supply forces, such as gender discrimination aspects of labour markets.

APPENDIX

Proof

The inversion of

$$u_y = \alpha\, s_f + \beta\, s_y + \gamma X + \epsilon = \alpha\, s_f + \gamma' X' + \varepsilon \tag{5.1}$$

$$s_f = -\delta\, u_f + \phi Z + \eta \tag{5.2}$$

$$u_f = \alpha_0\, s_f + \beta_0\, s_y + \gamma_0 X + \phi_0 Z + \theta = \alpha_0\, s_f + \gamma_0' X' + \phi_0 Z + \theta \tag{5.3}$$

gives

$$u_f = \frac{1}{1+\alpha_0\,\delta}\{\gamma_0' X' + (\phi_0 + \alpha_0\,\phi)\, Z + \theta + \alpha_0\,\eta\} = \pi_1 X' + \pi_2 Z + e_1$$

$$s_f = \frac{1}{1+\alpha_0\,\delta}\{(\phi - \delta\,\phi_0)\, Z - \delta\,\gamma_0' X' + \eta - \delta\,\theta\} = \pi_3 Z + \pi_4 X' + e_2$$

$$u_y = \frac{\beta}{1+\alpha_0\,\delta}(\phi - \delta\,\phi_0)\, Z + \left(\gamma' - \frac{\beta\,\delta\,\gamma_0'}{1+\alpha_0\,\delta}\right) X' + \varepsilon + \beta(\eta - \delta\theta)$$

$$= \pi_5 Z + \pi_6 X' + e_3$$

and $\delta = -\pi_4/\pi_1$ and $\beta = \pi_5/\pi_3$. The system is however estimated by 2LS or GMM, not by the indirect least square method.

Data sources
Yearly Data: OECD Labour Force Statistics, 1962–82, 1970–90, 1973–93, OECD Quarterly Labour Force Statistics, 1994–95.

---

[11] These aspects are explored in Wasmer (1998).

Shares of the Labour Force and Instruments: Education at a Glance (OECD), Report on Human Development, United Nations 1996, and UN Demographic Yearbook, 1992.

Microdata: USA: March Current Population Survey, 1964–97, provided by CPS Utilities, Unicon Research Corporation, Release 97.3.

Software: Stata under Unix for Microdata; E-Views 3.1 (32 bits) for Windows.

REFERENCES

Ben Porath, (1967). The production of human capital and the life-cycle of earnings, *Journal of Political Economy*, 75, 352.

Berger, M. C., (1983). Changes in labor force composition and male earnings: A production approach, *The Journal of Human Resources*, XVII(2), Mass, MIT Press.

Bloom, D., R. Freeman, and S. Korenman, (1987). The labour market consequences of generational crowding, *European Journal of Population*, 3, 131–76.

Calmfors, L. and J. Driffill (1988). Centralization of wage bargaining, *Economic Policy*, 6.

Goux, D. and E. Maurin (1994). Education, expérience et salaires: tendances récentes et évolution de long terme, *Economie et Prévision*, 116, 1994–5.

—— (1995). Demand for skilled labour, technical changes and international trade, the French case, 1970–93 mimeo, INSEE, *Review of Economics and Statistics, 2000* (forthcoming).

Grant, J. H. and D. S. Hamermesh (1982). Labour market competition among youths, white women and others, *Review of Economics and Statistics*, 354–60.

Gregg, P. and J. Wadsworth (1995). A short history of labour turnover, job tenure and job security 1975–1993, *Oxford Review of Economic Policy*.

Hamermesh, D. S. (1986). The demand for labour in the long run, in *Handbook of Labour Economics*, vol. I, Ashenfelter, O. and R. Layard (eds.), Elsevier Science Publisher BV.

—— (1979). Econometric studies of labour–labour substitution and their implications for policy, *The Journal of Human Resources*, XIV (4).

Juhn, C., K. Murphy, and B. Pierce (1993). Wage inequality and the rise in return to skill, *Journal of Political Economy*, 410–42.

Katz, L. and K. Murphy (1992). Changes in relative wages, 1963–1987: Supply and demand factors, *Quarterly Journal of Economics*, 75.

Korenman, S. and D. Neumark (1997). Cohort-crowding and youth labour markets: A cross-national analysis, *NBER working paper* 6031.

Layard, N., S. Nickell, and R. Jackman, (1991). *Unemployment. Macroeconomic Performance and the Labour Market*, Oxford University Press.

NBER Conference (1996). On Youth employment and joblessness in advanced countries, Blanchflower, D. and R. Freeman (eds.), 12–14 December 1996.

O'Neill, J. (1985). The trends in the male–female wage gap in the United States, *Journal of Labor Economics*, 3 (1), Part 2, S91–116.

Snower, D. and G. de la Dehesa (eds.) (1997). *Unemployment Policy. Government Options for the Labour Market*, Cambridge, University Press.

Topel Robert, H., (1994). Wage inequality and regional labour market performance in the US in Toshiaki Tachibanaki (ed.), *Savings and Bequests*, Ann Arbor University Michigan Press.

Wasmer, E. (1997). Can labour supply explain the rise in unemployment and wage inequality in the OECD?, *IIES working paper* 97–629.

—— (1998). Labour supply dynamics, unemployment and human capital investments, *IIES discussion paper* 98–651.

—— (1999). Between-group competition in the labour market and the rising return to skills, US and France, 1964–97 mimeo Ecare, ULB.

Welch, F., (1979). Effects of cohort size on earnings: The baby boom babies' financial bust, *Journal of Political Economy*, S65–97.

6

Pareto-Improving Immigration in an Economy with Equilibrium Unemployment

JAVIER ORTEGA

The existence and the nature of the effects of immigration on the economic situation of natives is a subject of debate in industrialized 'host' countries, particularly in Europe. The idea that the presence or arrival of immigrants may deteriorate the economic prospects of natives is widely spread. From the available empirical literature, the conclusion is, however, far from clear-cut, for the US as well as for Europe. As stressed by Borjas (1994) in his survey, 'the most important lesson is that the economic impact of immigration will vary by time and by place, and can be either beneficial or harmful'.[1]

While Harris and Todaro (1970) present an explanation of why immigration might have negative effects on the situation of natives, the theoretical literature hardly provides any example of a 'counter-balancing' effect, i.e., an explanation of why immigration might also have positive effects. The only exception is a model by Schmidt et al. (1994).[2] Their main hypotheses are that the wage in the host

This chapter is based on Chapter IV in my Ph.D. dissertation at DELTA, and was revised during my stay at the Institute for International Economic Studies (IIES Working Paper No. 618) and at Universitat Pompeu Fabra. I would like to thank Richard Barwell, Alberto Bennardo, Olivier Blanchard, Michel Martinez, Giorgio Negroni, Laurence Rioux, Gilles Saint-Paul, Akiko Suwa-Eisenmann, André Zylberberg, two anonymous referees, the editor of *The Economic Journal*, and seminar participants at Universidad Carlos III, CEPREMAP, CORE, IIES, CREST, FIEF, EEA-ESEM 96, Universitat Pompeu Fabra, CEPR Conference 'Social Inequalities and Social Mobility', GREMAQ and JEREM (Perpignan) for interesting comments and helpful discussions. I am also grateful to Christina Lönnblad for her editorial assitance. During my Ph.D., I benefited from a scholarship from the Banco de España. Funding from the Wenner-Grenska Samfundet and from the Spanish Ministry of Education (P5-153918) is gratefully acknowledged. Remaining errors are my own.

Previously published in *The Economic Journal* 110 (2000), 92–112 and reproduced with the permission of Blackwell Publishing Ltd. © Royal Economic Society.

[1] Positive impacts of immigration on the labour market situation of natives are found for the US by, for example, Bean *et al.* (1988), Winegarden and Khor (1991), and Altonji and Card (1991). Concerning Europe, Pischke and Velling (1994) find no detrimental effect of immigration on the unemployment rate in Germany and Winter-Ebmer and Zweimüller (1996) find that in 1991 the regional and industry share of foreign workers had a positive effect on the earnings of young native blue-collar workers.

[2] Berry and Soligo (1969) study this question in a Walrasian framework with perfectly flexible wages. They conclude that the arrival of immigrants generally improves the economic situation of

J. Ortega

country is set by a union caring only about the situation of natives and that the (scarce) jobs available are distributed proportionally among immigrants and natives. In this framework, they show that the arrival of immigrants leads to a loss of the effective power of the union, which chooses lower wages in order to relax job scarcity. In this case, immigration is not explicitly modelled however (i.e., it is exogenous).

The objective of this chapter is to provide a theoretical rationale for positive effects of immigration on natives' wages and unemployment, where the migration decision is fully integrated into the model. The general family of models that is chosen to accomplish this task is the search-matching analysis of labour markets, and particularly that of Pissarides (1990). The main advantage of this type of model (as opposed to a more traditional 'Walrasian' approach) is to provide a basic structure for the (labour) market that opens the door for (manageable) analyses of coordinational issues.

Our economy consists of two countries differing in their structural characteristics (separation rate from employment). Workers are born in either of the countries and, when unemployed, decide whether to look for a job in their country of origin or try their luck abroad (bearing a cost associated with emigration). Firms open job vacancies in each country, taking into account the average search costs of the population looking for a job in each country. The meetings between employers and job-seekers are determined by a constant returns to scale matching function in each country. Finally, wages are assumed to be the Nash cooperative outcome of a (non-cooperative) bargaining between each individual firm and worker.

The first result of this chapter is the existence of multiple (stationary state) equilibria, which underlines the idea that the outcome of such an economy *is not unequivocally determined* by the structural features of countries. More precisely, three equilibria can coexist: an equilibrium where each individual decides to search for a job in his country of origin ('no-migration'), a migration equilibrium where a fraction of the workers born in the 'structurally bad' country engage in search in the other country and finally a corner-migration equilibrium where all individuals born in the 'bad' country try their luck abroad. For workers, the existence of a cost associated with migration implies that they will choose to look for a job abroad only if the foreign employment prospects (i.e., the matching probability abroad) are sufficiently high to compensate for migration expenses. On the other hand, when deciding the number of vacancies to be posted in each country, firms anticipate that they will be able to pay 'low' wages to workers with a 'high' search cost, i.e., to immigrants. The multiplicity then arises from the interaction between these two optimizing behaviours in a matching context: if firms

natives. The interest of their analysis is, however, limited by the exogenous nature of immigration in their model and, more importantly, by the fact that unemployment cannot be an equilibrium outcome. Winter-Ebmer and Zweimüller (1996) present a two-tier insider–outsider framework without unemployment, where the earnings of natives may be positively linked to the number of immigrants. The idea is that the presence of competitively paid immigrants creates a rent that can be appropriated by natives (insiders).

believe that immigrants will come to country i, they expect to be able to pay (on average) relatively 'low' wages there, and this leads to a boost in their labour demand. The subsequent increase in matching probabilities for workers creates precisely the correct incentives for this migration to be profitable and occur (a 'self-fulfilling prophecy').[3]

Second, we prove that the equilibria are Pareto-ranked.[4] More precisely, the no-migration equilibrium is Pareto-dominated by the interior-migration equilibrium, which is, in turn, dominated by the full-migration equilibrium. Therefore, in this type of framework, everybody gains from migration, including the natives of the host country. Immigration enables firms to pay lower wages on average, and this compensates for the higher search costs they may bear in equilibrium. Immigrants will be better-off because the 'structural characteristics' of the host country allow them to enjoy better employment prospects and earn higher wages. Finally, natives are better-off because they benefit from the boost in labour demand following the arrival of immigrants in the country: they have access to the newly created jobs (lower unemployment rate) and earn higher wages (stronger bargaining position due to the relatively high availability of jobs).

6.1. THE MODEL

6.1.1. Environment

The economy consists of two countries[5] indexed by $i = 1, 2$. Assume that N individuals are born in each country (from now on, N is normalized to 1). Firms post vacancies in each country, and meetings are ruled by a standard matching function within each country.

Time is continuous and lasts forever. The entire analysis will be carried out in steady state. The structure of the model is depicted in Fig. 6.1. At any date, workers can be in four different states, namely unemployed or employed in each of the two regions (denoted by u_i and L_i respectively, $i = 1, 2$). The transition probabilities between these different states are assumed to be Poisson rates.

The flow from unemployment to employment (m_i) in each country is determined by a constant returns to scale matching function:[6]

$$m_i = m(v_i, u_i) \quad i = 1, 2 \tag{6.1}$$

[3] Other multiple equilibria mechanisms have been developed in the related literature (see for example Diamond (1982), Howitt and McAfee (1987) and Pissarides (1992)). Other related mechanisms are those of Matsuyama *et al.* (1993) or Trejos and Wright (1995) in the search theoretic approach to international currencies and Sánchez (1997) for rural–urban migrations. The presence of a 'self-fulfilling prophecy' indicates that the existence of sunspot equilibria may be an additional characteristic of the model.

[4] Murphy, Shleifer and Vishny (1989) and Chatterjee *et al.* (1993) find analogous results for their respective economic problems.

[5] The definition of a 'country' will become clear below. The term 'region' will also be used.

[6] The constant returns to scale assumption is the most widely accepted (or 'non-rejected') hypothesis in the empirical literature: see for example Blanchard and Diamond (1989) for US, Pissarides (1986) for UK, and Burda and Wyplosz (1994) for UK and Germany.

J. Ortega

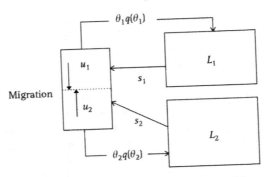

Figure 6.1. *Dynamic structure of the model.*

where v_i is the number of vacancies in region i. Given the CRS property of the technology and the standard random matching assumption, the probability of a firm contacting a worker and a worker contacting a firm are, respectively

$$q(\theta_i) \equiv \frac{m(v_i, u_i)}{v_i} = m\left(1, \frac{1}{\theta_i}\right) \quad i = 1, 2 \tag{6.2}$$

$$\frac{m_i}{u_i} = \frac{m(v_i, u_i)}{u_i} = m(\theta_i, 1) = \theta_i q(\theta_i) \tag{6.3}$$

with $\theta \equiv v_i/u_i$ being the 'market tightness' in country $i = 1, 2$. Denoting the exogenous separation rate in region i by s_i, the dynamic equations describing the model are

$$\frac{dL_i}{dt} = \theta_i q(\theta_i) u_i - s_i L_i. \tag{6.4}$$

6.1.2. The Employment and Unemployment Income of Workers

Individuals are assumed to be heterogeneous with respect to their search costs during unemployment.[7] More precisely, individuals have 'high' or 'low' search costs depending on whether they search in their native country or abroad. The additional per unit search cost implied by the decision of looking for a job abroad is intended to capture the costs (economic or social) associated with emigration. These costs can be diverse in nature: for example, they may be associated with learning a new language or (more generally) 'adapting' to the new environment.

---

[7] In addition to the heterogeneity with respect to search costs, some kind of heterogeneity regarding productivity (e.g., natives being more productive than immigrants) could have been assumed. This would have added a parameter to the model without changing the qualitative results. Had heterogeneity been defined *only* with respect to productivity differences, the multiple equilibria obtained as an outcome here would have vanished. The intuition is that y is a 'size of the cake' variable, while c_{ij} is a 'distribution of the cake' variable.

Let c_{ij} be the cost for an unemployed person born in country j of searching for a job in country i $(i, j = 1, 2)$. Assume that[8]

$$c_{11} = c_{22} = 0$$
$$c_{12} = c_{21} = 1. \tag{6.5}$$

Let U_{ij} be the expected discounted flow of income when unemployed in country i, for a native of country j $(i, j = 1, 2)$ and E_{ij} the corresponding value if the individual is employed. In a stationary environment

$$rU_{ij} = -c_{ij} + \theta_i q(\theta_i)(E_{ij} - U_{ij}), \tag{6.6}$$

the value of being unemployed in i for an individual born in j is given by the search costs (c_{ij}) one must pay while remaining in this state and the capital gain $(E_{ij} - U_{ij})$ from finding a job. Similarly, we have

$$rE_{ij} = w_{ij} + s_i(U_{ij} - E_{ij}), \tag{6.7}$$

i.e., when employed in country i, an individual born in j earns w_{ij}. Should a separation occur, one bears a capital loss of $U_{ij} - E_{ij}$.

6.1.3. Firms' Optimization Decision and Informational Hypothesis

Firms post vacancies that are filled with the endogenous probability $q(\theta_i)$. Let γ be the (per unit of time) cost of posting a vacancy and V_i its value while unfilled. We assume that firms cannot *ex ante* discriminate between natives and immigrants (i.e., they cannot post different *types* of vacancies for each group).[9] This hypothesis is reasonable if some kind of (enforced) legislation exists, forbidding vacancies specifying the national or ethnic origins of candidates.[10] Alternatively, it could be argued that the vacancy decisions of firms correspond to an investment, and that only information concerning the *average* characteristics of

---

[8] Two remarks can be made to explain this cost structure. First, the results are qualitatively the same if the search costs in the native and the foreign country are c_0 and c_1 respectively (with $c_0 < c_1$) or if there is an asymmetry (emigration is more costly for the natives of a given country). Second, the assumption on the homogeneity of workers born in the same country is also made for simplicity. Were there also heterogeneity among the workers of a given country, the results concerning wages would change, but the story would essentially remain the same.

[9] This type of hypothesis has been used in the literature by Pissarides (1992) in the context of a skill-loss model. For an analysis of its importance, see Ortega (1993).

[10] In contrast, this would not be the best hypothesis if networks for 'importing' foreign labour existed (linked to firms). Concerning countries with 'guest-worker' immigration policies (such as Switzerland or Austria), our hypothesis is only compatible with 'late stages' in the process of acceptance inside the country. For example, as described by Winter-Ebmer and Zweimüller (1996), in order to start working in Austria, an immigrant needs to find a firm that applies for a one-year permit issued specifically for her (also specifying the job and the task inside the firm). After one year, however, the immigrant may get a permit allowing job changes within a certain region and then (after another two years) 'free movements' (permanent permit).

J. Ortega

workers is available at the time the investment is decided. Then, the value of an unfilled vacancy can only be written in terms of the *expected* value from a filled job (J_i^e):

$$rV_i = -\gamma + q(\theta_i)(J_i^e - V_i). \tag{6.8}$$

However, once a firm meets a worker, it can observe whether she is an immigrant or a native. Then, given the wage bargaining process specified below, a firm producing in country i earns an income (J_{ij}) which depends on this characteristic:

$$rJ_{ij} = y - w_{ij} + s_i(V_i - J_{ij}) \tag{6.9}$$

where y is the productivity of the worker (which is assumed to be the same for all individuals),[11] w_{ij} the wage paid to a native of j and $(V_i - J_{ij})$ the capital loss borne with separation probability $s_i \, dt$.[12] The expression for the expected value of a filled job in region i is given by

$$J_i^e \equiv \eta_i J_{ii} + (1 - \eta_i)J_{ij} \quad i \neq j \tag{6.10}$$

where η_i denotes the probability that a vacancy is filled by a native worker in i, conditional on the event of meeting a worker. This probability can be written as

$$\eta_i = \frac{1 - \pi_i}{1 - \pi_i + \pi_j} \tag{6.11}$$

with π_j denoting the fraction of j-born individuals leaving j.

Firms are assumed to post vacancies in each country up to the point where the expected income from posting a further vacancy is zero $(V_i = 0$ for $i = 1, 2)$. Then, from (6.8)

$$J_i^e = \frac{\gamma}{q(\theta_i)} \quad i = 1, 2 \tag{6.12}$$

stating that in equilibrium, the expected income from a filled vacancy must equal the total costs of posting it.

6.1.4. Wage Setting and Unemployment Income

Wages are assumed to be the outcome of bilateral Nash bargaining between each individual firm and worker.[13] The worker receives an income equal to E_{ij} when an

---

[11] An equivalent way of modelling the production process is that of introducing explicit firms' demand for capital and a constant returns to scale production function (as in Pissarides, 1990). An implicit assumption of the model is the absence of fixed costs in production and the existence of no limits in the potential availability of factors. If capital were scarce, the arrival of immigrants in a country would decrease marginal productivity, and this would tend to reduce the benefits from emigration.

[12] Note that the size of the loss depends on the characteristics of the currently employed worker, since the income after a separation is the average (V_i).

[13] For the introduction of centralized (union) bargaining in a matching framework, see Ortega (1995).

agreement is reached. Her 'threat point' is U_{ij}.[14] The income of the firm when the match occurs is J_{ij} and its threat point V_i.[15] w_{ij} is then the solution to

$$\max_{w_{ij}}(E_{ij} - U_{ij})^{\beta}(J_{ij} - V_i)^{1-\beta}$$ (N)

where β is the worker's bargaining power. The wage solving this problem is (see the Appendix)

$$w_{ij} = \frac{\beta y(r + s_i + \theta_i q(\theta_i))}{r + s_i + \beta\theta_i q(\theta_i)} - \frac{(1 - \beta)(r + s_i)}{r + s_i + \beta\theta_i q(\theta_i)} c_{ij}.$$ (6.13)

As usual in these models, the wage depends positively on labour market tightness θ_i: the worker gets a larger part of the surplus whenever meeting alternative firms is easier.

It is important to note that the wage of immigrants will be lower than that of natives within a given country. Indeed, the position of an immigrant in the wage bargaining is 'weak', since in the absence of an agreement, she must continue to bear a high cost ($c_{ij} = 1$) while unemployed. This leads to a division of the surplus generated by the match which is more favourable for the firm. There is empirical evidence that this may be the case. Kee (1995) studies whether native–immigrant wage differentials in the Netherlands (in 1984–85) can be explained by 'wage discrimination' (lower pay for given productivity). His conclusion is that 'discrimination exists against Antilleans and Turks. Respectively, 11 percentage points (35 per cent) and 6 percentage points (15 per cent) of their log wage difference with natives is attributable to tastes for discrimination'.[16] Interpreting the higher search cost for immigrants in terms of the cost of learning a language, there is also an empirical literature analysing the effects of language proficiency on the earnings of immigrants.[17]

From the solution to the Nash bargain, we also find that the expected wage in country i is (see the Appendix)

$$w_i^e = \beta y + \beta\gamma\theta_i - (1 - \beta)c_i^e.$$ (6.14)

---

[14] This is true, for in a stationary environment, a worker having decided to search in a certain country will search again in that particular country whenever she is unemployed.

[15] Contrary to that of the worker, the threat point of the firm depends on the average characteristics of the workers searching in region i.

[16] However, for other groups (Surinamese and Moroccan workers) no indication of discrimination is found in this study. Another example is provided by Stalker (1995), who refers to a study for Germany which shows that (for a given job) the average wage of immigrants is 10 per cent lower than that of German citizens. According to this study, the wage differential does not come from the 'basic wage', but from the fact that natives receive bonuses and are allocated to the best-paid extra hours. See also Weiss and Gotlibovski (1995) for the wages of former Soviet Union immigrants in Israel.

[17] For example, Dustmann (1994) studies this issue in West Germany (1984) for Italian, Yugoslavian, Spanish, Turkish, and Greek immigrants. He concludes that 'those who report to speak German well or very well have earnings which are considerably higher than earnings of the base group (7.1 per cent for females and 6.9 per cent for males)'. Even stronger results are obtained for writing abilities. Chiswick

J. Ortega

Given the search costs structure (6.5), we know that country-i's average search cost also represents the proportion of immigrants in country i:

$$c_i^e = 1 - \eta_i. \tag{6.15}$$

Then, the average wage to be paid in region i depends negatively on the proportion of job searchers in i that are immigrants:

$$w_i^e = \beta y + \beta \gamma \theta_i - (1 - \beta)(1 - \eta_i). \tag{6.16}$$

Finally, the expected income during unemployment in i for a native of country j is (see Appendix)

$$rU_{ij} = \frac{\beta y \theta_i q(\theta_i) - (r + s_i)c_{ij}}{r + s_i + \beta \theta_i q(\theta_i)} \tag{6.17}$$

which depends negatively on the search costs the worker must bear (c_{ij}) and on the degree of precariousness of employment in that country (measured by the separation probability, s_i), and positively on how easily a job is found $[\theta_i q(\theta_i)]$. From this expression, we can see that the differences in the expected income from unemployment rU_{ij} among individuals can only be due to the region of origin of the agent (i.e., whether she is searching in her own country or not) and to the matching probability $\theta_i q(\theta_i)$.[18]

6.1.5. Migration Decision and Matching Probability

The relation between the individuals' migration decision and the matching probability will now be explained. The expected value of a filled vacancy for a firm depends on the average wage it expects to pay to its workers. Taking expectations in (6.9) and using $V_i = 0$,

$$J_i^e = \frac{y - w_i^e}{r + s_i}. \tag{6.18}$$

Moreover, remember that firms post vacancies up to the point where the expected value of a filled job is equal to the total cost of filling it, i.e., $J_i^e = \gamma/q(\theta_i)$. Equalizing these two equations and using the expression for the expected wage (6.16), we obtain the equation determining θ_i as a function of the (conditional) probability of meeting an immigrant $(1 - \eta_i)$:

$$\beta \gamma \theta_i + \gamma(r + s_i)\theta_i^{1/2} - (1 - \beta)y - (1 - \beta)(1 - \eta_i) = 0 \tag{6.19}$$

and Miller (1995) provide empirical evidence pointing in the same direction for other countries (Australia, US, and Israel).

[18] It is important to note that every meeting between a worker and a firm leads to their mutual acceptance as partners. This is true due to the assumption of constant returns in production (and the free-entry condition). If the number of jobs was fixed or there were other types of decreasing returns, a firm who has met a native would in some cases prefer to turn him down and wait for meeting an immigrant (because of the lower wage she could be paid).

where, for simplicity, a Cobb–Douglas matching function with parameter $\alpha = 0.5$ is assumed. The only positive solution to this equation is given by

$$\theta_i = \left(\frac{-\gamma(r + s_i) + \sqrt{\gamma^2(r + s_i)^2 + 4\gamma(1 - \beta)\beta(y + 1 - \eta_i)}}{2\gamma\beta} \right)^2. \tag{6.20}$$

Region-i's tightness (and therefore the matching probability of workers $\theta_i q(\theta_i)$) is a positive function of the proportion of immigrants looking for a job in that country. The economic intuition behind this result is as follows: if firms base their decision on the number of vacancies to post on the workers' average search cost and, at the same time, can pay a lower wage to workers with a higher search cost (i.e., immigrants), the presence of a high proportion of immigrants in a country leads to a boost in the labour demand of firms.

As concerns individuals, they will migrate whenever the higher unit search cost incurred during migration can be redeemed through better employment prospects, i.e., a higher matching probability. Let $rU(c, \theta)$ be the (flow) value of unemployment for a worker with search cost c, while in a market with tightness θ. Denoting by $\tilde{\theta}_i$ and θ_i^{**} country-i's labour market tightness when $\pi_j = 0$ and $\pi_j = 1$ respectively, the migration decision can be written as ($i = 1, 2$)

$$\pi_j = 0 \quad \text{if } rU(0, \theta_j) > rU(1, \tilde{\theta}_i)$$

$$\pi_j = 1 \quad \text{if } rU(0, \theta_j) < rU(1, \theta_i^{**}) \tag{M}$$

$$\pi_j = \pi_j^* / rU(0, \theta_j) = rU(1, \theta_i) \quad \text{otherwise.}$$

The first two equations describe corner situations. The first one shows that if the unemployment income for a native of country j is higher than that which she can obtain by emigrating to country i at a time when there is no emigration, then she stays in her country of origin and nobody emigrates ($\pi_j = 0$). The second equation presents the other extreme case: if the income from emigration is higher than that expected in country j when everybody emigrates, then every worker does so. Finally, the interior situation presents another possibility: there may exist a situation where emigration is only profitable for a part of the population of j.

6.2. EQUILIBRIA

In this model, regions differ in their exogenous separation rates (s_i). Country i will be considered the 'structurally bad' region if $s_i > s_j$, i.e., if it is subject to a larger number of negative employment shocks. In the rest of the chapter, region 1 will be assumed to be the structurally bad country.

6.2.1. No-migration Equilibrium

In the no-migration equilibrium, *each* agent prefers to search for a job in her country of origin. In other words, the matching probability in the foreign region is not high enough to redeem the costs of emigration. Let $\tilde{\theta}_i$ denote the labour market tightness in region i in the no-migration equilibrium. Agents do not migrate because $rU(0, \tilde{\theta}_1) > rU(1, \tilde{\theta}_2)$ and $rU(0, \tilde{\theta}_2) > rU(1, \tilde{\theta}_1)$ are verified: the matching probability 'offered' by the potential host country is not attractive enough to compensate for the increase in search expenditures.

As each worker searches for a job in her own country ($\pi_1 = \pi_2 = 0$), firms know that they can only meet natives ($\eta_1 = \eta_2 = 1$). Substituting in (6.20), this means, in particular, that the no-migration equilibrium is characterized by low labour market tightness in each country. The wages in this equilibrium ($\tilde{w}_{11}$ and $\tilde{w}_{22}$) are obtained by using $c_{11} = c_{22} = 0$ in (6.13) and substituting for $\tilde{\theta}_i$, using (6.20):

$$\tilde{w}_{ii} = \frac{y(2\beta - 1 + \sqrt{B_i})}{1 + \sqrt{B_i}} \quad \text{for } i = 1, 2 \tag{6.21}$$

where we see that the wage in a region depends only on the productivity level (y) and the region's structural characteristics summarized by $B_i \equiv 1 + 4\gamma^{-1}(r + s_i)^{-2}(1 - \beta)\beta y$.

Finally, the equilibrium values for the total employment level in each country ($\tilde{L}_1$ and $\tilde{L}_2$) are obtained imposing the stationarity conditions $dL_1/dt = dL_2/dt = 0$ in (6.4). We have

$$\tilde{L}_i = \frac{\tilde{\theta}_i^{1/2}}{s_i + \tilde{\theta}_i^{1/2}} N_i = \frac{\tilde{\theta}_i^{1/2}}{s_i + \tilde{\theta}_i^{1/2}} \tag{6.22}$$

as the number of agents searching in region i (N_i) is here equal to the number of agents born in the region ($N = 1$). A numerical example of this equilibrium is provided in the Appendix.

6.2.2. Migration Equilibria

6.2.2.1. *The Interior Solution*
Proposition 1 shows that, for certain parameter values, there exists an equilibrium where part of the population born in the structurally bad country emigrates to the other region.

Proposition 1. *If* $s_1 > s_2$ *and* $y\sqrt{B_2} - 1 < (1 + y)\sqrt{B_1} < 1 + y\sqrt{B_2} \times \sqrt{1 + (1 - B_2^{-1})/2y}$, *there exists an interior equilibrium with migration from country 1 to country 2 characterized by*

(1) *market tightness:* $\theta_1^* = \tilde{\theta}_2$ *and* $\theta_2^* = \left[\frac{r + s_2}{2\beta} \left(\frac{1 - y}{y} + \frac{1 + y}{y} \sqrt{B_1} \right) \right]^2 > \tilde{\theta}_2.$

(2) *migration:* $\dfrac{\pi_1}{1 + \pi_1} = 1 + y - \dfrac{\beta\gamma\theta_2^*}{1 - \beta} - \dfrac{\gamma(r + s_2)\theta_2^{*1/2}}{1 - \beta}.$

(3) *employment levels:* $(L_1^*, L_2^*) = \left(\dfrac{\tilde{\theta}_1^{1/2}}{s_1 + \tilde{\theta}_1^{1/2}} (1 - \pi_1), \dfrac{\theta_2^{*1/2}}{s_2 + \theta_2^{*1/2}} (1 + \pi_1) \right).$

(4) *wages:* $w_{11}^* = w_{21}^* = \tilde{w}_{11}$ *and* $w_{22}^* = \dfrac{\beta y (r + s_2 + \theta_2^{*1/2})}{r + s_2 + \beta \theta_2^{*1/2}} > \tilde{w}_{22}.$

Proof. See the Appendix.

In this equilibrium, as migration occurs from country 1 to country 2, the population of region 1 only consists of individuals born in that country, i.e., $\eta_1 = 1$. With constant returns to scale in matching, this implies that the number of vacancies per searching worker will be the same $(\theta_1^* = \tilde{\theta}_1)$ and that the wage earned by the natives of 1 who do not migrate will thus also be identical $(w_{11}^* = \tilde{w}_{11})$.

In region 2, the presence of immigrants boosts the labour demand of firms $(\theta_2^* > \tilde{\theta}_2)$ and employment.[19] As concerns wages, immigrants receive the same wage they would have earned had they stayed in their country of origin $(w_{21}^* = w_{11}^*)$. The economic intuition behind this result is that all adjustments due to the arrival of immigrants are channelled through the matching probabilities. In other words, the firms' willingness to post additional vacancies does not lead to an adjustment in prices (higher wages for immigrants) but to an adjustment in quantities (a higher number of immigrants). Finally, natives of region 2 enjoy a higher wage when immigrants search there (i.e., $w_{22}^* > \tilde{w}_{22}$). The reason for this is that the additional vacancies posted by the firms when the immigrants arrive can be also occupied by natives, and the increase in labour market tightness reinforces their wage bargaining position.[20]

It can be shown that no other interior equilibrium with migration exists. Two equilibria are, *a priori*, potential candidates. One might, for example, think that the fact that country 2 is 'better' than country 1 (in the sense that $s_1 \geq s_2$) does not preclude the existence of an equilibrium with migration from country 2 to country 1. However, this does not hold. If the economy of country 1 is subject to negative employment shocks to a larger extent than country 2, the employment opportunities with which it can provide immigrants are never good enough to 'convince' them to bear an additional (migration) cost.

Proposition 2. *If $s_1 \geq s_2$, there exists no equilibrium with migration from country 2 to country 1.*

Proof. See the Appendix.

---

[19] The arrival of immigrants decreases the duration of unemployment spells in country 2 (given by $\theta_2^{-1/2}$) and the unemployment rate. Although the effect on the unemployment *stock* in region 2 is ambiguous (due to the labour force growth in 2), the *total stock* of unemployed workers decreases as compared to the no-migration equilibrium.

[20] Here, we see that the assumption of an absence of *ex ante* discrimination is crucial: if firms were able to post different *types* of vacancies for natives and immigrants, then the demand for labour in the market for natives would probably fall in response to immigration. This suggests that making *ex ante* segregation based on nationality illegal may in some circumstances be more advantageous for natives.

The second (frustrated) candidate is an outcome with simultaneous migration in both directions: this cannot be an equilibrium since it is impossible to create simultaneous incentives for migration in both directions. If an incentive is created for migration from region 1 to region 2, the agents born in region 2 prefer to stay there, since the arrival of immigrants improves their employment prospects. We can then prove the following proposition:

Proposition 3. *There exists no equilibrium with simultaneous migration in both directions.*

Proof. See the Appendix.

6.2.2.2. *Corner Solution*

A corner solution here corresponds to an equilibrium where all agents from one country migrate to the other. The condition, in terms of expected values of unemployment, is

$$rU(0, \tilde{\theta}_1) < rU(1, \theta_2^{**}) \tag{6.23}$$

where $\tilde{\theta}_1$ is (as before) the tightness in country 1 when no immigrant searches in that country and θ_2^{**} the corresponding value in country 2 when all[21] natives of country 1 look for a job in country 2. As this condition is one of the necessary conditions for the existence of an interior equilibrium, this equilibrium exists (at least) whenever the interior equilibrium exists.

For the same reason as before, the higher probability of meeting immigrants in this equilibrium makes firms create (relatively) more vacancies ($\theta_2^{**} > \theta_2^* > \tilde{\theta}_2$) and consequently, wages become higher both for natives ($w_{22}^{**} > w_{22}^* > \tilde{w}_{22}$) and for immigrants ($w_{21}^{**} > w_{22}^* = w_{11}^* = \tilde{w}_{11}$). The wage of agents born in country 2 is higher (again) due to their stronger wage bargaining position. As concerns immigrants, both price and quantity effects are now present (which enables them to earn higher wages). Finally, it can be shown that the wage wedge between the natives and the immigrants is decreasing with the number of immigrants.

6.3. UNIQUENESS OR MULTIPLICITY OF EQUILIBRIA

In this section, we study the different qualitative equilibrium outcomes of the economy as a function of its structural characteristics.

As shown in Section 6.2, no equilibrium implying migration from the 'good' to the 'bad' country or simultaneous migration in both directions can exist. Therefore, the different outcomes of the model depend on the values of searching for a job without moving from the bad region ($rU(0, \theta_1)$) and migrating in order to search for a job abroad ($rU(1, \theta_2)$).

First, it must be kept in mind that the value for a given individual of staying in country 1 does not depend on the proportion of individuals leaving that country (π_1). Indeed, the population of country 1 is always homogeneous (since migration

---

[21] In order to avoid having no worker searching in country 1, we assume that there exist ε individuals born in country 1 who search in that region, with ε arbitrarily small.

from 1 to 2 cannot take place) and thus the wage firms expect to pay in region 1 remains unchanged notwithstanding the number of agents searching abroad. With constant returns to scale in the matching function, this implies that the number of vacancies in region 1 is proportional to the number of individuals searching for a job, and that therefore θ_1 (and $rU(0, \theta_1)$) do not depend on π_1. In other words, $rU(0, \theta_1) = rU(0, \tilde{\theta}_1) \ \forall \pi_1$, where $\tilde{\theta}_1$ is the labour market tightness of country 1 in the no-migration equilibrium.

Secondly, we have previously seen that labour market tightness in a given country depends positively on the number of immigrants looking for a job in that region, since the arrival of immigrants depresses the average wages (for a given matching probability), leads to the opening of a larger number of vacancies, and consequently, a higher matching probability (and labour market tightness). $rU(1, \theta_2)$ is therefore increasing in π_1.[22]

We can now present the possible equilibrium outcomes, depending on the structural characteristics of the regions. A first possibility (Fig. 6.2) arises when the two countries share very close structural features. In this case, the improved employment probabilities an agent can obtain by going abroad are never sufficient to redeem the migration cost, and the no-migration solution is the unique equilibrium.

The symmetrical (Fig. 6.3) situation corresponds to a case where the no-migration equilibrium does not exist: the characteristics of country 1 are so bad that they encourage migration even in the case where a very small number of individuals emigrate. In that case, C is the unique equilibrium.

By far the most interesting case is, however, the intermediate situation where multiple equilibria arise in this economy: the outcome of the economy is not *directly* determined by the structural characteristics of countries and depends on the interaction between agents. The situation in that case is represented in Fig. 6.4 (for a numerical example of multiple equilibria, see the Appendix).

The structural features of the regions are compatible with three different equilibria: a no-migration equilibrium (A'), an interior-migration situation (B), and finally, a full-migration solution (C').[23] A' and C' are stable equilibria, whereas B is not.[24]

---

[22] The second derivative $(\partial^2 rU(1, \theta_2)/\partial \pi_1^2)$ is negative. Note also that the effect of immigration is smaller the closer the characteristics of the countries are $(\partial^2 rU(1, \theta_2)/\partial \pi_1 \partial s_2 < 0)$.

[23] The structure of the model and the results share some formal features with the analyses of international currencies by Matsuyama *et al.* (1993) and Trejos and Wright (1995), although these chapters assume increasing returns to matching. In Matsuyama *et al.*, the heterogeneity between agents consists of different probabilities of meeting 'foreigners' and 'compatriots', and countries differ in size (number of agents). As agents are not obliged to choose what kind of agents to meet (they only have to decide whether to accept a currency or not), two types of equilibria not present in my chapter appear in Matsuyama *et al.*: an equilibrium where the currency of the small country becomes international (this would here correspond to the 'bad country' receiving immigrants), and another in which both currencies are used internationally (formally close to the simultaneous migration equilibrium in my framework). Trejos and Wright (1995) modify this framework to allow for endogenous prices and find multiple equilibria with essentially the same characteristics as Matsuyama *et al.*

[24] Indeed, any shock that locates the economy to the right or to the left of B gives rise to interactions between the profit maximization of firms and the workers' migration decision that move the economy

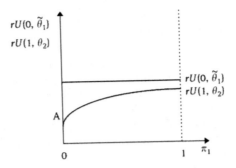

Figure 6.2. *Regions with close structural features.*

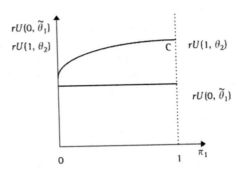

Figure 6.3. *Very bad structural features in country 1.*

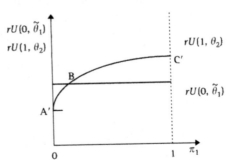

Figure 6.4. *Multiple equilibria.*

away from this point. This is a shortcoming of the model. In order to get a stable interior migration equilibrium, one possibility could be to introduce a decreasing marginal productivity of labour (scarcity of capital). However, in that case it will not be true any more that every meeting between a worker and a firm leads to their mutual acceptance (see footnote 18). An alternative way could be the presence of a counterbalancing congestion (threshold) effect that overcomes at some point the positive job creation externality, so that $rU(1, \theta_2)$ starts to be decreasing at some point in π_1.

In contrast to the unique equilibrium cases, the economy's equilibrium is not here *directly* determined by the structural characteristics of the countries. In other words, the interaction of workers' migration decision and firms' labour demand plays a crucial part here. Take equilibrium A', for example. This situation occurs when firms believe that no immigrants will arrive in country 2. If this is the case, firms believe that the position of workers in country 2 wage bargaining is relatively strong, since all potential employees are natives of the country and therefore bear small costs in case of disagreement. Then, firms present a relatively small number of vacancies in country 2. In other words, if firms believe that no immigrant will arrive in country 2, the matching probability in this region is not high enough to encourage migration. Thus, whenever firms (for some reason or other) believe that there will be no migration, no migration indeed occurs (a 'self-fulfilling prophecy'). The same type of argument applies for the full-migration equilibrium (C'): whenever firms believe that immigration will occur, the high labour demand induced by this belief creates the correct incentives for migration to be profitable, and for that expectation to be confirmed.[25]

6.4. WELFARE ANALYSIS FOR THE MULTIPLE EQUILIBRIA CASE

6.4.1. Pareto-ranking of the Equilibria

In this section, we show that the equilibria can be ranked according to Pareto's optimality criterion. More precisely, we prove that the no-migration equilibrium is Pareto-dominated by the interior-migration equilibrium, which, in turn, is dominated by the full-migration solution.[26] For this purpose, we compare in turn the situation of the different agents in each equilibrium, keeping as a convention that migration, whenever occurring, is from country 1 to country 2.

6.4.1.1. *No-migration versus Interior-migration*
In order to compare the situation of the individuals in the two equilibria, we define a welfare measure $W(c_{ij}, \theta_i)$ for workers, which takes into account the value of their expected discounted income when employed and when unemployed, and the respective probabilities of each of these states. This measure is given by

$$W(c_{ij}, \theta_i) \equiv e_i E(c_{ij}, \theta_i) + (1 - e_i) U(c_{ij}, \theta_i) \tag{6.24}$$

[25] As pointed out by a referee, the mechanism of the chapter is like that of an entry game with externalities: if no one enters, the fixed cost of entry is too high to be borne. On the other hand, with positive externalities, the pay-off from entry is increasing in the number of entrants (hence the multiplicity). Clearly, for some parameter values, entry (no entry) is a dominant strategy with low (high) fixed costs. For intermediate values, there is strategic interaction with the decisions of the other players.

[26] This does not mean that the full-migration equilibrium is Pareto-efficient. As shown in the matching literature (see, for example, Hosios (1989) or Pissarides (1990)), the existence of a thin-market externality leads to Pareto inefficiency (except under very special circumstances).

where e_i is the employment rate in the country where the individual considered lives. Concerning firms, as in both equilibria $V_i = 0$, we focus on the comparison of the value of filled vacancies. Remember that in this model all firms are *ex ante* identical and do not 'belong' to a specific country. A relevant criterion is therefore that the expected value of a filled vacancy (W_F) is higher in the interior-migration equilibrium. This is given by

$$W_F \equiv \frac{L_1}{L} J_1^e + \frac{L_2}{L} J_2^e. \tag{6.25}$$

Moreover, as the number of filled jobs in each equilibrium need not be the same, we must *also* check that the total number of filled jobs is larger ($L^* > \tilde{L}$). We can state the following proposition:

Proposition 4. *The interior migration equilibrium is Pareto-preferred to the no-migration equilibrium: the natives of country 1 who do not migrate are indifferent* ($W(0, \theta_1^*) = W(0, \theta_1)$), *immigrants and natives of country 2 are strictly better-off* ($W(1, \theta_2^*) > W(0, \tilde{\theta}_1)$) *and* $W(0, \theta_2^*) > W(0, \tilde{\theta}_2)$, *respectively). Firms are also strictly better-off* ($W_F^* > \tilde{W}_F$ *and* $L^* > \tilde{L}$).

Proof. See the Appendix.

The intuition for the result is as follows. After emigration, natives of country 1 who do not move face the same conditions in their region, i.e., the relative scarcity of jobs is unchanged. Immigrants are better-off, for while their income during unemployment is unchanged, their employment prospects are enhanced: finding a job abroad is easier than in their region of origin, and the value of holding a job is also higher. Natives benefit from the creation of new jobs following the inflow of immigrants both directly (increase in their employment opportunities) and indirectly (in a tight labour market, their bargaining position improves and they can get higher wages). Finally, firms are better-off because the allocation of labour across countries after migration enables them to concentrate job creation in the country where conditions are more favourable, i.e., in region 2: both the number of jobs and the expected value from a filled vacancy are now higher.

6.4.1.2. *Corner-migration versus Interior-migration*

Proposition 5. *The corner-migration equilibrium Pareto dominates the interior-migration equilibrium.*

Proof. Analogous to that of Proposition 4.

6.4.2. Subsidising Immigration

Although immigration improves everybody's welfare, there are situations where the gains will not be realized: for example, if the fixed costs from migration are 'high', the no-migration outcome may be the unique equilibrium (Fig. 6.2). As the natives of the 'good' country become unambiguously better-off through an inflow of immigrants, it will be in their interest to subsidize immigration to a certain extent: a system of Pareto improving transfers from natives to immigrants can be found. An example of such a system can be found in the Appendix.

6.5. CONCLUSIONS

This chapter presents a rationale for the existence of positive effects of immigration on the employment rates and wages of native workers. Previous analyses concentrated on the strength of competition between immigrants and natives (or a sub-group of these) over a scarce number of jobs. Our main idea is that this kind of analysis, which takes the number of jobs in the economy as given, may yield biased conclusions. Indeed, allowing for an endogenous determination of both the level of labour demand and labour supply (immigration) may, under certain conditions, lead to the existence of a multiplicity of Pareto-rankable equilibria. The ranking is characterized by the domination of migration equilibria since *immigration leads to an increased job creation in the host country*. In this model, the existence of decentralized labour markets, free-entry of firms with constant returns in production and the impossibility for these firms to present different *types* of vacancies for natives and immigrants are the conditions under which this occurs.

APPENDIX

Wage Setting

The optimality condition of problem (N) is given by

$$(1 - \beta)(E_{ij} - U_{ij}) = \beta(J_{ij} - V_i). \tag{6.A1}$$

Using the expressions for U_{ij}, E_{ij}, V_i, and J_{ij} (eqns (6.6)–(6.9)), the wage solving this problem is

$$w_{ij} = \beta y + 1(1 - \beta)rU_{ij}. \tag{6.A2}$$

Using (6.A1), (6.6) and the zero-profit condition for firms $V_i = 0$ in (6.9), we get

$$rU_{ij} = \frac{\beta(y - w_{ij})\theta_i q(\theta_i)}{(r + s_i)(1 - \beta)} - c_{ij}. \tag{6.A3}$$

Substituting (6.A3) in (6.A2), we get the wage of a worker native of j in country i:

$$w_{ij} = \frac{\beta y(r + s_i + \theta_i q(\theta_i))}{r + s_i + \beta\theta_i q(\theta_i)} - \frac{(1 - \beta)(r + s_i)}{r + s_i + \beta\theta_i q(\theta_i)} c_{ij}. \tag{6.A4}$$

Substituting (6.A4) in (6.A3),

$$rU_{ij} = \frac{\beta y \theta_i q(\theta_i) - (r + s_i)c_{ij}}{r + s_i + \beta \theta_i q(\theta_i)}. \tag{6.A5}$$

The expected wage level in country i of a native of country j is analogously obtained using the expected terms' versions of (6.A1) and (6.A2) and the free-entry condition for firms:

$$w_i^e = \beta y + \beta \gamma \theta_i - (1 - \beta)c_i^e. \tag{6.A6}$$

Proof of Proposition 1

(i) *Computation*
As $\pi_2 = 0$, $\theta_1^* = \tilde{\theta}_1$. From the migration condition $[rU(1, \theta_2^*) = rU(0, \theta_1^*) = rU(0, \tilde{\theta}_1)]$, we obtain the equilibrium value for θ_2^* (for $\alpha = 0.5$). π_1 is derived from the firms' optimization problem in country 2 (6.19), using $\eta_2 = 1/(1 + \pi_1)$. The wage and the employment level in each region are obtained as before.

(ii) *Set of Parameters for which the Equilibrium Exists*
If migration occurs from 1 to 2, the unemployment income of agents in region 1 $[rU(0, \tilde{\theta}_1)]$ does not depend on the proportion of agents leaving this region (π_1). On the contrary, from (6.17) $rU(1, \theta_2)$ depends positively on θ_2 and from (6.20) θ_2 is positively linked to π_1. It follows that $rU(1, \theta_2)$ also depends positively on π_1. Thus, the necessary and sufficient conditions for having $\pi_1 \in (0,1)$ such that $rU(0, \tilde{\theta}_1) = rU(1, \theta_2)$ are written as

$$rU(1, \tilde{\theta}_2) < rU(0, \tilde{\theta}_1) \tag{6.A7}$$
$$rU(1, \theta_2^{**}) > rU(0, \tilde{\theta}_1)$$

where $rU(0, \tilde{\theta}_2)$ is the expected value of being unemployed in country 1 when no country 1 worker migrates to country 2, and $rU(0, \theta_2^{**})$ is this same variable when everybody born in 1 goes to 2. Substituting the expression for $\tilde{\theta}_i$ ($\eta_i = 1$ in (6.20)) in that of $rU(0, \tilde{\theta}_i)$, we get $rU(0, \tilde{\theta}_i) = (-y + y\sqrt{B_i})/(1 + \sqrt{B_i})$ where $B_i \equiv 1 + 4\gamma^{-1}(r + s_i)^{-2}(1 - \beta)\beta y$.
   Analogously, $rU(1, \tilde{\theta}_i) = (-(y + 2) + y\sqrt{B_i})/(1 + \sqrt{B_i})$ for $i = 1, 2$. After some computation, condition (6.A7.1) becomes

$$(1 + y)\sqrt{B_1} > y\sqrt{B_2} - 1. \tag{6.A8}$$

Analogously to the above, condition (6.A7.2) can be rewritten as

$$(1 + y)\sqrt{B_1} < 1 + y\sqrt{B_2}\sqrt{1 + \frac{1 - B_2^{-1}}{2y}}. \tag{6.A9}$$

As $B_2 > B_1$, the set of parameters for which (6.A8) and (6.A9) are simultaneously verified is non-empty. A numerical example is provided below.

Proof of Proposition 2

Assume that $s_1 \geq s_2$ and let λ be such that $(r + s_1)^{-2} = \lambda^2(r + s_2)^{-2}$, where $\lambda^2 < 1$. Define μ^2 as $B_1 = \mu^2 B_2 (\mu^2 \leq 1)$. We argue by contradiction and assume that there exists an equilibrium with migration from 2 to 1. In this case, a necessary condition for its existence is given by $rU(0, \tilde{\theta}_2) < rU(1, \theta_1^{**})$. Analogously to the proof of Proposition 1, this inequality can be written as $1 + (1 + y)\sqrt{B_1}\mu^{-1} < y\sqrt{B_1}\sqrt{1 + (1 - B_1^{-1})/2y}$. Taking each side of the inequality to the square

$$1 + y^2 B_1 \mu^{-2} + B_1 \mu^{-2} + 2y B_1 \mu^{-2} + 2(1 + y)\sqrt{B_1}\mu^{-1} + \frac{y}{2} < y^2 B_1 + \frac{yB_1}{2}. \tag{6.A10}$$

But as $\mu^{-2} \geq 1$, we know that $y^2 B_1 \leq y^2 B_1 \mu^{-2}$ and $\frac{y}{2} B_1 < 2y B_1 \mu^{-2}$, and therefore eqn (6.A10) does not hold.

Proof of Proposition 3

Assume that such an equilibrium exists. In this case, we have simultaneously $rU(0, \theta_2) = rU(1, \theta_2)$ and $rU(0, \theta_1) = rU(1, \theta_2)$. We also know that the expected income during unemployment in a given region is always lower for immigrants than for individuals born in the region: $rU(0, \theta_1) > rU(1, \theta_1)$ and $rU(0, \theta_2) > rU(1, \theta_2)$. Using these equations, we arrive at a contradiction, since they imply $rU(1, \theta_1) > rU(1, \theta_2)$ and the opposite inequality.

Numerical Example of Multiple Equilibria

Assume that $y = 4.4$, $\gamma = 4$, $r + s_1 = 3.25 > r + s_2 = 0.95$ (i.e., country 1 is the 'structurally bad' region). Then, the three following equilibria coexist:

Table 6.1. *Numerical example of multiple equilibria*

	No migration	Interior migration	Full migration
θ_1	0.0272	0.0272	0.0272
θ_2	0.2163	0.2411	0.2587
$rU(0, \theta_1)$	0.1089	0.1089	0.1089
$rU(1, \theta_2)$	0.0619	0.1089	0.1403
$rU(0, \theta_1)$	0.8653	0.9036	0.9291
π_1	0	0.4209	1

Proof of Proposition 4

First, $\theta_1^* = \theta_1$ implies that $W(0, \theta_1^*) = W(0, \theta_1)$. Concerning immigrants, from $\theta_1^* = \theta_1$ and the migration condition, $[rU(0, \theta_1^*) = rU(0, \theta_1) = rU(1, \theta_2^*)]$. In addition, it is easy to show that $rE(1, \theta_2^*) > rE(0, \tilde{\theta}_1)$ whenever $s_1 > s_2$. As concerns employment rates, $e_1^* = \tilde{e}_1 = \tilde{\theta}_1^{1/2}/(s_1 + \tilde{\theta}_1^{1/2})$ and $e_2^* = \tilde{\theta}_2^{*1/2}/(s_2 + \tilde{\theta}_2^{*1/2})$ (from (6.22) and Proposition 1). As $\theta_2^* > \tilde{\theta}_1$ and $s_1 > s_2$, $e_2^* > \tilde{e}_1$. Then, from (6.24), $W(1, \theta_2^*) > W(0, \tilde{\theta}_1)$. Concerning individuals born in country 2, $\theta_2^* > \tilde{\theta}_2$ implies that $rU(0, \theta_2^*) > rU(0, \tilde{\theta}_2)$, $rE(0, \theta_2^*) > rE(0, \tilde{\theta}_2)$ and $e_2^* > \tilde{e}_2$. Consequently, $W(0, \theta_2^*) > W(0, \tilde{\theta}_2)$. For the total number of filled vacancies, from (6.21) and Proposition 1, $L^* - \tilde{L} = \pi_1(\theta_2^{*1/2}/(s_2 + \tilde{\theta}_2^{1/2}) - \tilde{\theta}_1^{1/2}/(s_1 + \tilde{\theta}_1^{1/2}) + \theta_2^{*1/2}/(s_2 + \theta_2^{*1/2}) - \tilde{\theta}_2^{1/2}/(s_2 + \tilde{\theta}_2^{1/2})$. As $\theta_2^* > \tilde{\theta}_2 > \tilde{\theta}_1$ and $s_2 < s_1$, $L^* > \tilde{L}$. We then compare $\tilde{W}_F = \frac{\tilde{L}_1}{\tilde{L}} \tilde{J}_1^e + \frac{\tilde{L}_2}{\tilde{L}} \tilde{J}_2^e$ and $W_F^* = \frac{L_1^*}{L^*} \tilde{J}_1^e + \frac{L_2^*}{L^*} J_2^{*e}$. $\theta_2^* > \tilde{\theta}_2 > \tilde{\theta}_1$ implies that $J_2^{e*} > \tilde{J}_2^e > \tilde{J}_1^e$. Furthermore as $\tilde{L}_1 > L_1^*$ and $\tilde{L} < L^*$, $\frac{\tilde{L}_1}{\tilde{L}} > \frac{L_1^*}{L^*}$ and $\frac{\tilde{L}_2}{\tilde{L}} < \frac{L_2^*}{L^*}$. Then, $W_F^* > \tilde{W}_F$.

Pareto-improving Transfers

Take an initial situation where the no-migration outcome is the unique equilibrium ($y = 4.4$, $\gamma = 4$, $r + s_1 = 2.8$, $r + s_2 = 0.95$). We consider a system of lump-sum taxes (t) paid by the natives of country 2 and of lump-sum subsidies (τ) received by immigrants, both independent of the labour market status of individuals (this simplifies things, since equilibrium wages are then unchanged). We want this system to make the full-migration equilibrium feasible and to be financially sustainable at that equilibrium (for this purpose, $t = \tau$ is the condition that must be imposed, since there are equal numbers of immigrants and natives in that equilibrium). $t = \tau = 0.03$ (therefore constituting 3 per cent of the fixed migration cost) is an example of such a Pareto-improving transfer (for natives, $rW(0, \theta_2^{**}, t) = 0.93 > rW(0, \tilde{\theta}_2) = 0.897$, for immigrants $rW(1, \theta_2^{**}, \tau) = 0.21 > rW(0, \tilde{\theta}_1) = 0.146$ with $rU(1, \theta_2^{**}, \tau) = 0.17 > rU(0, \tilde{\theta}_1) = 0.144$).

REFERENCES

Altonji, J. and D. Card (1991). The effects of immigration on the labor market outcomes of less-skilled natives, in Abowd, J. and R. B. Freeman (eds.), *Immigration, Trade, and the Labor Market*. Chicago: Chicago University Press.

Bean, F., B. Lowell, and L. Taylor (1988). Undocumented Mexican immigrants and the earnings of other workers in the United States, *Demography*, 35–52.

Berry, A. and R. Soligo (1969). Some welfare aspects of international migration, *Journal of Political Economy*, 77, 778–794.

Blanchard, O. and P. Diamond (1989). The Beveridge curve, *Brookings Papers on Economic Activity*, 2, 495–582.

Borjas, G. J. (1994). The economics of immigration, *Journal of Economic Literature.* Volume XXXII. (4) p 1668.

Burda, M. and C. Wyplosz (1994). Gross worker and job flows in Europe, *European Economic Review*, 38 (6), 1287–315.

Chatterjee S., R. Cooper, and B. Ravikumar (1993). Strategic complementarity in business formation: Aggregate fluctuations and sunspot equilibria, *Review of Economic Studies*, 60, 795–811.

Chiswick B. and P. Miller (1995). The endogeneity between language and earnings: International analyses, *Journal of Labor Economics*, 13 (2).

Diamond, P. (1982). Aggregate demand management in search equilibrium, *Journal of Political Economy*, 90 (5).

Dustmann, C. (1994). Speaking fluency, writing fluency, and earnings of migrants, *Journal of Population Economics*, 7, 133–56.

Harris, J. and M. Todaro (1970). Migration, unemployment and development: a two-sector analysis, *American Economic Review*, 60, 126–42.

Hosios, A. (1989). On the efficiency of matching and related models of search and unemployment, *Review of Economic Studies*, 57, 279–98.

Howitt, P. and R. McAfee (1987). Costly search and recruiting, *International Economic Review*, 28 (1) 89–107.

Kee, P. (1995). Native-immigrant wage differentials in the Netherlands: Discrimination? *Oxford Economic Papers*, 47, 302–17.

Matsuyama, K., N. Kiyotaki, and A. Matsui (1993). Toward a theory of international currency. *Review of Economic Studies*, 60, 283–307.

Murphy, K., A. Shleifer, and R. Vishny (1989). Industrialisation and the big push, *Journal of Political Economy*, 97 (5).

Ortega, J. (1993). Loss of skill during unemployment, complementarities in production and persistence of shocks, *DELTA Working Papers* 93.26.

—— (1995). Membership rules, matching, and unemployment, *DELTA Working Papers* 95.14.

Pischke, J. and J. Velling (1994). Wage and employment effects of immigration to Germany: An analysis based on local labour markets. Mimeo. MIT.

Pissarides, C. (1986). Unemployment and vacancies in Britain, *Economic Policy*, 3, 499–559.

—— (1990). *Equilibrium Unemployment Theory.* London: Basil Blackwell.

—— (1992). Loss of skill during unemployment and the persistence of employment shocks, *Quarterly Journal of Economics*.

Rioux, L. (1995). Heterogeneity, matching, and endogenous labour market segmentation, *DELTA Working Papers* 95.35.

Saint-Paul, G. (1992). Are the unemployed unemployable? *CEPR Discussion Series* 689.

Sánchez, G. (1997). Increasing political returns and rural-urban migrations. Mimeo. Universitat Pompeu Fabra.

Schmidt, M., A. Stilz, and K. Zimmermann (1994). Mass migration, unions, and government intervention, *Journal of Public Economics*, 55, 185–201.

Stalker, P. (1995). *Les travailleurs immigrés. Etude des migrations internationales de main d'œuvre.* Bureau international du Travail. Genève. (Available also in English).

Trejos, A. and R. Wright (1995). Toward a theory of international currency: A step further. Mimeo.

Weiss, Y. and M. Gotlibovski (1995). Immigration, search and loss of skill, *The Foerder Institute for Social Research Working Papers*, 34–95.

Winegarden, C. and L. Khor (1991). Undocumented immigration and unemployment of U.S. youth and minority workers: Econometric evidence, *Review of Economics and Statistics*, 73 (1), 105–12.

Winter-Ebmer, R. and J. Zweimüller (1996). Immigration and the earnings of young native workers, *Oxford Economic Papers* (forthcoming).

PART II

LIFETIME INEQUALITIES AND THE SCOPE FOR REDISTRIBUTION

7

Consumption Inequality and Income Uncertainty

RICHARD BLUNDELL AND IAN PRESTON

7.1. INTRODUCTION

The use of current income in studies of inequality is open to the obvious criticism that current income may not reflect the longer run level of resources available to a household or an individual. Temporarily high or low incomes may exaggerate the true position of the household when borrowing or saving is allowed to smooth the stream of consumption. Moreover, aggregate measures of inequality (or poverty) based on snapshots of income may fail to pick up changes over time associated with the duration rather than the depth of low-income spells. The importance of distinguishing long-run income inequality from inequality associated with transitory movements in income has been emphasized in a number of recent studies that have moved away from simply documenting the change in the cross-section distribution of income. For example, Gottschalk and Moffitt (1994), Moffitt and Gottschalk (1995), Buchinsky and Hunt (1996), and Gittleman and Joyce (1996) all use the time series of individual incomes to focus on this important distinction. Moffitt and Gottschalk (1995) study the autocovariance structure in US male earnings in the Panel Study of Income Dynamics over the 1970s and 1980s. They found a strong increase in the variance of the permanent

We are grateful to Daron Acemoglu, Orazio Attanasio, James Banks, François Bourguignon, Ian Crawford, Angus Deaton, Stephen Jenkins, Paul Johnson, Lawrence Katz, François Laisney, Costas Meghir, Christina Paxson, James Symons, Steven Webb, Guglielmo Weber, and two referees for helpful comments. This study is part of the programme of research of the Economic and Social Research Council Centre for the Microeconomic Analysis of Fiscal Policy at the Institute for Fiscal Studies. The financial support of the Economic and Social Research Council is gratefully acknowledged. Material from the Family Expenditure Survey made available by the Office for National Statistics through the Economic and Social Research Council Data Archive has been used by permission of the controller of Her Majesty's Stationery Office. Neither the Office for National Statistics nor the Economic and Social Research Council Data Archive bear responsibility for the analysis or the interpretation of the data reported here. The usual disclaimer applies.

component in income, mirroring the Buchinsky and Hunt (1996), and Gittleman and Joyce (1996) studies. However, they also show that the increase in income inequality over the later part of this period can be increasingly attributed to a rise in the variance of the transitory component of income, the transitory component showing no significant rise until the early 1980s.

The aim of this chapter is to see how consumption can help in this evaluation. The recognition that consumption expenditure may better reflect expected life-time resources has led to the increasing use of consumption[1] in the measurement of household welfare. Earlier work, such as Cutler and Katz (1991, 1992) and Slesnick (1993), has used repeated cross-section data on the distribution of consumption to examine changes in the distribution of permanent income and household welfare. Attanasio and Davis (1996) exploit the strong systematic movements in wage inequality over the 1980s in the US to evaluate the complete insurance hypothesis. They found that the distribution of consumption tends to follow the low frequency movements in real wages, but that consumption is well insulated from transitory movements. This provides strong evidence against complete insurance while giving tacit support to consumption smoothing.

This study seeks to advance the literature by formalizing some of the limitations of the use of consumption data alone in assessing changes in the distribution of economic welfare and permanent income. We further show how information on changes in the cross-section joint distribution of consumption and income can illuminate the nature of changes in inequality.

As consumption inequality tends to highlight the importance of permanent inequality, the arguments for consumption based measures of inequality are powerful. But, how reliable is consumption as a measure of welfare? Consumption expenditure does typically differ from income and these differences surely reflect differences in expected resources and needs. However, although comparisons within date of birth cohorts are likely to be reliable measures of inequality in living standards this is not so easily proven for comparisons across different cohorts. The different levels of income growth and the different intertemporal substitutions open to cohorts at similar points in their life-cycle make such comparisons less compelling. We, therefore, argue that there are strong welfare grounds for analysis within cohorts. Moreover, the evolution of distribution within the whole population is influenced by changes in age structure which obscure the role of permanent and transitory income uncertainty.

In this chapter, we examine the distinction between permanent and transitory income uncertainty in the evaluation of growth in consumption inequality within cohorts. We derive conditions under which the growth of variances and covariances of income and consumption can be used to separately identify the growth in the variance of permanent and transitory income shocks. We develop

---

[1] In this chapter, we tend to use the terms 'consumption' and 'expenditure' interchangeably while recognizing that in practical applications the distinction between the two is of considerable importance.

a difference in differences estimator for estimating the growth of the variance of the transitory component on this basis. This is based on a contrast between the growth in the variance of income and consumption. In addition we show that, where consumption and income are available in the same survey, the covariance between the two provides overidentifying information from which we can verify these results. These results are extended to income processes which include common shocks and cross-sectional correlation between shocks and past incomes. They are also generalized to consumers with preferences which permit precautionary saving. Household data from Britain for the period 1968–92 are used to show a strong growth in transitory inequality towards the end of this period while younger cohorts are shown to face significantly higher levels of permanent inequality in comparison to older cohorts at a similar age.

The chapter is organized as follows: Section 7.2 is concerned with exploring precisely when consumption does provide a suitable measure of welfare. The theory points to the importance of within-cohort comparisons of consumption and income inequality. Our analysis covers the case of prudent consumers by addressing the relationship between precautionary saving and the welfare cost of risk. Section 7.3 considers a variety of income processes and preferences and shows how growth in the variances and covariances of income and consumption can be used to identify growth in the variances of transitory and permanent shocks. These results are then used in Section 7.4 for an empirical evaluation of the differences in growth rates between income and consumption using British Family Expenditure Survey data over the 1970s and 1980s. We provide an analysis by cohort and compare this with the overall picture of changing inequality. Section 7.5 concludes.

7.2. DOES CONSUMPTION INEQUALITY MEASURE WELFARE INEQUALITY?

7.2.1. The Welfare Comparison Case for Within Cohort Comparisons

If one observes an individual's consumption, knowing the individual's age and the interest rates that link the periods of their life, it will always be possible to invert the Hicksian demand function to recover utility given real discount rates and age, assuming consumption in all periods to be a normal good. Given the assumption of common interest rates, comparisons of consumption within cohort at the same point in time do therefore suffice for welfare comparisons. However, if comparisons are between individuals who are differently aged or born in different years, as they will be if comparisons are across cohorts at a given date or across time within a cohort, then comparisons are more problematic.

Suppose individual i, reaching adulthood in year b_i has lifetime income Y_i. The real interest rate in year s is r_s and is assumed to be the same for all individuals. The individual seeks to maximize an increasing and quasiconcave lifetime welfare function $U_i = U(c_i)$, where $c_i \equiv (c_{i0}, c_{i1}, \ldots, c_{iT})$ and c_{it} is consumption at age t, subject to their lifetime budget constraint. Hicksian demands are $c_{it} = c_t(U_i, p_i)$ where $p_i \equiv (p_{i0}, p_{i1}, \ldots, p_{iT})$ and $p_{it} \equiv \prod_{s=0}^{t}(1 + r_{s+bi})^{-1}$. We assume interpersonal ordinal full comparability of welfare so that welfare comparisons are preserved only by common increasing transformations of utilities.[2]

The following proposition shows the conditions under which consumption comparisons suffice for welfare comparisons.

Proposition 1.

(i) *Comparisons within cohorts at same age: $c_{it} \geq c_{jt}$ implies $U_i \geq U_j$ whenever individuals i and j share the same year of birth if and only if consumption in all periods is a normal good.*

(ii) *Comparisons across cohorts at same age: $c_{it} \geq c_{jt}$ implies $U_i \geq U_j$ for all i and j whether or not individuals i and j share the same year of birth if and only if $c_t(U_i, p_i) = f_t(U_i)$ where $f_t(\cdot)$ is an increasing function for all t. This is so if and only if $U(c_i) = \min_t u_t(c_{it})$ where $u_t(\cdot)$ is an increasing function for all t.*

(iii) *Comparisons across ages: $c_{it} \geq c_{js}$ implies $U_i \geq U_j$ for all s and t whenever individuals i and j share the same year of birth if and only if $c_t(U_i, p_i) = f(U_i)$ where $f(\cdot)$ is an increasing function. This is so if and only if $U(c_i) = \min_t u(c_{it})$ where $u(\cdot)$ is an increasing function. The same conditions apply to ensure $c_{it} \geq c_{js}$ implies $U_i \geq U_j$ for all s and t whether or not individuals i and j share the same year of birth.*

Proof.   See Appendix.

In cases of cross-cohort or cross-age comparisons, all requisite information on welfare is available from consumption only if agents choose to equalize utilities across all periods of the life-cycle—an extreme case of antipathy to inter-temporal substitution. This is obviously an unrealistic degree of smoothing and as a result there is almost certain to be some weakness in the undiscriminating use of consumption as an indicator of lifetime standard of living.

Additive separability in the direct representation of lifetime utility $U_i = \sum_t u_t(c_{it})$ would be a more appealing assumption and one that is commonly adopted. With such preferences the first-order conditions for optimization imply that agents aim for a marginal utility of within-period expenditure equal at each age to the marginal utility of discounted lifetime income:

$$u_0'(c_{i0}) = u_t'(c_{it})/p_{it}. \tag{7.1}$$

This constancy of discounted marginal utility is the familiar Euler condition for consumption over the life-cycle (see Hall, 1978; Attanasio and Weber, 1989; Browning et al., 1985, for example). Even though direct utility is additive across periods, it is known that intertemporal substitution invalidates the use of the sum

---

[2] See, for instance, Sen (1977).

of compensating variations as a measure of lifetime compensating variation (see Blackorby *et al.*, 1984; Keen, 1990). Nevertheless, we might wish to categorize the circumstances under which consumption is likely to be reliable as a welfare measure.

Equation (7.1) points to a number of reasons why consumption could give a poor indication of welfare. If within-period utility functions $u_t(\cdot)$ vary much over the life-cycle and welfare comparisons are made across age, then comparisons could be undermined. In particular, subjective discounting will lead to consumption being pushed towards the earlier years of life. On the other hand, if real interest rates are high and welfare comparisons are made across age then incentives to push consumption towards the later period of life will lead the old to appear to be better off than they actually are in comparison to the young. Finally, if the interest rate is variable over time then differing incentives to substitute intertemporally could undermine welfare comparisons made across cohorts. The magnitude of this last problem can be shown to depend on the magnitude of intertemporal substitution elasticities.

7.2.2. The Welfare Cost of Income Risk

Risk-averse households with more uncertain incomes than others need to be considered worse off. This might show up to an extent in lower expenditure by such households, if their response is precautionary saving (see Kimball, 1990 for discussions of precautionary saving). This section explores the precise relationship between precautionary saving and the welfare cost of risk.

Suppose future income is uncertain and intertemporal utility takes the additive form. It will be useful to define $\widetilde{Y}_i$ as that certain present discounted value of income which would allow the individual to achieve the same expected utility. The consumption stream $\widetilde{c}_i = \widetilde{c}(EU_i)$ that would be chosen given $\widetilde{Y}_i$ satisfies

$$\sum_t u_t(\widetilde{c}_{it}) \equiv E\left(\sum_t u_t(c_{it})\right) = EU_i.$$

Focusing on within-cohort comparisons of $\widetilde{c}(EU_i)$, actual consumption differences will be indicative of welfare differences when households face differing degrees of uncertainty only if $c_i = \widetilde{c}(EU_i)$ for all households. We show below that the unique case in which this holds exactly is that of constant absolute risk aversion (CARA).[3]

Proposition 2. *Comparisons across individuals facing different income risk: $c_{it} \geq c_{jt}$ implies $EU_i \geq EU_j$ whenever individuals i and j share the same year of birth*

---

[3] Strictly speaking, this condition applies to subsequent periods' utility only since period 1 is not affected by uncertainty but it would seem sensible to maintain the same structure on within-period preferences in all periods.

if and only if $c_i = \tilde{c}(EU_i)$ whatever the distribution of future income. This is so if and only if

$$u_t(c_{it}) = -\alpha_t \exp(-\beta_t c_{it}) \quad \alpha_t, \beta_t > 0, \ t > 0. \tag{7.2}$$

Proof. See Appendix.

The sufficiency part of this is a special case of a more general result of Drèze and Modigliani (1972, p. 324) which also establishes that decreasing absolute risk aversion (DARA) implies $c_{i0} < \tilde{c}_{i0}$, i.e., that there is excess precautionary saving if higher incomes decrease risk aversion. Their result is not interpreted in terms of welfare considerations but rather in terms of the correspondence between CARA and the absence of substitution effects in response to uncertainty. This links the preference restrictions considered here nicely with those of the previous section. The validity of consumption as a welfare measure relies on the absence of substitution effects in response to intertemporal prices and to uncertainty.

7.3. PERMANENT INEQUALITY AND TRANSITORY UNCERTAINTY

Uncertainty concerned with unexpected transitory shifts in income is very different from the inequality associated with permanent shifts in the position of individuals in the income distribution. Growth in cross-section measures of income inequality (or poverty) cannot alone distinguish between these two phenomena. Here we show that taking income inequality together with consumption inequality and the life-cycle model, we are able to separate the growth in permanent inequality from the growth in transitory uncertainty.

7.3.1. A Stochastic Process for Income

We start by considering a permanent-transitory decomposition for income. Income for individual i in cohort k in period t is written as

$$y_{it} = y_{it}^p + u_{it} \quad \text{for } i \in k \tag{7.3}$$

where y_{it}^p represents the permanent component of income and u_{it} the transitory shock in period t. The permanent component is assumed to follow a random walk

$$y_{it}^p = y_{i,t-1}^p + v_{it} \tag{7.4}$$

where v_{it} is a permanent shock assumed orthogonal to u_{it}. We assume that the variances of the shocks are the same in any period for all individuals in any cohort but that these variances are not constant over time. The cross-sectional covariances of the shocks with previous periods' incomes are assumed to be zero. In this discussion, we assume that shocks are independently distributed across individuals. Section 7.3.4 considers a relaxation of this assumption and also considers models for income in which the cross-section distribution of shocks is correlated with the distribution of past income.

The process for income can be written as

$$y_{it} = y_{i,t-1} + u_{it} - u_{i,t-1} + v_{it}. \tag{7.5}$$

This covers the general MA(1) model in which

$$y_{it} = y_{i,t-1} + \epsilon_{it} - \theta_t \epsilon_{i,t-1} \tag{7.6}$$

though notice that in this representation the MA coefficient θ_t is time varying. The evolution of θ_t can be directly related to the evolution of the variances of the transitory and permanent innovations to income.[4] Defining $\text{Var}_{kt}(u)$ to be the cross-section variance of transitory shocks for cohort k in period t and $\text{Var}_{kt}(v)$ to be the corresponding variance of permanent shocks, the growth in the cross-section variance of income for cohort k can be seen from (7.5) to take the form:[5]

$$\Delta \text{Var}_{kt}(y) = \Delta \text{Var}_{kt}(u) + \text{Var}_{kt}(v). \tag{7.7}$$

Permanent inequality $(\text{Var}_{kt}(v))$ or growth in uncertainty $(\Delta \text{Var}_{kt}(u))$ both result in growth of income inequality. The cross-section distribution of income cannot, on its own, distinguish these.

7.3.2. Identifying the Growth in Transitory and Permanent Variances

Taking income inequality together with consumption inequality and the life-cycle model, we are able to separate the growth in permanent inequality from the growth in transitory uncertainty. Assuming quadratic preferences, with the discount rate equal to the real interest rate, we obtain the familiar martingale property for consumption[6]

$$\rho_t \Delta c_{it} = \eta_{it} \tag{7.8}$$

where ρ_t is an annuitization factor,[7] and η_{it} is the consumption innovation.[8] Relating η_{it} to the transitory and permanent innovations to income (7.5), we have

$$\eta_{it} = \rho_t v_{it} + \frac{r}{1+r} u_{it}. \tag{7.9}$$

That is, the consumption innovation is simply the sum of the annuity value of the transitory shock and permanent shock.

The derivation of (7.9) requires that the consumer can separately identify transitory u_{it} from permanent v_{it} income shocks, which we assume throughout

---

[4] See Blundell and Preston (1997).
[5] Note that $\text{Cov}_{kt-1}(yu) = \text{Var}_{kt-1}(u)$ where $\text{Cov}_{kt-1}(yu)$ is the cross-section variance of income with transitory shocks for cohort k in period $t-1$.   [6] See Hall (1978).
[7] $\rho_t = 1 - (1+r)^{-(T-t+1)}$.
[8] $\eta_{it} = r/(1+r) \sum_{k=0}^{T-t} (1+r)^{-k} (E_t - E_{t-1}) y_{t+k}$—see Deaton and Paxson (1994), for example.

unless otherwise stated. However, for a consumer who simply observed ϵ_{it}, we would have

$$\eta_{it} = \rho_t(1 - \theta_{t+1})\epsilon_{it} + \frac{r}{1+r}\theta_{t+1}\epsilon_{it} \tag{7.10}$$

which, by analogy with (7.9), provides a decomposition of the MA innovation ϵ_{it} into the component representing the new information concerning permanent effects and that representing a transitory innovation to income. The permanent effects component can be thought of as capturing news about both current and *past* permanent effects since

$$E\left(\sum_{j=0} v_{i,\,t-j}|\varepsilon_{it},\varepsilon_{i,\,t-1},\dots\right) - E\left(\sum_{j=0} v_{i,\,t-j}|\varepsilon_{i,\,t-1},\dots\right) = (1 - \theta_{t+1})\varepsilon_{it}.$$

The decomposition (7.10) therefore represents the best prediction of the split between permanent and transitory components given θ_{t+1}.

The connection between consumption and income innovations in (7.9) can be used to link the growth in the variance of consumption and in the covariance of consumption and income to the variances of the underlying components in the income process. From this expression, the identification of the growth in transitory and permanent variances can be related to the growth in consumption and income variances as is shown in the following proposition.

Proposition 3. *For individuals in a cohort k*

$$\Delta \mathrm{Var}_{kt}(c) = \frac{1}{\rho_t^2}\frac{r^2}{(1+r)^2}\mathrm{Var}_{kt}(u) + \mathrm{Var}_{kt}(v), \tag{7.11}$$

$$\Delta \mathrm{Cov}_{kt}(c, y) = \Delta\left[\frac{1}{\rho_t}\frac{r}{(1+r)}\mathrm{Var}_{kt}(u)\right] + \mathrm{Var}_{kt}(v), \tag{7.12}$$

$$\Delta \mathrm{Var}_{kt}(y) - \Delta \mathrm{Var}_{kt}(c) = \left[1 - \frac{1}{\rho_t^2}\frac{r^2}{(1+r)^2}\right]\mathrm{Var}_{kt}(u) - \mathrm{Var}_{kt-1}(u). \tag{7.13}$$

Proof. Equations (7.11) and (7.12) follow from (7.8) and (7.9). Substituting for $\mathrm{Var}_{kt}(v)$ in (7.7) from (7.11) gives (7.13).

Intuitively, the growths in the variance of consumption and in the covariance of consumption and income are dominated by permanent inequality. The proposition shows that the difference of differences in the variances eliminates the variance of the permanent shocks. For large $T - t$ and small r, these results take a particularly simple form.

Corollary. *For T − t large and r small*

$$\Delta \mathrm{Var}_{kt}(c) \simeq \mathrm{Var}_{kt}(v). \tag{7.14}$$

$$\Delta \mathrm{Cov}_{kt}(c, y) \simeq \mathrm{Var}_{kt}(v). \tag{7.15}$$

$$\Delta \mathrm{Var}_{kt}(y) - \Delta \mathrm{Var}_{kt}(c) \simeq \Delta \mathrm{Var}_{kt}(u). \tag{7.16}$$

Removing the growth in the consumption variance from the growth in the income variance eliminates the permanent inequality term. A higher growth in income variance than in consumption variance must imply a rise in the variance of transitory shocks. In general, the difference provides a lower bound on the growth in transitory uncertainty but for large $T - t$ and small r the corollary shows that growth in short-run income uncertainty is exactly measured by the difference in growth between income inequality and in consumption inequality. To measure the growth in the variance of the transitory shocks to income we therefore suggest the use of a difference of differences estimator (7.16).

Moreover, for large $T - t$ and small r, individuals consume their permanent income, so that $\Delta \mathrm{Var}_{kt}(c)$ and $\Delta \mathrm{Cov}_{kt}(c, y)$ each equal the variance of the permanent shocks. A rise in the variance of permanent income shocks would be reflected in an *acceleration* in their growth. If we have data on both then (7.14) and (7.15) provides one overidentifying restriction per period to use in improving precision of estimates.

Liquidity constraints, by exaggerating the effect of transitory shocks on consumption growth for some consumers, can be thought of in the same way as the finite T model. It remains true that changes in the variance of incomes that are not reflected also in changes in the variance of expenditures can be attributed to transitory shocks. In a simple model in which a fixed proportion of consumers is constrained to consume their income, the difference in the growth of the variance in consumption and income now only identifies the growth in the variance of transitory shocks to the unconstrained group.

Even if u_{it} and v_{it} are not distinguished by the consumer, who observes only ϵ_{it} in (7.6), then

$$\Delta \mathrm{Var}_{kt}(y) - \Delta \mathrm{Var}_{kt}(c) \simeq \Delta \left(\frac{1 - (1 - \theta_{t+1})^2}{\theta_{t+1}} \right) \mathrm{Var}_{kt}(u).$$

A similar path for both variances still suggests a stable pattern of short-run income uncertainty over time.

7.3.3. Prudent Consumers and Precautionary Saving

Proposition 3 extends naturally to preferences that admit precautionary saving. An analogous relationship between the variances of consumption and income can be seen to hold under Constant Absolute Risk Aversion (CARA) preferences.

Caballero (1990, p. 128) has shown that for such preferences and for income processes of the sort considered here with non-constant variances

$$\Delta c_{it} = \Gamma_{kt} + \zeta_{kt} + \frac{1}{\rho_{kt}} \eta_{it} \qquad (7.17)$$

where $(1/\rho_{kt})\eta_{it}$ is the annuitized income innovation as previously, Γ_{kt} is the slope of consumption paths within the cohort and ζ_{kt} is a term taking into account revisions to variance forecasts. With normally distributed innovations Γ_{kt} is proportional to the expected variance of next period's consumption innovations.[9] Since both Γ_{kt} and ζ_{kt} are assumed constant within cohorts the results of Proposition 3 continue to hold in this setting. It is important, therefore, to choose cohort groups which, wherever possible, are sufficiently homogeneous for these constancy assumptions to be valid.[10]

To extend to the case of decreasing absolute risk aversion, we consider Constant Relative Risk Averse preferences. Assume, as above, that the discount rate equals the real interest rate and suppose that a stochastic process similar to that described above applies to the logarithm of income

$$\ln y_{it} = \ln y_{it}^p + u_{it} \quad \text{for } i \in k$$
$$\ln y_{it}^p = \ln y_{it-1}^p + v_{it}$$

where u_{it} and v_{it} are assumed orthogonal with properties as above. In such a case it is possible to approximate[11] the growth of individual consumption by an expression similar to (7.17)

$$\Delta \ln c_{it} \simeq G_{kt} + z_{kt} + \ln \left(\frac{L_{it}}{E_{t-1} L_{it}} \right) \qquad (7.18)$$

where G_{kt} and z_{kt} have similar interpretations as the slope of consumption paths within the cohort and as a term taking into account revisions to variance forecasts. Here L_{it} denotes the value of current financial wealth plus the present value of future earnings. If $(1/E_{t-1} L_{it}) \sum_{k=0}^{T-t} (1 + r)^{-k} E_{t-1} y_{it+k} \simeq 1$, that is, L_{it} consists mainly of the present value of future earnings, as would seem reasonable for younger cohorts, then[12]

$$\Delta \ln c_{it} \simeq G_{kt} + z_{kt} + v_{it} + \frac{r}{\rho_t(1 + r)} u_{it} \qquad (7.19)$$

---

[9] $\Gamma_{kt} = (1/\beta)\ln E_t \, e^{-\beta(1/\rho_k)\eta_{it} + \zeta_{kt}}$ where β is the coefficient of absolute risk aversion.
[10] If individuals within a cohort group k are subject to different changes in the variance of permanent shocks, divergences in the growth in variances of consumption and income could not necessarily be given the simple interpretation we establish here.
[11] The proof of the approximation is in the Appendix and has some similarity to that in Skinner (1988, p. 252), though Skinner establishes his result only for a case in which all shocks are transitory and normally distributed with constant variance.
[12] For proof of this further step refer again to the Appendix.

which is analogous to the consumption growth process in (7.8) and the decomposition results of Proposition 3 and the Corollary apply. However, they now refer to identification of the growth in variances of *proportionate* transitory and permanent shocks.

7.3.4. Alternative Income Processes

In this section, we investigate the robustness of these results to modifications to the income process such as allowance for common shocks, deterministic trends and cross-sectional correlation between the distributions of shocks and of past incomes.

7.3.4.1. *Common Shocks*

Common shocks to the income process that impact in the same way across all individuals in the cohort will be captured by the Γ_{kt} term in (7.17) and will have no impact on within-cohort consumption or income inequality. However, we may wish to allow for common effects that are distributed unevenly across individuals. For example,[13] suppose we define e_{kt} to be a common transitory shock to incomes in cohort k at time t and suppose that it is distributed across individuals in the cohort according to an individual parameter γ_i. The income process (7.3) then becomes

$$y_{it} = y_{it}^p + u_{it} + \gamma_i e_{kt} \quad \text{for } i \in k \tag{7.20}$$

where u_{it} is again the purely idiosyncratic transitory shock in period t. Suppose the permanent component has an analogous decomposition

$$y_{it}^p = y_{i,t-1}^p + v_{it} + \delta_i \upsilon_{kt}. \tag{7.21}$$

Assuming $\text{Cov}_{kt}(y_{-1}\gamma) = \text{Cov}_{kt}(y_{-1}\delta) = 0$, in this case the decomposition results in Proposition 3 generalize to allow the identification of permanent and transitory components in the sum of both idiosyncratic and common contributions to the growth in income uncertainty.[14]

7.3.4.2. *Cross-section Correlation between Shocks and Past Incomes*

Although, when averaging across time, transitory or permanent shocks will be uncorrelated with historical events, this may not be true in a given cross-section. That is in any particular period the distribution of shocks to income may be related to the position of individuals in the income or consumption distribution. For example, this would occur if the γ_i in income process (7.20) were correlated in the cross-section with $y_{i,t-1}$ even though e_{kt} is uncorrelated with $y_{i,t-1}$ over time. In this case $\text{Cov}_{kt}(y_{-1}\gamma e) \neq 0$ but $\lim_{T \to \infty}(1/T)\sum_t \text{Cov}_{kt}(y_{-1}\gamma e) = 0$.[15]

---

[13] See, for instance, the use of this process in Deaton (1992, p. 148).

[14] For CRRA preferences the impact would be a common proportionate effect across all individuals.

[15] See also Attanasio and Jappelli (1997).

With income processes of this general type, the covariances $\text{Cov}_{kt}(y_{-1}, v)$ and $\text{Cov}_{kt}(c_{-1}, v)$ and the covariance $\text{Cov}_{kt}(y_{-1}, u)$ and $\text{Cov}_{kt}(c_{-1}, u)$ would be non-zero. In general, if either permanent or transitory shocks are correlated with past incomes and expenditures then it is clear that $\Delta\text{Var}_{kt}(c) \neq \Delta\text{Cov}_{kt}(c, y)$ and the overidentifying restrictions discussed above will fail to hold. Our assumptions are therefore testable against alternatives of this sort. To evaluate whether it is still possible to use cross-sectional variances and covariances of incomes and expenditures to draw inferences about changes in the variances of the permanent and transitory shocks it is interesting to consider the following separate cases.

Suppose that transitory shocks are uncorrelated with past incomes and consumptions, $\text{Cov}_{kt}(y_{-1}, u) = \text{Cov}_{kt}(c_{-1}, u) = 0$, but allow for correlations with permanent shocks, so that $\text{Cov}_{kt}(y_{-1}, v)$ and $\text{Cov}_{kt}(c_{-1}, v)$ are both non-zero. The simple difference of differences estimator $\Delta\text{Var}_{kt}(c) - \Delta\text{Var}_{kt}(y)$ will no longer serve as an estimate of the change in the variance of transitory shocks. However, writing[16]

$$\Delta\text{Var}_{kt}(c) + \Delta\text{Var}_{kt}(y) - 2\Delta\text{Cov}_{kt}(c, y) = \Delta\text{Var}_{kt}(u) \tag{7.22}$$

it can be seen that knowledge of the covariance term $\Delta\text{Cov}_{kt}(c, y)$ is sufficient to identify the growth in the variance of transitory shocks. Notice, incidentally, that (7.22) can also be written in terms of the growth of the variance of deviations of income and consumption as

$$\Delta\text{Var}_{kt}(y - c) = \Delta\text{Var}_{kt}(u). \tag{7.23}$$

In contrast, suppose that permanent shocks are uncorrelated with past incomes and consumptions, $\text{Cov}_{kt}(y_{-1}, v) = \text{Cov}_{kt}(c_{-1}, v) = 0$, but allow for correlations with transitory shocks, $\text{Cov}_{kt}(y_{-1}, u)$ and $\text{Cov}_{kt}(c_{-1}, u)$ both non-zero. Then $\Delta\text{Var}_{kt}(c)$ still provides an estimate of the variance of permanent shocks but there is no way, in general, to combine this or $\Delta\text{Cov}_{kt}(c, y)$ with $\Delta\text{Var}_{kt}(y)$ to recover the change in the variance of transitory shocks.

7.3.4.3. Idiosyncratic Trends

A further generalization results in the incorporation of idiosyncratic deterministic trends ϕ_i in the income processes[17]

$$y_{it} = y_{it-1} + u_{it} - u_{it-1} + v_{it} + \phi_i. \tag{7.24}$$

Then, for large $T - t$ and small r

$$\Delta\text{Var}_{kt}(y) = \Delta\text{Var}_{kt}(u) + \text{Var}_{kt}(v) + \text{Var}_k(\phi) + 2\text{Cov}_{kt-1}(y, \phi),$$
$$\Delta\text{Var}_{kt}(c) \simeq \text{Var}_{kt}(v).$$

---

[16] See Blundell and Preston (1997) for the derivation.

[17] We could derive this by supposing permanent income to be the sum of a stochastic component y_{it}^p as before and a deterministic component $y_{it}^d = y_{it-1}^d + \phi_i$.

Thus,

$$\Delta \text{Var}_{kt}(y) - \Delta \text{Var}_{kt}(c) \simeq \Delta \text{Var}_{kt}(u) + \text{Var}_k(\phi) + 2\text{Cov}_{kt-1}(y, \phi)$$

and the difference between the growth in income and expenditure variances fails to identify the growth in the transitory variance.

The presence of idiosyncratic deterministic trends would also undermine the testable moment restriction (7.14) on equality of growth in the consumption variance and consumption-income covariance since

$$\Delta \text{Cov}_{kt}(c, y) \simeq \text{Var}_{kt}(v) + 2\text{Cov}_{kt}(c, \phi) \neq \Delta \text{Var}_{kt}(c).$$

Thus, unless such trends are absent the growth in the expenditure variance will not equal the growth in the expenditure-income covariance.[18] Our assumptions are therefore also testable against alternatives of this sort.

7.4. THE GROWTH IN SHORT TERM INCOME RISK

7.4.1. Data

The data used in this study are drawn from the 1968–92 British Family Expenditure Survey (FES) and are described in the Data Appendix. The long time-series of household level data on consumption and income available in Britain and the rapid change in income inequality over this period make it an ideal base for this analysis.

The measure of income used in this chapter is current weekly net income of the household and the measure of expenditure is total current weekly spending by the household on all goods excluding durables but including housing. Expenditure and income of different family types are adjusted onto a comparable basis using equivalence scales which take account of numbers of adults and children in different age ranges, the precise form of the scale being given in the Data Appendix. There are clearly advantages and disadvantages to excluding durables from our measure of consumption. Durable expenditure does not measure consumption of service flows and this discrepancy is likely to vary systematically over the cycle. However, by excluding durables, we are assuming that there is little substitution between durables and non-durables over time and with age. Although our preference is to exclude durable expenditures, given the potential sensitivity of our conclusions to this, we have repeated all our analysis including durable expenditures and briefly comment on specific comparisons when we discuss the results below. In summary, the conclusions we draw at both the cohort and aggregate level are unaffected by the inclusion of durable expenditures.[19]

As argued above we base most of our analysis on date-of-birth cohorts to avoid some of the obvious biases that result from inequality across cohorts. We know,

---

[18] Blundell and Preston (1997) consider other similar processes.
[19] A full set of comparison figures and tables are available from the authors on request.

for instance, from Deaton and Paxson (1994) that one should expect within-cohort inequality to rise with age (see (7.14)) and also that the age composition of our population is changing. The cohorts are defined by 10-year bands for age of birth of head of household. This enables us to calculate measures of inequality in each year for groups of fairly similar age. Sample sizes for each cohort are given in Table 7.5 of the Appendix.

7.4.2. Results

For each cohort we calculate the sample variances and covariances of income and expenditure in each year and the associated variance–covariance matrix of these statistics. Figure 7.1 presents within-cohort paths of the same statistics for the four central cohorts. (These figures can be interpreted as the outcome of non-parametric regressions on a complete set of interacted year and cohort dummies.)

There is a systematic evolution of the within-cohort variances over the whole 25-year period considered. Figure 7.1 shows that within-cohort income and expenditure variances increase with age as predicted. However, there is little evidence of the sort of acceleration in expenditure inequality that would be indicative of increasing within-cohort variance of permanent shocks. Nonetheless, income variance rises faster than expenditure variance in the latter half of the 1980s. According to (7.16) this points to evidence of rising short term uncertainty. These within-cohort results are robust to the inclusion of durable expenditures in our definition of expenditure. Similar results also come through if we use only those who have stayed in education beyond the compulsory school leaving age.

Two sets of estimates were calculated for the changes in the variances of the underlying shocks. First (Table 7.1) we estimate $\Delta \mathrm{Var}_{kt}(u)$ by the difference between the first differences of the sample income and expenditure variances (as suggested by (7.16)) and $\Delta \mathrm{Var}_{kt}(v)$ by the second difference of the sample expenditure variance. A second set of estimates make use also of the information in the sample covariances, imposing the full set of moment restrictions in (7.14), (7.15) and (7.16) by minimum distance estimation (MDE). These imply one over-identifying moment restriction per period and the method provides a χ^2 test of these overidentifying restrictions (which can be interpreted as a test for the specification of the income process). These procedures were repeated using the logarithms of income and expenditure. We concentrate in the body of the paper on the results using logs but report also the results using levels in Table 7.9 of the Appendix.

The estimates in Table 7.2 use the difference of differences result in equation (7.16) of Proposition 3.1 to calculate the growth in the transitory variance $\Delta \mathrm{Var}_{kt}(u)$ from the difference in rates of growth of consumption and income variances and these results are illustrated in Fig. 7.2.[20] For all cohorts there is

---

[20] For clarity, Tables 7.2 and 7.3 present estimates of total changes over three subperiods. Year-by-year changes are presented in Tables 7.7 and 7.8 of the Appendix. Figures 7.2 and 7.3 present year-by-year changes smoothed by taking five year moving averages.

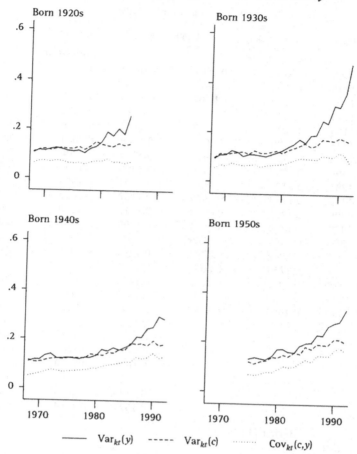

Figure 7.1. *Variances of expenditures and income and their covariance by cohort, 1968–92.*

strong evidence of growth in transitory income variance, particularly in the late 1980s where the 95 per cent confidence bands for these changes lie well above zero. This provides strong support for the evidence from the income panel data study by Moffitt and Gottschalk (1995) based on United States Panel Study of Income Dynamics data. Table 7.3 contains estimates of the growth in the permanent variance $\Delta\mathrm{Var}_{kt}(v)$ based on the acceleration in the expenditure variance and these are illustrated in Figure 7.3. It is clear that none of these changes is significantly different from zero.

7.4.2.1. *Using Covariance Information*
Since the FES contains detailed information on income *and* expenditure for each household we can use covariances to test the robustness of our results.

R. Blundell and I. Preston

Table 7.1. *Variances and covariances*

Year	$\text{Var}_{kt}(c)$	$\text{Var}_{kt}(y)$	$\text{Cov}_{kt}(c, y)$	$\text{Var}_{kt}(c)$	$\text{Var}_{kt}(y)$	$\text{Cov}_{kt}(c, y)$
		Born 1920s			Born 1930s	
1968	0.1064	0.1033	0.0607	0.0960	0.0934	0.0546
1969	0.1145	0.1143	0.0693	0.1126	0.1069	0.0662
1970	0.1188	0.1119	0.0701	0.1109	0.1080	0.0641
1971	0.1143	0.1179	0.0676	0.1127	0.1272	0.0742
1972	0.1199	0.1222	0.0717	0.1164	0.1188	0.0690
1973	0.1231	0.1179	0.0688	0.1209	0.1021	0.0636
1974	0.1196	0.1112	0.0627	0.1116	0.1106	0.0647
1975	0.1194	0.1090	0.0599	0.1266	0.1101	0.0695
1976	0.1285	0.1130	0.0631	0.1191	0.1065	0.0609
1977	0.1156	0.1029	0.0576	0.1167	0.1042	0.0659
1978	0.1299	0.1201	0.0653	0.1217	0.1120	0.0667
1979	0.1479	0.1279	0.0691	0.1259	0.1202	0.0700
1980	0.1385	0.1469	0.0689	0.1192	0.1259	0.0719
1981	0.1324	0.1882	0.0781	0.1293	0.1436	0.0799
1982	0.1282	0.1729	0.0657	0.1345	0.1524	0.0869
1983	0.1420	0.2015	0.0668	0.1444	0.1724	0.0960
1984	0.1349	0.1799	0.0620	0.1578	0.1605	0.0934
1985	0.1392	0.2544	0.0668	0.1445	0.1896	0.0919
1986				0.1521	0.1923	0.0943
1987				0.1737	0.2485	0.1055
1988				0.1725	0.2401	0.1057
1989				0.1695	0.3109	0.1035
1990				0.1811	0.3047	0.1220
1991				0.1725	0.3619	0.1132
1992				0.1621	0.4784	0.0769
		Born 1940s				
1968	0.1093	0.1065	0.0519			
1969	0.1038	0.1145	0.0588			
1970	0.1071	0.1168	0.0632			
1971	0.1147	0.1326	0.0698			
1972	0.1184	0.1374	0.0759			
1973	0.1205	0.1213	0.0696			
1974	0.1181	0.1203	0.0685		Born 1950s	
1975	0.1199	0.1237	0.0704	0.1199	0.1324	0.0686
1976	0.1234	0.1219	0.0714	0.1132	0.1394	0.0682
1977	0.1217	0.1190	0.0735	0.1233	0.1349	0.0729
1978	0.1223	0.1229	0.0756	0.1261	0.1297	0.0800
1979	0.1384	0.1247	0.0794	0.1383	0.1446	0.0808
1980	0.1344	0.1323	0.0810	0.1380	0.1715	0.0922
1981	0.1338	0.1568	0.0883	0.1488	0.1727	0.1028
1982	0.1430	0.1514	0.0940	0.1428	0.1620	0.0999
1983	0.1441	0.1637	0.0971	0.1557	0.1596	0.1033
1984	0.1538	0.1557	0.1016	0.1522	0.1852	0.1134

Table 7.1. *(Continued)*

Year	Var$_{kt}$(c)	Var$_{kt}$(y)	Cov$_{kt}$(c, y)	Var$_{kt}$(c)	Var$_{kt}$(y)	Cov$_{kt}$(c, y)
		Born 1940s			Born 1950s	
1985	0.1544	0.1668	0.1064	0.1824	0.1950	0.1315
1986	0.1823	0.1759	0.1092	0.1737	0.1991	0.1227
1987	0.1787	0.2088	0.1261	0.1938	0.2297	0.1461
1988	0.1824	0.2101	0.1222	0.1916	0.2263	0.1492
1989	0.1734	0.2430	0.1263	0.1883	0.2655	0.1468
1990	0.1947	0.2503	0.1438	0.2139	0.2790	0.1698
1991	0.1767	0.2928	0.1251	0.2120	0.2872	0.1813
1992	0.1801	0.2836	0.1300	0.2004	0.3337	0.1658

This table presents variances of log expenditure and log income per equivalent adult and their covariances within cohorts.

Table 7.2. *Estimates of changes in the variances of transitory shocks to income*

Year	Born 1920s ΔVar$_{kt}$(u)	Born 1930s ΔVar$_{kt}$(u)	Born 1940s ΔVar$_{kt}$(u)	Born 1950s ΔVar$_{kt}$(u)
Estimates based on variances alone				
1969–76	−0.0153 (0.0077)	−0.0070 (0.0075)	−0.0121 (0.0082)	
1976–84	−0.0605 (0.0105)	0.0154 (0.0099)	0.0034 (0.0093)	0.0068 (0.109)
1984–92		0.3135 (0.0623)	0.1015 (0.0201)	0.1002 (0.0273)
Minimum distance estimates				
1969–76	0.0036 (0.0054)	0.0038 (0.0053)	−0.0064 (0.0061)	
1976–84	0.0641 (0.0088)	0.0213 (0.0074)	0.0042 (0.0065)	−0.0021 (0.0082)
1984–92		0.2949 (0.0620)	0.0991 (0.0172)	0.0967 (0.0259)

Estimates based on variances alone are calculated from (7.14) using log expenditure and log income per equivalent adult. Minimum distance estimates are calculated from (7.14), (7.15), and (7.16) using the same data. Associated χ^2 tests are presented in Table 7.4. Full year-by-year estimates are given in the Appendix.

Tables 7.2 and 7.3 also provide estimates using minimum distance estimation applied to the moment conditions (7.14), (7.15) and (7.16).[21] These estimates are also represented in Figs 7.2 and 7.3 where they are presented with confidence bands.[22] The evidence of growing within-cohort variance of transitory shocks and static within-cohort variance of permanent shocks is strengthened, at least for the two younger cohorts, by the use of covariance information. Although we

[21] These are calculated by minimum distance estimation with the asymptotically optimal weights. Conscious of the arguments of Altonji and Segal (1994) for preferring equally weighted minimum distance estimates in small samples, we also recalculated results (available on request) using equal weights but found very little difference in results.

[22] These estimates are also smoothed in the figures by taking five-year moving averages. Confidence bands are adjusted accordingly.

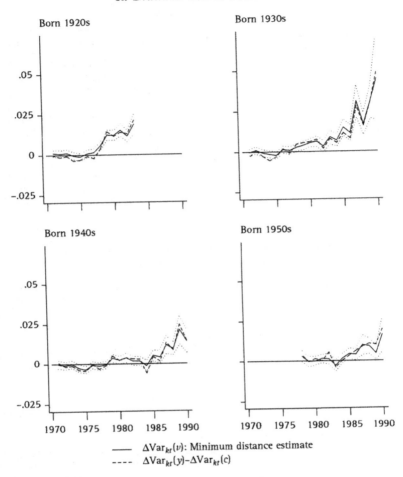

Figure 7.2. *Estimated changes in the variance of transitory income shocks by cohort, 1968–92.*

document an increase in permanent inequality over time for each cohort, there is no evidence of an increase in the variance of the permanent component of income shocks. The growth in permanent inequality within each cohort comes purely from the accumulation of permanent shocks in the consumption growth equation (7.19).

Note that the overidentifying restrictions based on (7.14), (7.15) and (7.16) in the Corollary are acceptable for the younger two cohorts only, in other words exactly those for whom $T - t$ is largest (Table 7.4).[23] In principle, for older cohorts

---

[23] These overidentification tests fail when we include durable expenditures in our expenditure definition, although only marginally for the youngest cohort and the test statistics remain largest for the older cohorts.

Table 7.3. *Estimates of changes in the variances of permanent shocks to income*

Year	Born 1920s $\Delta\mathrm{Var}_{kt}(v)$	Born 1930s $\Delta\mathrm{Var}_{kt}(v)$	Born 1940s $\Delta\mathrm{Var}_{kt}(v)$	Born 1950s $\Delta\mathrm{Var}_{kt}(v)$
Estimates based on variances alone				
1969–76	0.0010 (0.0090)	−0.0241 (0.0093)	0.0090 (0.0103)	
1976–84	−0.0162 (0.0106)	0.0208 (0.0114)	0.0062 (0.0107)	0.0033 (0.0127)
1984–92		−0.0238 (0.0137)	−0.0063 (0.0129)	−0.0080 (0.0133)
Minimum distance estimates				
1969–76	−0.0040 (0.0074)	−0.0215 (0.0074)	0.0000 (0.0083)	
1976–84	−0.0115 (0.0087)	0.0116 (0.0095)	0.0045 (0.0087)	0.0093 (0.0108)
1984–92		−0.0201 (0.0122)	−0.0023 (0.0116)	−0.0208 (0.0123)

Estimates based on variances alone are calculated from (7.16) using log expenditure and log income per equivalent adult. Minimum distance estimates are calculated from (7.14), (7.15) and (7.16) using the same data. Associated χ^2 tests are presented in Table 7.4. Full year-by-year estimates are given in the Appendix.

it would be possible to estimate the permanent and transitory variances by minimum distance by choosing an appropriate value for r and fixing values for $(1/\rho_t)r/(1+r)$ in (7.11) to (7.13).

7.4.2.2. Cross-sectional Correlation between Shocks and Past Incomes

It was shown above that neither the difference in differences nor the MDE estimate of the change in the variance of transitory shocks would be robust to cross-sectional correlation between permanent shocks and past incomes and expenditures. However, an alternative robust estimate using variance and covariance information was proposed in (7.22). This estimate is presented, together with the simpler difference in differences estimate, in Figure 7.4. It is evident that the picture of increasing transitory uncertainty is preserved even if one allows for permanent shocks correlated with past incomes with estimated growth in the transitory variance consistently positive throughout the 1980s using either estimate.

7.4.2.3. The Overall Picture

What is also interesting however is the comparison of the growth in inequality within and across cohorts. This can be gauged from Figure 7.5 which presents the evolution over time of the variances and covariance of logarithms[24] for the whole sample.[25] There is no *a priori* reason why the consumption rule (7.19) itself should

---

[24] It should be noted that the variance of logarithms is not a wholly satisfactory index of inequality since progressive transfers of income or expenditure can cause it to increase. Results using the variance of levels give a similar picture and are available from the authors on request.

[25] This picture is unaffected by the inclusion of durable expenditures.

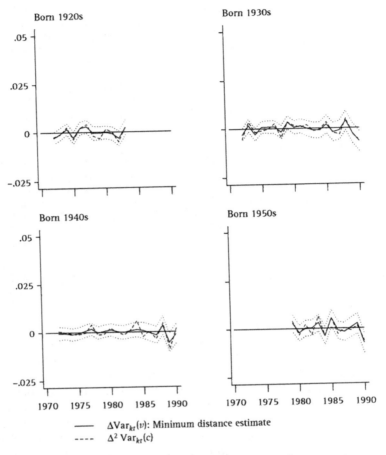

Figure 7.3. *Estimated changes in the variance of permanent income shocks by cohort, 1968–92.*

Table 7.4. *Tests of overidentifying restrictions*

Born 1920s	Born 1930s	Born 1940s	Born 1950s
$\chi^2_{17} = 81.05$	$\chi^2_{24} = 65.38$	$\chi^2_{24} = 34.46$	$\chi^2_{17} = 27.55$
$P = 0.000$	$P = 0.000$	$P = 0.077$	$P = 0.051$

These are χ^2 tests of the overidentifying moment restrictions in (7.14), (7.15), and (7.16) using log expenditure and log income per equivalent adult.

produce such a picture even though for each cohort there is growth of consumption inequality. The growth of consumption inequality in Figure 7.5 reflects one or more of three possible explanations. First it may reflect the aging population. Second it may reflect a higher level of permanent inequality for younger

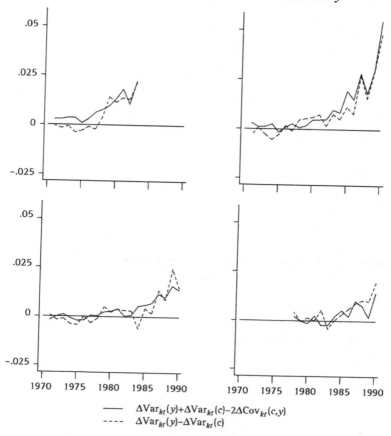

Figure 7.4. *Estimated changes in the variance of transitory income shocks by cohort, 1968–92: robustness to permanent shocks correlated with past incomes.*

cohorts when comparison is made for the same age. Third it may reflect a growth in within-cohort variance of permanent components. The later explanation is ruled out from our discussion of Figure 7.3. The first could explain part of the growth in the overall picture but the second explanation is also supported by the data. To see this, consider Figure 7.5. Figure 7.5 plots the variances against age for all cohorts in one diagram. The results are striking. Inequality in both income and consumption was sharply greater in the late 1980s for all cohorts than it had been for preceding cohorts at a similar age. We can now see that younger cohorts face not only an increase in the variance of transitory components by comparison with older cohorts when they were at a similar age but that this is also true for permanent income inequality. As the variance of permanent shocks does not appear

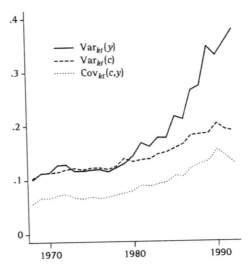

Figure 7.5. *Variances of expenditure and income and their covariance for the whole sample, 1968–92.*

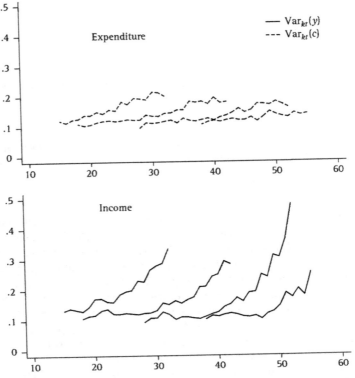

Figure 7.6. *Variances of expenditures and income for each cohort by age, 1968–92.*

to have risen for any cohort the implication is that this difference reflects an increase in initial permanent income inequality for younger cohorts. The explanation for a growth in overall consumption inequality can therefore be attributed in part to an aging population and in part to new cohorts facing higher levels of initial income inequality.

7.5. CONCLUSIONS

This chapter has shown how a comparison of the growth paths of income and consumption inequality can together be used to document the growth in short-term income risk. We derive conditions under which the growth of variances and covariances of income and consumption can be used to separately identify the growth in the variance of permanent and transitory income shocks. This sheds new light on the debate concerning the use of consumption versus income in assessing the evolution of inequality.

Comparisons within cohorts are shown to carry more reliable welfare implications than comparisons across cohorts at any point in time. Increasing short-term risk will inflict a welfare cost on risk averse households and we derive the set of preferences under which the level of precautionary saving can be used as a money metric measure of the individual welfare loss from income risk.

We use a sample of households from the United Kingdom Family Expenditure Survey over the period 1968–92. Over this period, both income and consumption inequality are shown to have risen for all cohorts. However, there is striking evidence that income inequality has risen faster than consumption inequality in recent years especially for younger cohorts. By plotting the difference of differences between consumption and income inequality across this period we are able to measure the precise path of growth in short-term income risk over this period. The paths of consumption–income covariances within cohorts provide corroborative evidence of growing short-term uncertainty.

Appendix

The data used here are from the 1968–92 United Kingdom Family Expenditure Survey (FES). The FES is an annual survey conducted with the principal purpose of determining the basket of goods used to construct the Retail Price Index. In a typical year the FES contains information on around 7000 households. In general, the households form a representative sample, but excluded are those not living in private houses, such as residents of residential homes.

The measure of income used in this chapter is current weekly net income of the household and consists of earnings from main and subsidiary jobs (net of tax and national insurance contributions), net profits from self-employment, all social security benefits received, allowances from non-members of the household, benefits from friendly societies and children's incomes.

Households participating in the FES are asked to complete a diary detailing all their spending.[26] In this chapter, expenditure is defined as total current weekly spending by the household on all goods excluding durables but including housing.[27]

Expenditure and income of different family types are adjusted onto a comparable basis, using the equivalence scales based on McClements (1977), and favoured by the United Kingdom Department of Social Security, and expressed in 1992 pounds for a childless couple. These equivalence scales depend on number of adults and numbers of children in various age ranges.[28] We remove the households with the highest and lowest 2 per cent of incomes and expenditures in each year so as to enhance robustness of the results.

We split the samples into cohorts defined by 10-year bands for age of birth of head of household. Table 7.5 shows a cross-tabulation of the numbers of households in each annual FES with the head of household's date of birth falling into particular ranges. We drop from the analysis any such cohort in any year in which it could include households with head aged over the statutory retirement age of 65 or in which the sample size falls below 300. This leads us to concentrate on the four central cohorts with head born between 1920 and 1960. Sample sizes and summary statistics for income and expenditure by year for households belonging to these cohorts are given in Table 7.6.

Sensitivity of results to the use of levels rather than logarithms is shown in Table 7.7. It is clear that the restrictions implied by the theory are more acceptable when using logs though the main conclusions about rising transitory variances remain evident when using levels. Sensitivity to choice of equivalence scales was investigated and results found to be qualitatively similar with alternative scales (Tables 7.8 and 7.9).[29]

Proof of Propositions

Proof *of Proposition 1*

(i) If $b_i = b_j$ then $p_i = p_j$. The result then follows trivially.

(ii) If $b_i \neq b_j$ then it may be that $p_i \neq p_j$. Hence $c_t(U, p)$ cannot depend on p, i.e. $c_t(U, p) = f_t(U)$. If $e(U, p)$ is the expenditure function then Shephard's lemma requires

$$\frac{\partial e(U, \mathbf{p})}{\partial p_t} = f_t(U) \quad \Leftrightarrow \quad e(U, \mathbf{p}) = \sum_t p_t f_t(U) + \varphi(U) \qquad (7.25)$$

---

[26] All of what has been said so far assumes that income and expenditure are accurately recorded in the data. We would not wish to ignore the consideration that expenditure may often be better measured, particularly for groups such as the self-employed. On the other hand, infrequency of purchase may well be important given that diary records are kept over a two week period (see Kay et al., 1984).

[27] For a detailed consideration of the issues involved in treatment of housing costs, see Johnson and Webb (1991).

[28] Specifically, the scale assigns a first adult 0.55 times the cost for a couple, second and third adults 0.45 and subsequent adults 0.40. Children have a cost of 0.07 times that of a couple if aged 2 or under, 0.18 if aged 3 or 4, 0.22 if aged 5 to 10, 0.27 if aged 11 to 16 and 0.38 if aged 17 or 18.

[29] For details see Blundell and Preston (1997).

Table 7.5. *Cohort sample sizes*

Year	Born 1920s	Born 1930s	Born 1940s	Born 1950s
1968	1227	1079	653	2
1969	1156	1066	734	8
1970	1020	966	805	26
1971	1155	1040	980	82
1972	1160	1025	1073	142
1973	1154	949	1076	214
1974	995	920	1033	266
1975	1080	1016	1154	407
1976	1091	1006	1105	558
1977	1055	987	1170	631
1978	1107	930	1148	717
1979	979	914	1108	832
1980	1011	954	1167	852
1981	1090	1003	1253	987
1982	1107	988	1226	1084
1983	993	941	1105	1043
1984	1091	926	1098	1081
1985	1009	923	1124	1068
1986	**1001**	891	1091	1116
1987	**1118**	855	1092	1192
1988	**1003**	880	1085	1105
1989	**1083**	882	1050	1089
1990	**998**	819	987	1065
1991	**973**	851	936	1078
1992	**1066**	852	1061	1129

Numbers in bold represent cohorts where some members may be over 65 or sample size is below 300. These cells are not used in the analysis.

and $\varphi(U) = 0$ by homogeneity. If $U = \min_t u_t(c_t)$ then

$$e(U, \mathbf{p}) = \min_c \left[\sum_t p_t c_t \mid \min_t u_t(c_t) \geq U \right] = \sum_t p_t f_t(U) \text{ where } u_t(f_t(U))$$
$$\equiv U$$

as required. Note also that (7.25) implies that the distance function $d(U, \mathbf{c})$ (see Deaton and Muellbauer, 1980, p. 53) takes the form

$$d(U, \mathbf{c}) = \min_{\mathbf{p}} \left[\sum_t p_t c_t \mid \sum_t p_t f_t(U) = 1 \right] = \min_r \frac{c_t}{f_t(U)}$$
$$\Rightarrow U = \min_t u_t(c_t).$$

Hence both necessity and sufficiency are established.

Table 7.6. *Summary statistics*

Year	Expenditure		Income		Sample size
	Mean	Std Dev	Mean	Std Dev	
1968	136.33	47.38	161.76	52.48	2961
1969	142.67	51.13	162.93	55.36	2964
1970	145.94	53.71	167.83	58.50	2817
1971	146.19	53.07	168.65	61.47	3257
1972	153.80	57.45	179.45	64.79	3400
1973	161.50	60.96	186.66	64.28	3393
1974	165.04	61.77	185.97	63.68	3214
1975	160.78	60.11	182.80	62.94	3657
1976	157.02	59.05	177.14	61.18	3760
1977	155.40	57.63	174.24	58.86	3843
1978	162.55	61.89	189.36	65.80	3902
1979	171.97	68.41	195.50	69.28	3833
1980	167.59	65.61	195.47	72.94	3984
1981	168.12	67.55	189.82	75.81	4333
1982	163.05	64.78	183.33	73.06	4405
1983	171.17	71.03	185.34	76.71	4082
1984	173.14	72.55	186.43	76.49	4196
1985	176.81	76.39	192.31	84.90	4124
1986	184.56	82.91	197.02	90.18	4099
1987	188.46	88.78	206.23	104.71	4257
1988	191.43	88.94	212.08	107.86	4073
1989	195.12	90.76	211.35	111.18	4104
1990	198.75	98.51	214.40	121.29	3869
1991	200.06	94.36	212.00	120.02	3838
1992	200.91	93.97	208.74	118.18	4108
Total	170.99	74.73	190.27	84.47	94473

This table presents summary statistics for levels of expenditure and income per equivalent adult.

(iii) Since it is possible that $s \neq t$ then $c_t(U, \mathbf{p})$ cannot depend on t i.e., it must be that $c_t(U, \mathbf{p}) = f(U, \mathbf{p})$. By quasiconcavity of preferences this can be so only if $f(U, \mathbf{p}) = f(U)$. It is obvious that the same condition would ensure welfare comparisons across cohorts. Then similar reasoning establishes $U = \min_t u(c_t)$ as the corresponding direct representation for preferences.

Proof of Proposition 2
Define $\hat{c}_{it}$ by $u_t(\hat{c}_{it}) \equiv E u_t(c_{it})$. Then

$$\sum_{t=0} u_t(\tilde{c}_{it}) = u_t(c_{i0}) + \sum_{t=1} u_t(\hat{c}_{it}). \tag{7.26}$$

Table 7.7. Estimates of changes in the variances of transitory and permanent shocks to income based on log expenditure and log income variances alone

Year	Born 1920s $\Delta \mathrm{Var}_{kt}(u)$	Born 1920s $\Delta \mathrm{Var}_{kt}(u)$	Born 1930s $\Delta \mathrm{Var}_{kt}(u)$	Born 1930s $\Delta \mathrm{Var}_{kt}(u)$	Born 1940s $\Delta \mathrm{Var}_{kt}(u)$	Born 1940s $\Delta \mathrm{Var}_{kt}(v)$	Born 1950s $\Delta \mathrm{Var}_{kt}(u)$	Born 1950s $\Delta \mathrm{Var}_{kt}(u)$
1969	0.0028 (0.0068)		−0.0031 (0.0069)		0.0135 (0.0090)			
1970	−0.0067 (0.0074)	−0.0039 (0.0107)	0.0028 (0.0077)	−0.0183 (0.0114)	−0.0010 (0.0086)	0.0088 (0.0126)		
1971	0.0106 (0.0075)	−0.0088 (0.0114)	0.0174 (0.0079)	0.0035 (0.0123)	0.0082 (0.0087)	0.0043 (0.0120)		
1972	−0.0013 (0.0075)	0.0101 (0.0108)	−0.0121 (0.0080)	0.0020 (0.0116)	0.0012 (0.0083)	−0.0040 (0.0121)		
1973	−0.0075 (0.0080)	−0.0023 (0.0113)	−0.0212 (0.0082)	0.0006 (0.0122)	−0.0183 (0.0079)	−0.0015 (0.0116)		
1974	−0.0032 (0.0080)	−0.0067 (0.0118)	0.0178 (0.0086)	−0.0137 (0.0129)	0.0015 (0.0079)	−0.0046 (0.0117)		
1975	−0.0020 (0.0077)	0.0033 (0.0118)	−0.0155 (0.0084)	0.0243 (0.0130)	0.0016 (0.0078)	0.0042 (0.0118)		
1976	−0.0052 (0.0078)	0.0094 (0.0115)	0.0039 (0.0078)	−0.0225 (0.0126)	−0.0053 (0.0077)	0.0017 (0.0117)	0.0138 (0.0124)	
1977	0.0028 (0.0079)	−0.0220 (0.0119)	0.0001 (0.0076)	0.0050 (0.0119)	−0.0012 (0.0074)	−0.0052 (0.0120)	−0.0146 (0.0106)	0.0170 (0.0159)
1978	0.0030 (0.0079)	0.0271 (0.0117)	0.0029 (0.0083)	0.0074 (0.0121)	0.0033 (0.0071)	0.0024 (0.0116)	−0.0080 (0.0097)	−0.0074 (0.0152)
1979	−0.0103 (0.0092)	0.0038 (0.0128)	0.0039 (0.0089)	−0.0007 (0.0131)	−0.0143 (0.0080)	0.0155 (0.0120)	0.0027 (0.0096)	0.0094 (0.0144)
1980	0.0284 (0.0102)	−0.0274 (0.0143)	0.0124 (0.0089)	−0.0109 (0.0132)	0.0115 (0.0086)	−0.0201 (0.0130)	0.0272 (0.0106)	−0.0125 (0.0150)
1981	0.0475 (0.0109)	0.0032 (0.0139)	0.0076 (0.0095)	0.0167 (0.0130)	0.0251 (0.0087)	0.0034 (0.0131)	−0.0096 (0.0108)	0.0111 (0.0151)
1982	−0.0111 (0.0108)	0.0019 (0.0130)	0.0036 (0.0101)	−0.0049 (0.0133)	−0.0146 (0.0088)	0.0098 (0.0125)	−0.0047 (0.0099)	−0.0168 (0.0146)
1983	0.0147 (0.0123)	0.0181 (0.0129)	0.0101 (0.0112)	0.0047 (0.0138)	0.0112 (0.0096)	−0.0081 (0.0128)	−0.0153 (0.0095)	0.0189 (0.0136)
1984	−0.0145 (0.0132)	−0.0210 (0.0140)	−0.0253 (0.0120)	0.0035 (0.0149)	−0.0177 (0.0104)	0.0086 (0.0137)	0.0292 (0.0106)	−0.0165 (0.0142)
1985	0.0702 (0.0165)	0.0114 (0.0142)	0.0423 (0.0141)	−0.0266 (0.0158)	0.0105 (0.0107)	−0.0091 (0.0145)	−0.0204 (0.0116)	0.0337 (0.0145)
1986			−0.0049 (0.0150)	0.0208 (0.0157)	−0.0188 (0.0114)	0.0273 (0.0153)	0.0127 (0.0118)	−0.0389 (0.0157)
1987			0.0346 (0.0164)	0.0140 (0.0172)	0.0365 (0.0123)	−0.0316 (0.0168)	0.0105 (0.0120)	0.0288 (0.0161)
1988			−0.0073 (0.0179)	−0.0227 (0.0189)	−0.0024 (0.0133)	0.0074 (0.0170)	−0.0012 (0.0122)	−0.0224 (0.0167)
1989			0.0739 (0.0301)	−0.0019 (0.0183)	0.0419 (0.0195)	−0.0128 (0.0170)	0.0425 (0.0178)	−0.0010 (0.0168)
1990			−0.0177 (0.0315)	0.0146 (0.0185)	−0.0140 (0.0203)	0.0303 (0.0170)	−0.0121 (0.0198)	0.0289 (0.0175)
1991			0.0657 (0.0287)	−0.0201 (0.0202)	0.0605 (0.0251)	−0.0393 (0.0185)	0.0101 (0.0168)	−0.0275 (0.0188)
1992			0.1269 (0.0663)	−0.0019 (0.0189)	−0.0126 (0.0293)	0.0214 (0.0176)	0.0581 (0.0287)	−0.0096 (0.0186)

Estimates are calculated from (7.14) and (7.16) using log expenditure and log income per equivalent adult.

Table 7.8. *Minimum distance estimates of changes in the variances of transitory and permanent shocks to income using logs*

Year	Born 1920s		Born 1930s		Born 1940s		Born 1950s	
	$\Delta\mathrm{Var}_{kt}(u)$	$\Delta\mathrm{Var}_{kt}(v)$	$\Delta\mathrm{Var}_{kt}(u)$	$\Delta\mathrm{Var}_{kt}(v)$	$\Delta\mathrm{Var}_{kt}(u)$	$\Delta\mathrm{Var}_{kt}(v)$	$\Delta\mathrm{Var}_{kt}(u)$	$\Delta\mathrm{Var}_{kt}(v)$
1969	0.0012 (0.0048)		0.0007 (0.0050)	−0.0156 (0.0089)	0.0037 (0.0068)	0.0027 (0.0107)		
1970		−0.0068 (0.0089)	0.0034 (0.0054)	0.0086 (0.0096)	−0.0031 (0.0063)	0.0028 (0.0101)		
1971	0.0094 (0.0054)	−0.0063 (0.0095)	0.0085 (0.0058)	−0.0084 (0.0096)	0.0099 (0.0064)	−0.0028 (0.0101)		
1972	−0.0003 (0.0056)	0.0096 (0.0091)	−0.0029 (0.0060)	−0.0014 (0.0097)	−0.0008 (0.0064)	−0.0065 (0.0100)		
1973	−0.0020 (0.0057)	−0.0060 (0.0093)	−0.0116 (0.0057)	0.0020 (0.0096)	−0.0114 (0.0059)	0.0006 (0.0095)		
1974	−0.0009 (0.0058)	−0.0045 (0.0097)	0.0075 (0.0056)	0.0083 (0.0098)	0.0003 (0.0059)	0.0034 (0.0095)		
1975	0.0000 (0.0057)	0.0035 (0.0099)	−0.0048 (0.0054)	−0.0149 (0.0099)	0.0015 (0.0057)	−0.0003 (0.0094)	0.0074 (0.0089)	0.0101 (0.0137)
1976	0.0004 (0.0056)	0.0065 (0.0096)	0.0038 (0.0052)	0.0103 (0.0094)	−0.0029 (0.0056)	−0.0005 (0.0093)	−0.0093 (0.0079)	−0.0011 (0.0129)
1977	−0.0038 (0.0054)	−0.0128 (0.0094)	−0.0065 (0.0050)	−0.0006 (0.0094)	−0.0048 (0.0053)	0.0004 (0.0093)	−0.0124 (0.0070)	−0.0014 (0.0127)
1978	0.0083 (0.0055)	0.0183 (0.0092)	0.0069 (0.0053)	0.0018 (0.0102)	0.0023 (0.0052)	0.0056 (0.0097)	0.0138 (0.0072)	0.0035 (0.0127)
1979	0.0022 (0.0063)	−0.0008 (0.0103)	0.0046 (0.0061)	−0.0053 (0.0108)	−0.0026 (0.0056)	−0.0069 (0.0102)	0.0158 (0.0078)	0.0028 (0.0128)
1980	0.0217 (0.0070)	−0.0134 (0.0115)	0.0043 (0.0062)	0.0104 (0.0111)	0.0058 (0.0057)	0.0045 (0.0103)	−0.0092 (0.0075)	−0.0146 (0.0123)
1981	0.0332 (0.0086)	0.0066 (0.0114)	0.0096 (0.0068)	−0.0027 (0.0112)	0.0170 (0.0061)	0.0022 (0.0106)	−0.0077 (0.0070)	0.0102 (0.0115)
1982	−0.0054 (0.0094)	−0.0112 (0.0111)	0.0015 (0.0073)	0.0029 (0.0118)	−0.0108 (0.0064)	−0.0046 (0.0108)	−0.0052 (0.0068)	−0.0002 (0.0118)
1983	0.0251 (0.0108)	0.0153 (0.0108)	0.0117 (0.0090)	−0.0053 (0.0130)	0.0095 (0.0075)	0.0038 (0.0115)	0.0121 (0.0074)	0.0163 (0.0127)
1984	−0.0172 (0.0118)	−0.0135 (0.0116)	−0.0109 (0.0098)	−0.0099 (0.0134)	−0.0124 (0.0079)	−0.0024 (0.0119)	−0.0052 (0.0086)	−0.0311 (0.0136)
1985	0.0586 (0.0161)	0.0147 (0.0118)	0.0316 (0.0117)	0.0106 (0.0135)	0.0055 (0.0074)	0.0070 (0.0123)	0.0135 (0.0087)	0.0313 (0.0141)
1986			−0.0004 (0.0126)	0.0122 (0.0148)	0.0016 (0.0087)	−0.0004 (0.0138)	0.0065 (0.0090)	−0.0217 (0.0151)
1987			0.0419 (0.0141)	−0.0171 (0.0165)	0.0213 (0.0097)	−0.0104 (0.0146)	−0.0073 (0.0093)	−0.0036 (0.0155)
1988			−0.0056 (0.0155)	−0.0006 (0.0163)	0.0048 (0.0103)	−0.0025 (0.0153)	0.0414 (0.0156)	0.0271 (0.0161)
1989			0.0852 (0.0255)	0.0147 (0.0166)	0.0263 (0.0151)	0.0224 (0.0159)	−0.0091 (0.0175)	−0.0204 (0.0175)
1990			−0.0383 (0.0273)	−0.0220 (0.0181)	−0.0074 (0.0154)	−0.0379 (0.0172)	−0.0081 (0.0137)	−0.0187 (0.0178)
1991			0.0668 (0.0271)	−0.0080 (0.0172)	0.0614 (0.0224)	0.0219 (0.0167)	0.0650 (0.0269)	
1992			0.1136 (0.0659)		−0.0144 (0.0266)			
	$\chi^2_{17} = 81.05$ $P = 0.000$		$\chi^2_{24} = 65.38$ $P = 0.000$		$\chi^2_{24} = 34.46$ $P = 0.077$		$\chi^2_{17} = 27.55$ $P = 0.051$	

Estimates are calculated from (7.14), (7.15), and (7.16) using log expenditure and log income per equivalent adult. Associated χ^2 tests are presented below.

Table 7.9. *Minimum distance estimates of changes in the variances of transitory and permanent shocks to income using levels*

Year	Born 1920s $\Delta\mathrm{Var}_{kt}(u)$	$\Delta\mathrm{Var}_{kt}(v)$	Born 1930s $\Delta\mathrm{Var}_{kt}(u)$	$\Delta\mathrm{Var}_{kt}(v)$	Born 1940s $\Delta\mathrm{Var}_{kt}(u)$	$\Delta\mathrm{Var}_{kt}(v)$	Born 1950s $\Delta\mathrm{Var}_{kt}(u)$	$\Delta\mathrm{Var}_{kt}(v)$
1969	0.0018 (0.0159)		−0.0016 [0.0176]		0.0104 (0.0247)			
1970	0.0240 [0.0199]	0.0063 (0.0238)	0.0157 [0.0201]	−0.0227 (0.0245)	−0.0050 [0.0247]	0.0147 (0.0283)		
1971	0.0301 [0.0221]	−0.0441 (0.0280)	0.0197 [0.0224]	−0.0015 (0.0293)	0.0275 [0.0251]	−0.0031 (0.0292)		
1972	−0.0094 [0.0218]	0.0618 (0.0270)	0.0121 [0.0235]	−0.0018 (0.0288)	0.0404 [0.0255]	0.0074 (0.0305)		
1973	0.0215 [0.0240]	−0.0351 (0.0298)	−0.0264 [0.0233]	−0.0183 (0.0302)	−0.0339 [0.0259]	−0.0144 (0.0311)		
1974	−0.0215 [0.0248]	−0.0080 (0.0342)	0.0275 [0.0245]	0.0112 (0.0308)	−0.0191 [0.0255]	−0.0308 (0.0326)		
1975	−0.0043 [0.0231]	−0.0316 (0.0372)	−0.0349 [0.0231]	0.0163 (0.0326)	0.0025 [0.0247]	0.0180 (0.0327)		
1976	−0.0117 [0.0212]	0.0321 (0.0329)	0.0151 [0.0201]	−0.0606 (0.0331)	−0.0150 [0.0234]	−0.0152 (0.0321)	−0.0131 (0.0342)	
1977	−0.0147 [0.0191]	−0.0338 (0.0308)	−0.0337 [0.0190]	0.0453 (0.0301)	−0.0412 [0.0203]	0.0249 (0.0306)	−0.0254 (0.0270)	0.0319 (0.0415)
1978	0.0579 [0.0214]	0.0868 (0.0286)	0.0546 [0.0222]	0.0251 (0.0288)	0.0653 [0.0230]	0.0064 (0.0316)	0.0138 (0.0272)	0.0152 (0.0402)
1979	0.0217 [0.0267]	−0.0203 (0.0357)	0.0245 [0.0270]	0.0052 (0.0342)	−0.0145 [0.0264]	0.0062 (0.0350)	0.0311 (0.0301)	0.0164 (0.0426)
1980	0.0643 [0.0297]	−0.0473 (0.0421)	0.0218 [0.0282]	−0.0314 (0.0398)	0.0341 [0.0277]	−0.0094 (0.0382)	0.0763 (0.0339)	−0.0392 (0.0476)
1981	0.0364 [0.0315]	0.0360 (0.0422)	0.0282 [0.0301]	0.0185 (0.0417)	−0.0089 [0.0270]	−0.0076 (0.0400)	−0.0288 (0.0351)	0.0531 (0.0477)
1982	−0.0210 [0.0324]	−0.0896 (0.0418)	−0.0154 [0.0298]	−0.0250 (0.0416)	0.0101 [0.0257]	0.0094 (0.0411)	−0.0434 (0.0314)	−0.1106 (0.0477)
1983	0.0269 [0.0330]	0.1164 (0.0398)	0.0213 [0.0313]	0.0853 (0.0424)	0.0063 [0.0294]	0.0013 (0.0413)	−0.0241 (0.0291)	0.0937 (0.0441)
1984	−0.0554 [0.0317]	−0.0805 (0.0467)	0.0070 [0.0351]	−0.0951 (0.0523)	−0.0465 [0.0289]	−0.0043 (0.0452)	0.0338 (0.0297)	−0.0134 (0.0482)
1985	0.0626 [0.0344]	0.0517 (0.0484)	0.0927 [0.0407]	0.0266 (0.0545)	0.0717 [0.0312]	0.0575 (0.0487)	0.0282 (0.0335)	0.0523 (0.0523)
1986			0.0466 [0.0501]	0.0287 (0.0588)	0.0478 [0.0410]	−0.0092 (0.0562)	0.1052 (0.0415)	−0.0649 (0.0601)
1987			0.1732 [0.0642]	0.0311 (0.0738)	0.1436 [0.0547]	0.0688 (0.0705)	0.0902 (0.0513)	0.1848 (0.0724)
1988			0.0967 [0.0733]	−0.0270 (0.0859)	−0.0101 [0.0580]	−0.1371 (0.0819)	0.0323 (0.0581)	−0.1896 (0.0864)
1989			−0.0001 [0.0730]	−0.0866 (0.0848)	0.0500 [0.0552]	0.0589 (0.0848)	0.0672 (0.0624)	−0.0093 (0.0877)
1990			0.0922 [0.0840]	0.1457 (0.0906)	0.1956 [0.0709]	0.1370 (0.0960)	0.0207 (0.0677)	0.2001 (0.0935)
1991			0.0079 [0.0897]	−0.1526 (0.1093)	0.0475 [0.0823]	−0.3522 (0.1098)	0.0178 (0.0726)	−0.1875 (0.1120)
1992			0.0272 [0.0837]	−0.0309 (0.1003)	0.0287 [0.0794]	0.1975 (0.1000)	0.0149 (0.0703)	−0.0862 (0.1134)
	$\chi^2_{17} = 158.5$ $P=0.000$		$\chi^2_{24} = 212.9$ $P=0.000$		$\chi^2_{24} = 105.4$ $P=0.000$		$\chi^2_{17} = 31.95$ $P=0.015$	

Estimates are calculated from (7.14), (7.15), and (7.16) using levels of expenditure and income per equivalent adult. Associated χ^2 tests are presented below.

Note that

$$\frac{u_0'(\tilde{c}_{i0})}{u_t'(\tilde{c}_{it})} = \frac{u_0'(c_{i0})}{Eu_t'(c_{it})} = p_{it}. \tag{7.27}$$

Since $U(\cdot, \cdot)$ is quasiconcave and noting (7.26), $c_{i0} = \tilde{c}_{i0}$, if and only if

$$\frac{u_0'(c_{i0})}{u_t'(\tilde{c}_{it})} = p_{it}$$

for all t which is true given (7.27) if and only if $u_t'(\hat{c}_{it}) = Eu_t'(c_{it})$.
To see that CARA is sufficient for this, note that, given CARA,

$$u_t'(\hat{c}_{it}) = -\beta_t u_t(\hat{c}_{it}) = -\beta_t Eu_t(c_{it}) = Eu_t'(c_{it}).$$

To establish necessity, consider the case where risk is small. A Taylor expansion around $c_{it} = \hat{c}_{it}$ yields

$$Eu_t'(c_{it}) \simeq u_t'(\hat{c}_{it}) + E(c_{it} - \hat{c}_{it})\, u_t''(\hat{c}_{it}) + \frac{1}{2}E(c_{it} - \hat{c}_{it})^2\, u_t'''(\hat{c}_{it}). \tag{7.28}$$

Similarly, by another Taylor expansion,

$$Eu_t(c_{it}) \simeq u_t(\hat{c}_{it}) + E(c_{it} - \hat{c}_{it})\, u_t'(\hat{c}_{it}) + \frac{1}{2}E(c_{it} - \hat{c}_{it})^2\, u_t''(\hat{c}_{it}).$$

$$\Rightarrow \frac{E(c_{it} - \hat{c}_{it})}{E(c_{it} - \hat{c}_{it})^2} \simeq -\frac{1}{2}\frac{u_t''(\hat{c}_{it})}{u_t'(\hat{c}_{it})}$$

Substituting into (7.28) gives

$$Eu_t'(c_{it}) \simeq u_t'(\hat{c}_{it}) + \frac{1}{2}E(c_{it} - \hat{c}_{it})^2 \left[u_t'''(\hat{c}_{it}) - \frac{u_t''(\hat{c}_{it})^2}{u_t'(\hat{c}_{it})} \right]$$

Hence $u_t'(\hat{c}_{it}) = Eu_t'(c_{it})$ for small enough risks only if

$$\frac{u_t'''(\hat{c}_{it})}{u_t''(\hat{c}_{it})} = \frac{u_t''(\hat{c}_{it})}{u_t'(\hat{c}_{it})}$$

which holds for all $\hat{c}_{it}$ iff

$$u_t(c_{it}) = A\,\exp(Bc_{it}) + C$$

for some constants A, B, and C. Without affecting behaviour we can set $C=0$ and the requirement that $U(\cdot, \cdot)$ be increasing and quasiconcave ensures $A < 0$, $B < 0$.

Proof of (7.18) and (7.19)
Let L_{it} denote the value of current financial wealth plus the present value of future earnings at period t and let $\xi_{it} = L_{it} - E_{t-1}L_{it}$ denote the innovation to L_{it}. Let

preferences be Constant Relative Risk Aversion (CRRA) with γ denoting the Arrow-Pratt measure of CRRA (see Skinner, 1988, p. 241) and let the constant interest rate r equal the consumer's subjective discount rate.

Suppose that optimal consumption c_{it} is approximately proportional to L_{it}

$$c_{it} \simeq \phi_{it} L_{it}$$

for some ϕ_{it} which could depend on uncertain current and future moments of the income process. We know that this is trivially true for $t = T$ since $c_{iT} = L_{iT}$.

By the Euler equation and intertemporal budget constraint

$$c_{it-1}^{-\gamma} \simeq E_{t-1}(\phi_{it} L_{it})^{-\gamma}$$
$$= E_{t-1}(\phi_{it}\{(L_{it-1} - c_{it-1})(1+r) + \xi_{it}\})^{-\gamma}.$$

Taking a Taylor expansion around $\phi_{it} = E_{t-1}\phi_{it} \equiv \bar{\phi}_{it}$ and $\xi_{it} = 0$ i.e., $L_{it} = E_{t-1}L_{it} = (L_{it-1} - c_{it-1})(1+r) \equiv \bar{L}_{it}$ and assuming ϕ_{it} and ξ_{it} to be independent

$$c_{it-1}^{-\gamma} \simeq (\bar{\phi}_{it}\bar{L}_{it})^{-\gamma}\left[1 + \frac{\gamma(\gamma+1)}{2}\left\{\frac{\text{Var}(\xi_{it})}{\bar{L}_{it}^2} + \frac{\text{Var}(\phi_{it})}{\bar{\phi}_{it}^2}\right\}\right]$$
$$\equiv (\bar{\phi}_{it}\bar{L}_{it})^{-\gamma}[1 + K_{it}].$$

Substituting from the budget constraint

$$c_{it-1} \simeq \bar{\phi}_{it}(L_{it-1} - c_{it-1})(1+r)(1 + K_{it})^{-1/\gamma}$$

and thus

$$c_{it-1} \simeq \frac{\bar{\phi}_{it}(1+r)(1 + K_{it})^{-1/\gamma}}{1 + \bar{\phi}_{it}(1+r)(1 + K_{it})^{-1/\gamma}} L_{it-1}$$
$$\equiv \phi_{it-1} L_{it-1}.$$

Hence the supposed approximate proportionality of consumption is established by induction. Furthermore,

$$\frac{c_{it}}{c_{it-1}} \simeq \frac{\phi_{it}}{\bar{\phi}_{it}} \frac{L_{it}}{\bar{L}_{it}} (1 + K_{it})^{1/\gamma}$$

and thus

$$\Delta \ln c_{it} \simeq \frac{1}{\gamma} \ln(1 + K_{it}) + \ln\left(\frac{\phi_{it}}{\bar{\phi}_{it}}\right) + \ln\left(\frac{L_{it}}{E_{t-1}L_{it}}\right)$$
$$\equiv G_{kt} + z_{kt} + \ln\left(\frac{L_{it}}{E_{t-1}L_{it}}\right).$$

By a series of further approximations

$$
\ln\left(\frac{L_{it}}{E_{t-1}L_{it}}\right) \simeq \frac{L_{it} - E_{t-1}L_{it}}{E_{t-1}L_{it}}
$$

$$
\simeq \frac{1}{E_{t-1}L_{it}} \sum_{k=0}^{T-t} (1+r)^{-k}(E_t - E_{t-1})y_{it+k}
$$

$$
\simeq \frac{1}{E_{t-1}L_{it}} \sum_{k=0}^{T-t} (1+r)^{-k}E_{t-1}y_{it+k}(E_t - E_{t-1}) \ln y_{it+k}
$$

$$
\simeq v_{it} + \frac{r}{\rho_t(1+r)} u_{it}
$$

if

$$
\frac{1}{E_{t-1}L_{it}} \sum_{k=0}^{T-t}(1+r)^{-k}E_{t-1}y_{it+k} \simeq 1.
$$

REFERENCES

Altonji, Joseph G. and Lew M. Segal (1994). Small sample bias in GMM estimation of covariance structures, *Journal of Business and Economic Statistics*, XIV, 353–66.

Attanasio, Orazio P. and Steven J. Davis (1996). Relative wage movements and the distribution of consumption, *Journal of Political Economy*, CIV, 1227–62.

—— —— and Tullio Jappelli (1997). The life-cycle hypothesis and consumption inequality, *Institute for Fiscal Studies working paper*, Institute for Fiscal Studies.

—— —— and Guglielmo Weber (1989). Intertemporal substitution, risk aversion and the Euler equation for consumption, *Economic Journal*, IC, 59–73.

Blackorby, Charles, David Donaldson, and David Moloney (1984). Consumer's surplus and welfare change in a simple dynamic model, *Review of Economic Studies*, LI, 171–6.

Blundell, Richard and Ian Preston (1997). Consumption inequality and income uncertainty, *Institute for Fiscal Studies working paper* W97/15, Institute for Fiscal Studies.

Browning, Martin J., Angus S. Deaton, and Margaret J. Irish (1985). A profitable approach to labor supply and commodity demands over the life-cycle, *Econometrica*, LIII, 503–43.

Buchinsky, Moshe and Jennifer Hunt (1996). Wage mobility in the United States, *National Bureau of Economic Research working paper* 5455, National Bureau of Economic Research.

Caballero, Ricardo (1990). Consumption puzzles and precautionary savings, *Journal of Monetary Economics*, XXV, 113–36.

Cutler, David and Lawrence Katz (1991). Macroeconomic performance and the disadvantaged, *Brookings Papers on Economic Activity*, II, 1–61.

—— and —— (1992). Rising inequality? Changes in the distribution of income and consumption in the 1980s, *American Economic Review*, LXXXII, 546–61.

Deaton, Angus S (1992). *Understanding Consumption*. Oxford: Clarendon Press.

—— and Christina H. Paxson (1994). Intertemporal choice and inequality, *Journal of Political Economy*, CII, 437–67.

Drèze, Jacques H. and Franco Modigliani (1972). Consumption decisions under uncertainty, *Journal of Economic Theory*, V, 308–35.

Gittleman, Maury and Mary Joyce (1996). Earnings mobility and long-run inequality: An analysis using matched CPS data, *Industrial Relations*, XXXV, 180–95.

Gottschalk, Peter and Robert Moffitt (1994). The growth of earnings instability in the U.S. labor market, *Brookings Papers on Economic Activity*, II, 217–72.

Hall, Robert E. (1978). Stochastic implications of the life-cycle permanent income hypothesis: Theory and evidence, *Journal of Political Economy*, XXXVI, 971–88.

Johnson, Paul and Steven Webb (1991). *UK poverty statistics: a comparative study*, Institute for Fiscal Studies Commentary 27, Institute for Fiscal Studies.

Kay, John A., Michael J. Keen, and C. Nicholas Morris (1984). Estimating consumption from expenditure data, *Journal of Public Economics*, XXIII, 169–81.

Keen, Michael J. (1990). Welfare analysis and intertemporal substitution, *Journal of Public Economics*, XLII, 47–66.

Kimball, Miles S. (1990). Precautionary saving in the small and in the large, *Econometrica*, LVIII, 53–73.

McClements, Leslie (1977). Equivalence scales for children, *Journal of Public Economics*, VIII, 191–210.

Moffitt, Robert and Peter Gottschalk (1995). Trends in the covariance of earnings in the United States: 1969–1987, *Discussion Paper 1001*, Institute for Research on Poverty.

Poterba, James (1989). Lifetime incidence and the distributional burden of excise taxes, *American Economic Review*, LXXIX, 325–30.

Sen, Amartya K. (1977). On weights and measures: Informational constraints in social welfare analysis, *Econometrica*, XLV, 1539–72.

Skinner, Jonathan (1988). Risky income, life-cycle consumption and precautionary savings, *Journal of Monetary Economics*, XXII, 237–55.

Slesnick, David (1993). Gaining ground: Poverty in the postwar United States, *Journal of Political Economy*, CI, 1–38.

8

Income Redistribution Within the Life Cycle Versus Between Individuals: Empirical Evidence Using Swedish Panel Data

ANDERS BJÖRKLUND AND MÅRTEN PALME

8.1. INTRODUCTION

Most empirical analyses on income inequality have focused on the distribution of income measured over a single year. Not least the Luxembourg Income Study has spurred an impressive amount of comparative research on income distribution using annual data for a large number of countries.[1] One result that has emerged as almost a stylized fact from this literature is that the distribution of post-tax and benefit family income is more equal than the distribution of pre-tax and benefit income, i.e., taxes and benefits make the income distribution less unequal. Sweden is no exception in this respect; rather the equalizing impact of the Swedish 'welfare state' seems to be quite high by international standards.

However, an obvious limitation of studies of annual income inequality is that they blend, and attach equal weights to, two conceptually different sources of income inequality, namely (i) transitory variation of individual incomes over time and (ii) variation in long-run (or lifetime) incomes. In the public policy discussion one can commonly hear claims that the distribution of lifetime income is the most important one. Indeed, in a world of complete credit markets that enables perfectly smooth consumption by the individual, the only interesting income redistributions, from a social welfare point of view, would be those that take place between individuals with different 'permanent' or lifetime income. Due to several well known problems, markets that provide such opportunities will not always be

Previous versions of this paper were presented at the IARIW conference in Lillehammer, 18–24 August 1996, at Uppsala University, and at a workshop organized by the Danish Ministry of Finance. We thank Jonas Agell, Stephen Jenkins, Markus Jäntti, and Anders Klevmarken for useful comments. Björklund acknowledges financial support from the Swedish Council for Social Research (SFR) and Palme from the Swedish Council for Research in the Humanities and Social Sciences (HSFR).

[1] See Atkinson *et al.* (1995) for comprehensive results from the Luxembourg Income Study.

available. Therefore, progressive income taxes and public benefits will to some extent serve as insurance against temporarily low incomes. In the famous Beveridge Report (Beveridge, 1942), which provided guidelines for post-war British social policy, the following text could be read:

'Abolition of want cannot be brought about merely by increasing production, without seeing to correct distribution of the product... Better distribution of purchasing power is required among wage earners themselves, as between times of earning and not earning, and between times of heavy family responsibilities and light or no family responsibilities. Both social insurance and children's allowances are primary methods of redistributing wealth'.

That also progressive income taxation can be considered as a social insurance has been suggested in the literature more recently (for example, Varian, 1980). The idea is that the individual is exposed to exogenous shocks that affect his or her earnings capacity. Progressive income taxation might serve as welfare enhancing social insurance against such shocks. Luck is likely to vary over the life cycle and therefore the progressive income tax will serve the purpose of equalizing income and consumption over the life cycle. Maasoumi and Zandvakili (1986) and Bird (1995) analyse the individual welfare improvements brought about by income security.

Thus, the literature obviously offers arguments for why equalization of *both* long-run (permanent) income *and* of income variability over time can improve social welfare and, therefore, be interesting to analyse empirically. But from the discussion above, it is also obvious that these two types of income redistribution are conceptually quite different and it is not clear that equal weights should be attached to them in a policy evaluation. In order to gain a more thorough understanding of the income redistribution process in a welfare state, it is therefore important to separate out these effects. In the policy debate it has been claimed that several welfare state benefits 'only' equalize income between different phases of the life cycle and have no effect on the distribution of lifetime income.[2] Indeed, it is even possible that some benefits have regressive effects on lifetime income, so that there is a conflict between reducing the two types of inequality.

The family is another institution that affects income distribution. Provided that there is a less than perfect correlation between the income positions of the spouses, family formation will have an equalizing effect on the income distribution. Several empirical studies have shown that this is in fact the case (see, for example, Lehrer and Nerlove, 1981, or, on Swedish data, Björklund, 1992). A natural extension of these studies is to examine to what extent pooling of economic resources within the family affects the distribution of long-run income and income variability over time for men and women.

---

[2] It has also been suggested that public benefit programmes designed for a single phase of the life cycle can be replaced by 'personal savings accounts' by means of which families can handle the intertemporal allocation of income themselves. See e.g., Fölster (1996).

The aim of this study is to assess to what extent income redistribution caused by the family, income taxes and welfare state benefits, reflect income redistribution between different phases of the life cycles of the same individuals, and to what extent it reflects income redistribution between individuals with different long-run income. Our technique is to apply an income inequality measure, the generalized entropy measure, that is decomposable between different population sub-groups. The 'within-group' inequality component represents income variability over each individual's life cycle and the 'between-group' component represents inequality of long-run income between different individuals. Income redistribution, caused by, for example, income taxes, is measured as the difference between the measured income inequality when we have and have not considered income taxes in the income concept. This technique is also applied to the analysis of income redistribution caused by the family and by welfare state benefits.

We also analyse the empirical relationship between income variability and long-run income. Is income variability higher or lower for those with low long-run income? Or is it independent of long-run income? Furthermore, we examine to what extent income redistribution between different phases of the same individual's life cycle differ between different quartiles of the distribution of long-run income.

Our analysis requires longitudinal data, ideally for the whole life cycle. We have been able to construct a representative sample of Swedes that we can follow over 18 years, from 1974 to 1991. For this sample of individuals, we have information on family composition, income and taxes of both adults in the family, and their major welfare state benefits. Even though this data set does not cover a whole life cycle, it allows us to extend the previous analyses of inequality of annual income to a considerable extent. We can compute long-run income as the individual's average income over the whole period, as well as her (or his) income variability over the 18 years.

To sum up, the contribution of this study is that it suggests a technique for, and carries out an empirical analysis of, how income redistribution can be separated into one effect on the distribution of long-run income and one effect on intertemporal income variability of the same individual. But we should also stress that the study has some limitations. The most obvious one is that it relies on mechanical comparisons between income distributions where we have and have not included the income component we analyse the effect of. More specifically, we ignore behavioural effects as well as general equilibrium effects on prices in the economy, i.e., in our implicit counterfactual labour supply is inelastic to changes in taxes and benefits. Moreover, we do not cover the entire life cycle of each individual.

The chapter proceeds as follows. Section 8.2 explains the methodology, the statistical technique as well as the income concepts. The data sources are described in Section 8.3. The results are presented in Section 8.4, and Section 8.5 concludes and discusses the main findings.

8.2. METHODOLOGY

8.2.1. Decomposition of Inequality

Following the discussion in the introduction, our goal is to distinguish between inequality of long-run income and individual intertemporal income variability. To achieve this goal, we suggest the use of the generalized entropy measure.[3] This measure is defined as

$$I_\gamma = \frac{1}{n} \sum_{i=1}^{n} \frac{[(y_i/\bar{y})^\gamma - 1]}{\gamma(\gamma - 1)}$$

where y_i is the income of unit i, n is the number of units in the sample, $\bar{y}$ is sample mean income, and γ is a parameter for degree of 'poverty aversion' chosen by the researcher. This inequality measure could be decomposed in order to measure to what extent the total inequality in the population could be attributed to different population sub-groups. This decomposition is defined as

$$I_\gamma = \sum_{r=s1}^{R} \left[\frac{y_r}{\sum_{j=1}^{n} y_j} \right]^\gamma \left(\frac{n_r}{n} \right)^{1-\gamma} I_\gamma^r + I_\gamma^B$$

where r is an index for the R different population sub-groups; $y_r/\sum_{j=1}^{n} y_j$ is the share of total income attributed to a particular group r (i.e., y_r is total income of subgroup r); n_r is the number of individuals in group r; I_γ^r is the generalized entropy measure within group r; and I_γ^B is the generalised entropy measure for the distribution of group mean incomes.

In this chapter, we investigate income inequality and mobility for a sample of annual incomes over the time period 1974–91 (18 years). In the framework outlined above, we interpret *each unit* (individual)[4] in the sample as 'one group'. Hence, what is usually measured as 'within (demographic) group inequality' in studies where the generalized entropy measure is used (see, for example, Cowell, 1984) is in this study interpreted as 'intertemporal variability' in income streams for each individual. Obviously we attach the same weight to each individual since each individual is one group ($n_r = 1$ for all r). What is usually interpreted as the 'between group inequality component', I^B, is here interpreted as 'long-run inequality' or inequality of mean income over the period of 18 years. 'Overall inequality' will in our framework be the inequality in the complete panel of data covering 18 years and all individuals of the sample to be analysed.

The parameter for poverty aversion, γ, has a meaningful interpretation in this framework. For the component measuring intertemporal variability, relatively

---

[3] This measure has been used in several empirical studies, see, for example, Cowell (1984).
[4] As explained below, we use the individual as the unit of analysis even though we use the household as the unit of income.

high poverty aversion reflects high aversion to temporarily very low individual incomes. High poverty aversion for the component measuring long-term income inequality reflects high aversion to 'lifetime' poverty.

Bird (1995) and Maasoumi and Zandvakili (1986) use additive individual utility functions in order to measure efficiency losses of high variability in individual annual income. This is an alternative approach. Because our ambition is to distinguish between inequality of long-run income on the one hand, and intertemporal variability on the other, we believe that the proposed approach is more informative.

We have chosen two alternative values of γ: 0 and 1. These measures are known as Theil-0 and Theil-1 inequality indices, respectively. The former represents a higher aversion to poverty. This gives the following estimation formulas:[5]

$$I_1 = \frac{1}{n} \sum_{i=1}^{n} \frac{y_i}{\bar{y}} \log\left(\frac{y_i}{\bar{y}}\right)$$

and

$$I_0 = \frac{1}{n} \sum_{i=1}^{n} \log\left(\frac{\bar{y}}{y_i}\right).$$

8.2.2. Income Concepts

Our basic income concept, which we call *market income*, consists of labour earnings as well as income from capital, capital gains, real estate, and own business. Market income also includes a number of public benefits that are 'work related' in the sense that they are subject to income tax and that the magnitude of the benefits are determined by previous earnings. The most important benefits that are included in market income are sickness pay, unemployment compensation,[6] early retirement pensions, and parental leave payment.

We start by examining inequality of *individual market income*, i.e., the individual is used both as the unit of analysis and as the unit of income. In the next step we look at *household market income*. We add the income of the spouse (for those who have one), assume equal sharing of income among members of the household, but retain the individual as the unit of analysis. At this stage, we must also take a stand on the issue of differences in needs that might exist between single and cohabiting persons, and between families with different numbers of children, i.e., make a choice of equivalence scale. In order to illustrate the role of children as determinants of income inequality among adults, we make two separate analyses with two different scales. One analysis applies a standard equivalence

---

[5] Formally, these two formulas are obtained from the limit of generalized entropy measure when $\gamma \to 0$ and $\gamma \to 1$, respectively (see, for example, Cowell, 1984).

[6] All compensations to participants in labour market programmes are also subject to income tax and hence included in our measure of market income.

scale on all the members of the households, namely one or two adults plus the number of children below 18 years of age. We use the simple square root scale; the equivalent number of adults in the household is equal to the square root of the number of persons in the household as defined above. Such an analysis implies that children are considered a financial burden for the adults. In a separate analysis we treat a child as a pure consumption good, i.e., children incur no costs to the adults of the household. In this analysis we only consider the economies of scale of the second adult of the household. We use the square root scale and hence divide total household income of two adults by 1.41 (the square root of 2.0) in order to arrive at the equivalent income of the individual that we use in our computations. By comparing the results from these two equivalence scales, we can shed light on the role of children in generating long-run inequality as well as income variability over time.

In defining household market income we also include one transfer designed for single parents, called the maintenance advance (bidragsförskott). In about half of all cases, the absent parent—in general the father—pays this amount to the custodial parent—in general the mother. But in other cases the custodial parent receives the amount as a public transfer.

In the next step we proceed to study the impact of taxes on the distribution of income. We do this by simply deducting taxes (of both spouses) from household market income as defined above. We confine ourselves to income taxes and do not treat wealth and property taxes. In the period 1974–91, Swedish income taxes were changed a number of times. The most well known changes are the two 'tax-reforms' in 1983–85 and 1990–91. In these reforms the highest marginal taxes were markedly reduced, some generous deductions were eliminated or reduced, and benefits to families with children (see below) were raised.[7] However, even after the last tax reform, income taxation was progressive. Basically, the flat tax rate of 30 per cent was applied on all income for 80 per cent of Swedish income earners and the marginal rate of 50 per cent for the other 20 per cent of income earners.

Then we proceed to analyse the impact of two central welfare state benefits for families with children. The first one is the universal child allowance (barnbidrag) that is paid directly to each mother of a child irrespective of her, or of her husband's, income and wealth. It is not taxable. The amount of this transfer was raised several times in nominal as well as in real terms during the time-period included in this analysis. There is a fixed amount that is paid for every child, but in 1982 a progressive amount was introduced that gave a larger benefit amount for the third and each subsequent child. Both the general and the progressive part of the child allowance were considerably raised in 1991 as one part of the tax reform. Even though this transfer by tradition has been politically popular, it has been claimed in the public discussion during recent years that it is too general and could be replaced by more means tested programmes. Pressed by the budget

---

[7] Björklund et al. (1995) examine the impact of these reforms on income distribution.

deficit, the Swedish government decided to reduce the universal child allowance (effective 1 January 1996) for the first time ever, and a large part of the reduction was made on the progressive part.

The second benefit to families with children is the means tested housing allowance *(bostadsbidrag)*. Its primary purpose is to guarantee a decent quality of housing for low-income families. The specific rules deciding the housing allowance have changed several times as well as the groups that are eligible; at times also some categories of retired and single persons have been eligible. In general, though, a certain fraction of the cost of housing for low-income families has been covered by the programme.

We conduct these analyses of benefits by adding one benefit at a time to the previous income concept and examine the impact of each benefit on inequality of income.

8.3. THE DATA SOURCE

Our basic data source is the Swedish Level of Living Survey.[8] This is a survey of a representative sample of individuals living in Sweden and aged 15–75 years. The first survey was made in 1968 with interviews of around 6000 individuals. Subsequent interviews were carried out in 1974, 1981, and 1991. At these later interviews the original sample was retained to make it a longitudinal data base, but youths and immigrants were added to the sample to make it representative for the whole population in these years as well.

Most of the information that we use does not stem from the interviews in the surveys, but from various public registers that have been merged with the information from the interviews. For example, we define cohabitation status by means of register information on tax status. Those who live together and are either formally married or have (or have had) common children get tax status as cohabitants.[9] Unfortunately, some cohabiting persons will in this way be treated as single, namely those who live together with an adult person without being married or without having had common children.[10] Even though we regard this as a shortcoming, it should not be too severe. Many of those who live together

---

[8] See Erikson and Åberg (1987) for more information.

[9] The formal Swedish concept is *samtaxerad.* Two persons get this tax status for a specific year if they (1) lived together at the beginning of the year and during most of the year and (2) were either formally married or had (or had had) common children born at the beginning of the year.

[10] The only way of getting complete information about cohabitation is to ask questions in a survey. This is for example done by Statistics Sweden in their Income Distribution Survey (*HINK*). In the Level of Living Survey, questions are asked about cohabitation status during 'most of the year' preceding the interview. For 1980 and 1990 we compared this broader definition of cohabitation with the more narrow one defined by tax status. For the young sample we found that at most 12 per cent were counted as cohabitants in the survey but not by tax status; for the old sample the corresponding number was at most 4 per cent. These discrepancies consist of (1) persons who lived together the whole year without being formally married and without having common children and (2) persons who moved together during the year and spent most of the year together.

without being married or having had common children have probably not merged their economic resources as much as other cohabiting couples have, although such couples make some economies of scale by sharing capital goods.

In order to compute household size, we also need to know the number of children in the family of the individual in our data set. This variable is also obtained from public registers.[11] Our variable for the number of children covers children who are 17 years of age or younger. As a consequence, those who are 18 years old are treated as 'adults' (as individuals in our data set) even if they still live with their parents.

The variables market income and taxes are also obtained from register information.[12] The universal child allowance is imputed from the information on the number of children in the family, whereas the data on housing allowance are obtained from public registers. We do not have direct observations on the special transfer for single parents (advance maintenance) and can therefore only impute the amount of it to all single parents according to the number of children.[13]

We do not have complete information on social assistance benefits over the whole period and therefore we cannot include this transfer in any of our income concepts. Neither do we have information about student loans and some other minor tax exempt benefits. The omission of social assistance benefits is not overly restrictive for our results. The expenditure on those benefits is comparatively low, only about one third of the expenditure on universal child allowances in the period that we cover.

We use two different samples. The first one—called the young sample—was 18–32 years old in 1974. The second one—called the old sample—was 33–47 years old in 1974. For both samples we require that the individuals were living in Sweden every year from 1974 to 1991.[14] Hence we also require that they survived the whole period of our analysis. The sizes of the two samples are 1388 and 991 individuals, respectively. Descriptive statistics of some of the most important variables of the two samples are presented in tables in the Appendix (Tables 8.5 and 8.6). All income variables in these tables and in our analysis have been deflated to the price level of 1980 by using the consumer price index.

These two samples cover different parts of the life cycle and consequently capture different types of intertemporal income variability. The young sample consists of quite a number who at the beginning of the period were students with zero or very low income and later on entered the labour market. Hence, the (proportionate) growth of income is higher in the young sample than in the old one. The young sample also consists of quite a number who change cohabiting

[11] The exception is 1990 for which year we use interview data about the number of children.

[12] For the years 1974–90 the income concept was called *sammanräknad inkomst*. This concept disappeared when the tax system was changed in 1991, and for 1991 we instead use *förvärvsinkomst plus kapitalinkomst* as our measure of market income.

[13] This procedure is subject to two errors. First, the transfer is tax-free but nonetheless we add it to market income before taxes. Second, we cannot deduct the payment of this transfer from the income of those absent parents who actually pay the amount themselves.

[14] We define living in Sweden by the Swedish concept *mantalsskrivning*.

status from living as a single person to becoming married or living with another adult as unmarried. Because of the age limits of the sample, quite a number had their first child during the period that we cover. The second sample, on the other hand, covers the period in life when children typically leave their parents. The data in the tables in the Appendix (Tables 8.5 and 8.6) confirm these demographic characteristics of the two samples.

8.4. RESULTS

8.4.1. Individual versus Family Income

We display our results for the young sample in Table 8.1(a), and for the old sample in Table 8.1(b). We start by looking at the nature of inequality of individual market income in the two samples (rows 1–3 in the tables). Overall inequality is sensitive to the degree of poverty aversion (γ) and it appears clearly that this sensitivity can be attributed to the intertemporal variability of income. Intuitively this is not surprising: if a heavy weight is attached to temporarily low incomes, overall inequality will become high. In both samples and for both degrees of inequality aversion, we find that overall inequality of individual market income is much higher for women than for men. Both components of inequality contribute to this male–female differential, but the component capturing intertemporal variability is the most important one.

By comparing inequality of individual market income (rows 1–3) with inequality of household market income (rows 4–6), we can see how the cohabitation pattern

Table 8.1(a). *Components of inequality, alternative income concepts. Young sample*

	$\gamma = 1$			$\gamma = 0$		
	Overall inequality	Intertemporal variability	Long-run inequality	Overall inequality	Intertemporal variability	Long-run inequality
Individual market income	0.1829	0.0731	0.1098	0.4133	0.2941	0.1192
Individual market income, men	0.1261	0.0545	0.0716	0.3164	0.2449	0.0715
Individual market income, women	0.1955	0.1040	0.0916	0.8294	0.7251	0.1044
Household market income (children no financial burden)	0.1211	0.0604	0.0607	0.2128	0.1501	0.0627
Household market income (children no financial burden), men	0.1190	0.0570	0.0620	0.2900	0.2251	0.0648
Household market income (children no financial burden), women	0.1230	0.0640	0.0590	0.2817	0.2215	0.0602
Household market income (children financial burden)	0.1225	0.0641	0.0584	0.2123	0.1509	0.0615

Source: Author's calculations from Level of Living Surveys.

Table 8.1(b). *Components of inequality, alternative income concepts. Old sample*

	$\gamma = 1$			$\gamma = 0$		
	Overall inequality	Intertemporal variability	Long-run inequality	Overall inequality	Intertemporal variability	Long-run inequality
Individual market income	0.1957	0.0453	0.1504	0.7013	0.4938	0.2075
Individual market income, men	0.1170	0.0320	0.0850	0.2003	0.1192	0.0811
Individual market income, women	0.2176	0.0683	0.1493	1.0992	0.8543	0.2449
Household market income (children no financial burden)	0.1045	0.0300	0.0745	0.1562	0.0808	0.0754
Household market income (children no financial burden), men	0.1059	0.0344	0.0715	0.1600	0.0895	0.0705
Household market income (children no financial burden), women	0.1026	0.0256	0.0770	0.1520	0.0724	0.0797
Household market income (children financial burden)	0.1178	0.0411	0.0767	0.1688	0.0912	0.0776

Source: Author's calculations from Level of Living Surveys.

affects for inequality of income. For all three cases—both sexes, men, and women—we get more equal distributions when the household is used as the unit of income. This equalization is most marked for women (rows 3 and 6). For the high degree of inequality aversion, in particular the intertemporal component for women is reduced. This is expected since women are likely to have low incomes when they are married (or are cohabiting) and can live out of the income of their husbands. It is also notable that incomes are equalized for men (rows 2 and 5) when household income rather than individual income is used, although the effect to a larger extent is attributable to long-run income.

Next we compare rows 4 and 7 (both sexes only) in the tables to examine the consequences of considering children as a financial burden for their parents. For the old sample, overall inequality increases for both degrees of inequality aversion. Most of the increase comes from the intertemporal variation. For the young sample, the effects on overall inequality are negligible with, by and large, counteracting effects on intertemporal variation (increase) and long-run inequality (decrease).

8.4.2. Impacts of Taxes and Benefits

Tables 8.2(a) and 8.2(b) show the impact of taxes and benefits on the components of inequality. Rows 1–4 show results for the case when children are not considered a financial burden, and rows 5–8 for the case when they are. Further, we start by presenting inequality of household market income, then subtract taxes, then add universal child allowances, and finally add housing allowances. So by comparing

Table 8.2(a). *The impact of taxes and benefits on inequality components. Young sample*

	γ = 1			γ = 0		
	Overall inequality	Intertemporal variability	Long-run inequality	Overall inequality	Intertemporal variability	Long-run inequality
Children no financial burden						
Household market income (children no financial burden)	0.1211	0.0604	0.0607	0.2128	0.1501	0.0627
Household market income-taxes	0.1041	0.0563	0.0478	0.1943	0.1450	0.0494
Household market income-taxes + universal child allowance	0.1008	0.0540	0.0468	0.1774	0.1289	0.0485
Household market income-taxes + universal child allowance + housing allowance	0.0967	0.0524	0.0443	0.1631	0.1175	0.0456
Children financial burden						
Household market income	0.1225	0.0641	0.0584	0.2123	0.1509	0.0615
Household market income-taxes	0.1032	0.0586	0.0446	0.1909	0.1441	0.0468
Household market income-taxes + universal child allowance	0.0944	0.0539	0.0405	0.1675	0.1254	0.0421
Household market income-taxes + universal child allowance + housing allowance	0.0891	0.0518	0.0373	0.1515	0.1132	0.0383

Source: Author's calculations from Level of Living Surveys.

the results of row 1 with those of row 4, and row 5 with those of row 8, the combined income redistribution effect of income taxes and the two welfare state benefits can be studied. The results show that *overall* inequality is reduced between 20 and 35 per cent depending on the sample, equivalence scale, and the degree of poverty aversion that is used. The proportionate reduction in inequality is consistently higher in the old sample, when children are considered a financial burden, and if γ is set to 0, whereas there is no consistent difference between the two samples.

The proportionate redistribution effects on long-run income are higher than the effects on overall inequality. Further, the redistribution of long-run income is somewhat higher when children are considered a financial burden and when γ equals 0. There are no consistent differences between the two samples. The proportionate effects on intertemporal variability are lower than the overall effects. These effects are very sensitive to the degree of poverty aversion chosen. For example, in the old sample when children are considered a financial burden, the inequality reduction is close to 5 per cent when γ is set to 1, and almost 30 per cent when it is set to 0. The explanation to this is that temporarily very low incomes

Table 8.2(b). *The impact of taxes and benefits on inequality components. Old sample*

	$\gamma = 1$			$\gamma = 0$		
	Overall inequality	Intertemporal variability	Long-run inequality	Overall inequality	Intertemporal variability	Long-run inequality
Children no financial burden						
Household market income	0.1045	0.0300	0.0745	0.1562	0.0808	0.0754
Household market income-taxes	0.0855	0.0308	0.0547	0.1359	0.0810	0.0549
Household market income-taxes + universal child allowance	0.0824	0.0291	0.0533	0.1197	0.0662	0.0535
Household market income-taxes + universal child allowance + housing allowance	0.0796	0.0286	0.0510	0.1080	0.0574	0.0506
Children financial burden						
Household market income	0.1178	0.0411	0.0767	0.1688	0.0912	0.0776
Household market income-taxes	0.0969	0.0409	0.0561	0.1465	0.0902	0.0563
Household market income-taxes + universal child allowance	0.0902	0.0370	0.0532	0.1258	0.0728	0.0530
Household market income-taxes + universal child allowance + housing allowance	0.0867	0.0360	0.0507	0.1133	0.0633	0.0500

Source: Author's calculations from Level of Living Surveys.

are weighted more heavily if γ is set to 0. These incomes are to a larger extent affected by welfare state benefits.

We can also examine the separate effects of income taxes and welfare state benefits. By comparing rows 1 and 2 as well as rows 5 and 6, it can be seen that in all eight cases, post-tax income is more equally distributed than pre-tax income. Further, by focusing on the two components in the decomposition it can be seen that this redistribution primarily can be attributed to equalization of long-run income inequality. For all eight cases long-run inequality is reduced by income taxes.[15] The impact of income taxation on intertemporal variation is in all eight cases very small.

Adding the universal child allowance to the previous income concept, we find, not surprisingly, that overall inequality is reduced by this transfer in all our eight cases of analysis. The component showing intertemporal variation is uniformly reduced. This result is expected, at least when we consider children a financial

[15] Using another technique and another income concept, Björklund *et al.* (1995) found an equalizing impact of income taxes on both annual and long run income.

burden, as the aim of child allowances is to give economic support in times of heavy family responsibilities, which is reflected in the equivalence scale. A more interesting finding, however, is that the impact on long-run inequality goes in the same direction, i.e., that child allowances also equalize long-run income. Even though this impact is quite small, the reduction of long-run inequality takes place even when we consider a child as a pure consumption good.

The means tested housing allowance, finally, also reduces inequality in all cases. Although both components are reduced for both choices of γ, the magnitude of each component is very much dependent on the choice of poverty aversion: with high poverty aversion the bulk of the reduction is attributed to the intertemporal component, and otherwise to the component showing long-run inequality.

To sum up, income taxes are the most important component for redistribution of long-run income: between 63–84 per cent, depending on the choice of sample, equivalence scale and poverty aversion, of total long-run income redistribution is due to income taxes. Turning to the reduction in income variability, the picture is reversed: most of the reduction in income variability can be attributed to welfare state benefits, although it is important to stress that our results suggest that these benefits also redistribute long-run income.[16]

8.4.3. Accounting for Trends

Income variability that can be foreseen is likely to be less costly for the individual. If an income decline can be planned for, it is easier for the individual, through access to credit markets, to smooth consumption. Consequently, assuming concave utility functions, the welfare loss will be less than it otherwise would have been. As we cannot observe whether or not the income variability can be foreseen by the individual, we are unable to take this into account. However, it is less likely that income mobility in the form of erratic variability, rather than a smooth trend, can be foreseen and planned for. Individual exogenous income shocks are more likely to appear as sharp deviations from a smooth trend, rather than as a declining trend over several years. Thus, one way of discriminating between different forms of income variability is to account for trends in the individual's income path.

The obvious problem with this approach is that the functional form of this trend has to be more or less arbitrary. From Mincer's (1962) pioneering work on the on-the-job-training hypothesis, and later also e.g., Lillard and Weiss (1979) or Hause (1980), we know that individual preference heterogeneity on the discount rate for how to value future income streams, may generate, disregarding all sorts of income shocks, heterogeneous earnings growth rates. Taking these results into account, we estimate separate quadratic trends for the income path of each

---

[16] The magnitude of these results is likely to be affected by the order we chose to add benefits and deduct income taxes from household income. However, the observed difference between the effect of income taxes and welfare state benefits is so large that the qualitative result is unlikely to be affected by this choice.

individual in the sample, i.e.,

$$y_{it} = \alpha_i + \beta_{1,i}t + \beta_{2,i}t^2 + \varepsilon_{it}$$

where i is a subindex for individual, t is a time trend, and ε is assumed to be an i.i.d. error term.

In order to investigate if all individuals have a trend in their income paths, we performed an F-test of joint significance of the two coefficients that constitute the quadratic trend for each individual. In the case of individuals for whom we could not detect a significant trend (at the 5 per cent level), we simply use their mean income over their income path as predicted income.

To estimate if the family, income taxes, and welfare state benefits smooth income over the life cycle, we again use the generalized entropy measure. But instead of calculating the deviation from the sample mean, we use the predicted income $\hat{y}_{it}$, i.e.,

$$I_\gamma^i = \frac{1}{t}\sum_{j=1}^{t}\frac{\left[(y_j/\hat{y})^\gamma - 1\right]}{\gamma(\gamma-1)}$$

where t is the number of time-periods considered, i.e., here 18.

Tables 8.3(a) and 8.3(b) show the results for the young and old samples, respectively. We use the same values for the poverty aversion, 0 and 1, as in the preceding analysis. We also report the average R^2 for the entire sample. As a comparison the tables also report some of the results from the preceding analysis under the heading 'Raw income variability'. But to save space we do not report the results for all income concepts from the preceding analysis.

Let us first note a counter-intuitive result in Tables 8.3(a) and 8.3(b). If γ is set to 1, i.e., when less weight is attached to the lower end of the distribution, detrended income variability is generally much larger than raw income variability. This result is not what we would have expected. However, examining the data more carefully, we discovered that the number of outliers, which are more than four times the predicted or the mean individual income, is somewhat larger when we control for an individual trend compared to 'Raw' income variability. If we reduce the value of these outliers to four times the predicted or the mean individual income, the order of the estimates is reversed for all income concepts considered.

As can be seen in Tables 8.3(a) and 8.3(b), the most important results from the previous section are retained when we account for a smooth trend in individual income paths. Comparing the rows for 'Household income (children financial burden)' with the row for 'Disposable income (children financial burden)' it can be seen that income taxes and benefits reduce income variability even when we account for a trend. This result applies for both sub-samples and for both values of γ. For $\gamma = 0$, the magnitudes of the difference between the estimates for 'Household market income' and 'Disposable income' are about the same for 'Raw income variability' and 'Detrended income variability' in both sub-samples. The estimate of the variability measure decreases by about one third. By comparing

Table 8.3(a). *Income variability when accounting for a quadratic trend. Young sample*

	$\gamma = 1$		$\gamma = 0$		
	Raw income variability	Detrended income variability	Raw income variability	Detrended income variability	Average R^2
Individual market income	0.0731	0.4611	0.2941	0.1925	0.5211
Household market income (children no financial burden)	0.0604	0.6424	0.1501	0.0975	0.5599
Household market income (children financial burden)	0.0641	0.4807	0.1509	0.1000	0.5435
Disposable income (children financial burden)	0.0518	0.2800	0.1132	0.0756	0.4858

Source: Author's calculations from Level of Living Surveys.

Table 8.3(b). *Income variability when accounting for a quadratic trend. Old sample*

	$\gamma = 1$		$\gamma = 0$		
	Raw income variability	Detrended income variability	Raw income variability	Detrended income variability	Average R^2
Individual market income	0.0453	3.1026	0.4938	0.4139	0.2521
Household market income (children no financial burden)	0.0300	3.0852	0.0808	0.0615	0.3760
Household market income (children financial burden)	0.0411	2.7472	0.0912	0.0621	0.4617
Disposable income (children financial burden)	0.0360	2.4534	0.0633	0.0417	0.4016

Source: Author's calculations from Level of Living Surveys.

the rows for 'Individual market income' and 'Household market income', it can be seen that also the conclusion that the family smooths out income paths is retained, except for the young sub-sample with $\gamma = 1$. Again, for $\gamma = 0$ the magnitude of the differences is about the same for the 'Detrended' and 'Raw' income variability measures.

8.4.4. Who Suffers from Income Variability?

In a world of imperfect capital markets, and assuming concave utility functions, income variability represents a welfare loss for the individual. We would like to know if these welfare losses are larger among those with low than among those with high long-run income. For this purpose, we have computed ordinary correlation coefficients between individual income variability and long-run income in our two samples and with the two measures of poverty aversion. In order to find out whether there are non-linearities in the relationships, we have also divided the distribution of long-run income into quartiles and computed average income variability in each quartile.

Tables 8.4(a) and 8.4(b) contain the results for the young and old samples. We can see that the correlation for household market income before taxes and

Table 8.4(a). *Correlation coefficients (ρ) between income variability and long-run income, and average income variability in each quartile of the distribution of long-run income. Young sample*

| | $\gamma = 1$ | | | | | $\gamma = 0$ | | | |
	ρ	1st qu.	2nd qu.	3rd qu.	4th qu.	ρ	1st qu.	2nd qu.	3rd qu.	4th qu.
Individual market income	−0.394 (−16.0)	0.213	0.072	0.041	0.054	−0.391 (−15.8)	0.805	0.190	0.086	0.096
Household market income (children no financial burden)	−0.250 (−9.6)	0.104	0.053	0.053	0.051	−0.280 (−10.9)	0.318	0.099	0.110	0.079
Household market income (children financial burden)	−0.259 (−10.0)	0.103	0.060	0.053	0.058	−0.282 (−11.0)	0.298	0.116	0.102	0.088
Disposable income (children financial burden)	−0.213 (−8.1)	0.078	0.049	0.041	0.049	−0.250 (−9.6)	0.219	0.094	0.073	0.068

Note: Disposable income equals household market income + universal child allowances + housing allowances − taxes. T-ratios within parentheses.

Source: Author's calculations from Level of Living Surveys.

Table 8.4(b). *Correlation coefficients (ρ) between income variability and long-run income, and average income variability in each quartile of the distribution of long-run income. Old sample*

| | $\gamma = 1$ | | | | | $\gamma = 0$ | | | |
	ρ	1st qu.	2nd qu.	3rd qu.	4th qu.	ρ	1st qu.	2nd qu.	3rd qu.	4th qu.
Individual market income	−0.362 (−12.2)	0.174	0.047	0.016	0.033	−0.394 (−13.5)	1.781	0.116	0.030	0.053
Household market income (children no financial burden)	−0.050 (−1.6)	0.050	0.022	0.016	0.037	−0.168 (−5.4)	0.239	0.028	0.024	0.033
Household market income (children financial burden)	−0.031 (−1.0)	0.061	0.032	0.028	0.048	−0.157 (−5.0)	0.246	0.041	0.037	0.042
Disposable income (children financial burden)	0.094 (3.0)	0.044	0.025	0.025	0.048	−0.097 (−3.1)	0.149	0.030	0.033	0.041

Note: Disposable income equals household market income + universal child allowances + housing allowances − taxes. T-ratios within parentheses.

Source: Author's calculations from Level of Living Surveys.

benefits is negative for all cases, i.e., individuals with relatively low long-run income also tend to have more income variability. Overall, the negative relationship is much stronger in the young than in the old sample. From the average income variability in the four quartiles we can see that the income variability is markedly highest in the first quartile, but does not consistently fall from the second to the fourth quartile. Hence, the relationship seems to be non-linear.

Taxes and welfare state benefits seem to smooth out income fluctuations in all quartile groups. However, the magnitude of this income smoothing is largest in the lowest quartile. That is, individuals with relatively low long-run income make the largest gain from income smoothing from income taxes and welfare state benefits.[17] Therefore, for disposable income, the negative relationship between long-run income and income variability is weaker, and for the old sample and low aversion towards poverty ($\gamma = 0$) the correlation even turns positive.

8.5. CONCLUSIONS

By means of an 18 year long panel we have extended the traditional analysis of annual inequality and distinguished between (i) individual income variability over time and (ii) inequality of long-run (18 years) income. As in the traditional analysis, we found that household income is more equally distributed than individual income (assuming equal sharing of income within the household). For women, this equalizing effect of the household could be mainly attributed to income variability over time, whereas for men, the main effect showed up in long-run income. Treating children as a financial burden for their parents raises mainly intertemporal variation of income.

Turning to taxes and benefits, we found that the main equalizing impact of income taxes is on long-run income rather than on intertemporal variation of income. Our analyses of one universal and one means tested transfer programme for families with children showed, not surprisingly, that both programmes reduce individual income variability. We found it more striking, though, that even the universal programme had an equalizing impact on long-run income and this impact was robust to a number of alternative assumptions about the cost of having children and the degree of 'poverty aversion'. This transfer is often classified as 'only' redistributing income over the life cycle rather than redistributing lifetime income. Our results therefore imply that there is no conflict between the goals of equalizing long-run income and reducing income variability. Instead the two goals reinforce each other. The main conclusions about the effect of income taxes and welfare state benefits on income variability were retained when we measured variability as deviations from a smooth trend in individual income.

In our analysis of the pre-tax and benefit relationship between long-run income and income variability, we found that income variability is unambiguously highest in the lowest quartile of the distribution of long-run income. In some cases income variability is higher in the top quartile of long-run income than in the second and third quartiles, so the relationship is not linear. Furthermore, we found that the proportionate impact of taxes and benefits on income variability is, in general, highest in the lowest quartile of the distribution of long-run income. These findings help us understand why there is no conflict between the goals of equalizing long-run income and income variability.

---

[17] These results, which can be obtained from the authors upon request, prevail also when we account for a quadratic trend using the same method as in the preceding analysis.

APPENDIX

Table 8.5. *Sample characteristics of the young sample, 18–32 years old in 1974, n = 1388. Coefficients of variation within parentheses*

Year	Individual market income, 1000 SEK	Household market income of both spouses, 1000 SEK	Fraction of cohabitants	Fraction of lone parents	# of children	Disposable income, 1000 SEK
1974	44.2 (0.78)	46.6 (0.63)	0.460	0.056	0.69	34.7 (0.57)
1975	50.2 (0.68)	52.1 (0.56)	0.492	0.038	0.73	37.5 (0.47)
1976	54.2 (0.65)	56.1 (0.56)	0.543	0.039	0.82	40.0 (0.45)
1977	56.3 (0.59)	57.7 (0.48)	0.569	0.045	0.93	41.5 (0.39)
1978	58.2 (0.60)	58.5 (0.49)	0.597	0.050	1.01	41.0 (0.39)
1979	60.1 (0.61)	60.1 (0.46)	0.610	0.053	1.08	42.4 (0.42)
1980	60.5 (0.62)	62.2 (0.43)	0.646	0.059	1.15	44.9 (0.38)
1981	60.2 (0.71)	61.4 (0.46)	0.658	0.055	1.22	45.2 (0.49)
1982	59.9 (0.64)	58.2 (0.47)	0.670	0.071	1.34	42.6 (0.44)
1983	59.2 (0.56)	62.3 (0.45)	0.686	0.070	1.35	46.3 (0.45)
1984	60.9 (0.53)	62.2 (0.40)	0.697	0.076	1.35	45.9 (0.34)
1985	63.3 (0.53)	64.9 (0.41)	0.699	0.079	1.34	48.1 (0.34)
1986	67.0 (0.61)	68.6 (0.45)	0.697	0.079	1.33	49.5 (0.37)
1987	71.0 (0.58)	73.5 (0.44)	0.713	0.072	1.25	51.5 (0.34)
1988	74.2 (0.56)	77.3 (0.43)	0.717	0.066	1.20	53.5 (0.33)
1989	79.2 (0.66)	83.5 (0.47)	0.728	0.064	1.16	56.9 (0.39)
1990	81.7 (0.56)	84.7 (0.49)	0.741	0.071	1.26	57.9 (0.37)
1991	80.5 (0.64)	84.8 (0.51)	0.737	0.058	1.14	60.9 (0.42)

Note: All zero incomes (and a few negative ones) have been set to 1 SEK. For household and disposable income the square root equivalence scale is applied for all members of the household including the children.

Source: Author's calculations from Level of Living Surveys.

Table 8.6. *Sample characteristics of the old sample, 33–47 years old in 1974, n = 991. Coefficients of variation within parentheses*

Year	Individual market income, 1000 SEK	Household market income of both spouses, 1000 SEK	Fraction of cohabitants	Fraction of lone parents	# of children	Disposable income, 1000 SEK
1974	59.2 (0.71)	63.0 (0.53)	0.846	0.039	1.53	46.0 (0.46)
1975	64.2 (0.71)	68.1 (0.48)	0.836	0.047	1.48	48.0 (0.40)
1976	65.5 (0.66)	70.4 (0.48)	0.831	0.046	1.42	48.5 (0.38)
1977	66.2 (0.64)	72.6 (0.47)	0.825	0.046	1.30	49.9 (0.37)
1978	66.2 (0.61)	72.6 (0.45)	0.814	0.053	1.21	48.5 (0.35)
1979	67.6 (0.61)	75.5 (0.46)	0.803	0.058	1.10	50.0 (0.37)
1980	66.9 (0.58)	75.7 (0.44)	0.798	0.054	0.97	51.3 (0.36)
1981	66.4 (0.79)	76.5 (0.56)	0.788	0.047	0.85	51.9 (0.59)
1982	64.8 (0.58)	75.6 (0.45)	0.783	0.042	0.75	50.9 (0.39)
1983	64.8 (0.75)	78.6 (0.50)	0.781	0.031	0.64	52.6 (0.45)
1984	64.2 (0.57)	79.1 (0.44)	0.771	0.026	0.52	53.3 (0.36)
1985	66.2 (0.58)	82.6 (0.43)	0.773	0.021	0.42	55.8 (0.36)

Table 8.6. *(Continued)*

Year	Individual market income, 1000 SEK	Household market income of both spouses, 1000 SEK	Fraction of cohabitants	Fraction of lone parents	# of children	Disposable income, 1000 SEK
1985	66.2 (0.58)	82.6 (0.43)	0.773	0.021	0.42	55.8 (0.36)
1986	68.3 (0.57)	85.7 (0.43)	0.770	0.015	0.35	56.5 (0.36)
1987	71.1 (0.54)	90.5 (0.49)	0.769	0.010	0.29	58.5 (0.36)
1988	72.1 (0.55)	91.4 (0.44)	0.765	0.009	0.24	58.8 (0.35)
1989	76.0 (0.60)	96.5 (0.48)	0.759	0.009	0.19	62.1 (0.37)
1990	75.6 (0.54)	95.8 (0.43)	0.761	0.010	0.15	62.7 (0.36)
1991	77.5 (1.44)	99.6 (1.39)	0.759	0.005	0.12	69.9 (1.36)

Note: All zero incomes (and a few negative ones) have been set to 1 SEK. For household and disposable income the square root equivalence scale is applied for all members of the household including the children.

Source: Author's calculations from Level of Living Surveys.

REFERENCES

Atkinson, Anthony B., Tim Smeeding, and Lee Rainwater (1995). Income distribution in the OECD countries: The evidence from the Luxembourg income study, *Social Policy Studies*, OECD, Paris.

Beveridge, William (1942). *Social Insurance and Allied Services*, Macmillan, New York.

Bird, Edward (1995). An exploratory comparison of income risk in Germany and the United States, *Review of Income and Wealth*, 41, 405–26.

Björklund, Anders (1992). 'Rising female labour force participation and the distribution of family income—the Swedish experience, *Acta Sociologica*, 35 (4), 299–310.

——, Mårten Palme, and Ingemar Svensson (1995). Tax reforms and income distribution: An assessment using different income concepts, *Swedish Economic Policy Review*, 2 (2), 229–66.

Cowell, Frank (1984). The structure of American income inequality, *Review of Income and Wealth*, 30, 351–75.

Erikson, Robert and Rune Åberg (1987). *Welfare in Transition—Living Conditions in Sweden 1968–1981*, Clarendon Press, Oxford.

Fölster, Stefan (1996). Social insurance based on personal savings accounts: A possible reform strategy for overburdened welfare states? *IUI Working Paper* 454, The Industrial Institute for Social and Economic Research, Stockholm.

Hause, John C. (1980). The fine structure of earnings and the on-the-job training hypothesis, *Econometrica*, 48, 1013–29.

Lehrer, Evelyn and Marc Nerlove (1981). The impact of female work on family income distribution in the United States: Black–white differentials, *Review of Income and Wealth*, 27 (4), 423–31.

Lillard, Lee A. and Yoram Weiss (1979). Components of variation in panel earnings data: American scientists 1960–70, *Econometrica*, 47, 437–54.

Maasoumi, Esfandiar and Sourushe Zandvakili (1986). A class of generalized measures of mobility with applications, *Economics Letters*, 22, 97–102.

Mincer, Jacob (1962). On the job training: Cost, returns and some implications, *Journal of Political Economy*, 70, 50–79.

Varian, Hal (1980). Redistributive Taxation as Social Insurance, *Journal of Public Economics*, 14, 49–68.

9

Earnings Dispersion, Low Pay, and Household Poverty in Italy, 1977–98

ANDREA BRANDOLINI, PIERO CIPOLLONE, AND PAOLO SESTITO

9.1. INTRODUCTION

Last decade was a period of considerable transformation for the Italian labour market. Employment fell sharply in the early 1990s, in the course of the deepest recession of the post-war period, and returned to growth only after 1995. This recovery coincided with a profound modification in the composition of the work force by sex, age, and educational attainment, and it went along with a rapid increase in part-time and fixed-term jobs as well as other forms of contingent work. At the same time, important institutional changes affected the wage formation mechanism, such as the abolition of automatic indexation in 1991 and the phasing-out of contribution relief for firms in the South since 1994.

It is common opinion that these changes, by their sheer magnitude, must have had a significant impact on the distribution of earnings and household incomes. Some suggest that low-paid positions are on the rise, and the concern has been frequently voiced that holding a job is no longer sufficient to avoid poverty. The higher volatility of employment opportunities has exacerbated the deficiencies of the Italian social safety net, which is largely ineffective in protecting persons with poor work experience or trapped in contingent jobs. The debate on the reform of the Italian welfare state has begun, but changes have been minor to date; a fully fledged reform of existing unemployment benefit schemes has been repeatedly delayed; trials of a social inclusion income support mechanism (*reddito minimo di inserimento*) only began in 1998.

In this context, we need to ground the discussion on a factual documentation of developments in the distribution of earnings. To appreciate the importance of

We are grateful for the helpful comments of Tony Atkinson, Matteo Bugamelli, Luigi Cannari, and Daniele Checchi, and of participants in the Lower Conference on 'Low-paid in Europe' (Bordeaux, January 1997), the CEPR workshop on 'New Inequalities' (La Coruña, February 1997), and the XV National Conference of AIEL (Ancona, September 2000), where preliminary versions of the paper were presented. We thank Roger Meservey and Raffaella Nizzi for the excellent editorial assistance. The views expressed herein are those of the authors and do not necessarily reflect those of the Bank of Italy or the Ministry of Labour.

recent changes, one must put them in historical perspective and hence evaluate the information over a sufficiently long period of time. With this objective in mind, our contribution is two-fold.

First, we offer fresh statistical evidence on the evolution of the earnings distribution in the period from 1977 to 1998, revising and updating what little information is currently available (Section 9.3). We focus on changes at the bottom of the distribution by measuring the extent of low-paid work, its trend over time and its socio-demographic composition (Section 9.4). Our results are based on the most coherent database at our disposal, namely the microdata of the Historical Archive (HA) of the Bank of Italy's Survey of Household Income and Wealth (SHIW), which is extensively described in Section 9.2 and Appendix.

Second, we exploit the richness of the database to study the link between the poverty status of households and the labour market conditions of their adult members (Section 9.5). In particular, we look at the differential impact of employment status and low wages on poverty.

Two important limitations need to be stressed at the beginning. In the first place, we pay no attention to workers' earnings mobility and to transitions into and out of low-paid jobs. The concern over low-paid work would clearly be attenuated were such status mostly a temporary situation from which exit is easy. However, according to the evidence reported by Lucifora (1998) for employees in the private sector present continuously from 1975 to 1988, about half of the workers in the bottom tenth of the distribution in 1975 were still in the same tenth in 1988; the proportion rose to 60 per cent for the bottom fifth of the distribution. Thus, for a significant number of workers low pay may represent a permanent rather than a transitory condition. Moreover, we focus on salaried employment only. However debatable in the light of their numerical importance in Italy, the exclusion of the self-employed derives from the intrinsic difficulty of correctly measuring their labour earnings.[1]

9.2. A DESCRIPTION OF THE DATA

In this chapter, we use the microdata of the HA of the Bank of Italy's SHIW, which covers the period 1977–98. Details about the structure and quality of the survey, especially with regard to the questions concerning employees and earnings, are provided in the Appendix.

The use of microdata from a household survey like the SHIW poses a number of problems. First, the pattern of non-responses may alter the representativeness of

---

[1] See Brandolini (2000a) for a full discussion of these issues. A growing number of independent contractors, consultants or free-lance workers, often called *parasubordinati* (i.e., quasi-employees), are engaged in marginal activities, in conditions frequently not very different from those of an employee except for being less well paid and less well protected. Data for 1995 indicate that the lower tail of the distribution of monthly after-tax labour earnings is much thicker among the self-employed than among employees (see Brandolini, 2000a, Figure 9.1).

the sample, and earnings may be under-reported, or not reported at all. Second, earnings are recorded net of taxes and social security contributions. As the amounts reported are the result of computations performed by respondents, we cannot control the extent to which they reflect respondents' personal situation (e.g., the inclusion of family allowances; whether the implicit tax rate accounts for other sources of income, where taxation is progressive). Third, the relatively small size of the survey calls for some caution in interpreting the evidence, and it makes the coverage of some segments of the labour market insufficient (e.g., farm employees, workers with a university degree). Despite these problems, the SHIW is the only source of individual data that allows us to measure the changes in the *whole* Italian wage distribution consistently over a long period of time, and to relate labour earnings to households' total income.[2]

The basic sample examined in the chapter includes all *primary* job positions but excludes *secondary* job positions, i.e., the jobs that people may have in addition to their main occupation as employees or self-employed (they accounted for about 2 per cent of total positions at the beginning of the period, less than 0.5 per cent in the mid-1990s and 1.4 per cent in 1998). The size of the basic sample ranges from around 3000 observations in the late 1970s to over 7000 in the late 1980s (Table 9.1).

Employees working for the whole year account for the great majority of the sample, about 87 per cent on average. This proportion reflects, somewhat loosely, the business cycle, as the peak was reached in the expansion years 1989 and 1991; after dropping below 85 per cent during the recession of 1993, it returned near the average in 1998, despite the recent spread of fixed-term contracts. The share of self-declared part-time jobs, which is only available from 1986 on,[3] was about 5 per cent in 1986–87; it fell in 1989 and 1991 at the peak of the expansion

---

[2] The administrative database of the National Social Security Institute (INPS) (see Abbate and Baldassarini, 1995; Lucifora, 1996; Casavola *et al.*, 1999) provides precise figures on pre-tax earnings and a few individual characteristics since the mid-1970s, but it covers only employees in the private sector who comply with the social security regulations (with the exclusion of certain employees at the managerial level) and it lacks information about their households and other sources of income. The new longitudinal household survey inititated by the national statistical institute (Istat) in 1994 to supply the Italian data in the European Community Household Panel shares most of the problems of the SHIW.

[3] Until 1984 part-time contracts were permitted but not explicitly regulated by the law; their provisions were set out directly by firms and workers, through individual negotiation or, more recently, collective agreements. Regular statistics did not exist, but scattered evidence suggests that their diffusion was marginal (see Istituto italiano per la promozione del lavoro a tempo parziale, 1980). Part-time work was first recognized and regulated by Law 863 of 19 December 1984, where it was defined with reference to the standard working time fixed in collective agreements. The share of part-time workers in total employment remained fairly modest until the early 1990s; it has been steadily increasing ever since. National contracts have accommodated this tendency by raising the ceiling on the use of part-time work and by relaxing the restrictions on its application (see the chapter 'The Labour Market' in Banca d'Italia, 2000a). For further details on part-time work in Italy, see Addabbo (1997).

Table 9.1. *Characteristics of the samples, 1977–98 (percentage shares, except for observations)*

| Year | Observations | All primary job positions | | | | | | Full-time job positions | | Non-farm prime-age male workers employed year-round | |
| | | Whole-year | | | Part-year | | | | | | |
		Total	Full-time	Part-time	Total	Full-time	Part-time	Observations	Whole-year	Observations	Part-time
1977	2815	88.2			11.8					854	
1978	3262	85.1			14.9					909	
1979	2988	86.2			13.8					844	
1980	3013	86.4			13.6					852	
1981	4151	85.7			14.3					1196	
1982	4172	85.6			14.4					1168	
1983	4123	87.4			12.6					1201	
1984	3853	86.2			13.8					1201	
1986	6988	83.7	81.7	2.0	16.3	13.4	2.9	6627	85.9	2196	0.5
1987	7156	87.3	84.5	2.8	12.7	10.3	2.4	6776	89.1	2178	1.0
1989	7061	92.6	90.3	2.3	7.4	6.1	1.3	6783	93.7	2249	0.4
1991	6762	91.5	88.6	2.9	8.5	7.3	1.2	6462	92.4	2207	0.3
1993	6479	84.8	81.4	3.4	15.2	12.5	2.7	6096	86.6	1955	0.8
1995	6453	84.9	80.4	4.5	15.1	13.0	2.1	5994	86.1	1929	1.2
1998	5837	86.3	81.1	5.2	13.7	9.8	3.9	5312	89.2	1796	1.1

Source: Authors' elaboration on data from SHIW-HA (Release 1.0).

and has steadily increased since, reaching 9 per cent in 1998. Nevertheless, the diffusion of part-time contracts in Italy is still well below the levels recorded in most advanced countries.

From 1977 to 1998, the share of female workers rose steadily from 31 to 41 per cent (Table 9.2). This tendency was paralleled by an increase in the proportion of jobs held by spouses from 17 to 26 per cent, while those held by household heads declined, mainly in the 1990s, from 55 to 48 per cent. The proportion of workers resident in Southern regions oscillated between 27 and 30 per cent, roughly reflecting the asymmetric business cycle. There was an appreciable improvement in educational attainment: the incidence of employees with high-school degrees doubled from 22 to 45 per cent; that of university graduates from 6 to 13 per cent. With regard to the age structure, the shares both of persons younger than 30 and of those older than 50 declined considerably. The first phenomenon reflects demographic evolution as well as the interaction of factors such as increasing education, the growing difficulty of finding a job for new entrants in the labour market, and the strength of family support, which allows young people to wait for better job opportunities. The falling proportion of persons older than 50 was facilitated by generous seniority pension schemes; the acceleration in 1993 and 1995 was brought about by people retiring early as the reform of the Italian pension system restricted eligibility conditions. As a result of these tendencies, workers in the middle age groups came to account for 59 per cent of the total in 1998, compared with 47 per cent in 1977, and the age-profile of Italian employment turned out to be considerably different from the EU average. Lastly, the decrease in the proportions of production workers and of industrial employment were matched by increasing shares of clerical workers and employment in sundry services.

In addition to the basic sample just described, we focus on two sub-samples. The first is constructed by excluding self-declared part-time workers, and is consequently limited to the period from 1986 onwards. The share of workers employed for the whole year turns out to be slightly higher than in the basic sample (Table 9.1); the sub-sample composition is virtually unchanged, except for a somewhat lower proportion of females (and spouses), among whom part-time is more frequent (Table 9.2). The second sub-sample tries to isolate what is conceivably *core employment*: non-farm male employees, aged 30 to 50, working year-round. We did not exclude part-time workers in order to have longer time-series, but the results should not be significantly altered as the incidence of part-time in this sub-group is minimal (below 1 per cent; Table 9.1). In this sub-sample, the share of workers living in the South rises considerably in the period examined. It is higher than in the basic sample from the late 1980s on (except in 1991), which might reflect a difference in participation by men and women. In comparison with the basic sample, core employment shows a higher proportion of persons with a university degree (except in 1998), and a lower share of production workers (Table 9.2).

Table 9.2. Composition of the samples, 1977–98 (percentage shares)

Personal characteristic	All job positions															Full-time job positions						
	1977	1978	1979	1980	1981	1982	1983	1984	1986	1987	1989	1991	1993	1995	1998	1986	1987	1989	1991	1993	1995	1998
Sex																						
Male	68.9	68.6	66.6	64.8	65.7	65.6	66.2	65.4	64.3	64.8	63.4	62.4	61.4	60.2	59.2	66.1	66.7	64.8	64.1	63.9	63.1	62.1
Female	31.1	31.4	33.4	35.2	34.3	34.4	33.8	34.6	35.7	35.2	36.6	37.6	38.6	39.8	40.8	33.9	33.3	35.2	35.9	36.1	36.9	37.9
Household position																						
Head	54.7	53.7	52.1	51.0	52.2	53.0	51.2	54.2	54.5	53.5	52.7	50.5	48.1	47.2	48.2	55.9	55.2	53.6	51.8	49.8	48.7	50.6
Spouse	16.8	17.1	19.4	20.2	18.9	20.0	18.9	21.1	21.7	20.5	21.9	21.7	25.5	25.4	26.1	20.4	19.4	21.1	20.5	24.0	23.6	23.9
Child	26.1	27.3	26.2	25.9	27.0	25.3	28.1	23.4	21.9	24.5	23.5	25.7	24.3	25.5	23.8	21.8	24.0	23.5	25.6	24.1	25.7	23.6
Other member	2.4	1.9	2.3	2.9	2.0	1.8	1.8	1.3	2.0	1.5	1.9	2.1	2.1	1.9	1.9	1.9	1.4	1.8	2.1	2.1	1.9	1.8
Age																						
Under 30	35.5	34.1	35.1	34.9	36.9	32.9	34.4	29.8	28.9	31.2	31.9	30.4	29.3	29.3	26.0	28.7	30.7	31.6	30.1	28.7	29.1	25.0
31–50	47.3	47.5	48.0	48.0	46.9	49.5	49.2	53.4	55.1	51.8	52.9	54.4	56.8	56.8	59.2	55.5	52.4	53.1	54.6	56.9	56.7	59.8
51 and over	17.3	18.4	16.9	17.1	16.2	17.6	16.3	16.8	15.9	17.0	15.2	15.2	13.9	13.9	14.8	15.9	17.0	15.3	15.3	14.3	14.2	15.2
Education																						
None or primary	42.7	38.0	37.8	30.2	30.3	27.4	26.4	24.5	26.2	23.1	19.1	18.2	15.6	13.1	10.8	25.1	22.4	18.7	17.8	15.3	12.4	10.4
Secondary	29.7	29.8	29.7	31.8	32.8	33.0	35.7	32.6	33.8	35.2	34.7	32.1	38.4	33.6	32.0	34.1	35.7	35.0	32.2	38.2	33.4	31.5
High school	21.6	24.8	24.5	29.3	29.3	31.4	29.8	33.3	32.2	32.1	36.4	38.9	36.1	42.5	44.6	32.7	32.1	36.5	39.1	36.1	42.8	45.0
University	6.1	7.4	8.0	8.7	7.5	8.2	8.0	9.5	7.9	9.6	9.8	10.7	10.0	10.8	12.5	8.1	9.8	9.8	10.9	10.3	11.4	13.0
Geographical area																						
North	72.2	71.2	71.2	71.6	72.2	70.6	69.9	69.6	71.2	73.1	73.1	71.7	71.6	70.8	70.5	71.4	72.8	73.2	71.8	71.5	70.6	71.0
South	27.8	28.8	28.8	28.4	27.8	29.4	30.1	30.4	28.8	26.9	26.9	28.3	28.4	29.2	29.5	28.6	27.2	26.8	28.2	28.5	29.4	29.0
Economic branch[a]																						
Agriculture and fishery	4.6	5.7	5.9	4.9	4.1	4.8	4.4	4.4	4.7	4.1	4.5	4.7	4.7	3.8	3.2	3.8	5.2	4.3	4.5	3.4	3.1	4.4
Industry	43.6	43.1	41.8	41.0	41.3	38.3	34.8	29.9	36.8	34.0	37.4	35.3	35.8	35.0	33.6	37.5	34.7	37.7	36.1	36.6	36.0	35.3
Trade and lodging	8.8	8.3	8.2	9.3	8.5	10.4	14.8	12.5	11.2	11.7	12.6	9.5	8.1	8.9	9.9	10.9	12.0	9.3	7.8	8.4	9.1	9.4
Transport and credit	11.5	10.2	10.1	9.2	9.0	10.6	12.6	12.3	11.3	11.7	10.1	8.3	8.3	6.6	7.0	11.8	12.2	10.3	8.4	6.7	6.8	7.2
Other services	31.5	32.7	34.0	35.6	37.2	36.0	33.4	40.5	36.5	38.5	35.9	43.6	44.9	45.2	44.5	35.9	35.9	38.3	43.1	44.9	44.9	43.7
Job status[a]																						
Production workers	67.3	62.2	63.1	54.2	55.6	51.6	55.3	56.1	52.5	52.0	47.5	45.2	46.8	47.5	46.0	51.4	51.2	47.4	44.9	46.1	46.7	46.0
Clerical workers	30.7	35.3	34.2	43.3	42.1	45.9	42.7	41.4	46.2	46.2	50.2	52.6	51.2	50.4	51.7	47.2	46.9	50.2	52.9	51.7	51.1	51.7
Managerial workers	2.0	2.5	2.6	2.5	2.2	2.4	1.9	2.5	1.3	1.8	2.3	2.1	2.1	2.1	2.3	1.4	2.0	2.3	2.2	2.2	2.2	2.3
Total	100.0	100.0	100.0	100.0	100.0	100.0	100.0	100.0	100.0	100.0	100.0	100.0	100.0	100.0	100.0	100.0	100.0	100.0	100.0	100.0	100.0	100.0

Non-farm prime-age male workers employed year-round

Sex															
Male	100.0	100.0	100.0	100.0	100.0	100.0	100.0	100.0	100.0	100.0	100.0	100.0	100.0	100.0	100.0
Female	—	—	—	—	—	—	—	—	—	—	—	—	—	—	—
Household position															
Head	92.4	93.9	92.9	93.6	91.2	92.8	94.1	92.4	93.3	92.9	91.1	89.1	81.8	81.7	82.3
Spouse	0.1	0.2	0.1	0.2	0.2	0.0	0.1	0.3	0.1	0.2	0.8	0.8	9.1	8.9	6.8
Child	5.6	4.8	5.9	4.5	6.7	6.4	5.2	6.2	5.7	6.5	6.9	8.6	7.6	8.5	9.3
Other member	1.8	1.1	1.1	1.7	1.9	0.7	0.6	1.1	1.0	0.4	1.2	1.6	1.5	0.9	1.6
Age															
Under 30	—	—	—	—	—	—	—	—	—	—	—	—	—	—	—
31–50	100.0	100.0	100.0	100.0	100.0	100.0	100.0	100.0	100.0	100.0	100.0	100.0	100.0	100.0	100.0
51 and over	—	—	—	—	—	—	—	—	—	—	—	—	—	—	—
Education															
None or primary	45.5	37.2	39.2	31.4	33.5	26.2	27.1	23.0	22.5	22.8	20.8	18.8	14.0	13.1	8.2
Secondary	28.9	29.5	30.9	33.0	29.4	34.3	33.6	34.7	34.2	36.3	34.4	33.0	40.2	33.6	36.9
High school	17.8	24.6	18.6	26.2	28.7	30.2	30.3	31.2	32.9	30.6	33.6	35.7	34.5	41.2	44.0
University	7.7	8.7	11.3	9.4	8.4	9.3	9.0	11.1	10.3	10.3	11.2	12.5	11.3	12.1	10.9
Geographical area															
North	77.1	75.2	75.0	74.3	76.4	73.3	73.1	69.9	71.2	70.5	69.6	72.0	71.3	70.1	70.0
South	22.9	24.8	25.0	25.7	23.6	26.7	26.9	30.1	28.8	29.5	30.4	28.0	28.7	29.9	30.0
Economic branch[a]															
Agriculture and fishery	—	—	—	—	—	—	—	—	—	—	—	—	—	—	—
Industry	50.2	45.7	46.4	50.7	46.6	43.2	40.0	37.8	41.2	38.0	41.7	40.4	39.2	40.8	43.0
Trade and lodging	4.9	6.1	4.0	5.1	5.6	4.8	9.5	8.2	6.7	10.4	6.8	7.0	5.6	7.8	7.6
Transport and credit	16.7	17.7	17.4	13.2	14.3	17.8	20.0	19.9	18.1	18.0	15.1	12.7	11.1	8.8	9.0
Other services	28.2	30.5	32.2	31.0	33.4	34.2	30.5	34.0	34.0	33.6	36.4	39.9	44.1	42.7	40.4
Job status[a]															
Production workers	64.9	58.2	58.4	51.5	51.2	48.2	51.0	53.1	42.8	48.5	45.2	43.1	43.7	46.2	47.6
Clerical workers	31.2	37.1	36.1	43.6	44.8	47.7	45.7	42.0	54.8	48.7	51.1	53.3	52.6	50.4	49.2
Managerial workers	3.9	4.7	5.5	4.9	4.0	4.1	3.2	4.9	2.4	2.8	3.7	3.6	3.6	3.4	3.2
Total	100.0	100.0	100.0	100.0	100.0	100.0	100.0	100.0	100.0	100.0	100.0	100.0	100.0	100.0	100.0

Source and Notes: Authors' elaboration on data from SHIW-HA (Release 1.0). Figures might not add up to 100 because of rounding. (a) Population shares were calculated after elimination of a few missing values.

9.3. CHANGES IN THE DISTRIBUTION OF EARNINGS

9.3.1. The SHIW Evidence for 1977–98

We focus on the distribution of *real monthly net earnings*, obtained by dividing total earnings, net of taxes and social security contributions, by the number of months worked in the year in each job and deflating by the consumer price index for the population as a whole.[4] We cannot compute hourly earnings because hours worked are only available for some years and are imprecisely estimated, so we control for differences in working time by looking at the sample of full-time workers only. The moments of the distributions are characterized by some considerable year-to-year changes, both for the full sample and for the sub-samples. This is probably due in part to the small size of the sample, but to some extent it is also the outcome of the staggered renewal of labour contracts, the operation of the wage indexation system, and the modifications in the composition of the labour force. Whatever the reasons for such variability, we shall mainly concentrate on medium-term movements rather than annual changes.

Between 1977 and 1989, both mean and median real monthly net earnings rose by about one fourth, or 1.8 per cent per year (Fig. 9.1; Table 9.3). In the following 9 years, they declined by around 1 per cent per year; some of this reduction was due to the spread of part-time work, as is shown by the much smaller drop in monthly earnings of full-time employees. In the 1990s, the decline in monthly wages was compounded with a reduction in the average number of months worked (from 11.6 in 1989 to 11.0 in 1995, and 11.3 in 1998), causing a pronounced fall in annual income from employment. Data on gross wages are not available in the SHIW, but a rough comparison with the national accounts suggests that much of the fall in net earnings in the 1990s may have been caused by the rising fiscal burden.

In Fig. 9.1 we plot the time profile of two measures of dispersion of real monthly net earnings,[5] the Gini index of concentration and the decile ratio.[6] The Gini index of the overall distribution shows a narrowing during the 1980s,

---

[4] By adopting the *national* consumer price index, we neglect the differences in purchasing power induced by the variability of price levels across regions—a choice that is unavoidable due to the lack of official data. Caruso *et al.* (1993) have found that prices, particularly housing prices, rose more rapidly in the North than in the South in the 1970s and 1980s, and Cannari (1993) has estimated that, in 1989, price levels were higher in the North than in the South, and were positively correlated with town size. On the basis of this evidence, we are probably overestimating the inequality of *real* net earnings as well as biasing its changes over time.

[5] As positions held for part of the year account for a sizeable proportion of jobs (see Table 9.1), the dispersion of *annual* earnings is significantly greater than that of monthly earnings. It would, however, exhibit a rather similar pattern over time, possibly with larger year-to-year changes.

[6] The Gini index of concentration is defined as one-half of the arithmetic average of the absolute values of difference between all pairs of monthly earnings divided by their mean; it is equal to twice the area between the 45° line and the Lorenz curve, and it ranges between 0 (perfect equality) and 1 (maximum inequality). The decile ratio is obtained by dividing the 90th percentile by the 10th percentile of the distribution.

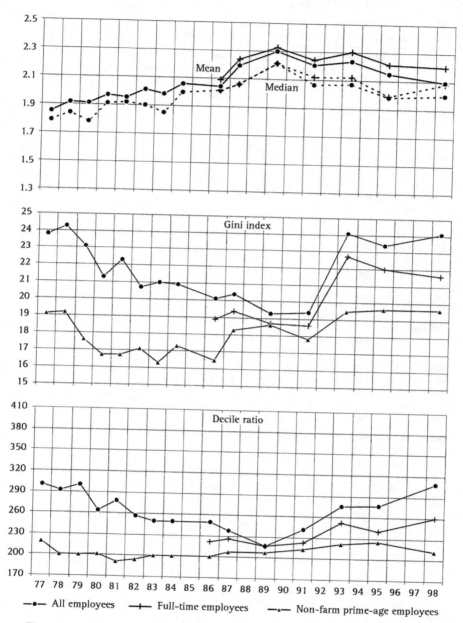

Figure 9.1. *Distribution of real monthly net earnings, 1977–98 (million lire at 1998 prices and per cent)*

Source: Authors' elaboration on data from SHIW-HA (Release 1.0).

Table 9.3. *Mean, median and measures of dispersion of the distribution of real monthly net earnings, 1977–98 (thousand lire at 1998 prices and percentage values)*

Year	Mean	Median	Mean logarithmic deviation	Theil index	Half coefficient of variation squared	Wolfson polarization index	Quintile ratio	Decile ratio
All primary jobs								
1977	1852	1789	11.7	10.9	14.4	16.3	179	300
1978	1916	1841	12.4	11.7	15.3	15.9	180	292
1979	1911	1781	11.4	10.5	12.9	15.9	167	300
1980	1969	1911	9.7	8.4	8.8	15.0	171	264
1981	1954	1919	11.0	10.2	13.8	15.1	168	278
1982	2012	1901	8.9	7.9	8.6	14.8	171	257
1983	1982	1851	8.7	8.0	8.7	15.6	167	250
1984	2056	1995	8.8	8.3	9.6	14.1	167	250
1986	2042	2014	7.7	7.3	7.9	13.4	167	250
1987	2193	2060	7.5	7.6	8.9	14.4	160	238
1989	2299	2214	6.5	7.0	8.5	13.4	157	217
1991	2204	2066	6.6	6.9	8.7	14.5	167	242
1993	2235	2073	11.0	11.1	14.4	17.3	184	275
1995	2149	1983	9.8	10.2	13.0	16.9	188	277
1998	2094	2000	12.1	11.2	13.9	15.9	167	308
Full-time jobs								
1986	2090	2014	6.6	6.4	7.1	12.7	167	222
1987	2238	2060	6.6	6.9	8.2	14.0	163	226
1989	2326	2214	5.9	6.5	8.1	13.0	157	217
1991	2241	2120	5.9	6.3	8.2	13.8	167	223
1993	2302	2122	9.5	9.9	13.2	16.4	175	252
1995	2215	1992	8.5	9.2	11.9	16.3	176	240
1998	2202	2083	8.9	9.2	12.2	14.2	163	260
Non-farm prime-age male workers employed year-round								
1977	2281	2064	6.5	7.7	12.4	14.7	167	219
1978	2397	2115	6.8	8.2	13.0	13.1	163	200
1979	2334	2138	5.7	6.3	8.0	11.1	150	200
1980	2390	2205	4.8	5.2	6.1	12.1	155	202
1981	2361	2214	5.2	6.5	10.7	11.4	149	191
1982	2417	2281	5.0	5.2	5.8	13.1	165	195
1983	2410	2210	5.1	4.9	5.2	12.1	150	200
1984	2450	2294	5.3	5.9	7.5	11.6	153	200
1986	2461	2244	4.6	4.9	5.6	12.7	154	200
1987	2560	2321	5.6	6.2	7.6	13.7	157	208
1989	2634	2399	5.8	6.6	8.2	13.5	156	208
1991	2607	2392	5.2	5.6	6.6	13.6	158	213
1993	2686	2468	6.3	6.9	8.3	14.0	160	222
1995	2557	2299	6.4	7.0	8.6	14.6	170	225
1998	2499	2250	6.6	7.4	9.6	14.2	164	212

Source: Authors' elaboration on data from SHIW-HA (Release 1.0).

somewhat stronger at the beginning, a sharp widening in the early 1990s and substantial stability between 1993 and 1998 (Table 9.4). The decile ratio, which is insensitive to movements in the middle of the distribution, shares this same pattern, though its increase from 1989 to 1998 is more regular (Table 9.3).[7] The dispersion of real earnings among full-time employees is less than in the whole sample, but it moved in a similar way over the period 1977–98. Some difference emerged in the mid-1990s, as the spread of part-time jobs turned a decreasing Gini index for the distribution among full-time workers into an increasing one overall. This difference should not be overemphasized, however, as it is within the bounds of sampling error. The evidence changes if we look at prime-age non-agricultural male workers employed year-round: their wage distribution is much more equal than that of the entire sample. Inequality diminished until the early 1980s and then tended to increase, through ups and downs, during the remainder of the decade, anticipating the trend reversal undergone by the full sample. Changes for this sub-group are much less marked, however.

In the overall sample, the narrowing of the distribution stemmed from gains at the bottom as well as (relative) losses at the top. Between 1977 and 1989, the ratio to the median of the monthly pay of employees at the 10th percentile rose from 51 to 67 per cent, while that of employees at the 90th percentile fell from 154 to 144 per cent; gains and losses were smaller, the closer workers were to the median (Fig. 9.2; Table 9.5). The rise in inequality in the 1990s reversed the changes of the previous decade, with earnings at different percentiles returning to their 1977 levels. Between 1995 and 1998 noticeable losses for employees at the top (80th and 90th percentiles) and bottom (10th percentile) resulted in the relative stability of overall inequality.

9.3.2. The SHIW Evidence for 1977–98 by Sex and Region

In order to shed further light on the evolution of the overall distribution we broke down the population along two relevant dimensions: sex and geographical area. Gender differentials showed fairly large variations from year to year, probably amplified by the small size of the female sub-sample (Fig. 9.3). However, a rather clear tendency towards closing the gap emerged from 1977 to 1989, as the ratio of women's to men's mean earnings rose by 10 percentage points to over 80 per cent; the ratio declined in the mid-1990s, but returned to 81 per cent in 1998. The narrower gap based on median earnings exhibited the same pattern. Differentials were smaller and somewhat more stable for full-time workers, part-time work being concentrated among women. In the 1980s, the bottom two deciles of the

---

[7] A substantially similar story is told by the polarization index, a measure ranging from 0 to 1 proposed by Wolfson (1994, p. 354) to capture '... the 'spreadoutness' from the middle...'. This index for all primary jobs showed some fluctuations but it declined from 16.3 per cent in 1977 to 13.4 per cent in 1989, suggesting some 'thickening' of the middle of the distribution; it then rose abruptly to 17.3 per cent in 1993, falling back below 16 per cent by 1998 (Table 9.3). If we restrict the sample to non-farm prime-age male workers, polarization rose in the mid-1980s but remained fairly stable afterwards.

Table 9.4. *Gini index of concentration for real monthly net earnings by sex and region, 1977–98 (per cent; asymptotic standard error × 100 in parentheses)*

Year	All	Males	Females	North		South	
All primary jobs							
1977	23.8 (0.58)	22.0 (0.70)	23.6 (0.76)	22.7	0.55	25.6	1.61
1978	24.3 (0.61)	22.5 (0.73)	24.2 (0.91)	24.3	0.72	22.8	0.95
1979	23.1 (0.59)	21.7 (0.73)	22.6 (0.84)	21.7	0.56	25.7	1.57
1980	21.3 (0.43)	20.3 (0.52)	20.9 (0.67)	20.9	0.51	21.2	0.69
1981	22.3 (0.64)	20.1 (0.77)	24.1 (1.06)	21.2	0.73	24.7	1.28
1982	20.7 (0.44)	19.8 (0.52)	19.7 (0.72)	20.2	0.54	21.3	0.65
1983	21.0 (0.42)	19.7 (0.47)	21.0 (0.79)	20.7	0.52	21.2	0.70
1984	20.9 (0.52)	20.4 (0.66)	18.8 (0.63)	20.8	0.67	20.4	0.62
1986	20.1 (0.45)	19.2 (0.53)	18.6 (0.63)	19.7	0.56	20.4	0.64
1987	20.4 (0.49)	20.1 (0.59)	18.3 (0.70)	20.8	0.58	18.7	0.77
1989	19.3 (0.42)	19.6 (0.52)	17.2 (0.61)	19.9	0.53	17.9	0.56
1991	19.4 (0.46)	19.2 (0.56)	17.9 (0.66)	19.6	0.55	18.8	0.78
1993	24.1 (0.65)	23.3 (0.70)	23.2 (1.32)	23.3	0.78	25.9	1.19
1995	23.4 (0.52)	23.2 (0.69)	21.7 (0.67)	23.2	0.64	23.8	0.87
1998	24.1 (0.54)	23.5 (0.66)	23.4 (0.91)	23.1	0.64	26.1	0.95
Full-time jobs							
1986	18.9 (0.44)	18.8 (0.53)	16.2 (0.61)	18.4	0.55	19.5	0.65
1987	19.5 (0.49)	19.7 (0.59)	16.3 (0.72)	19.6	0.58	18.1	0.78
1989	18.7 (0.42)	19.4 (0.53)	15.6 (0.57)	19.2	0.53	17.2	0.54
1991	18.6 (0.45)	19.0 (0.56)	16.2 (0.63)	18.7	0.54	18.2	0.78
1993	22.7 (0.66)	22.9 (0.70)	20.6 (1.40)	21.9	0.78	24.6	1.21
1995	22.0 (0.53)	23.0 (0.69)	18.6 (0.66)	21.8	0.64	22.5	0.88
1998	21.6 (0.52)	22.0 (0.64)	19.7 (0.92)	21.0	0.63	22.6	0.88
Non-farm prime-age male workers employed year-round							
1977	19.1 (1.01)						
1978	19.2 (1.15)						
1979	17.6 (0.82)						
1980	16.7 (0.67)						
1981	16.7 (1.26)						
1982	17.1 (0.65)						
1983	16.3 (0.65)						
1984	17.3 (0.90)						
1986	16.5 (0.74)						
1987	18.3 (0.80)						
1989	18.6 (0.72)						
1991	17.8 (0.72)						
1993	19.5 (0.94)						
1995	19.6 (0.81)						
1998	19.6 (0.77)						

Source: Authors' elaboration on data from SHIW-HA (Release 1.0). Asymptotic standard errors calculated according to the formula derived by Cowell (1989), assuming known mean of sample weights.

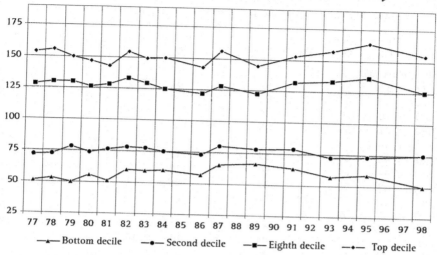

Figure 9.2. *Percentile ratios to median for real monthly net earnings, 1977–98 (percentage ratios; median = 100).*

Source: Authors' elaboration on data from SHIW-HA (Release 1.0).

female distribution gained sharply relative to the national median, whereas in the 1990s a rise at the top corresponded to a deterioration for the lowest deciles (Fig. 9.4).

Inequality, as measured by the Gini index, diminished in 1979 and 1980 for both men and women (Fig. 9.5). Equalization continued over the 1980s at a somewhat slower pace for men than for women.[8] Between 1991 and 1993, the reduction in inequality over the previous 15 years was completely undone: for workers of either sex the Gini index rose above 23 per cent, as against 22 for men and 24 for women in 1977–78 (Table 9.4). Inequality did not change from 1993 to 1998 for male employees, while it first declined and then went back to the 1993 value for female employees. The picture is broadly similar for the decile ratio, although the fall during the 1980s is less pronounced for men's earnings and the rise in the mid-1990s is more modest for women's. Monthly earnings of women employed full-time were considerably less dispersed than in the full sample, but the behaviour over time was similar. For men, the exclusion of part-time workers, a small minority, makes virtually no difference to the inequality pattern except in 1998, which shows a fall instead of a stability.

With regard to geographical differences, at the end of 1970s mean real monthly earnings in the South were 15 per cent lower than in the North (Fig. 9.3). This difference shrank in the 1980s, especially in the second half, and in 1989 the gap was virtually closed. In the following decade the geographical differential

[8] The composition of the sample for 1981 is at odds with other external information, particularly for women. We therefore disregard the dispersion of women's wages measured in this year.

Table 9.5. *Ratios to the median of percentiles of the distribution of real monthly net earnings, 1977–98 (percentage values)*

Year	P_{05}	P_{10}	P_{20}	P_{30}	P_{40}	P_{60}	P_{70}	P_{80}	P_{90}	P_{95}
All primary jobs										
1977	31	51	72	82	90	103	115	128	154	180
1978	33	53	72	83	89	107	111	130	156	178
1979	36	50	78	86	96	110	120	130	150	180
1980	37	55	74	85	92	108	115	126	146	175
1981	36	51	76	83	92	106	115	128	143	167
1982	42	60	78	89	94	111	117	133	154	178
1983	44	60	78	90	96	110	119	129	149	179
1984	43	60	75	83	92	108	115	125	150	167
1986	43	57	73	86	93	104	111	121	143	171
1987	50	66	80	87	93	107	117	128	156	180
1989	56	67	78	83	89	100	111	122	144	167
1991	55	63	79	84	95	105	116	132	153	174
1993	43	57	72	83	92	110	119	133	157	191
1995	46	59	73	82	91	109	118	136	164	191
1998	38	50	75	83	92	107	117	125	154	188
Full-time jobs										
1986	53	64	77	86	93	107	114	129	143	171
1987	60	69	80	87	93	107	120	130	157	180
1989	61	67	78	83	89	103	111	122	144	167
1991	61	67	77	86	92	103	115	128	149	174
1993	48	63	74	84	93	109	116	130	158	187
1995	54	68	77	86	91	109	118	136	163	190
1998	48	60	76	84	92	104	113	124	156	180
Non-farm prime-age male workers employed year-round										
1977	67	71	80	89	93	111	118	133	156	178
1978	70	77	83	91	97	106	116	135	155	193
1979	67	75	83	90	100	108	117	125	150	183
1980	67	77	80	91	93	107	113	124	155	173
1981	67	76	82	89	94	106	111	122	144	162
1982	65	74	79	88	93	108	111	130	144	167
1983	71	75	83	92	100	108	117	125	150	181
1984	65	73	80	87	94	104	109	123	145	174
1986	71	77	83	90	96	109	115	128	154	192
1987	71	74	83	89	95	107	118	130	154	186
1989	67	74	82	87	92	108	118	128	154	185
1991	68	73	82	89	91	109	114	130	155	182
1993	64	72	80	86	92	104	116	128	160	184
1995	63	71	78	86	94	110	118	133	159	195
1998	67	73	82	89	96	111	119	133	156	185

Source: Authors' elaboration on data from SHIW-HA (Release 1.0).

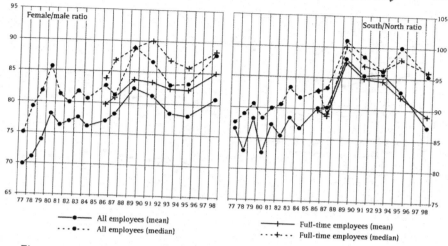

Figure 9.3. *Gender and geographical differentials, 1977–98 (percentage ratios).*
Source: Authors' elaboration on data from SHIW-HA (Release 1.0).

widened again. Between 1989 and 1998 mean real earnings fell by 5.8 per cent in the North and by 16.3 per cent in the South so that at the end of the period the average southern wage was 13 per cent lower than the average northern wage.[9] The narrowing of the gap in the 1980s mainly reflected substantial improvements in the bottom half of the southern wage distribution, which were completely undone in the 1990s; conversely, the top southern deciles gained nothing relative to the national median in the first sub-period but did better their positions in the following decade (Fig. 9.4). Measures of income inequality display the same basic behaviour in both areas of the country, although variations are larger in the South, partly as a consequence of the smaller sample size (Fig. 9.6). Earnings dispersion tended to be less in the North than in the South at the beginning and at the end of the period but greater in 1987, 1989, and 1991, when it was at its lowest in the country as a whole.

[9] The changes in geographical differential for net monthly earnings per job position in the SHIW are much more marked than for gross earnings per full-time equivalent employee in national accounts. The latter show small fluctuations around a flat trend. The discrepancy may be partly explained by the different definitions of earnings, and in particular by their being *net* of personal income taxes and employees' social security contributions in the SHIW but *gross* in national accounts. However, most of the discrepancy is likely to arise from the intrinsic differences between the two sources. On the one hand, the SHIW figures are liable to erratic movements induced by small sample size. On the other hand, the method used in the national accounts to impute mean values to employed standard labour units may tend to smooth out earnings variability, leading to more stable dynamics. Data drawn from INPS (2001), which refer to pre-tax earnings in the non-farm private sector, show North–South differentials similar both in levels and in their widening tendency over the period 1991–97 to those found in the SHIW.

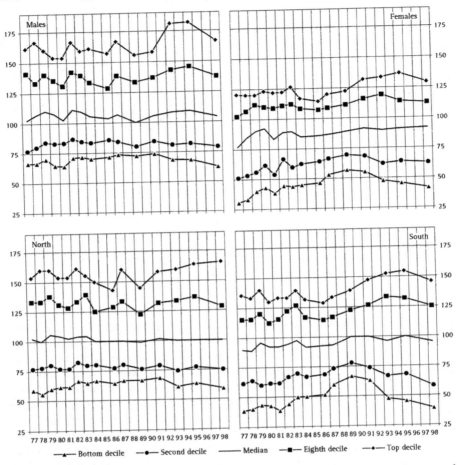

Figure 9.4. *Percentile ratios to national median of real monthly net earnings by sex and region, 1977–98 (percentage values; national median = 100).*

Source: Authors' elaboration on data from SHIW-HA (Release 1.0).

9.3.3. Summing Up

To sum up, the SHIW evidence suggests a definite temporal pattern for overall wage inequality in Italy. The distribution of net earnings narrowed from the late 1970s until the end of the 1980s, and especially in the first part of the period; it abruptly widened in the early 1990s and underwent little modification in the rest of the decade. The intensity of changes and year-to-year variations may differ, but this pattern broadly describes the evolution of earnings inequality in the main sub-groups of the population: full-time employees, both male and female salaried workers, both residents in the North and in the South. However, this picture must be rectified for prime-age non-agricultural male workers employed throughout the

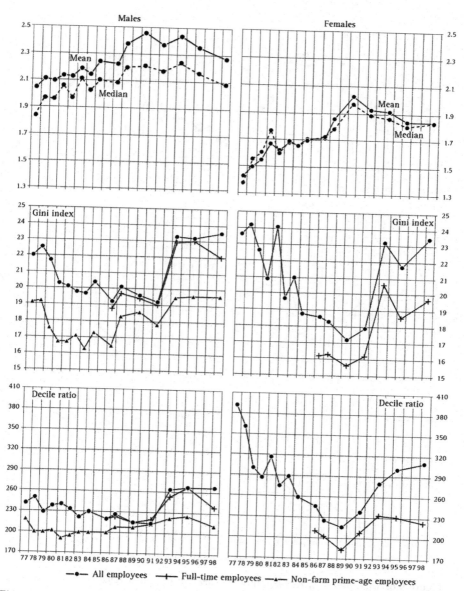

Figure 9.5. *Distribution of real monthly net earnings by sex, 1977–98 (million lire at 1998 prices and per cent).*

Source: Authors' elaboration on data from SHIW-HA (Release 1.0).

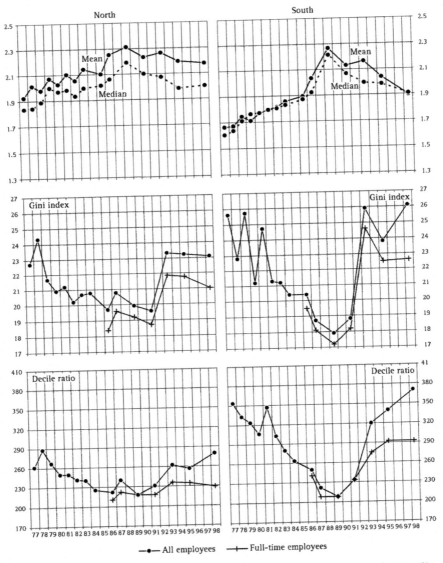

Figure 9.6. *Distribution of real monthly net earnings by region, 1977–98 (million lire at 1998 prices and per cent).*

Source: Authors' elaboration on data from SHIW-HA (Release 1.0).

whole year, for whom the tendency towards greater inequality had already emerged in the mid-1980s and manifested itself in a less extreme form. This asymmetry between core employment and the full sample indicates that the relevant changes were concentrated among workers at the margins of the labour market.

The long phase of diminishing earnings inequality that ended in the 1980s is largely confirmed by the other scattered evidence available, including the information on wage differentials provided in national accounts (see Sestito, 1992; Erickson and Ichino, 1995; Brandolini, 2000b). There is also a fairly general consensus that this phase dates back to the late 1960s and early 1970s, the post-war period in which industrial conflict was at its highest. In those years, bargaining power shifted sharply in favour of workers and their strongly egalitarian demands, such as equal (lump-sum) pay raises for all workers regardless of grade (e.g., Regalia *et al.*, 1978; Erickson and Ichino, 1995). Later on, these demands translated into the 1975 reform of the wage indexation mechanism, which granted a flat-sum wage increase for each percentage point rise in the cost-of-living index. Until the early 1980s, the operation of this mechanism in the presence of double-digit inflation rates imparted a strong egalitarian push to the evolution of the earnings structure, which was only partially compensated by decentralized bargaining. On the basis of evidence up to 1991, Erickson and Ichino (1995, p. 298) concluded that 'the overall picture of Italy . . . is of a country with a compressed wage structure that is not yet undergoing the rapid decompression experienced elsewhere during the 1980s'.

The severe political and economic crisis of the early 1990s saw the number of resident employees, as measured in the national accounts, plummet by 670,000, or 4.0 per cent, in the fourth quarter of 1993 from the historical peak recorded in the second quarter of 1992. As is shown above, this drop in employment was accompanied by a substantial widening of wage spreads. In the rest of the 1990s, inequality did not revert to the low levels of the previous decade and, if anything, it showed a tendency to increase further.

The economic crisis as well as concomitant institutional changes may have unleashed a decompression of the wage structure, originating in factors already at work in other advanced countries. Manacorda (2000), for instance, argues that a tendency comparable in amplitude to that experienced in the US was latent since the early 1980s but failed to emerge because of the egalitarian wage indexation mechanism. Descriptive evidence hinting at a weakening of egalitarian demands during the 1980s is summarized by Regalia and Regini (1996), who report that, in the manufacturing sector, performance-related premia and individual bonuses gradually spread, with the support of unions, through bargaining agreements at company level. After 1994, the phasing-out of contribution relief for southern firms could partly account for the return to wider geographical differentials: some firms may have been able to transfer part of the higher labour cost burden[10] onto the most vulnerable workers, reducing their net earnings. A further factor in the 1990s may have been the spread of part-time and fixed-term employment contracts. In any case, our evidence suggests that changes in the wage

---

[10] According to the regional accounts (Istat, 2001a), the difference in the implicit payroll tax rates—computed as the ratio of employers' social security contributions to gross wages and salaries—narrowed from 9 to 6.6 percentage points between 1995 and 1998.

structure mostly affected marginal employees, or those at the bottom of the wage scale.

9.4. LOW-PAID EMPLOYMENT

After documenting changes in the entire distribution of net earnings, we now turn our attention to its lower tail, and more precisely to low-paid workers, i.e., those '. . . workers who earn less than two thirds of median earnings for all full-time workers' (OECD, 1996). As was seen in Section 9.2, part-time contracts were not separately regulated by law until 1984 and no information was gathered in the SHIW; their diffusion was, however, almost negligible. We have therefore chosen to set the low-pay cut-off by reference to the overall distribution until 1984 and to the distribution for full-time jobs only from 1986 onwards. That the medians of the two distributions coincide in 1986, 1987, and 1989 provides some support for this choice.

Before looking at the data on low-paid workers, a short digression on institutional arrangements is in order. In Italy there is no compulsory minimum wage, but 'minima' are fixed in the national contracts signed by unions and employers' associations. Despite relatively strong centralization and co-ordination of bargaining, a national contract is binding only for a firm which is a member of an employers' association signing the contract. No formal rule prevents an independent firm from paying wages lower than the contractual ones. On the other hand, several forces operate to extend the actual coverage of national minima: (1) courts tend to use them as a yardstick, providing an incentive for dissatisfied employees to call for the court's intervention and for unions to support such claims; (2) financial subsidies to firms are often made conditional on complying with contractual rates; (3) employers' social security contributions are computed on the greater between the actual earnings and the contractual minimum. In so far as it acts as a minimum wage, the national contract would imply a much higher floor, relative to the average or median wage, than that usually fixed by law or by wage councils where a mandatory system applies. To some degree this may adversely affect the level of employment, although the large size of the Italian underground economy testifies to the extent to which contractual minima are not applied.[11]

The evolution of the share of low-paid jobs parallels that of earnings inequality and, with opposite sign, that of the ratio of the bottom decile to the median (Fig. 9.7; Table 9.6). As was seen above, the gains at the bottom of the distribution for all job positions were rather substantial in the 1980s, and the incidence of low-paid workers halved from 16.9 per cent in 1977 to a minimum of 8.1 per cent in 1989. The proportion rose to 15.7 in 1993, and after a fall in 1995, reached a

---

[11] According to the old system of the national accounts (ESA, 1979), from 1980 to 1997 the share of non-regular salaried employment went up, along with a widening of the earnings gap relative to regular employment. Notwithstanding the substantial downward revision caused by the adoption of the new system (ESA, 1995), the proportion of non-regular employees increased from below 15 per cent in 1992 to 16.5 per cent in 1999 (Istat, 2001*b*).

Figure 9.7. *Share of low-paid workers, 1977–98 (percentage values).*
Source: Authors' elaboration on data from SHIW-HA (Release 1.0).

peak of 18.3 per cent in 1998. The incidence of low-paid employment is less among full-time workers but tends to move as in the full sample until mid-1990s. But the rise in low-paid jobs between 1993 and 1998 is fully accounted for by the spread of part-time work, as the incidence among full-time workers remains around 12 per cent. Among prime-age male non-farm workers employed year-round, the proportion of low-paid jobs remained fairly stable around 2 per cent until 1995; it rose to 4 per cent in 1998.

The time profile for the share of low-paid jobs is common across socio-demographic groups: for all groups, it declines more or less regularly up to 1989 and rises in the 1990s, with the exception of 1995 (Fig. 9.8; Table 9.6). While time patterns are homogeneous, levels differ greatly across groups. Women's probability of being low-paid is three times that of men; only in the 1990s did this difference narrow slightly. By contrast, the share of low-paid workers in the South in 1998 was twice as large as in the North; in that year the regional gap reached a record value, reversing the convergence that had characterized the 1980s. Spouses and children, mainly those younger than 30, are the groups most commonly affected by low pay. The relative position of the children of household heads deteriorated dramatically in 1998, when one in three of those employed had a low-paid job. Poorly educated and manual workers suffer a greater risk of being low-paid than persons with a university degree or employed in clerical positions. However, higher education has been losing the ability to shelter people from the risk of being low-paid: compared with 1977, the risk was greater in 1998 for all workers, regardless of their level of education.

In spite of the recent increase, in the mid-1990s the average incidence of low-paid employment (for full-time jobs) was relatively low by international

Table 9.6. Incidence of low-paid employees, 1977–98 (per cent)

Personal characteristic	All job positions															Full-time job positions						
	1977	1978	1979	1980	1981	1982	1983	1984	1986	1987	1989	1991	1993	1995	1998	1986	1987	1989	1991	1993	1995	1998
Sex																						
Male	9.9	8.4	9.0	10.4	10.2	6.7	7.3	8.0	8.6	6.1	4.9	6.1	9.7	8.2	13.0	7.6	5.3	4.5	5.5	8.8	7.5	9.8
Female	32.4	27.3	25.9	23.4	30.2	17.8	22.5	20.9	22.4	17.7	13.8	17.2	25.1	22.0	25.9	16.1	12.0	10.0	12.4	17.3	13.5	16.1
Household position [a]																						
Head	5.4	4.4	5.4	5.2	5.3	3.3	3.4	4.4	5.0	2.6	2.7	3.2	6.5	6.6	8.9	3.8	1.8	2.0	2.7	4.7	4.6	5.9
Spouse	27.0	22.4	22.5	20.9	26.3	16.5	20.7	18.0	18.8	15.6	10.8	15.5	19.1	16.7	20.6	11.5	9.9	7.3	10.1	11.8	8.3	10.0
Child	33.8	27.9	26.8	29.1	33.3	20.8	23.5	25.2	29.0	21.4	17.4	19.8	29.7	23.0	34.3	26.5	18.4	15.6	16.8	26.3	19.9	27.9
Age																						
Under 30	28.2	25.1	23.9	24.2	28.1	18.3	20.7	22.3	26.2	18.5	15.0	18.5	29.5	23.8	34.0	23.3	15.6	13.1	15.3	25.7	19.7	26.2
31–50	10.4	8.0	8.8	9.0	10.0	6.3	8.1	8.1	7.8	6.6	5.0	6.7	10.0	10.1	12.5	4.9	4.0	3.4	4.7	6.1	6.0	7.0
51 and over	11.2	10.8	11.8	12.8	12.2	7.9	8.0	8.8	10.3	5.8	4.6	6.7	9.7	7.0	13.6	7.1	3.8	3.2	4.9	6.9	4.0	9.6
Education																						
None or primary	19.2	18.9	19.4	20.6	22.8	16.5	19.0	20.1	19.8	15.2	10.8	13.0	22.3	18.7	26.6	14.6	11.1	7.9	9.7	17.0	12.8	19.0
Secondary	20.1	14.9	15.5	15.4	19.4	11.5	14.4	13.5	17.1	11.9	11.0	14.7	21.6	19.5	23.3	14.4	9.6	9.6	12.1	17.9	15.1	15.8
High school	11.1	9.5	9.7	10.8	10.9	6.0	7.2	8.8	7.4	6.9	5.9	7.6	10.0	9.8	15.7	5.5	4.6	4.3	5.4	6.4	6.1	10.3
University	5.0	5.4	4.0	7.8	7.3	3.6	1.8	2.1	2.8	2.4	1.0	2.2	3.0	4.6	7.3	1.6	1.1	0.4	1.8	1.3	4.2	4.7
Geographical area																						
North	14.1	12.0	11.7	13.7		7.5	10.5	9.3	11.2	9.1	8.1	9.2	13.7	11.4	14.4	8.0	5.8	6.2	6.7	9.4	7.0	8.6
South	23.9	20.3	21.2	23.2	25.6	17.8	16.9	19.6	19.3	13.1	8.2	13.0	20.6	19.2	27.6	16.7	12.0	7.0	11.2	18.1	16.3	20.9
Economic branch																						
Agriculture and fishery	29.7	33.2	32.6	33.3	47.3	32.6	32.1	40.4	38.4	18.6	17.3	23.2	49.3	26.2	45.1	38.3	17.4	17.7	22.5	44.8	25.2	39.7
Industry	14.4	12.9	13.7	13.8	18.5	10.7	10.3	8.8	11.4	9.9	9.0	10.8	14.7	12.3	16.6	9.8	8.6	7.5	9.5	12.9	10.5	13.4
Trade and lodging	31.8	20.7	25.4	25.0	30.4	18.2	24.4	23.5	26.6	19.9	12.8	13.7	29.1	25.0	24.9	21.8	14.4	10.1	9.1	22.4	16.8	14.6
Transport and credit	3.8	4.6	3.1	4.7	2.4	2.7	4.4	1.5	1.9	2.1	2.6	5.6	5.3	4.4	12.0	1.6	1.5	1.6	4.3	2.3	1.7	8.8
Other services	19.0	14.5	13.4	13.8	12.6	7.4	9.9	11.9	12.5	8.4	6.5	8.7	12.4	12.8	16.1	7.8	4.8	4.5	5.6	7.9	7.8	8.5
Job status [b]																						
Production workers	21.4	19.3	19.5	21.7	23.8	15.8	18.0	18.0	21.2	15.1	12.2	16.0	23.7	19.2	24.9	17.1	11.7	10.4	13.0	19.6	14.7	18.1
Clerical workers	7.9	6.7	6.8	7.4	8.8	5.0	5.8	5.7	5.2	5.0	4.5	5.1	6.8	7.3	10.2	3.5	3.2	2.9	3.4	3.9	4.1	6.4
Job length																						
All year	13.8	9.8	10.3	10.3	13.0	7.4	9.2	7.7	9.8	7.1	7.3	8.2	11.3	10.9	13.2	7.9	5.0	5.8	6.1	8.5	7.2	9.1
Part year	39.6	40.7	41.9	44.7	41.3	29.2	34.6	42.3	32.8	31.1	18.7	32.7	40.2	29.2	50.3	26.1	27.9	16.6	30.3	34.0	25.5	37.7
Prime workers [c]	3.0	0.9	2.4	2.2	2.0	1.7	2.0	1.6	1.5	1.4	1.7	1.7	2.0	2.4	4.1	1.3	0.7	1.6	1.5	1.8	2.1	3.3
All employees	16.9	14.4	14.6	15.0	17.1	10.5	12.4	12.5	13.5	10.2	8.1	10.3	15.7	13.7	18.3	10.5	7.5	6.4	7.9	11.9	9.7	12.2

Source: Authors' elaboration on data from SHIW-HA (Release 1.0). (a) Figures for 'other members' were not reported because of their small share in population. (b) Figures for 'managerial workers' were not reported because of their small share in population. (c) Non-farm prime-age male workers employed year-round.

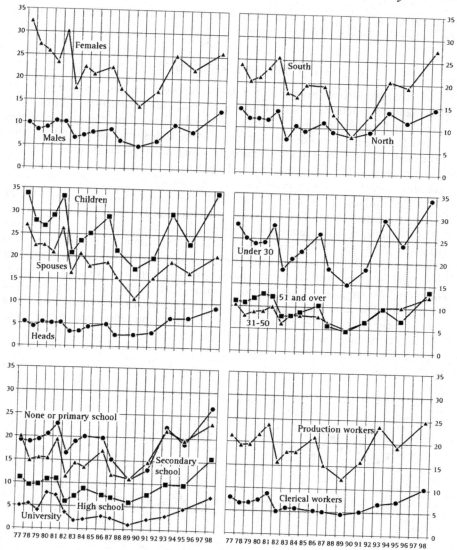

Figure 9.8. *Share of low-paid workers by personal characteristics, 1977–98 (percentage values).*

Source: Authors' elaboration on data from SHIW-HA (Release 1.0).

standards: it was much lower than in the Anglo-Saxon countries and Japan, more or less in line with the countries of continental Europe, and greater only than in the traditionally more equal countries, such as Belgium, Finland, and Sweden (OECD, 1996; Keese *et al.*, 1998). Also the composition of the low-paid employment according to several socio-demographic characteristics quite closely resembles the pattern in other countries.

9.5. LOW PAY AND POVERTY

In this final section, we examine the relationship between low pay and poverty. As is standard practice, we set the poverty line at half the median of household equivalent income. To check whether the results depend on the choice of the poverty line, we also consider two alternative thresholds set at 40 and 60 per cent of the median. The household's income is the sum of all after-tax incomes received by the members, including the imputed rent on owner-occupied dwellings but excluding interest and dividends, for they are recorded in the SHIW only after 1987. The equivalence scale used to deflate income is that utilized in official poverty statistics in Italy (see Inquiry Commission on Poverty, 1997).

The dynamics of poverty are shown in the left-hand panel of Fig. 9.9. Between 1977 and 1991, the proportion of persons in poor households ranged from 9 to 12 per cent, oscillating around a flat trend; it jumped to 14 per cent in 1993 and 1995, and to 15 per cent in 1998. The time pattern remains virtually the same, albeit on different levels, when the poverty line is set at either 40 or 60 per cent of the median. The ratio for employees is about half that of total population, being around 5 per cent until 1991 and over 7 per cent in the remainder of the 1990s (Fig. 9.9, right-hand panel).

The link between household poverty and low pay is summarized in Table 9.7. In 1998, 3.7 per cent of all primary jobs were low-paid and held by an employee

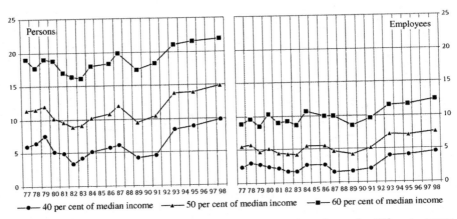

Figure 9.9. *Headcount poverty ratios among persons and employees by different poverty lines, 1977–98 (percentage values of persons or employees in poor households)*

Source: Authors' elaboration on data from SHIW-HA (Release 1.0). Income is defined as equivalent households' after-tax incomes, including imputed rental income from owner-occupied dwellings, but excluding net interest and dividends. The equivalence scale is that of the official Italian poverty commission (see Inquiry Commission on Poverty, 1997).

living in a household with equivalent income below the poverty line: the odds of being low-paid were 1 in 2 for poor employees against 1 in 6 for non-poor employees. On the other hand, having a low-paid job was not necessarily an indicator of poverty, as 4 out of 5 low-paid workers lived in non-poor households. The main reason is that wages and salaries are not the only source of income. On average, in 1998 they made up 34 per cent of total disposable income as defined here, while income from self-employment accounted for 17 per cent, pensions and other transfers for 30 per cent, and returns on real assets, including the imputed rent on owner-occupied dwellings, for the remaining 19 per cent. Moreover, as is shown in Table 9.6, low pay is predominantly a feature of supplementary earners, whose incomes tend to complement those of the primary earner, without altering the household's income status. The figures in Table 9.8 confirm these observations for the entire period: being low-paid is much more likely for poor employees, but the large majority of low-paid jobs are found in non-poor households. Table 9.8 also reports the Pearson χ^2 independence test, which shows that the null hypothesis of no association between low pay and poverty is strongly rejected in all years.

Low pay is only one dimension of the link between household poverty and the labour market, the other important dimension being the household's 'employment rate', i.e., the amount of work performed by its members. The interesting question is which characteristic—'employment rate' or 'low-paid status'—is more closely correlated with poverty. We have defined two further labour-market indicators: the total number of months worked and the number of months worked in self-employment, both expressed as ratios to the maximum number of months that a person can work (12 in general, 3 for students). We have also distinguished, for all variables, between the head and other adult members (i.e. aged between 18 and 65) pooled together (their low-paid status is the average of individual dummies). The Pearson χ^2 test of independence shows that all these variables, when considered separately, are closely correlated with poverty status.

Table 9.7. *Low-paid primary jobs and poverty, 1998*

	Numbers in thousands			Percentage shares of total		
	Low-paid	Non-low-paid	All	Low-paid	Non-low-paid	All
Poor	549	592	1,141	3.7	3.9	7.6
Non-poor	2,189	11,695	13,884	14.6	77.8	92.4
All	2,738	12,287	15,025	18.3	81.7	100.0

Source: Authors' elaboration on data from SHIW-HA (Release 1.0). An employee is considered poor when he/she lives in a household whose income is below 50 per cent of the median income. Income is defined as equivalent households' after-tax incomes, including imputed rental income from owner-occupied dwellings, but excluding net interest and dividends. The equivalence scale is the one utilized to compute official poverty statistics in Italy (see Inquiry Commission on Poverty, 1997).

Table 9.8. *Low-paid primary jobs and poverty, 1977–98 (percentage values)*

Year	Incidence of low-paid jobs		Distribution of low-paid jobs			Pearson χ^2 independence test[b]
	Poor employees[a]	Non-poor employees	Poor employees[a]	Non-poor employees	Total	
1977	40.8	15.4	13.4	86.6	100.0	62.7
1978	45.6	12.5	18.2	81.8	100.0	151.8
1979	44.0	13.2	14.1	85.9	100.0	104.7
1980	48.6	13.1	16.9	83.1	100.0	139.5
1981	49.1	15.6	12.7	87.3	100.0	127.4
1982	31.7	9.6	13.1	86.9	100.0	211.1
1983	34.8	11.4	11.8	88.2	100.0	143.6
1984	39.3	10.9	17.5	82.5	100.0	183.6
1986	32.8	12.4	13.4	86.6	100.0	194.6
1987	19.5	9.7	9.1	90.9	100.0	328.2
1989	14.7	7.8	7.5	92.5	100.0	491.7
1991	21.6	9.6	11.0	89.0	100.0	331.8
1993	47.4	13.2	21.8	78.2	100.0	369.3
1995	41.5	11.5	21.7	78.3	100.0	344.7
1998	48.1	15.8	20.0	80.0	100.0	286.6

Source: Authors' elaboration on data from SHIW-HA (Release 1.0). (a) An employee is considered poor when he/she lives in a household whose income is below 50 per cent of the median income. Income is defined as equivalent households' after-tax incomes, including imputed rental income from owner-occupied dwellings, but excluding net interest and dividends. The equivalence scale is the one utilized to compute official poverty statistics in Italy (see Inquiry Commission on Poverty, 1997). (b) Test of the null hypothesis that the classifications of low-paid jobs and poor employees are independent; since both classifications are binary, the test has 1 degree of freedom.

To compare the relative strength of the correlation, we have regressed household poverty against these labour-market variables, after inserting a number of controls (a dummy taking value zero when the head is older than 65 and value 1 otherwise; the household's size; the number of children; a dummy for home owners; and the amount of pensions and other transfers received, both divided by the number of equivalent persons). The results are not to be interpreted as the parameters of a structural model—as the labour-market indicators as well as most of the controls are endogenous variables that we are not trying to model—but rather as multivariate correlation coefficients. Robustness checks make us fairly confident that the endogeneity bias should not substantially alter our conclusions.[12]

---

[12] We run several regressions, of the type shown below, excluding one variable at a time, and we examine the changes in the estimated coefficients of the remaining variables. If the endogeneity bias is strong, we would expect substantial changes because of the correlation between the excluded variable and the remaining regressors. Our tests show that only the coefficient of the low paid variable is substantially altered by the sequential omission of one of the regressors, while the other coefficients, in particular those for months worked, are virtually unaffected.

Table 9.9. *Probability of being in poverty and poverty gap, pooled model, 1977–98*

	Probability of being in poverty				Poverty gap	
	Coefficient	Standard errors	Marginal effect[a]	Standard errors	Coefficient	Standard errors
Constant	−0.5652	0.0455	—	—	0.5722	0.0118
Household head						
Low-paid employee	0.0661	0.0237	0.0065	0.0023	0.0039	0.0082
Age 18–65	−0.0673	0.0249	−0.0912	0.0042	0.0052	0.0077
Months worked	−0.7040	0.0258	−0.0687	0.0026	−0.2578	0.0096
Months worked in self-employment	0.2791	0.0307	0.0272	0.0030	0.0818	0.0109
Other adult household members						
Low-paid employee	0.0555	0.0371	0.0054	0.0036	0.0070	0.0132
Months worked	−1.6198	0.0686	−0.1580	0.0060	−0.2182	0.0273
Months worked in self-employment	0.7619	0.0725	0.0743	0.0069	0.1382	0.0290
Number of members	0.1315	0.0089	0.0128	0.0009	−0.0066	0.0018
Number of children	0.1314	0.0058	0.0128	0.0006	−0.0023	0.0026
Home owner	−0.5913	0.0139	−0.0704	0.00207	−0.0677	0.0046
Pension per equivalent person (1 million lire at 1998 prices)	−0.1000	0.00023	−0.0098	0.0002	−0.0418	0.0012
Other transfers per equivalent person (1 million lire at 1998 prices)	−0.0126	0.0060	−0.0012	0.0006	−0.0291	0.0028
Log likelihood		−21,736				
Pseudo R^2		0.2030				
Number of observations		83,981			0.26 8,385	

Source: Authors' elaboration on data from SHIW-HA (Release 1.0). (a) The marginal effect is the partial derivative of the probability with respect to the regressor, evaluated at the sample means.

In Table 9.9 we report the results from estimating a probit model pooling together all years (year dummies not reported). The positive association between the probability of being poor and low wages is significant only for the household heads. More relevant is the number of months worked, especially when performed by household members other than the head, and in a salaried job. On the basis of the estimated coefficients, the head holding a low-paid job has roughly the same effect as working one month less as an employee. Results for control variables are in line with expectations. The household's size is positively associated with the risk of poverty, particularly when the additional members are minor children, whose marginal effect is twice as large as that of an adult. Home ownership and both types of transfers are negatively correlated with the probability of being poor. The modest effect of the other (non-pension) transfers confirms the poor targeting of the Italian welfare system.

Regressions conducted separately year-by-year allow us to qualify the picture (Table 9.10). In Fig. 9.10 we plot the marginal effects (including a four-standard-error symmetric band) estimated on a yearly basis for the four variables capturing labour-market status: the employment rate and low-paid status, separately for household heads and other adult members. (We ignore the effects of the other

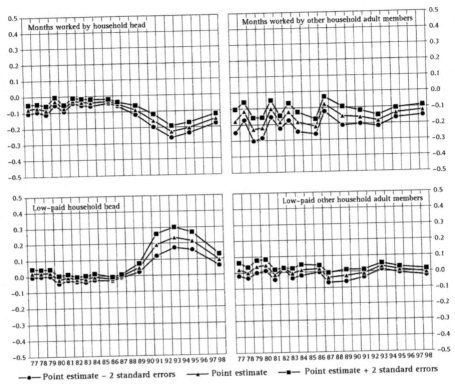

Figure 9.10. *Marginal effects on the probability of being in poverty, 1977–98.*

Source: Authors' elaboration on data from SHIW-HA (Release 1.0). A household is considered poor when its income is below 50 per cent of the median income. Income is defined as equivalent households' after-tax incomes, including imputed rental income from owner-occupied dwellings, but excluding net interest and dividends. The equivalence scale is the one utilized to compute official poverty statistics in Italy (see Inquiry Commission on Poverty, 1997).

covariates, which are reasonably stable over time.) The positive correlation between poverty and low-paid household head was statistically significant but quantitatively small in the late 1970s; it faded away in the following decade; it rose considerably between 1987 and 1993 and fell again by 1998, remaining four times higher than in 1977, however. While consistently significant over time, the marginal effect of the number of months worked by the head exhibited a rather similar, if opposite, pattern. Overall, both effects are now more substantial than they were at the beginning of our sample period. The changes are less dramatic for other adults: the coefficient of low-paid status is almost never statistically significant, while that of the employment rate is consistently negative and significant. To sum up, the separate regressions confirm that the probability of being in poverty is more strongly associated with the amount of employment in the

Table 9.10. Probability of being in poverty, separate regressions by year, 1977–98, marginal effects (standard errors in italics)

	1977	1978	1979	1980	1981	1982	1983	1984	1986	1987	1989	1991	1993	1995	1998
Household head															
Low-paid employee	0.0217	0.0213	0.0232	-0.0209	-0.0060	-0.0187	-0.0169	-0.0051	-0.0183	-0.0012	0.0492	0.1915	0.2364	0.2136	0.0944
	0.0131	*0.112*	*0.0112*	*0.0123*	*0.0094*	*0.0079*	*0.0100*	*0.0101*	*0.0059*	*0.0053*	*0.0133*	*0.0343*	*0.0321*	*0.0275*	*0.0178*
Age 18–65	-0.1838	-0.1392	-0.1289	-0.1562	-0.0769	-0.0564	-0.0882	-0.0754	-0.0974	-0.0615	-0.0451	-0.0794	-0.0550	-0.0725	-0.0879
	0.029	*0.0270*	*0.0270*	*0.0276*	*0.0178*	*0.0167*	*0.0196*	*0.0196*	*0.0155*	*0.0132*	*0.0102*	*0.0124*	*0.0105*	*0.0109*	*0.0126*
Months worked	-0.0787	-0.0715	-0.0858	-0.0295	-0.0737	-0.0273	-0.0370	-0.0411	-0.0330	-0.0518	-0.0910	-0.1576	-0.2290	-0.2049	-0.1489
	0.0140	*0.0125*	*0.0136*	*0.0126*	*0.0103*	*0.0081*	*0.0102*	*0.0108*	*0.0064*	*0.0065*	*0.0141*	*0.0202*	*0.0187*	*0.0165*	*0.0148*
Months worked in self-employment	0.0163	0.0312	0.0374	0.0104	0.0220	-0.0161	0.0106	-0.0118	0.0	0.0	0.0049	0.0032	0.0666	0.0598	0.0328
	0.0234	*0.0207*	*0.0187*	*0.0214*	*0.0169*	*0.0155*	*0.0164*	*0.0197*	*0.0*	*0.0*	*0.0057*	*0.0061*	*0.0079*	*0.0078*	*0.0072*
Other adult household members															
Low-paid employee	0.0222	0.0009	0.0389	0.0472	-0.0136	0.0266	-0.0060	0.0135	0.0199	-0.0363	-0.0247	-0.0112	0.0321	0.0106	-0.0055
	0.0210	*0.0171*	*0.0195*	*0.0178*	*0.0162*	*0.0010*	*0.0155*	*0.0170*	*0.0110*	*0.0153*	*0.0186*	*0.0119*	*0.0099*	*0.0094*	*0.0099*
Months worked	-0.1767	-0.1154	-0.2299	-0.2202	-0.1026	-0.1866	-0.1238	-0.1876	-0.2169	-0.0780	-0.1540	-0.1614	-0.1841	-0.1359	-0.1205
	0.0364	*0.0282*	*0.0366*	*0.0321*	*0.0262*	*0.01989*	*0.0270*	*0.0304*	*0.0234*	*0.0232*	*0.0291*	*0.0205*	*0.0171*	*0.0150*	*0.0157*
Months worked in self-employment	0.0757	-0.0589	-0.0116	-0.0195	-0.0184	0.0168	-0.0164	0.0560	0.0	0.0	0.0436	0.0974	0.0993	0.0628	0.0700
	0.0519	*0.0946*	*0.1085*	*0.0890*	*0.0653*	*0.0824*	*0.0848*	*0.0596*	*0.0*	*0.0*	*0.0301*	*0.0183*	*0.0147*	*0.0131*	*0.0138*
Number of members	0.0092	0.0088	0.009	0.0038	0.0128	0.0040	0.0111	0.0082	0.0149	0.0181	0.0144	0.0166	0.0113	0.0131	0.0138
	0.0035	*0.0033*	*0.0033*	*0.0031*	*0.0024*	*0.0018*	*0.0026*	*0.0028*	*0.0019*	*0.0019*	*0.0020*	*0.0020*	*0.0018*	*0.0018*	*0.0018*
Number of children	0.0110	0.0197	0.0159	0.0149	0.0024	0.0018	0.0026	0.0028	0.0019	0.0113	0.0120	0.0088	0.0131	0.0085	0.0119
	0.0054	*0.0050*	*0.0053*	*0.0050*	*0.0037*	*0.0031*	*0.0041*	*0.0044*	*0.0028*	*0.0027*	*0.0025*	*0.0022*	*0.0028*	*0.0026*	*0.0028*
Home owner	-0.0657	-0.0427	-0.0494	-0.0331	-0.0236	-0.0177	-0.0481	-0.0410	-0.0487	-0.0574	-0.0614	-0.0671	-0.1072	-0.1294	-0.1091
	0.0101	*0.0089*	*0.0096*	*0.0090*	*0.0068*	*0.0058*	*0.0083*	*0.0090*	*0.0058*	*0.0061*	*0.0070*	*0.0077*	*0.0081*	*0.0090*	*0.0095*
Pension per equivalent person (1 million lire at 1998 prices)	-0.0142	-0.0087	-0.0010	-0.0107	-0.0087	-0.0058	-0.0075	-0.0078	-0.01	-0.0063	-0.0045	-0.0052	-0.0102	-0.0105	-0.0113
	0.0018	*0.0015*	*0.0015*	*0.0014*	*0.0011*	*0.0011*	*0.0011*	*0.0011*	*0.0008*	*0.0006*	*0.0006*	*0.0006*	*0.0006*	*0.0006*	*0.0006*
Other transfers per equivalent person (1 million lire at 1998 prices)	-0.019	0.0187	0.0018	0.0047	-0.0060	-0.0033	-0.0030	-0.0043	0.0018	0.0012	0.0004	0.0018	-0.0035	-0.0043	-0.0065
	0.0416	*0.0188*	*0.0095*	*0.0061*	*0.0046*	*0.0037*	*0.0059*	*0.0056*	*0.0022*	*0.0016*	*0.0013*	*0.0009*	*0.0016*	*0.0017*	*0.0019*
Log likelihood	-814	-771	-806	-794	-992	-886	-973	-1,02	-2136	-1906	-1986	-1935	-2067	-2024	-1838
Pseudo R²	0.15	0.14	0.15	0.15	0.17	0.16	0.14	0.13	0.17	0.19	0.21	0.28	0.30	0.32	0.31
Number of observations	2915	3044	2886	2980	4091	3967	4107	4172	8022	8027	8260	8188	8089	8093	7140

Source: Authors' elaboration on data from SHIW-HA (Release 1.0). The marginal effect is the partial derivative of the probability with respect to the regressor, evaluated at the sample means.

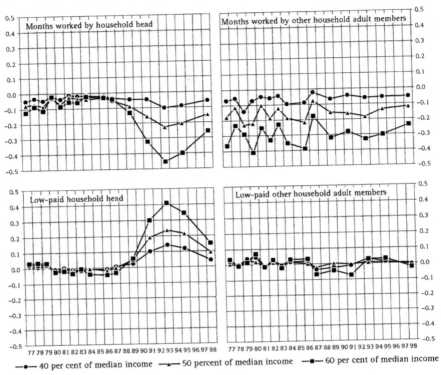

Figure 9.11. *Marginal effects on the probability of being in poverty, 1977–98.*
Source: Authors' elaboration on data from SHIW-HA (Release 1.0). A household is considered poor when its income is below 40, 50, and 60 per cent of the median income, respectively. Income is defined as equivalent households' after-tax incomes, including imputed rental income from owner-occupied dwellings, but excluding net interest and dividends. The equivalence scale is the one utilized to compute official poverty statistics in Italy (see Inquiry Commission on Poverty, 1997).

household, particularly of members other than the head, than with low pay. However, the low-paid status of the head has become more important in the last decade.

We looked for corroboration of the results discussed so far by considering two alternative poverty thresholds, and by looking at the deepness of poverty rather than the poverty risk. Re-estimating the probit models for poverty thresholds set at 40 and 60 per cent of the median equivalent income, we found that the absolute values of the marginal effects tend to be somewhat more pronounced, the higher the threshold, though their time patterns are very much unchanged (Fig. 9.11). Secondly, regressing the 'poverty gap' of poor households (i.e., the percentage shortfall of their income from the poverty line, set here at half the median) on the same set of explanatory variables shows a high correlation with the employment rate, although now the effect is stronger for the household head (Table 9.9, last

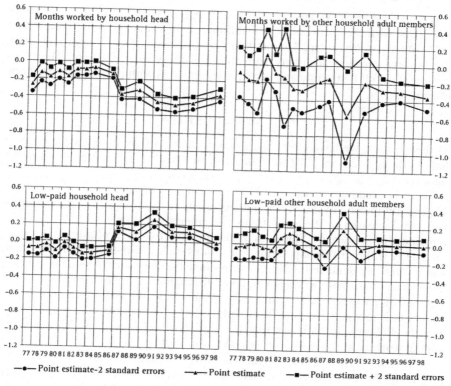

Figure 9.12. *Marginal effects on the poverty gap, 1977–98.*

Source: Authors' elaboration on data from SHIW-HA (Release 1.0). The poverty gap is the percentage ratio of the difference between poverty line and income of a poor household to the poverty line. A household is considered poor when its income is below 50 per cent of the median income. Income is defined as equivalent households' after-tax incomes, including imputed rental income from owner-occupied dwellings, but excluding net interest and dividends. The equivalence scale is the one utilized to compute official poverty statistics in Italy (see Inquiry Commission on Poverty, 1997).

two columns).[13] The difference between the two models is more evident in the year-by-year regressions: in the poverty risk model, the months worked by other members are more important than those worked by the head in most of the period, but not in the 1990s (Fig. 9.10); in the poverty gap model, they have similar effects, but the coefficient of the former is poorly estimated and becomes significant only in the 1990s (Fig. 9.12). Conversely, the poverty gap exhibits a weak correlation with the low-paid status of either the head or any other member.

---

[13] The importance of the employment status of the head in determining the household's total income was stressed by Rettore and Rizzi (1996) in a framework substantially different from ours. They found that spells of unemployment for members other than the head do not significantly affect the household's income, whereas those of the head can lead to a fall as large as 60 per cent.

Few other differences are notable. First, the number of children is positively associated with the household's probability of being in poverty, but is uncorrelated with the poverty gap. Second, household size is correlated negatively with the poverty gap and positively with the probability of being poor. Third, the income shortfall is strongly and negatively correlated with the size of both forms of transfer.

9.6. CONCLUSIONS

In this chapter, we have examined the distribution of net monthly earnings in Italy in the period from 1977 to 1998, on the basis of the data from the HA of the Bank of Italy's SHIW. The main results are the following.

First, the inequality in the distribution of net earnings decreased from the late 1970s until the end of the 1980s, and especially in the first part of the period; it abruptly increased in the early 1990s and underwent little modification in the remainder of the decade. This pattern also broadly fits the evolution of earnings inequality within major population sub-groups such as full-time employees, men and women, residents in the North and residents in the South. Among prime-age non-agricultural male workers employed throughout the whole year, however, the tendency towards greater inequality emerged in the mid-1980s and manifested itself in a less extreme form. This asymmetry between core employment and the full sample indicates that the significant changes were concentrated among workers at the margin of the labour market.

Second, the diffusion of low-paid jobs evolved in parallel with that of earnings inequality. The proportion of low-paid workers declined from 17 per cent in 1977 to a minimum 8 per cent in 1989, rose to 16 per cent in 1993, and after a fall in 1995, reached a peak of 18 per cent in 1998. The rise of low-paid jobs between 1993 and 1998 is entirely accounted for by the spread of part-time work, as the incidence of low pay among full-time workers remained around 12 per cent. As in the other advanced economies, young people, women and generally persons who are not household heads, the less educated and manual workers, employees in agriculture and trade and lodging are over-represented among the low-paid jobs.

Third, the probability of being in poverty is more closely correlated with the amount of employment in the household, particularly employment of members other than the head, than with low pay. However, the correlation with the low-paid status of the head has strengthened considerably in the last decade. Also the depth of poverty is correlated more with the employment rate than it is with low pay, irrespective of the earner's position in the household.

APPENDIX

Information about Employees in the SHIW, 1977–98

The Survey of Household Income and Wealth (SHIW) was conducted yearly by the Bank of Italy from 1965 to 1987 (except for 1985), every other year until 1995 and then in 1998, to gather information on personal income and wealth. Separate information is collected for each source of income for all household members, and the household income is obtained as the sum of these elementary components.

The survey's Historical Archive (SHIW-HA; see Banca d'Italia, 2000*b*) contains standardized information for years from 1977 onwards (microdata for preceding years are no longer available). The archive includes elementary variables gathered on a regular basis: among others, the personal characteristics of each household member and the incomes earned and job status of each income recipient. It also includes a set of sampling weights adjusted to bring some socio-demographic marginal distributions into line with the corresponding distributions found in Istat's population statistics and labour force survey. In the chapter, we use this set of adjusted weights (the use of the original weights would not alter the main results), multiplied by a factor equal to the ratio of the total Italian population to the number of individuals in the survey.

In spite of the many changes which have affected the SHIW (Brandolini, 1999), a set of basic questions about employees and their job positions has remained virtually unmodified over time; this set has been significantly broadened in the last few surveys. Full detail of the information gathered in each survey (except for a few questions asked only once), starting with 1977, is shown in Table 9.11. For the whole period we can distinguish between main and secondary jobs, and between jobs held for the whole year and jobs held for only part of the year; in the latter case, we know the number of months worked. The breakdown into full-time and part-time jobs is known since 1986 only, and age classes have to be used instead of persons' true ages because the information is missing before 1984.

The definition of earnings has remained stable, apart from minimal rewording: earnings are recorded net of taxes and social security contributions, and include all monetary and in-kind payments received by the worker in the year, though separate information is available only after 1980 (a minor discontinuity arises in 1986, since in-kind earnings were asked only of workers employed in the agricultural sector). Monthly earnings are obtained by dividing the annual amount by the number of months worked (set at 12 in the very few cases when it was missing).

The classification of occupations and economic branches has changed frequently (Tables 9.12 and 9.13). We distinguish among three occupations (production workers, clerical workers, managerial workers) and five economic branches: (1) agricultural, forestry, and fishery products; (2) industry (including energy products, manufacturing, and construction); (3) wholesale and retail trade, recovery and repair services, lodging and catering services; (4) transport and communication services, and services of credit and insurance institutions; (5) other market services to businesses and households, general public services and non-market services provided by general government (covering both market and non-market activities).

Table 9.11. *Information about employees and their job positions*

Type of information	1977	1978	1979	1980	1981	1982	1983	1984	1986	1987	1989	1991	1993	1995	1998

Information about the person
Sex
Age
Age class
Marital status
Level of education
Residence
Age at first job
Job change in the year
No. job changes in previous 2 years
No. job changes in the year
In search of new job
No. of job offers in the year
No. of rejected jobs in the year
No. of jobs held in the past
No. of weeks in training courses
No. of days out for illness

Information about main job
Manual job
Economic branch
Job status
All-year versus part-year

Table 9.11. *Continued*

Type of information	1977	1978	1979	1980	1981	1982	1983	1984	1986	1987	1989	1991	1993	1995	1998
Full-time versus part-time															
No. of months worked															
Total annual after-tax earnings	(a)	(a)	(a)												
– wages and salaries				(a)	(a)	(b)	(b)	(b)							
– payments in kind[d]				(c)	(c)	(c)	(c)	(c)							
Average hours worked per week[f]									(e)						
Average contract hours per week															
Average hours of overtime per week															
Job tenure															
Hours spent under CIG scheme															
Information about secondary jobs															
Economic branch															
Job status															
All-year versus part-year															
Full-time versus part-time															
No. of months worked															
Total annual after-tax earnings	(a)	(a)	(a)												
– wages and salaries				(a)	(a)	(b)	(b)	(b)							
– payments in kind[d]				(c)	(c)	(c)	(c)	(c)							
Average hours worked per week[f]									(e)						
Average contract hours per week															
Average hours of overtime per week															

Source: SHIW questionnaires. (a) For part-year jobs calculated as total monthly earnings by number of months worked. (b) Part-year jobs only, calculated as total monthly earnings by number of months worked. (c) All-year jobs only. (d) For part-year jobs collected on a yearly basis. (e) Only for workers in the agricultural sector. (f) Including overtime.

Table 9.12. *Classification of occupations*

1977–84	1986	1987[a]	1989–91	1993–98
Directors	Directors	Directors	Directors	Directors
		Administrators	Administrators	Administrators
Headmasters	Headmasters	Headmasters	Headmasters	Headmasters
		Judges	Judges	Judges
		University teachers	University teachers	University teachers
Clerical workers	Managerial workers	Managerial workers	Managerial workers	Managerial workers
	Foremen	Foremen	Foremen	Foremen
	Teachers	Teachers	Teachers	Teachers
	Clerical workers	Clerical workers	Clerical workers	Clerical workers
Other employees	Manual workers	Manual workers	Manual workers	Manual workers
	Other employees			

Source: SHIW questionnaires. (a) The questionnaire listed separately as an occupation: 'member of Parliament and of regional and local councils'; two persons (out of 9461) declared that such was their primary job and another three indicated it as their secondary job (out of 270).

Table 9.13. *Classification of economic branches*

Economic branch	1977–84	1986	1987	1989	1991	1993–98
Agricultural, forestry and fishery products						
Fuel and power products[a]						
Manufactured products[b]						
Building and construction						
Recovery and repair services						
Wholesale and retail trade services						
Lodging and catering services						
Transport and communication services						
Services of credit and insurance institutions						
Market services to businesses						
Other market personal services						
Non-market services provided by government						
General public services						
International organisations[c]						

Source: SHIW questionnaires. (a) Further separated into two branches in 1987. (b) Further separated into three branches in 1987. (c) Until 1989 this sector was not specified; in 1991 it was included among non-market services provided by general government. In 1993, eight persons (out of 8121) fell in this category.

Like most sample surveys on households' incomes, the SHIW suffers from problems of sample selection bias, non-reporting and under-reporting (e.g., Brandolini and Cannari, 1994; Cannari and Gavosto, 1995; Brandolini, 1999). In all the years of our sample, the number of salaried employees is higher in the SHIW than in the Istat's Labour Force Survey (LFS), while the number of wage-earners is closer; on balance, the employees appear to be over-represented, to a lesser extent in more recent surveys (Table 9.14). (To enhance comparability we re-scaled the total population size in the SHIW to equal that in the LFS.) Part of the discrepancy can be explained by the different definition of labour market status, which is defined as the prevalent occupation in the year in the SHIW, and

Table 9.14. *Employees in the LFS and the SHIW, 1977–98 (thousands of persons)*

Year	LFS[a]			SHIW (original weights)[b]			SHIW (adjusted weights)[c]		
	Wage earners	Salaried employees	Total	Wage earners	Salaried employees	Total	Wage earners	Salaried employees	Total
1977	9773	4589	14,362	10,903	5355	16,258	9416	4569	13,985
1978	9593	4770	14,363	10,989	6778	17,767	8695	5282	13,977
1979	9643	4968	14,611	11,099	6529	17,628	8925	5211	14,136
1980	9655	5153	14,808	9299	7900	17,199	7709	6500	14,209
1981	9500	5326	14,826	9719	7863	17,582	7880	6274	14,154
1982	9232	5568	14,800	9199	8786	17,985	7232	6821	14,053
1983	8959	5712	14,671	9474	7775	17,249	7801	6296	14,097
1984	8524	5954	14,478	9372	7509	16,881	7906	6188	14,094
1986	8364	6340	14,704	8365	7249	15,614	7526	6806	14,332
1987	8204	6505	14,709	8269	7964	16,233	7706	7134	14,840
1989	8161	6776	14,937	7881	8735	16,616	7217	7912	15,129
1991	8285	7194	15,479	7226	8581	15,807	7000	8470	15,470
1993	6981	7630	14,611	7024	7862	14,886	6731	7652	14,383
1995	7015	7189	14,204	7067	7666	14,733	6807	7481	14,288
1998	7441	7107	14,548	7013	8188	15,201	6601	7784	14,385

Source: SHIW: Authors' elaboration on data from SHIW-HA (Release 1.0). *LFS:* Istat, data from the labour force surveys. (a) Because of the extensive revisions carried out in 1984 and 1992, the figures cannot be interpreted as consistent time series. (b) Data computed using the original sample weights, which correct for the differential response rate in each stratum, with the SHIW total population size re-scaled to equal the LFS size. (c) Data computed using the adjusted weights derived from post-stratifying the sample according to the socio-demographic characteristics of the population, with the SHIW total population size re-scaled to equal the LFS size.

as the yearly average of conditions recorded at the moment of the interviews (conducted in January, April, July and October) in the LFS. The SHIW-HA (see Banca d'Italia, 2000b) provides an alternative set of weights adjusted to bring socio-demographic marginal distributions into line with the corresponding distributions found in the LFS and population statistics. Differences relative to the LFS statistics are somewhat attenuated, though not cancelled (last three columns of Table 9.14). In the chapter, we use the set of adjusted weights.

The number of employees as derived from the respondents' declaration may differ from the number of primary job positions for which information is available, either for a coding error, or, more likely, because some respondents moved to a new job or changed their status during the year. In the whole period, such differences in the SHIW are negligible, except in 1993, 1995, and 1998 where they are in the order of 4 per cent (Table 9.15). In the chapter we always refer to job positions. Apart from the relatively close correspondence with the LFS figures brought about by the use of the adjusted weights, we may note that the SHIW totals exceed the number of regular employees recorded in national accounts (NA), though they fall short of the total number of employees (Table 9.15). Thus, it seems that the SHIW manages to capture some part of non-regular employment. (Notice that the NA figures cover all persons employed in resident production establishments, including non-resident and institutionalized persons, while the SHIW and the LFS data refer to resident households.)

Table 9.15. *Employees in the NA, the LFS and the SHIW, 1986–98 (thousands of persons)*

Year	NA			LFS[a] Total	SHIW (adjusted weights)[b]		
	Regular workers	Non-regular workers	Total		Declared job status	Primary job positions	Adjusted primary job positions[c]
1977				14,362	13,985	13,900	13,205
1978				14,363	13,977	13,907	12,980
1979				14,611	14,136	14,079	13,140
1980				14,808	14,209	14,174	13,229
1981				14,826	14,154	14,110	13,052
1982				14,800	14,053	14,208	13,142
1983				14,671	14,097	14,025	13,207
1984				14,478	14,094	14,066	13,128
1986				14,704	14,332	14,301	13,110
1987				14,709	14,840	14,868	13,877
1989				14,937	15,129	15,096	14,592
1991				15,479	15,470	15,710	15,055
1993	13,916	2456	16,372	14,611	14,383	14,886	13,770
1995	13,539	2533	16,072	14,204	14,288	14,935	13,690
1998	13,759	2708	16,467	14,548	14,385	14,908	14,039

Source: *SHIW*: Authors' elaboration on data from SHIW-HA (Release 1.0). *LFS*: Istat, data from the labour force surveys. *NA*: Istat (2001b). (a) Because of the extensive revisions carried out in 1984 and 1992, the figures cannot be interpreted as consistent time series. (b) Data computed using the adjusted weights derived from post-stratifying the sample according to the socio-demographic characteristics of the population, with the SHIW total population size re-scaled to equal the LFS size. (c) Number of primary job positions multiplied by the average number of months worked divided by 12.

Wages and salaries appear to be imperfectly covered in the SHIW, but the under-estimation is less serious than for other income sources: on average, from 1977 to 1995, the grossed-up survey totals (based on the adjusted weights) fall short of the corresponding NA (ESA 1979) figures by 22 per cent (Brandolini, 1999, p. 219, Table 11). This discrepancy reflects a number of factors: (a) the underlying difference in definitions, which are often irreducible; (b) the incomplete coverage of non-regular employment just mentioned; (c) the difficulties encountered by the SHIW in capturing secondary jobs (see Brandolini, 1999, for a more extensive discussion).

REFERENCES

Abbate, C. and A. Baldassarini (1995). Contenuto informativo degli archivi INPS e confronto con altre fonti sul mercato del lavoro, *Economia & Lavoro*, 28 (2), 115–33.

Addabbo, T. (1997). Part-time work in Italy, in Blossfeld, H.-P. and C. Hakim (eds.), *Between Equalization and Marginalization. Women Working Part-Time in Europe and the United States of America*, 113–32. Oxford: Oxford University Press.

Banca d'Italia (2000a). *Annual Report*. Roma: Banca d'Italia.

—— (2000b). *Archivio storico dell'Indagine sui bilanci delle famiglie italiane, 1977–98. Versione 1.0. Aggiornamento al 18 aprile 2000*. D' Alessio, G. and I. Faiella (eds.), Roma: Banca d'Italia.

Brandolini, A. (1999). The distribution of personal income in post-war Italy: Source description, data quality, and the time pattern of income inequality, *Giornale degli Economisti e Annali di Economia*, 58, 183–239.

—— (2000a). The problematic measurement of income from self-employment: A comment, Paper presented at the *Seminar on Household Income Statistics* organised by Eurostat, Luxembourg, 13–14 December 1999.

—— (2000b). Appunti per una storia della distribuzione del reddito in Italia nel secondo dopoguerra. *Rivista di storia economica*, 16, 215–30.

—— and L. Cannari (1994). Methodological appendix: The Bank of Italy's Survey of Household Income and Wealth, in Ando, A., L. Guiso, and I. Visco (eds.), *Saving and the Accumulation of Wealth. Essays on Italian Households and Government Saving Behaviour*, 369–86. Cambridge: Cambridge University Press.

Cannari, L. (1993). Povertà e livello dei prezzi, in Commissione d'indagine sulla povertà e sull'emarginazione, *Terzo rapporto sulla povertà in Italia*. Roma: Istituto Poligrafico e Zecca dello Stato.

—— and A. Gavosto (1995). L'indagine della Banca d'Italia sui bilanci delle famiglie: una descrizione dei dati sul mercato del lavoro. *Economia & Lavoro*, 28 (1) 63–79.

Caruso, M., R. Sabbatini, and P. Sestito (1993). Inflazione e tendenze di lungo periodo nelle differenze geografiche del costo della vita. *Moneta e Credito*, 46, 349–78.

Casavola, P., P. Cipollone, and P. Sestito (1999). Determinants of pay in the Italian labor market: Jobs and workers, in Haltiwanger, J. C., J. I. Lane, J. R. Spletzer, J. J. M. Theeuwes, and K. R. Troske (eds.), *The Creation and Analysis of Employer–Employee Matched Data*, 25–58. Amsterdam: North Holland.

Cowell, F. A. (1989). Sampling variance and decomposable inequality measures. *Journal of Econometrics*, 42, 27–41.

Erickson, C. L. and A. Ichino (1995). Wage differentials in Italy: Market forces, institutions, and inflation, in Freeman, R. B. and L. F. Katz (eds.), *Differences and Changes in Wage Structures*, 265–305. Chicago, IL: University of Chicago Press.

Keese, M., A. Puymoyen, and P. Swaim (1998). The incidence and dynamics of low-paid employment in OECD countries, in Asplund, R., P. J. Sloane and I. Theodossiou (eds.), *Low Pay and Earnings Mobility, in Europe*, 223–65. Cheltenham: Edward Elgar.

Inquiry Commission on Poverty (1997). *Poverty in Italy. 1980–95*. Roma: Istituto Poligrafico e Zecca dello Stato.

INPS (2001). *Banche Dati Statistiche. Osservatorio sui lavoratori dipendenti*. At: http:// www.inps.it/doc/sas_stat/dipendenti/dipendenti.html.

Istat (2001a). *Conti economici territoriali secondo il Sec95. Dati analitici, anni 1995–1998*. At: http://www.istat.it/Primpag/contiter/presentazione.html.

—— (2001b). *L'occupazione non regolare nelle stime di contabilità nazionale secondo il Sec95. Anni 1992–1999. Dati analitici, maggio 2001*. At: http://www.istat.it/Anotizie/ Acom/connaz/occupazione.html.

Istituto italiano per la promozione del lavoro a tempo parziale (1980). *Il lavoro part-time. Realtà sociale e aspetti giuridico-sindacali*. Milano: Etas libri.

Lucifora, C. (1996). L'analisi del mercato del lavoro con micro-dati: l'utilizzo degli archivi amministrativi INPS. *Economia & Lavoro*, 29 (3), 3–20.

—— (1998). Working poor? An analysis of low-wage employment in Italy, in Asplund, R., P. J. Sloane, and I. Theodossiou (eds.), *Low Pay and Earnings Mobility in Europe*, 185–208. Cheltenham: Edward Elgar.

Manacorda, M. (2000). The fall and rise of earnings inequality in Italy. A semiparametric analysis of the role of institutional and market forces, UC Berkeley, Center for Labor Economics, Mimeo.

OECD (1996). Earnings inequality, low-paid employment and earnings mobility, in *Employment Outlook*, 59–108. Paris: OECD.

Regalia, I., M. Regini and E. Reyneri (1978). Labour conflicts and industrial relations in Italy, in Crouch, C. and A. Pizzorno (eds.), *The Resurgence of Class Conflict in Western Europe since 1968, vol. I. National Studies*, 101–58. London and Basingstoke: Macmillan.

—— and —— (1996). Sindacato e relazioni industriali, in *Storia dell'Italia repubblicana. Volume III. L'Italia nella crisi mondiale. L'ultimo ventennio. I. Economia e società*, 777–836. Torino: Einaudi.

Rettore, E. and D. Rizzi (1996). Indicatori settoriali di povertà: (non)occupazione, Mimeo.

Sestito, P. (1992). Costanti e variazioni nella struttura dei differenziali retributivi in Italia, in *Ricerche applicate e modelli per la politica economica*, 877–902. Roma: Banca d'Italia.

Wolfson, M. C. (1994). When inequalities diverge, *American Economic Review Papers and Proceedings*, 84, 353–8.

10

Changes in Home Production and Trends in Economic Inequality

PETER GOTTSCHALK AND SUSAN E. MAYER

10.1. INTRODUCTION

It is widely recognized that ignoring home production understates aggregate output. However, little attention has been paid to the impact of ignoring home production in assessing trends in economic inequality, even though many studies have shown that home production is important to economic well-being, and that the amount of home production has decreased as the labour force participation of women has increased. For instance, Gronau (1980) estimated that in 1973 among white married-couple households the value of home production was equal to 70 per cent of households' money income after taxes. Among households with young children, the value of home production was nearly equal to households' money income after taxes. Furthermore, Juster and Stafford (1991) show that women reduced time devoted to home production by more than 10 per cent between 1965 and 1981, a period of rapid increase in women's labour force participation.

Wage inequality has increased over the last two decades both because wages at the top of the wage distribution increased and because wages at the bottom of the income distribution declined.[1] Standard economic theory predicts that this change in the wage structure would, under most circumstances, increase home production among low-income families and reduce home production among high-income families.[2] This is because the change in the wage structure would raise the opportunity costs of home production for high-wage individuals while lowering the opportunity costs for those lower in the distribution. As opportunity costs decline, families substitute home production and leisure for goods produced in the market. This substitution effect would dominate unless income effects were sufficiently strong or the family was liquidity constrained. Thus, economic theory predicts that with sufficiently small income effects and no liquidity constraints, a decline in wages will be accompanied by a decline in the hours devoted to market work and an increase in home production and leisure.

We wish to thank Len Lopoo for excellent computer assistance.

[1] See Gottschalk (1997).

[2] For a recent review of the theory of home production see Gronau (1997).

Changes in family composition are also likely to affect the distribution of home production as well as money income.[3] We know that much of the increase in income inequality is accounted for by the increase in single-parent households. Since single-parent households have less total time to devote to the market and home production, the growth in single-parent households could contribute to a decline in both income and home production at the bottom of the income distribution.[4] In addition single-parent families potentially qualify for welfare benefits, which reduces the net monetary cost of substituting home for market production since the latter is subject to a benefit reduction rate while the former is not. On the other hand, wages at the bottom of the distribution declined more for men than for women (Waldfogel and Mayer, forthcoming). Because low-skilled women's wages declined relatively little, their opportunity costs also changed relatively little. The net effect of changes in the wage structure and changes in family composition, therefore, have an ambiguous effect.

If the reduction in home production were disproportionately large in families at the top of the distribution of money income, then the reduction in goods produced in the home would partially offset the increase in money income inequality. Measures of money income that place no value on home production would, therefore, overstate the gains of families at the top of the income distribution. In this chapter we first show trends in home production. Then we estimate trends in inequality using household money income and income adjusted for the value of home production and, in some cases, the value of leisure. The remainder of this chapter is divided into six sections. Section 10.2 describes the data that we use. Sections 10.3 and 10.4 review trends in money income and hours of home production, respectively. Section 10.5 discusses the methods we use to adjust income for the value of home production and leisure. Section 10.6 provides our results and Section 10.7 provides conclusions.

10.2. DATA

We use data from the Panel Study of Income Dynamics (PSID) for interview years between 1976 and 1992. Our sample includes households headed by persons 25–64 years old. The samples are between 3099 and 4060 households depending on the year. Sample weights are used throughout. (See Hill, 1992 for a description of the PSID.) Starting in 1976 the PSID has asked heads of households how many hours they, their spouse (if present), and other household members spend in an average week on housework and in labour market work.[5] The PSID also contains

---

[3] Cachian *et al.* (1991, Table 6.4) show that between 1978 and 1988 wives' earnings accounted for 64 per cent of the growth in household income among white couples and 70 per cent among black couples.

[4] For a review of this literature see Danziger and Gottschalk (1995).

[5] Hours of home production is measured as the respondent's response to a question that asks, 'About how much time do you spend on housework in the average week? (I mean time spent cooking, cleaning, and doing other work around the house.)' The respondent is also asked to report the average

the necessary income and earnings data to calculate the adjusted income measures we describe below.

An alternative source of data used in many home production studies is time-use diaries in which individuals keep detailed records of their activities for a short time period. These data presumably produce more accurate estimates of time use than the survey data collected in the PSID. However, they cannot be used to assess trends in the distribution of home production across income groups since there is no consistent time-series of data that include both diary entries and income for a sufficiently large sample of households.

Although the PSID includes much less detailed information on time use than diary surveys, it can be used to generate a consistent set of cross-sectional estimates of the total amount of time devoted to home and market production. Juster and Stafford (1991) note that survey questions like those asked in the PSID tend to over-state the use of time for specific tasks, but this bias will affect estimated trends in time use or the relative use of time for different household types only if the magnitude of the reporting error varies over time or by household type.[6]

10.3. CHANGES IN THE LEVEL AND DISTRIBUTION OF MONEY INCOME

As many studies document, the 1980s was a decade of slow growth in money income for non-elderly households (Danziger and Gottschalk, 1995; Karoly, 1993). Table 10.1 uses data from the PSID to show that median household income for households headed by someone 25–64 years old fluctuated between 1976 and 1992 but declined by 4.1 per cent between 1976 and 1992. While this decline partially reflects the recession of 1992, there is even a decline between 1979 and 1989, which were at similar points in the business cycle.

As many analysts have pointed out, trends in money income may understate growth in economic well-being for two reasons. First, average household size declined from 3.08 in 1979 to 2.92 in 1989 and has fallen only slightly since then. With fewer mouths to feed, households required fewer resources, so households' need for income declined while income increased. Using money income unadjusted for household size implicitly assumes that economies of scale are so large that additional household members imposed no cost on the household or, conversely, that reductions in household size do not reduce the household's needs. At the other extreme, per capita income assumes that there are no economies of scale and, therefore, that each additional household member adds the same

weekly hours of housework of the spouse and other household members. We omit hours of home production of household members other than the head and partner. The hours of housework contributed by other household members has hardly changed over time for any household type.

[6] PSID data cannot be used to assess trends in different kinds of home production. We therefore assume that the average value of an hour of home production is not a function of the kind of production. This is consistent with economic theory that predicts that the marginal value of an hour is equalized across activities.

Table 10.1. *Median income of households headed by persons 25–64 years old by household type and year*

Year	All	Married couple	Single parent	Single adult
Income				
1976	41,101	47,278	22,248	24,684
1977	42,368	50,841	23,730	25,003
1978	43,467	50,533	22,721	25,284
1979	42,090	50,245	21,814	25,167
1980	39,324	47,296	20,432	23,905
1981	38,586	46,427	20,404	24,849
1983	37,679	46,484	19,077	26,341
1984	39,405	49,422	19,309	26,735
1985	38,174	48,635	18,306	21,314
1986	40,103	51,460	20,630	26,882
1987	40,354	51,686	21,242	27,738
1988	42,042	52,265	22,113	28,463
1989	41,083	51,720	20,275	27,154
1990	39,717	51,915	21,606	25,870
1991	38,505	51,917	19,559	26,133
1992	39,413	53,500	19,798	25,529
Per cent change	− 4.1	13.2	− 7.9	− 3.4
Income per capita				
1976	14,065	13,808	7035	19,972
1977	14,769	14,060	7717	21,124
1978	14,671	14,450	7573	22,163
1979	14,547	14,300	7060	21,257
1980	13,837	13,639	6734	20,546
1981	13,968	13,923	6774	21,268
1983	14,573	14,156	6444	22,145
1984	15,016	14,846	6481	21,470
1985	14,994	14,535	6258	21,314
1986	15,804	15,607	7042	22,897
1987	16,055	15,800	7345	23,465
1988	16,010	15,947	7689	23,837
1989	16,542	16,406	6811	23,324
1990	16,262	16,101	7213	22,259
1991	16,044	15,932	6455	22,538
1992	16,893	16,732	6840	22,500
Per cent change	20.1	21.2	− 2.8	12.7

Source: Authors' calculations from the PSID.

Note: Income amounts are in 1992 dollars using the CPI-U-X1 price adjustment.

amount to the needs of the household. The 'right' equivalence scale is presumably between these extremes. Table 10.1 shows that median per capita household income grew by a substantial 20.1 per cent between 1976 and 1992. This is in contrast to the decline in unadjusted income over the same period.

A second factor that has affected growth in median income as well as growth in inequality is the shift from married-couple to single-parent households and other units with only one potential earner. Since overall growth in income is a weighted average of income growth for each type of household, it will be affected by changes in the weights as well as changes in the group specific means. As the weight shifts to single-adult and single-parent households who, as Table 10.1 shows, have lower average incomes than married-couple households, overall growth in household income declines. Between 1976 and 1992, median income unadjusted for household size grew by 13.2 per cent among married-couple households and declined by 7.9 per cent among single-parent households. Over the same period per capita income grew by 21.2 per cent for married-couple households and declined by 2.8 per cent among households headed by a single adult. In either case, inequality between these two family types grew. Whether one should focus on overall growth in income or on group-specific growth depends on whether one wants to include the effects of these demographic shifts in an assessment of changes in economic well-being. We leave it up to the reader by presenting our analysis by household type.

While median income did increase during the 1980s and early 1990s, at least moderately, the increase was not uniform throughout the income distribution. Table 10.2 shows that between 1976 and 1992 the income of the household at the 20th percentile fluctuated somewhat but declined by 16.7 per cent between 1976 and 1992, while the income of the household at the 80th percentile grew by 9.2 per cent. Per capita income declined much less than unadjusted income at the 20th percentile. But per capita income increased much more than unadjusted income at both the median and at the 80th percentile. Overall the increase in inequality was less for per capita income.

The increase in household income inequality was largely due to increased inequality in the labour market.[7] But it was also partly due to an increase in single-adult households combined with the increase in married-couple households with two earners. If changes in home production also have not been uniform throughout the income distribution, trends in a measure of income adjusted for the value of home production might not parallel trends in money income.

10.4. CHANGES IN THE LEVEL AND DISTRIBUTION OF HOME PRODUCTION

In order to see if trends in home production in the PSID are the same as trends using time-use surveys, we begin by showing overall trends in home production

---

[7] See Gottschalk (1997).

Table 10.2. *Income by income groups for households headed by an adult 25–64 years old*

Year	20th percentile	Median	80th percentile	20th percentile/ median	80th percentile/ median
Income					
1976	21,612	41,101	66,606	0.526	1.621
1977	22,920	42,368	68,414	0.541	1.615
1978	21,734	43,467	69,773	0.500	1.605
1979	22,031	42,090	68,332	0.523	1.623
1980	20,197	39,325	63,595	0.514	1.617
1981	19,532	38,586	61,738	0.506	1.600
1983	18,749	37,680	63,248	0.498	1.679
1984	19,445	39,406	65,491	0.493	1.662
1985	18,255	38,174	65,195	0.478	1.708
1986	19,330	40,103	69,126	0.482	1.724
1987	19,761	40,355	69,162	0.490	1.714
1988	20,547	41,569	71,277	0.494	1.715
1989	19,461	41,083	69,697	0.474	1.696
1990	18,785	39,718	68,701	0.473	1.730
1991	18,032	38,505	68,241	0.468	1.772
1992	18,000	39,413	72,700	0.457	1.845
Per cent change 1976–92	− 16.7	− 4.1	9.2	−13.2	13.8
Per capita income					
1976	7644	14,065	25,956	0.543	1.845
1977	7949	14,769	26,586	0.538	1.800
1978	8177	14,671	27,124	0.557	1.849
1979	8022	14,547	27,248	0.551	1.873
1980	7385	13,838	26,051	0.534	1.883
1981	7409	13,968	26,588	0.530	1.903
1983	6798	14,573	28,032	0.466	1.924
1984	7396	15,016	28,318	0.493	1.886
1985	7443	14,995	28,327	0.496	1.889
1986	7681	15,804	30,403	0.486	1.924
1987	7727	16,055	30,876	0.481	1.923
1988	8076	16,296	32,555	0.496	1.998
1989	7959	16,542	31,228	0.481	1.888
1990	7986	16,263	30,704	0.491	1.888
1991	7630	16,045	31,315	0.476	1.952
1992	7750	16,893	32,800	0.459	1.942
Per cent change 1976–92	1.4	20.1	26.4	−15.6	5.2

in the PSID. We then show changes in the distribution of home production and the impact of these changes on the distribution of economic well-being.

10.4.1. Trends in Hours of Home Production and Labour Market Work

Evidence on time use in the US, reviewed in Juster and Stafford (1991), shows that women have reduced their home production as they increased their market production. They show that between 1965 and 1981, women reduced their hours of home production by an average of 11.3 h per week (from 41.8 to 30.5). However, the number of hours spent in the labour market increased by an average of only 5.0 h (from 18.9 to 23.9 h per week). The result was a net decline of 6.3 h per week devoted to combined home and market production (or a 6.3 h increase in leisure).[8] These same studies also show that the number of hours men devote to home production is roughly a third of the number of hours women devote to home production, and that men increased their hours of home production by an average of 2.3 h per week (from 11.5 h to 13.8 h) between 1965 and 1981. On an average they decreased market work by 7.6 h per week, resulting in a net increase of 5.3 h per week devoted to leisure. We do not know from these studies if the decline in home production continued throughout the 1980s. We also do not know how it is distributed over income groups.

Figure 10.1 shows overall trends in annual hours of home production among all households and four sub-groups defined by whether the head was married and whether there was a child in the household. For all groups except married couples with no children, the number of hours of home production declined after 1977. It declined for all groups after 1981.

The decline in hours of home production for all households is a result of the decline in hours for each group and the changing relative size of the groups. Between 1976 and 1992 married-couple households declined from 60.0 per cent of all households to 46.9 per cent. The relative size of the other three household composition groups increased, with the largest increase coming from childless singles, who grew from 22.3 per cent to 33.9 per cent of all households. Since the shrinking group (married-couple families) had above average hours of home production and the fastest growing group (childless singles) had the fewest hours of home production, the compositional effect reduced aggregate hours of home production. The result was a decline of 331 h per year in aggregate hours of home production between 1977 and 1992.

Figure 10.1 shows that between 1976 and 1992 single-parent households always devoted fewer hours to home production than two-parent households. But the decrease in average hours of home production between 1977, when home production began to decline, and 1992 was 361 h per year (a decrease of 17.8 per cent)

---

[8] Some studies in psychology and sociology, as well as some in economics, emphasize the decrease in home production, especially the decrease in time spent with children, that occurs when mothers go to work outside the home (Kammerman and Hayes, 1982; Hewlett, 1991). But none of these studies estimates the impact of lost home production on the distribution of economic well-being.

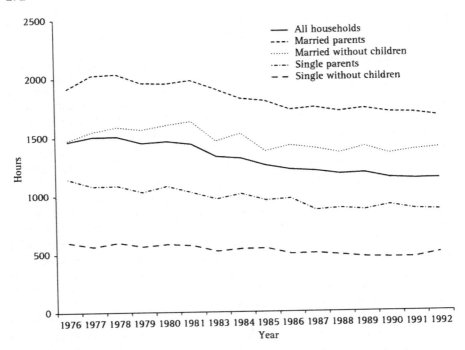

Figure 10.1. *Mean hours of housework among households with heads aged 25–64.*

for two-parent households. Housework declined by 217 h (20.0 per cent) for single-parent households. Thus, the gap in home production between single-parent and two-parent households decreased from 943 h in 1977 to 799 h in 1992. All else equal, this would raise income adjusted for the value of home production for single-parent families relative to two-parent families, thus reducing inequality between the two family types.

Households with no children headed by a single adult devote many fewer hours to home production than married couples with no children. But the decline in the absolute number of hours devoted to home production was similar for both household types.

Figure 10.2 shows trends in hours devoted to the labour market for different household types. Over this period the overall annual number of hours devoted to market work hardly changed, rising from 2434 in 1976 to 2540 in 1992, an increase of only 106 h. But this obscures the different trends for different types of households. The increase in annual hours of market work among two-parent households with children was 305 h. For single-parent households it was only 156 h. For married couples with no children, the increase was 305 h and for single-adult households with no children it was 187. The shift in household composition toward household types that worked relatively few hours in the market limited the increase in aggregate labour market hours.

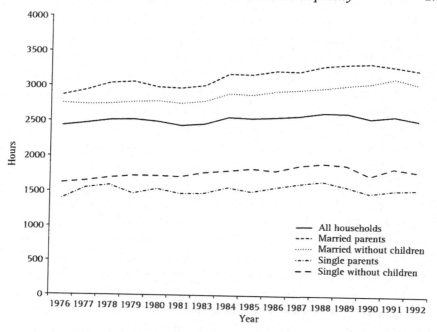

Figure 10.2. *Mean hours of labour market work among households with heads aged 25–64.*

The net result of the modest increase in market work and the decrease in housework between 1977 and 1992 is shown in Fig. 10.3. The average household devoted 225 fewer hours per year (a 6.1 per cent decrease) to total production in 1992 than in 1976. Consistent with findings from time-use studies, these results show a slight net increase in leisure over this decade. However, married-parent households devoted an additional 141 h per year to total production, while single-parent households devoted 122 fewer hours to total production. Hence the gap between these two family types increased.

10.4.2. Trends in the Distribution of Home Production and Earnings

Karoly and Burtless (1993) show that the increase in labour force participation among wives has been concentrated in the upper end of the income distribution, contributing to the rise in inequality of money income. If, as economic theory would predict, the decline in home production is also concentrated there, the increase in income among those at the upper end of the income distribution would overstate their increase in economic well-being. This implies that there might have been less growth in economic inequality than standard income measures suggest.

Figure 10.4 shows hours of home production for all households by money income quintiles. In all years households in the poorest income quintile allocate

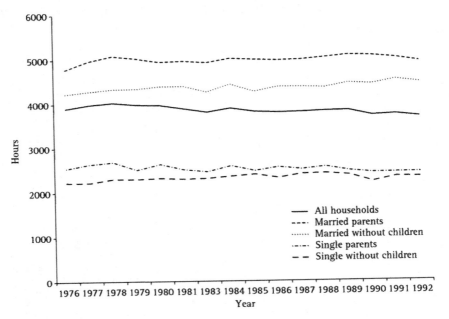

Figure 10.3. *Mean hours of total work (housework plus labour market) among households with heads aged 25–64.*

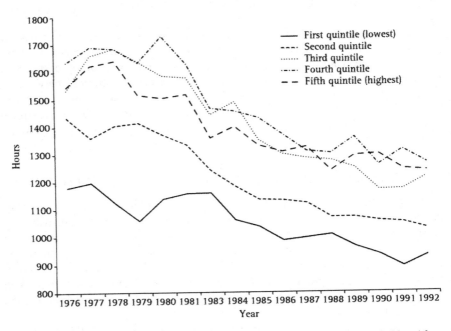

Figure 10.4. *Hours of housework by income quintiles among all households with heads aged 25–64.*

the fewest hours to home production.[9] Those in the third and fourth quintile allocate the most. This suggests that adding the value of home production would *increase* inequality in each year, though it does not inform us about trends in inequality.

The inclusion of the value of home production would affect the trend in inequality only if the decline in hours of home production varied by income. As noted above, economic theory predicts that under most circumstances home production would increase as wages decrease and decrease as wages increase. From this, we expect home production to increase for the poorest families and decrease for the richest families. Figure 10.4 shows that hours of home production decreased for all households but that the decline is largest for households in the highest quintiles. For example, between 1976 and 1992, households in the highest quintile reduced their hours of home production by 309 h. Because wages decreased for those at the bottom of the income distribution, economic theory predicts an increase in home production among that group. But Fig. 10.4 shows that home production declined by 249 h for households in the poorest income quintile.

Economic theory predicts that under most circumstances, as wages decline so will labour market work. Figure 10.5 shows hours of labour market work by the 'family wage rate'. The family wage rate is the sum of the head's and spouse's (if there is one) wage rate times the number of hours available for labour market work.[10] The number of hours available for work is 16 h per day (leaving 8 h for sleep.) Thus, the family wage rate is a function of the earning power of adults in the family and the number of adults in the family.[11] Wage rates increased for families in the top of the family wage rate distribution and declined for those at the bottom. Figure 10.5 shows that, as expected, the number of labour market hours increased for the top quintile and changed little for the second richest quintile. However, even tough wage rates declined for those in the bottom quintile, they did not reduce their hours of labour market work.

Overall, the gap in hours of home production between the rich and poor narrowed between 1977 and 1992. This suggests that increases in inequality over this period may be smaller when using income adjusted for the value of home production than when using money income.

10.5. METHODS FOR ADJUSTING INCOME FOR HOME PRODUCTION

Our first measure of income is the traditional money income measure, unadjusted for home production or leisure:

$$I_1 = M_h W_h + M_s W_s + O_f$$

---

[9] This partially reflects the concentration of single-parent families at the bottom of the distribution.
[10] An individual's wage rate is his or her observed wage if it is available or a wage predicted using a Heckman selection model when there is no observed wage. The selection model is estimated separately for men and women.
[11] This is equivalent to 'full income' less income from sources other than labour income.

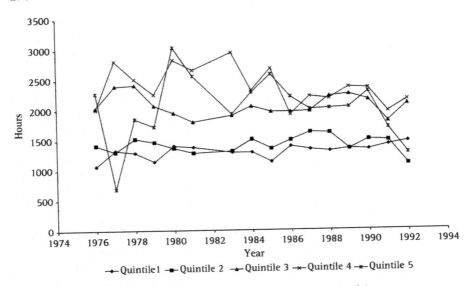

Figure 10.5. *Labour hours by 'family wage quintile'.*

where M_h and M_s are the hours of market work of the head and spouse (if present); W_h and W_s are their wages; and O_f is other income received by the household. Other income includes all non-labour sources such as interest, dividends, rents, public assistance, and private pensions.

Money income assigns a value of zero to hours spent not working in the market. An alternative approach is to value all hours the same, whether they are spent in market work, home production, or leisure. This approach uses the concept of full income in which all hours are valued at an individual's wage under the assumption that leisure and home production are priced at their opportunity cost, which is the income the individual could have earned had that time been spent in the market. Thus, our second measure of income (and our first measure of adjusted income) is

$$I_2 = (M_h + H_h + L_h)W_h + (M_s + H_s + L_s)W_s + O_f$$

where H_h and L_h are the hours of home production and leisure of the head, and H_s and L_s are the hours in the same activities for the spouse, if present.[12] Since the total hours devoted to market work, plus home production, plus leisure is the same for everyone, this measure reflects only differences in wage rates and non-labour income.

---

[12] Leisure is a residual category that includes all waking hours not devoted to market or home production. We assume that the total non-sleeping time is 16 h per day (or 5840 per year).

An intermediate approach, and one taken in the literature cited above, is to adjust income by the value of home production, but ignore the value of leisure. The drawback of this approach is, of course, that if additional market hours come at the cost of foregone leisure rather than home production, there will appear to be no off-setting cost. This measures the distribution of goods consumed (both market goods and home production), not the distribution of well-being.[13]

Adjusting income to reflect the value of home production requires two pieces of information: the number of hours each person devoted to home production and the value of an hour devoted to home production. Nearly all previous research has valued home production either as the cost of replacing the goods and services produced in the home (the replacement cost) or as the earnings that one could have obtained had that hour been spent in market production (the opportunity cost).

Replacement cost values home production at the price households would have to pay to purchase in the market the goods and services they produce in the home:

$$I_3 = (M_h W_h + M_s W_s) + R(H_h + H_s) + O_f$$

where R is the replacement cost of hours devoted to home production. In practice, the measures of replacement cost that are usually used are quite crude. We follow the standard practice of using the median hourly earnings of private household service workers as a measure of replacement cost.

If the opportunity cost of working in the home is the foregone income that would have been earned in the market, then both market work and home production should be valued at the market wage.[14] This leads to our final measure of adjusted income:

$$I_4 = (M_h + H_h)W_h + (M_s + H_s)W_s + O_f.$$

Using the opportunity cost to value home production implies that the time allocation across household members affects the value of home production for the unit. Husbands and wives typically have different market wages so their home production hours will be valued at different rates. This reflects the assumption that higher-wage spouses will undertake fewer low-return home production tasks than the lower-wage spouse because of the higher opportunity cost.

---

[13] For persons with zero earnings, we impute wages using standard techniques to correct for selection into the labour market. The wage equation includes a quadratic in age, education, an interaction of age and education, as well as three dummy variables for geographic region. In addition to these variables, the selection equation includes the following identifying variables: number of children, two dummy variables for child under age 3 and child aged 3–6, income of spouse, total transfer income, city size, county unemployment rate, and dummy variables for being married, disabled and owning a home.

[14] A crucial assumption of this approach is that individuals are free to adjust the number of hours they work in the market.

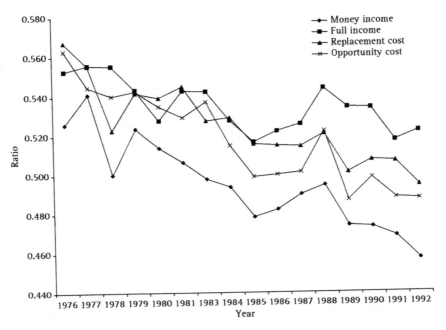

Figure 10.6. *Ratio of income at the 20th percentile to median.*

10.6. RESULTS: TRENDS IN ADJUSTED INCOME

We now put these pieces together by looking at the trends in inequality using these four different concepts of income. As a measure of inequality, we use the ratio of income at the 20th percentile to median income and the ratio of income at the 80th percentile to median income.[15] Figure 10.6 shows the first ratio and Fig. 10.7 shows the second. Table 10.3 shows these ratios for all years between 1976 and 1992.

Three conclusions can be reached from these two figures. First, income at the 20th percentile decreased relative to median income and income at the 80th percentile increased relative to the median, regardless of the income measure. Therefore, including the value of home production (and the value of leisure as in full income) does not overturn the main conclusion of the inequality literature: households at the bottom of the distribution lost ground, while those at the top gained.

Second, inequality is lower in any year when income is adjusted for the value of home production than when it is not. As Table 10.3 shows, in 1992 adding the value of both home production and leisure (full income) raises the 20th percentile from 45.9 per cent of the median (for money income alone) to 52.2 per cent. The ratio of the 20th percentile to the median is only slightly greater for income

---

[15] Percentiles are determined separately for each income concept. Thus, the 20/50 ratio for full income is the ratio of full income at the 20th percentile to the median full income.

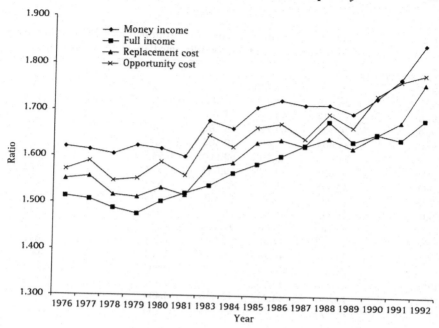

Figure 10.7. *Ratio of income at the 80th percentile to median.*

Table 10.3. *Various measures of income at the 20th, 50th, and 80th percentile*

Year	20th percentile	Median	80th percentile	20th percentile/ median	80th percentile/ median
Full income					
1976	77,652	140,481	212,623	0.553	1.514
1977	76,257	137,243	206,909	0.556	1.508
1978	76,229	137,315	204,361	0.555	1.488
1979	74,599	137,349	202,734	0.543	1.476
1980	68,415	129,660	194,899	0.528	1.503
1981	67,112	123,703	188,153	0.543	1.521
1983	65,715	121,203	186,423	0.542	1.538
1984	63,491	120,383	188,483	0.527	1.566
1985	61,685	119,446	189,336	0.516	1.585
1986	65,040	124,622	199,761	0.522	1.603
1987	64,310	122,385	199,072	0.525	1.627
1988	67,390	123,981	208,096	0.544	1.678
1989	65,086	121,925	199,407	0.534	1.635
1990	63,535	119,096	196,806	0.533	1.652
1991	60,413	116,855	191,724	0.517	1.641
1992	67,529	129,444	217,954	0.522	1.684
Per cent change 1976–92	− 13.0	− 7.9	2.5	−5.6	11.3

P. Gottschalk and S. E. Mayer

Table 10.3. *(Continued)*

Year	20th percentile	Median	80th percentile	20th percentile/ median	80th percentile/ median
Replacement cost					
1976	26,539	46,800	72,571	0.567	1.551
1977	26,579	47,855	74,488	0.555	1.557
1978	25,644	49,064	74,416	0.523	1.517
1979	26,928	49,723	75,182	0.542	1.512
1980	24,804	46,009	70,508	0.539	1.532
1981	24,620	45,196	68,570	0.545	1.517
1983	23,249	44,086	69,607	0.527	1.579
1984	23,948	45,284	71,916	0.529	1.588
1985	22,609	43,867	71,583	0.515	1.632
1986	23,619	45,893	75,208	0.515	1.639
1987	23,480	45,664	74,199	0.514	1.625
1988	24,504	47,072	77,303	0.521	1.642
1989	23,433	46,786	75,849	0.501	1.621
1990	23,042	45,448	75,027	0.507	1.651
1991	22,314	44,062	73,968	0.506	1.679
1992	21,902	44,324	78,048	0.494	1.761
Per cent change 1976–92	− 17.5	− 5.3	7.6	−12.9	13.6
Opportunity cost					
1976	32,564	57,861	90,914	0.563	1.571
1977	31,956	58,677	93,264	0.545	1.589
1978	32,402	59,991	92,830	0.540	1.547
1979	31,872	58,761	91,230	0.542	1.553
1980	29,349	54,880	87,166	0.535	1.588
1981	28,143	53,186	82,960	0.529	1.560
1983	27,430	51,084	84,135	0.537	1.647
1984	26,944	52,345	84,927	0.515	1.622
1985	25,332	50,793	84,558	0.499	1.665
1986	27,003	54,031	90,454	0.500	1.674
1987	27,197	54,281	89,088	0.501	1.641
1988	28,326	54,278	92,023	0.522	1.695
1989	26,275	53,998	89,986	0.487	1.666
1990	25,736	51,676	89,682	0.498	1.735
1991	24,262	49,743	87,894	0.488	1.767
1992	25,589	52,525	93,553	0.487	1.781
Per cent change 1976–92	− 21.4	− 9.2	2.9	−13.4	13.4

adjusted for the value of only home production than for money income alone. In 1992, the 20th percentile is 48.8 per cent of the median when we value home production at the opportunity cost and 49.4 per cent of the median when we value it at the replacement cost.

The fact that high-income households report more hours of home production might seem to imply that adding the value of home production would increase inequality. However, while the absolute increase in income from adding the value of home production is largest for high-income households, it is small relative to the base. As a result, adding the value of home production has a smaller proportionate impact on high-income than on low-income households.

Similarly, Fig. 10.7 shows that adding the value of both home production and leisure lowers the ratio of income at the 80th percentile to the median in each year. In 1992 it lowers it only slightly, from 1.8 to 1.7. Adding only the value of home production reduces this ratio more than adding both home production and leisure. However, the increase in the ratio of the 80th percentile to the median is slightly greater using adjusted income than using money income.

If we include the value of both home production and leisure, the decline in the ratio of the 20th percentile to the median and the increase in the 80th percentile to the median are smaller than the ratio for unadjusted income. Hence, the growth in income inequality is smaller once we include the value of home production. However, the difference in the trend in inequality is quite small when we value home production using either the replacement cost or the opportunity cost method.

We find analogous results for per capita income. Table 10.4 shows median per capita income and per capita income at the 20th and 80th percentile of the income distribution by year. These are plotted in Figs 10.6 and 10.7. Conclusions for per capita income are similar to those for unadjusted income, namely that measures of income adjusted for home production yield less inequality than money income in any one year, but inequality grows regardless of the income measure used. Growth in inequality is less when the value of home production is

Table 10.4. *Various measures of per capita income at the 20th, 50th, and 80th percentile*

Year	20th percentile	Median	80th percentile	20th percentile/ median	80th percentile/ median
Full income					
1976	27,960	48,541	82,690	0.576	1.704
1977	28,276	48,655	82,476	0.581	1.695
1978	28,426	49,149	84,025	0.578	1.710
1979	28,329	48,996	84,170	0.578	1.718
1980	26,459	46,884	81,742	0.564	1.743
1981	26,320	46,172	81,358	0.570	1.762
1983	25,206	47,347	82,500	0.532	1.742
1984	25,108	46,813	82,467	0.536	1.762
1985	25,672	46,257	82,456	0.555	1.783
1986	26,947	50,196	87,639	0.537	1.746
1987	26,549	49,974	88,432	0.531	1.770
1988	27,276	51,119	92,321	0.534	1.806
1989	26,946	50,331	89,377	0.535	1.776
1990	26,442	50,295	90,174	0.526	1.793

Table 10.4. *(Continued)*

Year	20th percentile	Median	80th percentile	20th percentile/ median	80th percentile/ median
1991	26,098	49,113	89,109	0.531	1.814
1992	29,675	56,570	101,333	0.525	1.791
Per cent change 1976–92	6.1	16.5	22.6	− 8.9	5.2
Replacement cost					
1976	9251	16,093	28,081	0.575	1.745
1977	9699	16,443	28,247	0.590	1.718
1978	9795	16,586	29,164	0.591	1.758
1979	10,088	17,065	30,007	0.591	1.758
1980	9280	16,215	28,540	0.572	1.760
1981	9372	16,472	28,651	0.569	1.739
1983	8860	16,729	29,777	0.530	1.780
1984	9313	17,370	30,536	0.536	1.758
1985	9266	17,064	30,584	0.543	1.792
1986	9395	18,143	32,386	0.518	1.785
1987	9630	18,097	32,638	0.532	1.804
1988	9642	18,267	34,040	0.528	1.863
1989	9750	18,659	32,960	0.523	1.766
1990	9763	18,311	33,074	0.533	1.806
1991	9469	18,093	33,500	0.523	1.852
1992	9666	18,758	34,809	0.515	1.856
Per cent change 1976–92	4.5	16.6	24.0	− 10.4	6.4
Opportunity cost					
1976	11,307	20,083	34,443	0.563	1.715
1977	11,881	20,520	34,594	0.579	1.686
1978	12,060	20,688	35,969	0.583	1.739
1979	12,004	20,749	35,777	0.579	1.724
1980	11,001	19,680	34,403	0.559	1.748
1981	11,010	19,716	33,488	0.558	1.699
1983	10,229	19,943	34,701	0.513	1.740
1984	10,575	20,203	35,706	0.523	1.767
1985	10,548	19,750	35,577	0.534	1.801
1986	10,967	21,557	37,311	0.509	1.731
1987	11,366	21,209	38,492	0.536	1.815
1988	11,218	21,775	39,713	0.515	1.824
1989	11,110	21,787	38,823	0.510	1.782
1990	11,102	20,999	38,644	0.529	1.840
1991	10,559	21,025	38,649	0.502	1.838
1992	11,476	22,489	41,427	0.510	1.842
Per cent change 1976–92	1.5	12.0	20.3	− 9.4	7.4

Table 10.5. *Changes in the median income of two-parent families relative to the median income of single-parent families*

Year	Two-parent families	Single-parent families	Ratio two-parent/single-parent
1976			
Money income	47,204	22,248	2.12
Income adjusted with replacement cost	56,997	28,495	2.00
1977			
Money income	48,079	23,730	2.02
Income adjusted with replacement cost	59,564	29,396	2.03
1992			
Money income	53,500	19,798	2.70
Income adjusted with replacement cost			

included mainly because the decline in income at the bottom of the distribution is less when home production is included.

Finally, Table 10.5 shows trends in household income and in adjusted income for single-parent and two-parent families. It shows that two-parent families had more than double the income of single-parent families in 1976 and 1992 regardless of whether we use unadjusted income or income adjusted for the value of home production. (Table 10.5 shows only money income adjusted with replacement cost because the conclusions are the same regardless of how we value home production.) But the gap between these two family types grew somewhat more if we take into account the value of home production. The same is true if we use per capita income.

10.7. CONCLUSIONS

Taken together these results show that (1) including the value of home production reduces inequality among households,[16] (2) hours of home production declined more for households with high money income, but (3) inequality of income adjusted for home production increased between 1976 and 1988. These conclusions hold regardless of the method we use to value home production and regardless of the adjustment for household size. The fact that the decline in hours of home production was greater for households that were more likely to have experienced an increase in the opportunity cost of home production is consistent with economic theory. Their above average decline in home production was,

---

[16] This may be one reason why there is less inequality in consumption than in measured income (Mayer and Jencks, 1993).

however, not sufficiently large to offset the increased dispersion of money income. As a result all of our measures of income continue to show an increase in inequality.

REFERENCES

Cachian, Maria, Sheldon Danziger, and Peter Gottschalk (1991). Working wives and family income inequality, in Sheldon Danziger and Peter Gottschalk (eds.), *Uneven Tides: Rising Inequality in America*, New York: Russell Sage Foundation.

Danziger, Sheldon and Peter Gottschalk (1995). *America Unequal*. Cambridge, MA: Harvard University Press.

Gottschalk, Peter (1997). Inequality, income growth, and mobility: The basic facts, *Journal of Economic Perspectives*, 11 (2) 21–40.

Gronau, Ruben (1980). Home production: A forgotten industry, *Review of Economics and Statistics*, 408–415.

Gronau, Rubin (1997). The theory of home production: The past ten years, *Journal of Labor Economics*, 15 (2), 197–205.

Hewlett, Sylvia Ann (1991). *When the Bough Breaks*. New York: Basic Books.

Hill, Martha S. (1992). *The Panel Study of Income Dynamics: A User's Guide*. Beverly Hills, CA: Sage Publications.

Juster, F. Thomas and Frank Stafford (1991). The allocation of time: Empirical findings, behavioral models and the problems of measurement, *Journal of Economic Literature* 24 (2), 471–523.

Kammerman, Sheila and Cheryl Hayes (eds.) (1982). *Families That Work: Children in a Changing World*. Washington, DC: National Academy Press.

Karoly, Lynn A. (1993). The trend in inequality among families, individuals, and workers in the United States: A twenty-five year perspective, in Sheldon Danziger and Peter Gottschalk (eds.), *Uneven Tides: Rising Inequality in America*. New York: Russell Sage Foundation.

—— and Gary Burtless (1993). The effects of rising earnings inequality on the distribution of US income, Paper presented at the *RAND/NICHD conference on Reshaping the Family*, January 1994.

Mayer, Susan and Christopher Jencks (1993). Recent trends in economic inequality in the United States: Income versus expenditures versus material well-being, in Wolfe, E. and D. Papadimitriou (eds.), *Poverty and Prosperity in the United States in the Late Twentieth Century*, London: Macmillan.

11

Unequal Societies: Income Distribution and the Social Contract

ROLAND BÉNABOU

The social contract varies considerably across nations. Some have low tax rates, others a steeply progressive fiscal system. Many countries have made the financing of education and health insurance the responsibility of the state. Some, notably the US, have left it in large part to families, local communities, and employers. The extent of implicit redistribution through labour-market policies or the mix of public goods also shows persistent differences. Can these societal choices be explained without appealing to exogenous differences in tastes, technologies, or political systems?

Adding to the puzzle is the fact that redistribution is often correlated with income inequality in just the opposite way than predicted by standard politico-economic theory: among industrial democracies the more unequal ones tend to redistribute less, not more. The archetypal case is that of the US versus Western Europe, but the observation holds within the latter group as well; thus Scandinavian countries are both the most equal and the most redistributive. In the developing world a similar contrast is found in the incidence of public education and health services, which is much more egalitarian in East Asia than in Latin America (e.g., South Korea versus Brazil). Turning finally to time trends, it is rather striking that the welfare state is being cut back in most industrial democracies at the same time that an unprecedented rise in inequality is occurring.

The aim of this chapter is to develop a joint theory of inequality and the social contract which can contribute to resolving some of these puzzles. In the process, it also seeks to reconcile certain empirical findings of the recent literature on political economy and growth. Several authors, such as Alberto F. Alesina and

This chapter was previously published in the *American Economic Review* (March 2000), and is reproduced here by kind permission of the American Economic Association.

This paper was written while I was at New York University, and visiting the Institut d'Economie Industrielle (IDEI-CERAS-GREMAQ) in Toulouse, France. I am grateful for helpful comments to Olivier Blanchard, Jason Cummins, John Geanakoplos, Mark Gertler, Robert Hall, Ken Judd, Jean-Charles Rochet, Julio Rotemberg, seminar participants at the NBER Summer Institute, Stanford University, Princeton University, and the Massachusetts Institute of Technology, as well as to three referees. Financial support from the National Science Foundation, the MacArthur Foundation, and the C.V. Starr Center is gratefully acknowledged. Frederico Ravenna provided excellent research assistance.

Dani Rodrik (1994) or Torsten Persson and Guido Tabellini (1994), have documented a negative relationship between initial disparities of income or wealth and subsequent aggregate growth. The proposed explanation is that greater inequality translates into a poorer median voter relative to the country's mean income, as in Alan H. Meltzer and Scott F. Richard (1981). This leads to increased pressure for redistributive policies, which in turn reduce incentives for the accumulation of physical and human capital. The cross-country data, however, do not seem very supportive of this explanation. Roberto Perotti (1994, 1996), and most of the other studies reviewed in Bénabou (1996c), find no relationship between inequality and the share of transfers or government expenditures in GDP. Among advanced countries the effect is actually negative, as suggested by the above examples (Francisco Rodriguez, 1998).[1] As to the effect of transfers on growth, most studies yield estimates which are in fact significantly positive.

The point of departure for this chapter is a rather different view of both the role of the state and the workings of the political process. When capital and insurance markets are imperfect, a variety of policies that redistribute wealth from richer to poorer agents can have a *positive* net effect on aggregate output, growth, or more generally *ex ante* welfare. Examples considered here will include social insurance through progressive taxes and transfers, state funding of public education, and residential integration. Net efficiency gains lead to very different political economy consequences from those of standard models: popular support for such re-distributive policies *decreases with inequality*, at least over some range. Intuitively, efficient redistributions meet with a wide consensus in a fairly homogeneous society but face strong opposition in an unequal one. Conversely, if agents engage in any type of investment, capital market imperfections imply that lower redistribution translates into more persistent inequality. The combination of these two mechanisms creates the potential for *multiple steady states*: mutually reinforcing high inequality and low redistribution, or low inequality and high redistribution. Temporary shocks to the distribution of income or the political system can then have permanent effects.

I formalize these ideas in a stochastic growth model with incomplete asset markets and heterogeneous agents who vote over redistributive policies, whether fiscal or educational. In the short run, redistribution is shown to be *U-shaped* with respect to inequality; in the long run they are *negatively* correlated across steady states. There are two important ingredients in the analysis. The first one is that redistribution enhances *ex ante* welfare, at least up to a point. I thus examine policies which reduce the variance and possibly increase the mean of family income, by providing insurance against idiosyncratic shocks and relaxing credit constraints. The second one is a simple extension of the standard voting model, reflecting the fact that some groups have more influence in the political process than others. I present extensive evidence that the propensities to vote, give political contributions,

---

[1] Using panel data for 20 OECD countries and controlling for national income, population, and the age distribution, Rodriguez finds that pretax inequality has a significantly negative effect on every major category of social transfers as a fraction of GDP, as well as on the capital tax rate.

work on campaigns, and participate in most forms of political activity rise with income and education. In the model, the pivotal agent is richer than the median, but need not be richer than the mean. It should be emphasized that I do not appeal to variations in political rights or participation to explain countries' different societal choices: this parameter is kept fixed across steady states. In the comparative statics analysis, I vary the efficiency costs and benefits of redistribution on the one hand (via the elasticity of labour supply and the degree of risk aversion), and the political system on the other, so as to identify their respective contributions to the results. In particular, I show that there exists a *critical level* for the gain in *ex ante* welfare from a redistributive policy, such that: (i) below this threshold, no allocation of political influence can sustain more than a single social contract; (ii) above this threshold, multiple steady states arise provided the political weight of the rich is neither too large nor too small.

When two 'unequal societies' arise from common fundamentals, they cannot be Pareto ranked. As to macroeconomic performance, the trade-off between tax distortions and liquidity-constraint effects allows for two interesting scenarios. One, termed 'growth-enhancing redistributions', is consistent with the positive coefficients of transfers in growth regressions, as well as the contributions of education and land policies in East Asian and Latin American countries to their respective developments (or lack thereof). The other, termed 'eurosclerosis', explains how European voters can choose to sacrifice more employment and growth to social insurance than their American counterparts, even though both populations have the same basic preferences. Another prediction of the model is that, depending on their source, exogenous shocks to income inequality will bring about sharply different evolutions of the social contract. Thus, an increased variability of sectoral shocks will lead to an expansion of the social safety net, while a surge in immigration may prompt large-scale cutbacks.

Some methodological features of the model may also be worth mentioning. The first is its analytical tractability. Individual transitions are linear, reflecting the absence of nonconvexities; yet there is multiplicity. The distribution of wealth remains lognormal, and closed-form solutions are obtained. The second is the progressivity of the redistributive schemes over which agents vote. The third is the intuitive formalization of political influence. These modelling devices could be useful in other settings.

The paper is related to three strands of literature. The first one emphasizes the political economy of redistribution (Giuseppe Bertola, 1993; Perotti, 1993; Gilles Saint-Paul and Thierry Verdier, 1993; Alesina and Rodrik, 1994; Persson and Tabellini, 1994, 1996). The second one is concerned with the financing and accumulation of human capital (Glenn C. Loury, 1981; Gerhard Glomm and B. Ravikumar, 1992; Oded Galor and Joseph Zeira, 1993; Bénabou, 1996b; Steven N. Durlauf, 1996a; Mark Gradstein and Moshe Justman, 1997; Raquel Fernández and Richard Rogerson, 1998). The third one stresses the wealth and incentive constraints which bear on entrepreneurial investment (Abhijit Banerjee and Andrew Newman, 1993; Philippe Aghion and Patrick Bolton, 1997; Thomas

R. Bénabou

Piketty, 1997). Most directly related are the models in Bénabou (1996*b*,*c*), upon which I build, and the paper by Saint-Paul (2001), which identifies another mechanism through which capital market imperfections can lead to multiple politico-economic regimes.[2] A rather different explanation for international differences in redistribution is provided in Piketty (1995), where agents' imperfect learning of the social mobility process allows different views of the equity-efficiency trade-off to persist in the long run.[3]

The chapter is organized as follows. Section 11.1 explains the main ideas using the simplest possible setup, which treats the aggregate impact of redistribution as exogenous. Section 11.2 presents the actual economic model, and Section 11.3 the political mechanism. Section 11.4 focuses on an endowment economy, in order to study whether social insurance will be more or less extensive in a more unequal country. Section 11.5 solves the full model with endogenous wealth dynamics. The range of economic and political 'fundamentals' that allow multiple steady states is characterized, and the growth rates under alternative regimes are compared. Section 11.6 recasts the model so as to explain differences in countries' systems of education finance. Section 11.7 discusses other applications such as altruism, residential integration, and the mix of public goods. Section 11.8 concludes. All proofs are gathered in the Appendix.

11.1. A SIMPLIFIED PRESENTATION OF THE MAIN IDEAS

As a prelude to the actual model, I present in this section a very stylized reduced form which provides a shortcut to the main intuitions and results.

11.1.1 The Standard View

Let there be a continuum of agents, $i \in [0, 1]$, with lognormally distributed endowments: $\ln y^i \sim \mathcal{N}(m, \Delta^2)$. The lognormal is a good approximation of empirical income distributions, leads to tractable results, and allows for an unambiguous definition of inequality, as increases in Δ^2 shift the Lorenz curve outward. This variance also measures the distance between median and per capita income: $m = \ln y - \Delta^2/2$, where $y \equiv E[y^i]$. Suppose now that agents are faced with the choice between two stylized policies:

($\mathcal{P}$) *laissez-faire*: each consumes his own endowment, $c^i = y^i$, for all i.

($\hat{\mathcal{P}}$) *complete redistribution*: resources are pooled, and everyone consumes $c^i = y$.

---

[2] Saint-Paul points out that increases in inequality whose adverse impact is concentrated in the lower tail of the income distribution may be accompanied by a rise in median income, relative to the mean, so that the politically decisive middle class will reduce its transfers to the poor. If exit from poverty requires some investment, credit constraints may then lead to multiple steady states: a large underclass that persists due to low redistribution, or one which is kept small by significant transfers.

[3] Piketty's mechanism is similar to a collective form of the bandit problem. Because individual experimentation is costly, agents never fully learn the extent to which income is affected by effort rather than predetermined by social origins. The citizens of otherwise identical countries may then end up with different distributions of beliefs over the disincentive effects of redistribution.

In this benchmark case where redistribution has no aggregate impact, how many people are in favour of it? Clearly, all those with endowment below the mean, i.e., a proportion

$$p = \Phi\left(\frac{\Delta^2/2}{\Delta}\right) = \Phi\left(\frac{\Delta}{2}\right) \tag{11.1}$$

where $\Phi(\cdot)$ is the cumulative distribution function of a standard normal. Because the income distribution is right-skewed, the median is below the mean, $p > 1/2$. A strict majority rule would thus predict that redistribution should always take place. In reality, the poor vote with lower probability than the rich and, to some extent, money buys political influence. Therefore the relevant threshold for redistribution to occur may not be $p^* = 50$ per cent $= \Phi(0)$, but $p^* = \Phi(\lambda)$, $\lambda > 0$. For instance if the π poorest agents never vote, $\Phi(\lambda) = (1 + \pi)/2$.[4]

What is important and robust in (11.1) is therefore not the level effect, $p > 1/2$, but the comparative statics, $\partial p/\partial \Delta > 0$: in a more unequal society there is greater political support for redistribution. For *any* degree of bias λ in the voting system, positive or negative, the likelihood that redistribution takes place increases with inequality—or more specifically, skewness.

This result is only reinforced under the standard assumption that redistribution entails some deadweight loss (endogenized later on), reducing available resources from y to ye^{-B}, $B > 0$. Given the choice between laissez-faire and sharing this reduced pie, the extent of political support for the *inefficient redistribution* is

$$p = \Phi\left(\frac{-B + \Delta^2/2}{\Delta}\right) = \Phi\left(-\frac{B}{\Delta} + \frac{\Delta}{2}\right). \tag{11.2}$$

Note that now $p \gtrless 1/2$ but $\partial p/\partial \Delta$ is even more positive than before. As inequality increases, so does the likelihood that a policy that reduces aggregate income gets implemented. This is, in essence, the mechanism by which inequality reduces growth in models such as Alesina and Rodrik (1994), Persson and Tabellini (1994), or some cases of Bertola (1993) and Perotti (1993).[5] The idea that distributional conflict hampers economic performance appears to be reasonably well supported by the evidence: a number of studies have confirmed Persson and Tabellini's and Alesina and Rodrik's findings of a negative effect of inequality on growth.[6] This correlation, however, does not seem to arise through increased redistribution. Perotti (1994, 1996), Philip Keefer and Stephen F. Knack (1995),

---

[4] Section 11.3 will formalize in more detail—as well as present extensive evidence on—the influence of income and human wealth on most forms of political activity.

[5] Naturally, this simple reduced form fails to capture the richness of the original models.

[6] See Bénabou (1996c) for a survey. As with nearly all growth regressions this finding is robust to some changes in specification but not to others. This caveat should be kept in mind, but in any case such a correlation is not essential to my results, which primarily involve inequality and redistribution. Thus, Section 11.5.2 will identify parameter configurations such that inequality and growth are positively, or negatively, correlated across steady states.

and Peter H. Lindert (1996) find no relationship between the income share of the middle class (which corresponds to the median voter) and any tax rate or share of government transfers in GDP. George R. G. Clarke (1992) finds no correlation between any measure of inequality and government consumption. As casual empiricism suggests, more unequal countries do not redistribute more. Among advanced nations, they typically redistribute *less* (Rodriguez, 1998). Furthermore, the coefficients on transfers in growth regressions are most often significantly positive: see, among others, Shantarayan Devarajan *et al.* (1993), Lindert (1996), Xavier Sala-i-Martin (1996), and especially Perotti (1994, 1996), who controls for the endogeneity of redistribution. While none of these findings should be viewed as definitive evidence, altogether they do suggest that something important may be missing from the traditional story.

11.1.2. Efficiency Gains and Redistribution: The Static Case

In a world of incomplete insurance and loan markets, some policies with redistributive features can have a positive effect on total welfare, and even output (as the evidence on transfers and growth may suggest). *Ex ante* welfare gains, in turn, imply a political support that varies with inequality in a radically different way from the traditional one. Indeed, suppose that by redistributing resources agents achieve increased efficiency, so that each gets to consume ye^B. For now I continue to take $B > 0$ as exogenous, but later on I shall derive it from a variety of channels: insurance, altruism, or credit constraints on the accumulation of human and physical capital. The fraction of people who support an *efficient redistribution* is

$$p = \Phi\left(\frac{B + \Delta^2/2}{\Delta}\right) = \Phi\left(\frac{B}{\Delta} + \frac{\Delta}{2}\right). \tag{11.3}$$

It is, of course, always higher than (11.1) and (11.2), but the important point is the one illustrated in Fig 11.1.

Proposition 1. *When a redistributive policy generates gains in ex ante efficiency, political support for it initially declines with inequality. In the present framework, the relationship is U-shaped.*

The intuition is simple: when dispersion is relatively small compared to the average gain, there is near-unanimous support for the policy. As inequality rises, the proportion of those who stand to lose from the redistribution increases. At high enough levels of inequality, however, the standard skewness effect eventually dominates: there are so many poor that they impose redistribution no matter what its aggregate impact may be. There is thus *no monotonic relationship* between income inequality or the relative position of the median agent (both measured here by Δ^2) and the likelihood of redistribution.[7]

---

[7] The fact that inequality affects political support for redistribution in opposite ways, depending on the sign of its aggregate impact, is essentially independent of distribution assumptions. For any symmetric distribution $F(x)$ with mean μ, a symmetric, mean-preserving spread leads to a decline in

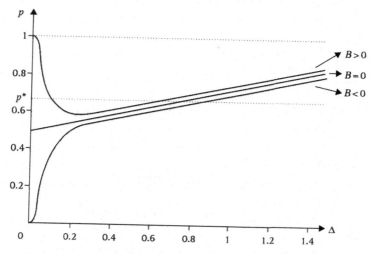

Figure 11.1. *Inequality and political support for redistribution.*
Note: $B = 5$ per cent, 0, -5 per cent.

To relate the extent of popular support for a policy to actual outcomes, one needs to specify the mechanism through which preferences are aggregated. I shall continue to assume that redistribution occurs if p exceeds a threshold $p^* \equiv \Phi(\lambda)$, where λ reflects the degree to which financial or human wealth contributes to political influence. More generally, the probability of implementation could be some increasing function of p. Figure 11.1 shows that *only if* redistribution's aggregate impact B is positive can the policy be abandoned as the result of greater inequality—no matter how biased the political system might be. Conversely, a positive λ is needed for the political outcome to reflect the drop in popular support. The full model will confirm the joint importance of *efficiency gains* and *wealth bias* in shaping a declining relationship between inequality and redistribution. The arguments seen here for a zero-one policy choice will then apply to marginal changes in the tax rate τ, i.e., to every electoral contest between τ and $\tau + d\tau$.

Finally, consider the dynamic implications of Proposition 1. A society that starts with enough wealth disparity to find itself below p^* on the U-shaped curve of Fig. 11.1 will not implement the redistributive policy; as a result, high inequality will persist into the next period or generation. Conversely, low inequality creates wide political support for efficient policies that prevent

---

popular support $p = F(\mu + B)$ for all $B > 0$, and an increase for all $B < 0$. With lognormally distributed wealth, a rise in Δ combines this general effect of dispersion with a fall in $m = \mu - \Delta^2/2$ due to increased skewness; hence the U shape. These properties remain true when B is a function of Δ, as long as $\Delta B'(\Delta)/B(\Delta) < 1$. Such will be the case when B is endogenized later on.

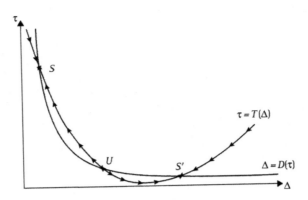

Figure 11.2. *Dynamics and steady states.*

disparities from growing. The *dynamic feedback* operates whenever some form of investment is credit constrained, so that current resources affect future earnings. Thus, the same type of market imperfections that can give rise to a (partly) decreasing relationship between inequality and transfers also provide the second ingredient required for *multiple steady states*. These dynamics are represented in Fig. 11.2 (which will be formally derived later on), for a continuous rate of redistribution $\tau \in [0, 1]$. The U-shaped curve $\tau = T(\Delta)$ is similar to that of Fig. 11.1, while the declining $\Delta = D(\tau)$ locus arises from the accumulation mechanism.

The main part of the chapter, to which I now turn, will show that all the intuitions obtained in this section carry over to a fully specified inter-temporal model of individual behaviour and collective choice, where the welfare gains and losses from redistribution are endogenous.

11.2. INCOMPLETE ASSET MARKETS AND PROGRESSIVE TAXATION

11.2.1. Technology, Preferences, and Decisions

The economy is populated by overlapping-generations families, $i \in I \equiv [0, 1]$. In generation t, adult i combines his (human or physical) capital endowment k_t^i with effort l_t^i to produce output, subject to an independently and identically distributed (i.i.d.) productivity shock z_t^i:

$$y_t^i = z_t^i (k_t^i)^\gamma (l_t^i)^\delta. \tag{11.4}$$

Taxes and transfers, specified below, transform this gross income y_t^i into a disposable income $\hat{y}_t^i$ which finances both the adult's consumption, c_t^i, and his

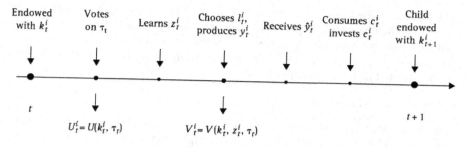

Figure 11.3. *Preferences and the timing of decisions.*

investment or educational bequest, e_t^i:

$$\hat{y}_t^i = c_t^i + e_t^i \qquad (11.5)$$

$$k_{t+1}^i = \kappa \xi_{t+1}^i (k_t^i)^\alpha (e_t^i)^\beta. \qquad (11.6)$$

Capital depreciates geometrically at the rate $1 - \alpha \geq \beta\gamma$, and investment is subject to i.i.d. productivity shocks ξ_t^i. There is no loan market for financing individual investment or educational projects (e.g., children cannot be held responsible for the debts of their parents) and no insurance or securities market where the idiosyncratic risks z_t^i and ξ_{t+1}^i could be diversified away. These are extreme forms of market incompleteness, but all that really matters is that there be some imperfections.[8] Both shocks are assumed to be lognormal with mean one, and initial endowments lognormally distributed across families: thus, $\ln z_t^i \sim \mathcal{N}(-v^2/2, v^2)$, $\ln \xi_t^i \sim \mathcal{N}(-w^2/2, w^2)$ and $\ln k_0^i \sim \mathcal{N}(m_0, \Delta_0^2)$.

Adults have preferences defined over their own consumption and effort, as well as their child's endowment of capital. Following David M. Kreps and Evan L. Porteus (1979), Larry G. Epstein and Stanley E. Zin (1989), and Philippe Weil (1990), these preferences are defined recursively over an individual's lifetime; see Fig. 11.3. Thus, upon discovering his productivity z_t^i, agent i chooses effort, consumption, and savings so as to maximize:

$$\ln V_t^i \equiv \max_{l_t^i, c_t^i}\{(1 - \rho)[\ln c_t^i - (l_t^i)^\eta] + \rho \ln ((E_t[(k_{t+1}^i)^r | k_t^i, z_t^i])^{1/r})\}. \qquad (11.7)$$

The disutility of effort is measured by $\eta > 1$, which corresponds to an intertemporal elasticity of labour supply equal to $1/(\eta - 1)$. The discount factor ρ defines the relative weights of the adult's own felicity and of his bequest motive,

[8] Perotti (1994) provides evidence that credit-market frictions reduce aggregate investment, especially where the income share of the bottom 40 per cent is low. Additional evidence on asset-market incompleteness as a constraint on investment decisions in education and farming is discussed in Bénabou (1996c).

while his (relative) risk aversion with respect to the child's endowment k_{t+1}^i is $1 - r'$. At the beginning of period t, however, when evaluating and voting over redistributive policies, the agent has not yet learned z_t^i. In other words, he knows his type (k_t^i, z_t^i) *imperfectly*.[9] The resulting uncertainty over his *ex post* utility level V_t^i is reflected in his *ex ante* preferences,

$$U_t^i \equiv \ln (E_t[(V_t^i)^r | k_t^i]^{1/r}), \tag{11.8}$$

with a risk-aversion coefficient of $1 - r$. When $r = 0$ preferences are time separable and $1/(1 - r)$ coincides with the intertemporal elasticity of substitution in consumption, which by (7) is fixed at one.[10] The more general specification allows $1 - r$ to parametrize the insurance value of redistributive policies, just as the labour-supply elasticity $1/(\eta - 1)$ parametrizes the effort distortions. Varying these parameters will make it possible to study how the set of politico-economic equilibria is shaped by the *costs and benefits of redistribution*—the central issue of this chapter. Finally, it should be noted that while I have assumed overlapping generations with 'imperfect' altruism, many of chapter's results can also be derived with infinitely lived agents.[11]

11.2.2. Fiscal Policy

Taxes and transfers map agent i's market income y_t^i into a disposable income $\hat{y}_t^i$, according to the following scheme:

$$\hat{y}_t^i \equiv (y_t^i)^{1-\tau_t} (\tilde{y}_t)^{\tau_t}. \tag{11.9}$$

The break-even level $\tilde{y}_t$ is determined by the government's budget constraint: net transfers must sum to zero or, denoting per capita income by y_t:

$$\int_0^1 (y_t^i)^{1-\tau_t} (\tilde{y}_t)^{\tau_t} di = y_t. \tag{11.10}$$

The elasticity τ_t of post-tax income measures the degree of *progressivity* (or regressivity) of fiscal policy.[12] An alternative interpretation is that of wage

---

[9] Therein lies the crucial difference between ξ_t^i and z_t^i, rather than in the fact that one affects human capital and the other production; the latter roles could be switched. Also, because the policies that I shall consider provide no insurance against ξ_{t+1}^i (only against z_t^i), the value of $1 - r'$ will turn out not to play an important role in the analysis. It could therefore be set (for instance) to zero, to one, or to $1 - r$, which is the more essential risk-aversion parameter defined in (11.8) below.

[10] This last assumption is made for analytical tractability, as in much of the literature on income distribution dynamics e.g., Glomm and Ravikumar (1992), Banerjee and Newman (1993), Galor and Zeira (1993), Saint-Paul and Verdier (1993), Aghion and Bolton (1997), or Gradstein and Justman (1997).

[11] See Bénabou (1996a, 2002). The infinite-horizon version of the preferences used here is obtained by replacing k_{t+1}^i with V_{t+1}^i in (11.7), with $r' = r$ and (11.8) unchanged.

[12] When $\tau_t > 0$ the marginal rate rises with pre-tax income, and agents with average income are made better off: $\tilde{y}_t > y_t$. Measuring progressivity by the (local) elasticity of after-tax to pretax income was first proposed by Richard A. Musgrave and Tun Thin (1948). Ulf Jakobsson (1976) and Nanak

compression through labour-market institutions favourable to workers with relatively low skills. Confiscatory rates $\tau_t > 1$ must be excluded as not incentive compatible, but nothing in principle prevents a regressive tax, so I shall allow it. Restricting τ_t to be non-negative would require dealing with corner solutions but would not change the nature of any result.

Proposition 2. *Given a tax rate τ_t, agents in generation t choose a common labour supply and savings rate:*

$$l_t = \chi (1 - \tau_t)^{1/\eta}$$

$$e_t^i = s \hat{y}_t^i$$

where $\chi^\eta \equiv (\delta/\eta)(1 - \rho + \rho\beta)/(1 - \rho)$ *and* $s \equiv \rho\beta/(1 - \rho + \rho\beta)$.

Because taxes are progressive rather than merely proportional they affect effort, $l_t = l(\tau_t)$, in spite of the fact that utility is logarithmic in consumption.[13] I will refer from here on to $1/\eta$ as 'the' elasticity of labour supply.[14]

11.2.3. Redistribution and Accumulation

Given Proposition 2, and substituting (11.9) into (11.6), capital accumulation simplifies to:

$$
\begin{aligned}
\ln k_{t+1}^i = {} & \ln \xi_{t+1}^i + \beta(1 - \tau_t)\ln z_t^i + \ln \kappa \\
& + \beta \ln s + (\alpha + \beta\gamma(1 - \tau_t))\ln k_t^i \\
& + \beta\delta(1 - \tau_t)\ln l_t + \beta\tau_t \ln \tilde{y}_t.
\end{aligned}
\tag{11.11}
$$

Due to the symmetry of agents' effort and savings decisions, wealth and income remain lognormally distributed over time. If $\ln k_t^i \sim \mathcal{N}(m_t, \Delta_t^2)$, the government's budget constraint (11.10) easily yields the break-even point of the redistributive scheme (see the Appendix):

$$\ln \tilde{y}_t = \gamma m_t + \delta \ln l_t + (2 - \tau_t)\gamma^2 \Delta_t^2/2 + (1 - \tau_t)v^2/2. \tag{11.12}$$

C. Kakwani (1977) showed this to be the 'right' measure of equalization: the post-tax distribution induced by a fiscal scheme Lorenz-dominates the one induced by another (for *all* pre-tax distributions), if and only if the first scheme's elasticity is everywhere smaller. A 'constant residual progression' scheme similar to (11.9) turns out to have been used in a couple of earlier but static models of insurance or risk taking (Martin S. Feldstein, 1969; S. M. Kanbur, 1979; Mats Persson, 1983).

[13] They would also affect savings, were it not for adults' simple bequest motive. Even with infinitely lived agents, however, the savings distortion can be fully offset by a balanced-budget combination of consumption taxes and investment subsidies; moreover, this can be shown to be Pareto optimal (Bénabou, 1996a, 2002). In any case, one distortion is enough to demonstrate how the trade-off between the costs and benefits of redistribution shapes the range of politico-economic equilibria.

[14] It is indeed the uncompensated elasticity to the net-of-tax rate $1 - \tau_t$, and varies monotonically with the usual intertemporal elasticity of substitution for proportional variations in the real wage, $1/(\eta - 1)$.

From (11.11), we then obtain two simple difference equations which govern the evolution of the economy:

$$m_{t+1} = (\alpha + \beta\gamma)m_t + \beta\delta\ln l_t + \beta\tau_t(2 - \tau_t)(\gamma^2\Delta_t^2 + v^2)/2$$
$$+ \ln(\kappa s^\beta) - (w^2 + \beta v^2)/2 \tag{11.13}$$

$$\Delta_{t+1}^2 = (\alpha + \beta\gamma(1 - \tau_t))^2\Delta_t^2 + \beta^2(1 - \tau_t)^2 v^2 + w^2. \tag{11.14}$$

The effect of redistribution on the dynamics of inequality is clear: the progressivity rate τ_t determines the *persistence of family wealth*, $\alpha + \beta\gamma(1 - \tau_t)$. The impact on the dynamics of aggregate income is more complex, as it involves a trade-off between labour supply and credit-constraint effects.

Proposition 3. *The distribution of pretax income at time t is $\ln y_t^i \sim \mathcal{N}(\gamma m_t + \delta\ln l_t - v^2/2, \gamma^2\Delta_t^2 + v^2)$, where m_t and Δ_t^2 evolve according to the linear difference equations* (11.13)–(11.14) *and $l_t = \chi(1 - \tau_t)^{1/\eta}$. The growth rate of per capita income is:*

$$\ln(y_{t+1}/y_t) = \ln\tilde{\kappa} - (1 - \alpha - \beta\gamma)\ln y_t + \delta(\ln l_{t+1} - \alpha\ln l_t) \tag{11.15}$$
$$- \mathcal{L}_v(\tau_t)v^2/2 - \mathcal{L}_\Delta(\tau_t)\gamma^2\Delta_t^2/2,$$

where $\ln\tilde{\kappa} \equiv \gamma(\ln\kappa + \beta\ln s) - \gamma(1 - \gamma)w^2/2$ is a constant and

$$\mathcal{L}_v(\tau) \equiv \beta\gamma(1 - \beta\gamma)(1 - \tau)^2 > 0,$$
$$\mathcal{L}_\Delta(\tau) \equiv \alpha + \beta\gamma(1 - \tau)^2 - (\alpha + \beta\gamma(1 - \tau))^2 > 0.$$

The term in $-\ln y_t$ reflects the standard convergence effect; it disappears under constant aggregate returns, namely when $\alpha + \beta\gamma = 1$ or when κ is replaced by an appropriate spillover κ_t (see Section 11.5.2). The next term, capturing the effects of labour supply on accumulation, is also of a 'representative agent' nature. The terms in $\mathcal{L}_v(\tau)$ and $\mathcal{L}_\Delta(\tau)$, on the other hand, represent growth losses specific to the heterogenous agent economy with imperfect credit markets. Suppose first that adults in generation t are *ex ante* identical ($\Delta_t^2 = 0$). Everyone then faces the same accumulation technology, with concavity (decreasing returns) $\beta\gamma(1 - \beta\gamma)$. The shocks z_t^i generate *ex post* income disparities (partially offset by redistribution), which credit constraints translate into inefficient variations in investment, reducing overall growth by $\mathcal{L}_v(\tau_t)v^2/2$. Consider now disparities in initial endowments, $\gamma^2\Delta_t^2$. When $\alpha = 0$ these have the same effect as income shocks: $\mathcal{L}_v \equiv \mathcal{L}_\Delta$. The marginal return to investment is higher for the poor than for the rich, because they are more severely liquidity constrained. When $\alpha > 0$, however, the preexisting capital stocks k_t^i represent *complementary inputs* which generate differential returns to investment, and thereby reduce the desirability of equalizing resources. Thus $\mathcal{L}_\Delta(\tau)$ is minimized for $\tau = (1 - \alpha - \beta\gamma)/(1 - \beta\gamma)$, which decreases with α.

11.2.4. Individual Welfare

I now turn from the evolution of the economy as a whole to individuals' evaluations of alternative policies. Given the optimal labour supply and savings responses to a tax rate τ_t, (11.7) gives agent i's *ex post* welfare V_t^i for any productivity realization z_t^i. Since he must vote before learning z_t^i, his preferences over τ_t are then defined by the *ex ante* utility U_t^i, according to (11.8).

Proposition 4. *Given a rate of fiscal progressivity τ_t, agent i's intertemporal welfare is:*

$$U_t^i = \bar{u}_t + A(\tau_t)(\ln k_t^i - m_t) + C(\tau_t) - (1 - \rho + \rho\beta)$$
$$\times (1 - \tau_t)^2 (\gamma^2 \Delta_t^2 + Bv^2)/2, \qquad (11.16)$$

where $\bar{u}_t$ is independent of the policy τ_t and

$$A(\tau) \equiv \rho\alpha + (1 - \rho + \rho\beta)\gamma(1 - \tau), \qquad (11.17)$$

$$C(\tau) \equiv (1 - \rho)(\delta \ln l(\tau) - l(\tau)^\eta) + \rho\beta\delta \ln l(\tau), \qquad (11.18)$$

$$B \equiv 1 - r + \rho r(1 - \beta) \geq 0. \qquad (11.19)$$

The first term in U_t^i depends only on the state variables m_t and Δ_t^2 and on the (endogenous but constant) investment rate s. The second term, which disappears through aggregation, makes clear the *redistributive* effects of tax policy, including its impact on the persistence of social positions, $\alpha + \beta\gamma(1 - \tau)$. The last two terms represent the *aggregate welfare cost* and *aggregate welfare benefit* of a progressivity rate τ_t. Thus $C(\tau_t)$, which is maximized for $\tau_t = 0$, reflects the distortions in labour supply entailed by such a policy. Conversely, the term $-(1 - \tau_t)^2$ $(\gamma^2 \Delta_t^2 + Bv^2)$, which is maximized for $\tau_t = 1$, embodies the efficiency gains that arise from better insurance and the redistribution of resources from low to high marginal-product investments. Note that B is now *endogenous*, and monotonically related to *risk aversion*, $1 - r$. More generally, by varying $1 - r$, β, v^2, and $1/\eta$, the net *ex ante* efficiency gain, $(1 - \rho + \rho\beta)(1 - \tau)^2 Bv^2/2 - C(\tau)$, can be made arbitrarily large or small relative to preexisting income inequality, $\gamma^2 \Delta_t^2$.

To make the role of market incompleteness more explicit, I consider again each source of heterogeneity in turn. By (11.16), idiosyncratic uncertainty lowers everyone's utility by $(1 - \rho + \rho\beta)B(1 - \tau)^2 v^2/2$. When $\beta = 1$ this simplifies to $(1 - r)(1 - \tau)^2 v^2/2$: with constant returns, the *ex ante* value of redistribution stems from the insurance it provides. In general, it also contributes to efficiency through the relaxation of credit constraints. This is best seen with risk-neutral parents who care only about their offspring: when $r = \rho = 1$ the utility loss is $\beta(1 - \beta)$ $(1 - \tau)^2 v^2/2$, which is the shortfall in expected (and aggregate) bequests resulting from idiosyncratic resource shocks and a concave investment technology. Turning now to pre-existing inequality, the loss in aggregate welfare is $(1 - \rho + \rho\beta)$ $(1 - \tau)^2 \gamma^2 \Delta_t^2/2$; it embodies two effects, only one of which is due to market incompleteness. First, reallocating investment resources towards the poor again increases the growth rate of total wealth, $\ln(k_{t+1}/k_t)$. Second, there is the standard effect of concave (logarithmic) utility functions, whereby average welfare increases when individual consumptions (of c_t^i and k_{t+1}^i) are distributed more equally.[15] Equivalently in this model, it captures the effect of *skewness*, as in Section 11.1: the median agent, who is poorer than average, gains when consumption and bequests are redistributed progressively.

11.3. THE POLITICAL SYSTEM

I now turn to the determination of the equilibrium policy. Each generation chooses, before the individual productivity shocks z_t^i are realized, the rate of fiscal progressivity τ_t to which it will be subject. Agent i's ideal policy would thus be to maximize U_t^i.[16] These individual preferences are aggregated through a political process in which some groups have more influence than others.

11.3.1. Preferred Policies

I first consider the simpler case where labour supply is inelastic, $1/\eta = 0$. The utility function U_t^i is then quadratic in τ_t, and maximized at:

$$\frac{1}{1-\tau_t^i} = \frac{\gamma^2 \Delta_t^2 + Bv^2}{\gamma \max\{\ln k_t^i - m_t, 0\}}. \tag{11.20}$$

Voters below the median desire the maximum feasible tax rate, $\tau_t^i = 1$, which is also the *ex ante* efficient one in the absence of distortions. Voters above the median desire a tax rate $\tau_t^i < 1$ that decreases with their initial wealth and increases with the variance of productivity shocks, for both insurance and investment reasons (concavity of preferences and concavity of the technology).

---

[15] One can rewrite $(1-\rho+\rho\beta)\gamma^2(1-\tau)^2$ as $\rho[\beta\gamma^2(1-\tau)^2 - (\alpha+\beta\gamma(1-\tau))^2] + (1-\rho)\gamma^2$ $(1-\tau)^2 + \rho(\alpha+\beta\gamma(1-\tau))^2 = -\rho\ln(k_{t+1}/\ln k_t) + (1-\rho)\mathrm{var}_{j\in I}[\ln c_t^j] + \rho\mathrm{var}_{j\in I}[\ln k_{t+1}^j] + \mu_t$, where $\mathrm{var}_{j\in I}[\cdot]$ denotes a cross-sectional variance, μ_t is independent of τ_t, and I have set $v=w=\delta=0$ for notational simplicity.

[16] Due to the overlapping-generations structure, no intertemporal strategic considerations are involved. Infinite horizons, by contrast, would generate a dynamic game where voters try to influence future political outcomes τ_{t+k} by altering the evolution of the wealth distribution Δ_{t+k}^2 through their choice of τ_t (see (11.14)). This problem is notoriously intractable, so the standard practice is to assume that voters are 'myopic,' either ignoring their influence on future outcomes or—as here—not caring about it due to a limited bequest motive. Notable exceptions are Saint-Paul (2001) and Gene M. Grossman and Elhanan Helpman (1998). Alternatively, Per Krusell *et al.* (1997) look for numerical solutions. In Bénabou (1996*a*) I considered a different form of political myopia, and obtained results similar to those presented here. In short, agents with fully dynastic preferences choose a *constitution* (namely a constant sequence $\{\tau_{t+k} = \tau_t\}_{k=0}^{\infty}$), ignoring the fact that future generations may revise it. In any steady state, however, ($\Delta_t^2 = \Delta_{t+1}^2$ in (11.14)), every generation, given the same choice set as its predecessors, validates the existing social contract.

With endogenous labour supply, complete redistribution is never chosen, as it would lead to zero effort and output. Agent i's desired policy is given by the first-order condition $\partial U_t^i / \partial \tau = 0$, or:

$$(1 - \tau)(\gamma^2 \Delta_t^2 + Bv^2) - \gamma(\ln k_t^i - m_t) - \frac{\delta}{\eta}\left(\frac{\tau}{1 - \tau}\right) = 0. \tag{11.21}$$

This quadratic equation always has a unique solution less than 1, which will be denoted τ_t^i.

Proposition 5. *Each agent's utility U_t^i is strictly concave in the policy τ_t. His preferred tax rate τ_t^i decreases with his wealth k_t^i and increases with Bv^2. Finally, $|\tau_t^i|$ decreases with the labour-supply elasticity $1/\eta$.*[17]

These results are intuitive. Lower personal wealth or greater *ex ante* efficiency benefits from redistribution increase an agent's demand for such policies. A more elastic labour supply increases the deadweight loss from taxes and transfers, whether progressive or regressive, that cause individuals to distort their labour supply away from the first-best level. Finally, as a prelude to the analysis of political equilibrium, note how (11.21) embodies the same intuitions as the stylized model of Section 11.1. For any $\tau < 1$, the proportion of agents who would like further redistribution at the margin,

$$p(\tau, \Delta_t) \equiv \text{card}\left\{ i \left| \frac{\partial U_t^i}{\partial \tau} > 0 \right. \right\}$$
$$= \Phi\left(\frac{(1 - \tau)Bv^2 - \delta\tau/(\eta(1 - \tau))}{\gamma\Delta_t} + (1 - \tau)\gamma\Delta_t\right), \tag{11.22}$$

is U-shaped in Δ_t, provided the resulting gain in *ex ante* efficiency $(1 - \tau)Bv^2$ dominates the distortion $\delta\tau/(\eta(1 - \tau))$. Otherwise, $p(\tau, \Delta_t)$ is strictly increasing in Δ_t. Also as in Figure 11.1, variations in popular support for efficient increases in τ all take place above the 50 per cent level, so they will influence policy outcomes only under some departure from the pure 'one person, one vote' democratic ideal.

11.3.2. Wealth and Political Influence

It is well known that poor and less educated individuals have a relatively low propensity to register, turn out to vote, and give political contributions. These are among the facts documented in Tables 11.1 and 11.2, which present data from Steven J. Rosenstone and John M. Hansen (1993); see also Raymond E. Wolfinger and Rosenstone (1980), Thomas B. Edsall (1984), or Margaret M. Conway (1991). For each form of participation in electoral or governmental politics, the *representation ratio* of a given socioeconomic group is the ratio between its share of the population engaged in this activity and its share of the general population.

---

[17] More specifically, for $\ln k_t^i \leq m_t + \gamma\Delta_t^2 + Bv^2/\gamma$ the ideal τ_t^i is positive and decreases towards zero as $1/\eta$ rises. For $\ln k_t^i > m_t + \gamma\Delta_t^2 + Bv^2/\gamma$, $\tau_t^i < 0$ and it increases towards zero as $1/\eta$ rises.

R. Bénabou

Table 11.1 *Political participation by income*

Political activity: Electoral Politics, 1952–1988	Total fraction taking part (in per cent)	Representation ratios by percentile family income					Pivot p^* (in per cent)
		0–16	17–33	34–67	68–95	96–100	
Vote	66.1	0.76	0.90	1.00	1.16	1.27	55.5
Try to influence others	26.7	0.63	0.79	0.98	1.25	1.54	60.6
Contribute money	8.9	0.25	0.51	0.98	1.54	3.25	73.6
Attend meetings	7.8	0.49	0.73	0.93	1.31	2.27	65.7
Work on campaign	4.6	0.48	0.74	0.85	1.37	2.42	67.6

Source: Rosenstone and Hansen (1993), Table 8.2, plus my computation of p^*.

Table 11.2 *Political participation by education*

Political activity	Total fraction taking part (in per cent)	Representation ratios by years of education (with corresponding percentage of population)					Pivot p^* (in per cent)
		0–8 (20.1)	9–11 (16.3)	12 (32.8)	13–15 (16.8)	16+ (14)	
Electoral Politics, 1952–88							
Vote	66.1	0.85	0.83	1.00	1.12	1.26	55.8
Try to influence others	26.7	0.61	0.75	0.94	1.33	1.61	63.5
Contribute money	8.9	0.33	0.51	0.87	1.37	2.41	73.7
Attend meetings	7.8	0.48	0.50	0.85	1.43	2.14	72.2
Work on campaign	4.6	0.48	0.50	0.87	1.33	2.25	72.0
Governmental Politics, 1976–88							
Sign petition	34.8	0.34	[←	0.87	→]	1.44	69.5
Attend local meeting	18.0	0.31	[←	0.78	→]	1.46	73.3
Write to Congress	14.6	0.38	[←	0.72	→]	1.56	75.9

Source: Rosenstone and Hansen (1993), Tables 8.1 and 8.2, plus my computation of p^*.

Thus the poorest 16 per cent account for only $0.76 \times 16 = 12.2$ per cent of the votes and $0.25 \times 16 = 4.0$ per cent of the number of campaign contributors, while the richest 5 per cent account for $1.27 \times 5 = 6.4$ per cent of the votes and $3.25 \times 5 = 16.3$ per cent of contributors.[18]

The data in Tables 11.1 and 11.2 are striking in several respects. The propensity to participate in *every* reported form of political activity rises with income and education. For voting itself the tendency is relatively moderate, whereas for contributing to political campaigns it is drastic. In the latter case, the actual bias is still understated since the data reflects only the number of contributions, and not their amounts. It is intuitive that the wealthy should be overrepresented in

---

[18] Put differently, the representation ratios are the slopes of the (piecewise linear) *Lorenz curve* that describes the concentration, by income or education, of a given form of political influence.

money-intensive channels of political influence: such lobbying is a form of collective investment where liquidity constraints are even more likely to bind than usual. One might have expected poorer, less skilled agents to have a countervailing advantage for attending meetings, working on campaigns, writing to Congress, and other time-intensive activities for which they have a lower opportunity cost. But, remarkably, the pro-wealth (financial and human) bias is here again not only positive, but extremely strong.

I shall not seek here to explain the source of these biases, only to model them in a plausible and convenient manner.[19] Let each agent's opinion be affected by a relative influence weight, or probability of voting, $\omega^i / \int_0^1 \omega^j dj$. If individual preferences are single-peaked and the preferred policy is monotonic in wealth, or more generally if preferences satisfy a single-crossing condition (as in Joshua S. Gans and Michael Smart, 1996), a median-voter-type result applies, but where the median is computed on an appropriately renormalized population. With a log-normal distribution, the following schemes yield particularly simple results.

Proposition 6. *Suppose that agents $i \in [0, 1]$ have preferences $U(k^i, \tau)$ over some policy variable $\tau \in \mathbb{R}$, such that: for all $k < k'$ and $\tau < \tau'$ if $U(k', \tau') > U(k', \tau)$ then $U(k, \tau') > U(k, \tau)$.*

1. *If an agent's political weight depends on his rank in the wealth distribution, $\omega^i = \omega(p^i)$, the pivotal voter is the one with rank $p^* = \Phi(\lambda)$ and (log) wealth $\ln k^* = m + \lambda \Delta$, where $\lambda \lessgtr 0$ is defined by $(\int_0^{\Phi(\lambda)} \omega(p) \, dp) / (\int_0^1 \omega(p) \, dp) = 1/2$.*
2. *If an agent's political weight depends on the absolute level of his wealth, with $\omega^i = (k^i)^\lambda$ for some $\lambda \lessgtr 0$, the pivotal voter has rank $p^* = \Phi(\lambda \Delta)$ and (log) wealth $\ln k^* = m + \lambda \Delta^2$.*

Ordinal schemes ensure that each person's weight and the identity of the pivotal voter remain invariant when the distribution of wealth shifts due to growth, or when it becomes more unequal.[20] Previous discussions have often assumed that political rights or influence depend on one's absolute level of wealth. This was motivated by historical examples such as voting franchises restricted to citizens owning enough property (Saint-Paul and Verdier, 1993; Persson and Tabellini, 1994) or costly membership in a ruling elite (Alberto Ades and Verdier, 1996). I find it more plausible that even such cutoffs should be relative ones, keeping up with aggregate growth and the competitive nature of bids for political influence. I shall therefore focus on ordinal schemes, but the second part of Proposition 6 shows that absolute income effects are just as easy to capture; the case $\lambda = 1$, for

---

[19] John E. Roemer (1998) shows how the presence of a second dimension in the political game (morals, religion) can result in a similar kind of bias, by splitting the coalition that would naturally arise in favour of redistribution. It is worth emphasizing again that I shall not appeal to differences in the allocation of political power or influence to explain why redistribution varies across countries (although the model can readily incorporate this 'easier' explanation).

[20] Also, for any ordinal scheme $\omega(\cdot)$ the associated λ is a sufficient statistic: it is as if the bottom $2\Phi(\lambda) - 1$ votes [or the top $1 - 2\Phi(\lambda)$ when $\lambda < 0$] systematically abstained. Note that even though $\lambda > 0$ is the more empirically relevant case, the model will be solved for all $\lambda \gtrless 0$.

instance, corresponds to a 'one dollar, one vote' rule. Moreover, this alternative formulation would only reinforce the paper's results, as it implies that the political system becomes more biased towards the wealthy as inequality rises.

In the last columns of Tables 11.1 and 11.2, I interpolated the empirical $\omega(p)$ function to compute the *position of the pivotal agent p^** for each separate form of political participation i.e., as if it were the only one that mattered.[21] No data exist that would allow me to weigh them by their relative importance in determining the political outcome. For voting, the wealth bias is moderate, with the pivot at the 56th percentile rather than the usually assumed median. For all other forms of influence it is much stronger, with the pivotal agent always above the 60th percentile, and quite often the 70th. From this evidence it seems safe to conclude that the decisive political group is located *above the median* in terms of income and human wealth. Depending on the relative efficacy of the different channels of political influence it may even be above the mean, which in the US income distribution falls around the 63rd percentile.[22]

11.3.3. Political Equilibrium, Inequality, and Redistribution

We are now ready to establish the chapter's first main result. By virtue of Propositions 5 and 6, the policy outcome is obtained by simply setting $\ln k_t^i - m_t = \lambda \Delta_t$ in the first-order condition $\partial U_t^i / \partial \tau = 0$, or equivalently $p(\tau, \Delta_t) = p^* = \Phi(\lambda)$ in (11.22). As before, I consider first the case where labour supply is inelastic $(1/\eta = 0)$; for $\lambda > 0$, this yields:

$$\frac{1}{1 - \tau_t} = \frac{\gamma^2 \Delta_t^2 + Bv^2}{\lambda \gamma \Delta_t}. \tag{11.23}$$

The equilibrium tax rate is clearly *U-shaped* in Δ_t, and minimized where $\gamma^2 \Delta^2 = Bv^2$. Similarly, in the general case it is the unique solution $T(\Delta_t) < 1$ to the quadratic equation derived from (11.21):

$$(1 - \tau_t)\left(\frac{\gamma^2 \Delta_t^2 + Bv^2}{\gamma \Delta_t}\right) - \frac{\delta}{\eta \gamma \Delta_t}\left(\frac{\tau_t}{1 - \tau_t}\right) = \lambda. \tag{11.24}$$

Proposition 7. *The rate of fiscal progressivity $\tau_t = T(\Delta_t)$ chosen in generation t has the following features:*

1. *τ_t increases with the ex ante efficiency gain from redistribution (gross of distortions) Bv^2, and decreases with the political influence of wealth, λ.*

---

[21] The weights ω^i are obtained by rescaling each group's representation ratios by the population's average propensity to participate in the activity under consideration (given in column 1). Concerning the relationship between voters' income and their political preferences, Nolan M. McCarthy *et al.* (1997) provide substantial evidence that US politics are highly—and increasingly—unidimensional, along the axis of rich/opposed to redistribution versus poor/favouring redistribution.

[22] We shall see below that the first condition, but not the second, is required for redistribution to decline with inequality in the model.

2. $|\tau_t|$ decreases with the elasticity of labour supply $1/\eta$.[23]

3. For $\lambda > 0$, τ_t is U-shaped with respect to inequality Δ_t. It starts at the ex ante efficient rate $T(0) = 1 - 2(1 + \sqrt{1 + 4\eta Bv^2/\delta})^{-1}$, declines to a minimum at some $\underline{\Delta} > 0$, then rises back towards $T(\infty) = 1$. The larger Bv^2, the wider the range $[0, \underline{\Delta}]$ where $\partial \tau_t/\partial \Delta_t < 0$. For $\lambda \leq 0$, τ_t is increasing in Δ_t.

The first two results show that the equilibrium tax rate depends on the costs and benefits of redistribution, as well as on the allocation of political influence, in a very intuitive manner. The third result provides an *endogenously derived* analogue to Fig. 11.1, with the continuous policy τ now replacing the proportion of people supporting redistribution in a zero–one decision. It also confirms several claims made earlier about the result that *redistribution may decline with inequality*. First, it is not predicated on the pivotal agent being richer than the mean, or becoming richer relative to the mean. Second, it is more likely to occur the larger the *ex ante* welfare gain from redistribution, e.g., the larger Bv^2.[24] Third, some bias $\lambda > 0$ with respect to pure majority rule is needed as well, because the median agent always wants to push redistribution beyond its range of efficiency. As shown in (11.22), it is only within that range that political support for a tax increase, $p(\tau, \Delta_t)$, can decline with higher inequality.

It is worth noting that the distinctive non-monotonic relationship predicted by the model has recently been tested by Paolo Figini (1999), who found in cross-country regressions a significant U-shaped effect of income inequality on the shares of tax revenues and government expenditures in GDP.

The above results apply equally in an endowment economy ($\beta = 0$) and in the presence of accumulation. In the first case the efficiency gains arise from insurance. In the second they also reflect the reallocation of resources to agents whose marginal product of investment is higher, due to tighter liquidity constraints. In studying which social contracts emerge in the long run, I shall consider each case in turn.

11.4. INEQUALITY AND SOCIAL INSURANCE IN AN ENDOWMENT ECONOMY

Should we expect a more generous welfare state in countries with greater disparities of income and wealth, as predicted by standard models, or a less generous one, as a comparison between Sweden and the US would suggest? To study the political economy of pure social insurance, let us focus on an endowment

---

[23] More specifically, if $Bv^2 > \lambda^2/4$ then $\tau_t > 0$ and $\partial \tau_t/\partial \eta > 0$. If $Bv^2 < \lambda^2/4$, then $\partial \tau_t/\partial \eta$ has the sign of τ_t.

[24] With respect to the first claim, note that $\ln k^* - \ln E[k] = \lambda \Delta - \Delta^2/2$ is increasing only on $[0, \lambda]$ and positive only on $[0, 2\lambda]$. Neither interval coincides with, nor contains, $[0, \underline{\Delta}]$. The second claim follows from Proposition 7, but even when $Bv^2 = 0$ one sees from (11.22) that for all $\Delta \in [0, \underline{\Delta}]$ a marginal rise in τ above $T(\Delta)$ increases *ex ante* efficiency. These gains now arise from lowering the effort distortions due to regressionary taxes, as $Bv^2 = 0$ implies $T(0) = 0$, hence $\tau_t < 0$ on $[0, \underline{\Delta}]$.

economy $(\beta = 0)$.[25] Each dynasty's endowment k_t^i then simply follows a geometric AR(1) process with serial correlation α (see (11.6)), and the equilibrium policy is $T(\Delta_t)$. In the long run inequality converges to $\Delta_\infty^2 \equiv w^2/(1 - \alpha^2)$, and the tax rate therefore to $\tau_\infty \equiv T(\Delta_\infty)$. When $1/\eta = 0$, for instance,

$$\frac{1}{1 - \tau_\infty} = \frac{w}{\lambda}\left[\frac{\gamma}{\sqrt{1 - \alpha^2}} + (1 - (1 - \rho)r)\left(\frac{v}{w}\right)^2\left(\frac{\sqrt{1 - \alpha^2}}{\gamma}\right)\right]. \tag{11.25}$$

More generally, the following results are immediate (focusing on the empirically relevant case of $\lambda > 0$).

Proposition 8. *The steady-state rate of fiscal progressivity τ_∞ increases with agents' degree of risk aversion $1 - r$ and with income uncertainty v^2, but is U-shaped with respect to the variability w^2 and the persistence α of the endowment process. It decreases with the political influence of wealth λ, and declines in absolute value with the labour-supply elasticity $1/\eta$.*

Recalling that steady-state income dispersion is $\gamma^2 w^2/(1 - \alpha^2) + v^2$, the above results indicate that the relationship between inequality and redistribution is not likely to be monotonic. What matters is not just the *amount* of income inequality, but also *its source*. To the extent that high income disparities in some countries reflect large uninsurable shocks (or more imperfect insurance markets), higher taxes and transfers should be observed. But if greater inequality is due to greater *ex ante* heterogeneity at the time of the policy decision—correlated for instance with ethnic or regional differences—the reverse correlation may be observed.[26] While greater persistence makes income more variable, it also increases the number of agents for whom the value of insurance is more than offset by their vested interest in the status quo.

11.5. HISTORY-DEPENDENT SOCIAL CONTRACTS

11.5.1. Dynamics and Multiple Steady States

I now turn to the paper's second main idea, sketched at the end of Section 11.1: if more inequality leads to less redistribution, and if investment resources depend on past transfers, multiple steady states can arise. To demonstrate this point I solve

---

[25] The important assumption here is the absence of insurance markets. The incompleteness of the loan market is inessential, and indeed this section's results remain unchanged with $\rho = 0$. This one-shot model is close to that of Persson (1983), except that he assumes no initial heterogeneity $(\Delta_0 = 0)$.

[26] A related result obtains in Persson and Tabellini (1996), where two regions bargain over the degree of risk sharing in the federal constitution. In both models the underlying assumption is the inability to make transfers contingent only on unpredictable innovations to individual or regional income, as distinguished from its permanent component. See also George Casamata *et al.* (2000) for a study of how *ex post* political equilibrium constrains the *ex ante* design of public health insurance systems.

the full model with capital accumulation subject to wealth constraints ($\beta > 0$). The critical difference with the endowment economy is that the wealth distribution is now endogenous, through the effect of fiscal policy on persistence, $\alpha + \beta(1 - \tau_t)$. The joint evolution of inequality and policy is thus described by the recursive dynamical system:

$$\begin{cases} \tau_t = T(\Delta_t) \\ \Delta_{t+1} = \mathcal{D}(\Delta_t, \tau_t) \end{cases} \tag{11.26}$$

where $T(\Delta_t)$ is the unique solution less than one to (11.24), while $\mathcal{D}(\Delta_t, \tau_t)$ is given by (11.14). Under a time-invariant policy, in particular, long-run inequality decreases with redistribution:

$$\Delta_\infty^2 = \frac{w^2 + \beta^2(1 - \tau)^2 v^2}{1 - (\alpha + \beta\gamma(1 - \tau))^2} \equiv D^2(\tau). \tag{11.27}$$

A steady-state equilibrium is an intersection of this downward-sloping locus, $\Delta = D(\tau)$, with the U-shaped curve $\tau = T(\Delta)$ described in Proposition 7; see Figure 11.2. Substituting (11.27) into (11.24), this corresponds to a rate of tax progressivity solving the equation:

$$f(\tau) \equiv (1 - \tau)\left(\frac{\gamma^2 D(\tau)^2 + Bv^2}{\gamma D(\tau)}\right) - \frac{\delta}{\eta \gamma D(\tau)}\left(\frac{\tau}{1 - \tau}\right) = \lambda. \tag{11.28}$$

This is a polynomial equation of degree eight, and therefore quite complex. Yet, by exploiting geometric intuitions on the shape of f, one can establish a series of results that formalize the chapter's main ideas.[27] As illustrated in Fig. 11.4, two countries with the same economic and political fundamentals can nonetheless evolve into *different societies*, provided:

(1) the *ex ante* welfare benefits of redistribution are high enough, relative to the costs;

(2) the political power of the wealthy lies in some intermediate range.

Theorem 1. *Let* $1 - \alpha < 2\beta\gamma$. *When the normalized efficiency gain* $B \equiv 1 - r(1 - \rho + \rho\beta)$ *is below some critical value* $\underline{B}$ *(equivalently, when risk-aversion* $1 - r$ *is less than some* $1 - \underline{r}$*), there is a unique, stable, steady state. When* $B > \underline{B}$,

---

[27] The intuition behind the proofs is the following. Consider $f(\tau)$ as a function of $1 - \tau \in (0, (1 - \alpha)/\beta\gamma)$. Since D is monotonic, the first fraction in (11.28) is U-shaped in $1 - \tau$. After multiplication by $1 - \tau$ the product typically becomes N-shaped, so that it will have three intersections with the horizontal λ, for some range of values of λ. The larger B, the more pronounced this N shape, which is also that of the vertical difference $T(\Delta) - D^{-1}(\Delta)$ on Figure 11.2. Conversely, the last term in (11.28), reflecting effort distortions, tends to make f strictly increasing in $1 - \tau$ (at least where $\tau > 0$), and therefore works towards uniqueness.

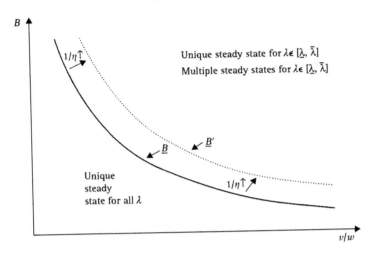

Figure 11.4. *Multiplicity or uniqueness of stable steady states.*
Note: The dotted line corresponds to $1/\eta' > 1/\eta$.

on the other hand, there exist $\underline{\lambda}$ and $\bar{\lambda}$ with $0 < \underline{\lambda} < \bar{\lambda}$, such that:

(1) *For each λ in $[\underline{\lambda}, \bar{\lambda}]$ there are (at least) two stable steady states.[28] Inequality is lower, and social mobility higher, under a more redistributive social contract.*
(2) *For $\lambda < \underline{\lambda}$ or $\lambda > \bar{\lambda}$ the steady state is unique.*

Where multiple steady states occur, *history matters.* Temporary shocks to the distribution of wealth (immigration, educational discrimination, shifts in demand or technology) as well as to the political system (slavery, voting-rights restrictions) can permanently move society from one equilibrium to the other, or more generally have long-lasting effects on the economy and the social contract.

This history-dependence contrasts sharply with traditional politico-economic models, where countries can deviate at most temporarily from a common steady-state level of inequality and redistribution (given stable 'fundamentals'). In particular, fiscal policy operates there as a stabilizing force on the distribution of wealth: more inequality today means more redistribution, hence less inequality tomorrow.[29] Here, on the contrary, there emerges in the long run a *negative*

---

[28] Specifically, there are $2 \leq n \leq 4$ stable steady states. If $1/\eta$ is small enough then $n \leq 3$, and if α is also small enough then $n = 2$. See the theorem's proof in the Appendix.

[29] In Persson and Tabellini (1994) income inequality, hence the equilibrium policy, depends only on the exogenous distribution of talent. In Bertola (1993) and Alesina and Rodrik (1994) the deterministic nature of the models allows any distribution of initial endowments to persist indefinitely. Incorporating idiosyncratic shocks would normally lead to a unique steady-state distribution. Uniqueness also obtains in Perotti (1993) and Saint-Paul and Verdier (1993). In Saint-Paul and Verdier (1992) greater inequality again results in higher taxes and spending on public education (which is problematic in view of the empirical evidence), but this stabilizing effect is more than offset by a divergence in the incentives of rich and poor to invest privately in additional human capital. Hence two possible steady

correlation between inequality and redistribution, as indeed one observes between the US and Europe, or among advanced countries in general (Rodriguez, 1998).[30]

Also of interest is the predicted negative correlation between inequality and *social mobility,* which is consistent with the results obtained by Robert Erikson and John H. Goldthorpe (1992) for a sample of 15 developed countries. But what of the conventional wisdom of the US as an exceptionally mobile society? In fact, most econometric studies of intergenerational income mobility find either no significant difference, or even somewhat greater mobility in European 'welfare states': see Anders Björklund and Markus Jäntti (1997a) for a survey.[31] Indeed, the most extreme forms of social immobility at the lower end, such as urban ghettos or the persistence of welfare dependency across generations, do seem more exacerbated in American society. Things could well be different for the middle class, so a more satisfactory comparison across countries would take into account such nonlinearities in the mobility process (e.g., Suzanne J. Cooper *et al.,* 1994). These remain beyond the scope of the present model and of most existing comparative studies.

Having demonstrated how the *sustainability of different societal choices* depends on the importance of risk aversion and credit constraints (both summarized in Section 11.5.2), as well as on the allocation of power in the political system (λ), I now consider the role of income and endowment shocks (v^2 and w^2) and that of tax distortions ($1/\eta$). Due to the complexity of the problem, their effects on the multiplicity threshold $\underline{B}$ are studied under additional assumptions.

Proposition 9. *Let* $1/\eta = 0$. *The efficiency threshold for multiplicity* $\underline{B}$ *is a decreasing function of* v/w, *with* $\lim_{v/w \to 0}(\underline{B}) = +\infty$ *and* $\lim_{v/w \to +\infty}(\underline{B}) = 0$.

This result appears in Fig. 11.4. The intuition is that income uncertainty interacts with market incompleteness in generating efficiency gains from redistribution, as reflected by the term Bv^2 in (11.16). For a given B, multiplicity therefore occurs when v^2 is large enough compared to the variance w^2 of the shocks that agents learn prior to choosing policy. The concrete implications are important: depending on their source, changes in the economic environment which have similar short-run effects on income inequality can bring about radically *different evolutions of the social contract.* Thus, an increase in the variability of sectoral shocks (similar to v^2) may lead to an expansion of the welfare state and

---

states: high (low) inequality and public education expenditures, with private accumulation by the rich only (by both classes).

[30] Multiple steady states due to a negative impact of inequality on redistribution is the distinguishing feature which the present model shares with Saint-Paul (2001). Consistent with the general argument that this entails redistributions that increase the size of the pie, Saint-Paul's model has the property that transfers raise aggregate income in the long run.

[31] For instance, Kenneth A. Couch and Thomas A. Dunn (1997) find greater mobility—especially in terms of education—in Germany than in the US, and Björklund and Jäntti (1997b) find similar results for Sweden. Aldo Rustichini *et al.* (1999), on the other hand, find lower mobility in Italy than in the US.

public education. Conversely, a surge in immigration that results in a greater heterogeneity of the population (similar to a rise in w^2) may lead to cutbacks or even a large-scale dismantling. In the first case the policy response will mitigate the shock's impact on long-run inequality, while in the second it will aggravate it.

Just as greater benefits of redistribution increase the likelihood of multiplicity, greater distortions reduce it. This is also illustrated in Fig. 11.4, where the efficiency threshold $\underline{B}$ *shifts up* as $1/\eta$ rises. The formal proposition is somewhat more complicated, as it is only for positive values of τ that labour-supply distortions rise with $1/\eta$.[32] I shall not present it here due to space constraints, and because a somewhat similar result appears in Theorem 2 below. Basically, when regressive fiscal policy is ruled out, or more generally for economies that operate in a region where $\tau > 0$, distortions do rise monotonically with $1/\eta$, and the scope for multiple regimes correspondingly declines.

11.5.2. Growth Implications of Different Social Contracts

The steady states corresponding to two different social contracts are clearly not Pareto rankable. How do they compare in terms of aggregate performance? Recall from (11.5) that the effect of τ_t on short-run growth reflects the trade-off between tax distortions and credit-constraint effects; taking limits shows that this remains true for long-run income. Moreover, any comparison of long-run levels is easily transposed to *long-term growth rates*, through knowledge spillovers or public goods complementing private investment. For instance, let κ in (11.6) be replaced by $(\kappa_t)^\phi$, where the human or physical capital aggregate

$$\kappa_t \equiv \left(\int_0^1 (k_t^i)^\gamma di \right)^{1/\gamma} \tag{11.29}$$

captures external effects of the economic environment on accumulation, other than those of policy. As κ_t does not enter into determination of the politico-economic equilibrium (Δ_t, τ_t), all previous results remain unchanged, with κ simply replaced by κ_t everywhere. The presence of the spillover only affects the growth rate along each equilibrium trajectory, transforming for instance finite steady states (when $0 \le \phi < 1 - \alpha - \beta\gamma$) into endogenous growth paths (when $\phi = 1 - \alpha - \beta\gamma$).[33] The following results therefore apply equally to short- and to long-run economic growth.

---

[32] Where effort is distorted by regressionary taxes and transfers, on the contrary, a rise in τ represents an efficiency gain which increases with $1/\eta$: recall that $C(\tau)$ is maximized for $\tau = 0$.

[33] Because it aggregates individual contributions with the same elasticity of substitution as total output, κ_t is *heterogeneity neutral*, in the sense that it does not introduce any additional effects of income distribution on growth. It just makes more permanent those due to imperfect credit markets, by reducing or even eliminating the 'convergence' term $-(1 - \alpha - \beta\gamma) \ln y_t$ from (11.15). Alternative constant elasticity of substitution (CES) aggregates with elasticities other than $1/(1 - \gamma)$ could easily be dealt with, as in Bénabou (1996b).

Proposition 10. *A more redistributive social contract:*

(1) *has higher income growth when* $1/\eta = \alpha = 0$ *and* $\beta\gamma < 1$;
(2) *has lower income growth when* $1/\eta > 0$, $\alpha = 0$ *and* $\beta\gamma = 1$.

Since both conditions are compatible with Theorem 1's requirement that $1 - \alpha < 2\beta\gamma$, they allow the comparison of steady states corresponding to different, self-sustaining values of τ. Two interesting empirical scenarios can thus be accounted for by the model.

Case 1: Growth-enhancing redistributions
The fact that all equilibria have (endogenously) the same savings rate makes clear that the faster growth under the most redistributive social contract arises from a more efficient allocation of investment expenditures.[34] Tax distortions, meanwhile, remain relatively small. This scenario is particularly relevant for human capital investment (which is considered in more detail in the next section) and public health expenditures, where the contrasted paths followed by East Asia and Latin America come to mind. More generally, it offers a potential explanation, in a context of endogenous policy choice, for the fact that regression estimates of the effects of social and educational transfers on growth are often significantly positive.

Case 2: Eurosclerosis and the welfare state
In this converse case, the credit-constraint effect is weak compared to the tax distortions. European countries, it is often argued, have chosen a higher degree of social insurance and compression of inequalities than the US, at the cost of higher unemployment and slower growth.[35] Whether this is viewed as enlightened policy or dismal 'Eurosclerosis', it begs the question of why voters on both sides of the Atlantic would choose such different points on the equity-efficiency, or insurance-growth, trade-off. In the present model, Europeans choose more redistribution than Americans not because they are intrinsically more risk averse, but because in more homogeneous societies there is less erosion of the consensus over social insurance mechanisms which, *ex ante*, would be valued enough to compensate for lesser growth prospects.

Consider finally average welfare, which here is also that of the median voter; see (11.16). Since multiplicity requires some political bias ($\lambda > 0$), it is clear from (11.21) that, in each steady state, a *marginal* increase in redistribution would raise $\int_0^1 U_t^i \, di$. This corresponds to the requirement, in the stylized model of Section 11.1, of an aggregate gain from the policy $\hat{\mathcal{P}}$ relative to $\mathcal{P}$. Comparing steady states, on the other hand, involves discrete variations in τ. When tax distortions are small

---

[34] The equality of investment rates is true in the infinite-horizon version of the model as well. A higher τ implies a lower private savings rate, but this is exactly offset by a higher equilibrium rate of consumption taxation and investment subsidization.

[35] It is only in recent years that European growth has fallen short of US growth, but unemployment has been higher in Europe for nearly two decades.

enough ($1/\eta$ is low), a more redistributive steady state does have higher total welfare; but in general this need not be the case.

11.6. EXPLAINING INTERNATIONAL DIFFERENCES IN EDUCATION FINANCE

11.6.1. Alternative Systems of School Funding

Education finance provides perhaps the most compelling case of a redistributive policy with positive efficiency implications. Loan market imperfections are more likely to affect investment in human than in physical capital, which can serve as collateral. The same is true for decreasing returns. The financing of elementary and secondary education also constitutes a striking example of international differences in redistributive policy. Japan and most European countries have state-funded public schools that largely equalize expenditures across pupils. The US, by contrast, relies in large part on local financing; because communities are heavily income segregated, expenditures reflect parental resources to a large extent, making education a quasi-private good. In Bénabou (1996b) I show how a move from local to state funding of schools can raise the economy's long-run income, or even its long-term growth rate. Calibrating a model with local funding to US data, Fernández and Rogerson (1998) find that a move to state finance could raise steady-state GDP by about 3 per cent. Whether or not one subscribes to this view, differences in national education systems that persist for over a century represent a puzzle.[36]

To examine this issue, let k_t^i now specifically represent human wealth. The term $(k_t^i)^\alpha$ in (11.6) captures the transmission of human capital or ability within the family, while the shocks ξ_{t+1}^i represent the unpredictable component of innate talent. Finally, instead of progressive taxes and transfers I now consider *progressive subsidies* to educational investment. Thus (11.9) is replaced by $\hat{y}_t^i = y_t^i$, while in (11.6) parental savings e_t^i are replaced by the net (after-tax) resources invested in their child's education, namely:

$$\hat{e}_t^i = e_t^i (\tilde{y}_t / y_t^i)^{\tau_t}, \tag{11.30}$$

with $\tilde{y}_t$ still determined by (10). Because agents will still choose a common savings rate, the government's budget constraint, which is now

$$\int_0^1 (\hat{e}_t^i - e_t^i)\, \mathrm{d}i = 0 \tag{11.31}$$

---

[36] In Glomm and Ravikumar (1992) private finance of education leads to higher long-run growth than public funding, as it generates better incentives to accumulate human wealth. Bénabou (1996b) shows that allowing for idiosyncratic shocks (e.g., children's ability) tends to reverse this ranking, as do economy-wide spillovers. Gradstein and Justman (1997) study similar issues in a model with endogenous labour supply, then examine voters' choice among different funding regimes. They obtain a unique equilibrium.

will again be satisfied. The progressivity rate τ_t is the *elasticity of the tax price of education with respect to wealth*. Given agents' savings behaviour, $e_t^i = s\hat{y}_t^i$, it also measures the extent to which education is *publicly and equally* provided: thus $\tau = 0$ corresponds to private finance, while $\tau = 1$ is equivalent to a European-style system where universal public education is funded by a proportional income tax.

Proposition 11. *Given a rate of education finance progressivity τ_t, agents in generation t choose a common labour supply and savings rate: $e_t^i/\hat{y}_t^i = \rho\beta/(1 - \rho + \rho\beta) \equiv s$, as before, while*

$$l_t = \left(\frac{\delta}{\eta}\right)^{1/\eta}\left(\frac{1 - \rho + \rho\beta(1 - \tau_t)}{1 - \rho}\right)^{1/\eta}.$$

The effort distortion is smaller than with fiscal redistribution, because the education-based policy leaves untouched the part of their income that adult agents consume. Up to that difference in $l_t = l(\tau_t)$, individual and aggregate wealth dynamics are exactly identical to (11.11)–(11.15), and the resulting *ex ante* utility function resembles closely the one which arose under fiscal redistribution.

Proposition 12. *Given a rate of education finance progressivity τ_t, agent i's intertemporal welfare is*

$$U_t^i = \bar{u}_t + A(\tau_t)(\ln k_t^i - m_t) + C(\tau_t) - \rho\beta(1 - \tau_t)^2\gamma^2\Delta_t^2 + B(\tau_t)v^2/2,$$

$$(11.32)$$

where $\bar{u}_t$ is independent of the policy τ_t and

$$A(\tau) \equiv \rho\alpha + (1 - \rho + \rho\beta(1 - \tau))\gamma \tag{11.33}$$

$$C(\tau) \equiv (1 - \rho)(\delta \ln l(\tau) - l(\tau)^\eta) + \rho\beta\delta \ln l(\tau) \tag{11.34}$$

$$B(\tau) \equiv -(1 - \rho + \rho\beta(1 - \tau)^2) + r(1 - \rho + \rho\beta(1 - \tau))^2. \tag{11.35}$$

Two differences with Proposition 4 are worth mentioning. On the cost side, $C(\tau)$ is the same function of effort $l(\tau)$ as before, but $l(\tau)$ is now different. In particular, distortions remain bounded, so U_t^i may be maximized at $\tau = 1$ for a poor enough agent. The other difference occurs in the benefits term. For $\rho = 1$, $B(\tau) = -\beta(1 - r\beta)(1 - \tau)^2$ as in (11.16), and with the same interpretation in terms of insurance and reallocation of liquidity-constrained investments. But in general $B(\tau)$ is no longer proportional to $-(1 - \tau)^2$, and when $r > 0$ it is not even monotonic in τ. While the education model is sufficiently close to the tax model to ensure that the political equilibrium remains qualitatively similar, the formal analysis is made more difficult by these differences. Moreover, deriving an exact analogue to Theorem 1 would be repetitious. I shall therefore focus instead on a simpler case, which yields new and more explicit comparative statics results.

11.6.2. Sustainability of Centralized and Decentralized Education Systems

From here on, policy is restricted to two options. Under laissez-faire or *decentralized funding*, $\tau = 0$, education expenditures are determined by family or community resources; the two are essentially equivalent when communities are stratified by socioeconomic status. *Public funding* of education corresponds to $\tau = 1$ or more generally to $\tau = \bar{\tau}$, where $0 < \bar{\tau} \leq 1$. Given an initial distribution of human capital Δ_t, this system is adopted if $U_t^i(\bar{\tau}) > U_t^i(0)$ for at least a fraction $p^* \equiv \Phi(\lambda)$ of the population. Setting $\ln k_t^i - m_t = \lambda \Delta_t$ in (11.32), this means:

$$\lambda < \left((B(\bar{\tau}) - B(0)) \left(\frac{v^2}{2} \right) - (C(0) - C(\bar{\tau})) \right) \left(\frac{1/\rho\beta\bar{\tau}}{\gamma\Delta_t} \right) + \left(\frac{2 - \bar{\tau}}{2} \right) \gamma \Delta_t. \quad (11.36)$$

Intuitively, the *political influence of wealth* must not be too large compared to the *aggregate welfare benefit* of redistributive education finance (relative to laissez-faire). Preexisting inequality *raises the hurdle* that public policy must overcome, as reflected by the term $1/\gamma\Delta_t$ multiplying the net welfare benefit. This effect tends to make adoption of state finance more difficult where it has not previously been in place (e.g., the US), because of the greater human capital disparities that result over time from a decentralized system. Conversely, the term in $\gamma\Delta_t$ incorporates the combined effects of skewness and credit constraints, which both intensify the demand for redistribution. As a result of these offsetting forces the right-hand side of (11.36) has the usual U shape in Δ_t, and is in fact very similar to (11.3) in the stylized model of Section 11.1. To focus now on the long run, let us replace Δ_t with $\Delta_\infty = D(\bar{\tau})$, given by (11.27). Public funding of education (partial or complete) is thus a steady state when

$$\lambda < \left((B(\bar{\tau}) - B(0)) \left(\frac{v^2}{2} \right) - (C(0) - C(\bar{\tau})) \right) \times \left(\frac{1/\rho\beta\bar{\tau}}{\gamma D(\bar{\tau})} \right)$$
$$+ \left(\frac{2 - \bar{\tau}}{2} \right) \gamma D(\bar{\tau}) \equiv \bar{\lambda}. \quad (11.37)$$

Conversely, private or local financing is a steady state, with inequality $\Delta_\infty = D(0)$, when

$$\lambda > \left((B(\bar{\tau}) - B(0)) \left(\frac{v^2}{2} \right) - (C(0) - C(\bar{\tau})) \right) \times \left(\frac{1/\rho\beta\bar{\tau}}{\gamma D(0)} \right)$$
$$+ \left(\frac{2 - \bar{\tau}}{2} \right) \gamma D(0) \equiv \underline{\lambda}. \quad (11.38)$$

The two regimes can coexist if and only if $\underline{\lambda} < \bar{\lambda}$, which occurs when the differential gain

$$B(\bar{\tau}) - B(0) = \rho\beta\bar{\tau}[2 - \bar{\tau} - r(2 - 2\rho + \rho\beta(2 - \bar{\tau}))] \quad (11.39)$$

exceeds the differential cost

$$C(0) - C(\bar{\tau}) = \frac{\delta}{\eta} \left[(1 - \rho + \rho\beta) \ln \left(\frac{1 - \rho + \rho\beta}{1 - \rho + \rho\beta(1 - \bar{\tau})} \right) - \rho\beta\bar{\tau} \right] \qquad (11.40)$$

by a sufficient amount, specified below. It is easily seen that the distortion $C(0) - C(\bar{\tau})$ is positive and increasing $1/\eta$. I will assume that $B(\bar{\tau}) > B(0)$, so that there is an actual gain to compare to this cost. Such is the case provided agents care enough about insurance $(1 - r \geq 1)$ or about investment in their children's education $(\rho(2 + \beta) \geq 1)$, or alternatively provided $\bar{\tau}$ is not too large.

Theorem 2. *If the gain in ex ante welfare from progressive public financing of education, relative to private or decentralized financing, is large enough, namely*

$$B(\bar{\tau}) - B(0) \geq (C(0) - C(\bar{\tau}))(2/v^2) + G(\bar{\tau}, v^2/w^2) \equiv \underline{B},$$

where $G(\bar{\tau}, v^2/w^2) > 0$ is given in the Appendix, then there exist $0 < \underline{\lambda} < \bar{\lambda}$ such that:

(1) *For each λ in $[\underline{\lambda}, \bar{\lambda}]$ both public and decentralized school funding are stable steady states. The first regime has lower inequality and greater social mobility than the second.*

(2) *For $\lambda < \underline{\lambda}$ public funding is the only steady state, while for $\lambda < \bar{\lambda}$ it is decentralized funding.*

The efficiency threshold for multiplicity $\underline{B}$ decreases with income uncertainty v^2 and increases with endowment variability w^2, with $\lim_{v/w \to 0}(\underline{B}) = +\infty$. It rises with the labour-supply elasticity $1/\eta$.

These results demonstrate how such different systems of school finance as those of the US and Western European countries can be self-perpetuating, once arisen from historical circumstances.[37] As to which one leads to faster growth, this depends once again on the trade-off between the positive impact of redistributive education finance on wealth constraints and its adverse effect on incentives: Proposition 10 applies unchanged. Because the distortions are less severe than with fiscal policy, however, the likelihood that state funding enhances growth is now greater.

Theorem 2 also makes clear how the efficiency threshold for multiplicity $\underline{B}$ (or equivalently, the minimal risk aversion $1 - \underline{r}$) varies with the costs of redistributive school finance, as well as with different sources of income inequality. These results can again be represented in Fig. 11.4, with $B \equiv B(\bar{\tau}) - B(0)$ now on the vertical axis, and the same interpretations as for Proposition 9. The only difference is that for $B < \underline{B}$ there might be no steady state, as $\bar{\lambda}$ is then less than $\underline{\lambda}$. The economy can instead be shown to cycle between the two regimes, as in

---

[37] Generalizing Theorem 2 to any policy pair $\{\underline{\tau}, \bar{\tau}\}$ with $0 \leq \underline{\tau} < \bar{\tau} \leq 1$ is straightforward.

R. Bénabou

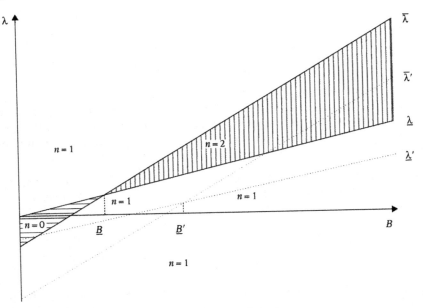

Figure 11.5. *The number of steady states.*
Note: The dotted lines correspond to $1/\eta' > 1/\eta$.

Gradstein and Justman (1997).[38] Actual instances of such cycling are hard to come by, and indeed Theorem 1 indicates that non-existence is largely an artifact of restricting the policy τ to discrete values.[39]

I now return to the central issue, namely the coexistence of multiple regimes. The *range of political systems* that allow this indeterminacy is illustrated in Fig. 11.5.

Proposition 13. *The scope for the political system to generate multiple equilibria increases with the efficiency benefits of redistribution and decreases with their efficiency costs: as $B \equiv B(\bar{\tau}) - B(0)$ increases, due to greater risk aversion or more decreasing returns, both $\underline{\lambda}$ and $\bar{\lambda}$ rise but the interval $[\underline{\lambda}, \bar{\lambda}]$ widens. A higher labour-supply elasticity $1/\eta$ has the opposite effects.*

[38] Equations (11.37)–(11.38) show that for $\lambda \notin [\bar{\lambda}, \underline{\lambda}]$ there is a unique (and intuitive) steady state, but for $\lambda \in [\bar{\lambda}, \underline{\lambda}]$ there is none. The model of Gradstein and Justman (1997) corresponds to the case where $1 - r = 1$ (time-separable, logarithmic utility), the disutility of effort $-l^\eta$ is replaced by $\ln(1 - l)$, $\tau \in \{0, 1\}$ (pure public or private system), $\lambda = 0$ (pure democracy), and $v^2 = 0$ (no uncertainty at the time of voting). From Theorem 2 we see that the restrictions $\lambda = 0$ and $v^2 = 0$ preclude multiple equilibria.

[39] With a continuous τ the analogue of eqn (11.28) for education funding is easily shown to always have at least one stable steady state. Conversely, an analogue of Theorem 2 can be derived for *fiscal policy*, with the progressivity rate τ restricted to $\{0, \bar{\tau}\}$. This shows that the non-linear redistributive schemes used in the chapter, namely (11.9) and (11.30), are not driving the results: for $\tau = 0$ and $\tau = \bar{\tau} \equiv 1$ the geometric specification and the standard linear one coincide exactly.

11.7. OTHER APPLICATIONS

11.7.1. Concern for Equity

Apart from social insurance and capital market imperfections, one of the main reasons for income redistribution is simply that most people dislike living in a society which is too unequal. This may be due to pure altruism or to the fact that inequality generates social tensions, crime, and similar problems that have direct costs. To capture these ideas one can simply augment (11.7) as follows:

$$\ln \hat{V}_t^i = \ln V_t^i - (\mathcal{A}/2) \times [(1 - \rho) \operatorname{var}_{j \in I}[\ln c_t^j - (l_t^j)^\eta]$$
$$+ \rho \operatorname{var}_{j \in I}[\ln k_{t+1}^j]]. \tag{11.7'}$$

The coefficient $\mathcal{A}$ represents everyone's aversion to disparities in felicity, measured by the cross-sectional variances of consumption (including leisure) and bequests. It is easily seen that the economy's laws of motion remain unchanged, and the political equilibrium quite similar. In an endowment economy ($\beta = 0$), for instance, the only difference is that the ubiquitous $\gamma^2 \Delta_t^2 + B v^2$ is replaced by $(1 + \mathcal{A})\gamma^2 \Delta_t^2 + (B + \mathcal{A})v^2$: inequality aversion is equivalent to a simultaneous increase in risk aversion and in the concavity of aggregate welfare (previously logarithmic). Thus, with $1/\eta = 0$ the steady-state tax rate becomes

$$\frac{1}{1 - \tau_\infty} = \frac{w}{\lambda}\left[(1 + \mathcal{A})\left(\frac{\gamma}{\sqrt{1 - \alpha^2}}\right) + (1 + \mathcal{A} - (1 - \rho)r)\left(\frac{v}{w}\right)^2\left(\frac{\sqrt{1 - \alpha^2}}{\gamma}\right)\right]. \tag{11.25'}$$

If one observed two countries, the first with low pretax inequality yet extensive redistribution, the other with the reverse situation, one would indeed be tempted to conclude that the citizens of the first country were more altruistic, or their poor better organized politically. In fact it could be that preferences are identical and political institutions equivalent (same $\mathcal{A}$ and λ), but that the second country's more unequal distribution reflects a more persistent income process. This could be due to exogenous factors, as with α here, or be endogenous, as in the case of multiple steady states.

11.7.2. The Mix of Public Goods

Some public services such as the legal system, the protection of property, prisons, etc., benefit citizens largely in proportion to their levels of wealth or investment. Others have more uniformly or even regressively distributed benefits. Klaus Deininger and Lyn Squire (1995) find in cross-country regressions that public investment affects income growth equally for all quintiles, while public schooling benefits the bottom 40 per cent most, the middle class to a lesser extent, and the rich not at all. Consider therefore a government choosing (at the margin) a single public good or service from a menu of options: if g_t is spent on a good with characteristics $(\kappa, \alpha, \beta, \gamma)$, the private sector faces the accumulation technology $k_{t+1}^i = \kappa \xi_{t+1}^i (k_t^i)^\alpha (e_t^i)^\beta (g_t)^\gamma$. A public good or institution with high $\alpha + \beta$ makes wealth more persistent, so relatively well-off agents may prefer it to an alternative that has higher overall productivity (larger κ or $\alpha + \beta + \gamma$). The problem is thus analogous to the earlier ones, implying that countries can sustain different choices without any underlying differences in tastes. In reality, many public goods are provided simultaneously and the debate is over the appropriate mix, but the same intuitions should remain applicable.

11.7.3. The Socioeconomic Structure of Cities

The presence in human capital accumulation of peer effects, role models, and other neighbourhood interactions implies that residential stratification increases the *persistence* of income disparities across families (e.g., Bénabou, 1993; Durlauf, 1996a). Urban ghettos are but the most extreme example of this phenomenon, which is the subject of a large empirical literature.[40] Moreover, I show in Bénabou (1993, 1996b) that equilibrium segregation generally tends to be *inefficiently high*. The two conditions identified in this chapter for multiple politico-economic regimes are thus again satisfied, leading to the following predictions: (a) more highly segregated cities are also those where socioeconomic disparities are greater; (b) in such cities public policy (on housing, schooling, transport, or infrastructure) will tend to accommodate and even facilitate segregation, while in better integrated (and more equal) cities more public support and resources will be mobilized to prevent further polarization.[41]

11.8. CONCLUSIONS

In this chapter I have asked how countries with similar preferences and technologies, as well as equally democratic political systems, can nonetheless make very different choices with respect to fiscal progressivity, social insurance, and

---

[40] Recent references include Cooper *et al.* (1994), George J. Borjas (1995), and Giorgio Topa (2001). Christopher Jencks and Susan E. Mayer (1990) provide an extensive survey of earlier empirical studies, and Charles F. Manski (1993) a critical discussion of methodology. Indeed the identification of these social spillovers remains the subject of some controversy; see for instance William N. Evans *et al.* (1992).

[41] At the heart of this class of models (e.g., Bénabou, 1996b) lies a general law of motion for human capital of the form: $h_{t+1}^i = F(\xi_{t+1}^i, h_t^i, L_t^i, H_t)$, where L_t^i and H_t are human capital averages capturing respectively *local externalities* (e.g., peer effects) and *economy-wide* interactions (production complementarities, knowledge spillovers, etc.). Where families have sorted into socioeconomically homogeneous communities, $L_t^i = h_t^i$ for all i, so $h_{t+1}^i = F(\xi_{t+1}^i, h_t^i, h_t^i, H_t)$. Conversely, under perfect integration $L_t^i = L_t^j = L_t$, hence $h_{t+1}^i = F(\xi_{t+1}^i, h_t^i, L_t, H_t)$. The similarity with the cases $\tau = 0$ and $\tau = 1$ in the present model is readily apparent. An alternative source of multiplicity is explored in Durlauf (1996b), where it is only when socioeconomic disparities are not too large that rich families are willing to share with poorer ones the fixed costs of running a community and its schools.

education finance. The proposed answer is a simple theory of inequality and the social contract, based on two mechanisms that arise naturally in the absence of complete insurance and credit markets. First, redistributions that would increase *ex ante* welfare command less political support in an unequal society than in a more homogeneous one. A lower rate of redistribution, in turn, increases inequality of future incomes due to wealth constraints on investment in human or physical capital. This leads to two stable steady states, the archetypes for which could be the US and Western Europe: one with high inequality yet low redistribution, the other with the reverse configuration. These two societies are not Pareto rankable, and which one has faster income growth depends on the balance between tax distortions to effort and the greater productivity of investment resources (particularly in education) reallocated to more severely credit-constrained agents.

These ideas were formalized in a stochastic growth model with missing markets, progressive fiscal or education finance policy, and a more realistic political system than the standard median voter setup. The resulting distributional dynamics remain simple enough to allow a number of extensions. In Bénabou (2002) I develop and calibrate an infinite-horizon version of the incomplete markets model, then use it to quantify the effects of fiscal and educational redistribution on growth, risk, and welfare. Another interesting problem is to endogenize the kind of wealth-biased political mechanism used here, where those with more resources command more influence; François Bourguignon and Verdier (2000) and Rodriguez (1998) are recent examples of such models. Finally, the original question of why the social contract differs across countries, and whether these choices are sustainable in the long run, remains an important topic for further research.

APPENDIX

Proof of Proposition 2. Once agent i knows his productivity z_t^i, hence also his pre- and posttax incomes $y_t^i = z_t^i (k_t^i)^\gamma (l_t^i)^\delta$ and $\hat{y}_t^i = (y_t^i)^{1-\tau_t} (\tilde{y}_t)$, his decision problem takes the form:

$$
\ln V_t^i = \max_{l,\nu} \{(1-\rho)[\ln((1-\nu)\hat{y}_t^i) - l^\eta] + (\rho/r)\ln E_t[(k_{t+1}^i)^r] \, | k_{t+1}^i
$$

$$
= \kappa \xi_{t+1}^i (k_t^i)^\alpha (\nu \hat{y}_t^i)^\beta \}
$$

$$
= \max_\nu \{(1-\rho)\ln(1-\nu) + \rho\beta \ln \nu\}
$$

$$
+ \max_l \{-(1-\rho)l^\eta + (1-\rho+\rho\beta)(1-\tau_t)\delta \ln l\}
$$

$$
+ \rho(\ln \kappa - (1-r')w^2/2) + [\rho\alpha + (1-\rho+\rho\beta)\gamma(1-\tau_t)] \ln k_t^i
$$

$$
+ (1-\rho+\rho\beta)[(1-\tau_t) \ln z_t^i + \tau_t \ln \tilde{y}_t], \tag{11.A1}
$$

R. Bénabou

where $\nu_t^i \equiv e_t^i / \hat{y}_t^i$ is the savings rate. Strict concavity in ν and l is easily verified, and the first-order conditions directly yield the stated results.

Proof of Proposition 3. Let us start by computing the redistributive scheme's cutoff level $\tilde{y}_t$. If $\ln k_t^i \sim \mathcal{N}(m_t, \Delta_t^2)$, then (11.4) implies that aggregate income is:

$$\ln y_t = \ln E[z_t^i] + \ln E[(k_t^i)^\gamma] + \delta \ln l_t = \gamma m_t + \delta \ln l_t + \gamma^2 \Delta_t^2 / 2. \quad (11.A2)$$

The level of transfers $\tilde{y}_t$ which satisfies the government budget constraint (11.10) is then given by:

$$\begin{aligned}
\tau_t \ln \tilde{y}_t &= \ln y_t - \delta(1 - \tau_t) \ln l_t - \ln E[(z_t^i)^{1-\tau_t}] - \ln E[(k_t^i)^{\gamma(1-\tau_t)}] \\
&= \ln y_t - \delta(1 - \tau_t) \ln l_t + ((1 - \tau_t) - (1 - \tau_t)^2) v^2 / 2 \\
&\quad - ((1 - \tau_t)\gamma m_t + (1 - \tau_t)^2 \gamma^2 \Delta_t^2 / 2),
\end{aligned}$$

since the z_t^i, and k_t^i's are independent. Thus:

$$\begin{aligned}
\tau_t \ln \tilde{y}_t &= \gamma \tau_t m_t + \delta \tau_t \ln l_t + \tau_t (2 - \tau_t) \gamma^2 \Delta_t^2 / 2 \\
&\quad + \tau_t (1 - \tau_t) v^2 / 2,
\end{aligned} \quad (11.A3)$$

as claimed in (11.12). Equation (11.14) follows from taking variances in (11.11), while (11.13) follows from taking averages with $\tau_t \ln \tilde{y}_t$ replaced by (11.A3). Finally, combining both laws of motions with (11.A2) yields:

$$\begin{aligned}
\ln y_{t+1} &= \delta \ln l_{t+1} + \gamma[(\alpha + \beta\gamma)m_t + \beta\delta \ln l_t + \beta\tau_t(2 - \tau_t)(\gamma^2 \Delta_t^2 + v^2)/2 \\
&\quad + \ln(\kappa s^\beta) - (w^2 + \beta v^2)/2] + \gamma^2[(\alpha + \beta\gamma(1 - \tau_t))^2 \Delta_t^2 \\
&\quad + \beta^2(1 - \tau_t)^2 v^2 + w^2]/2 \\
&= \gamma(\ln \kappa + \beta \ln s - (1 - \gamma)w^2/2) + \delta(\ln l_{t+1} - \alpha \ln l_t) \\
&\quad + (\alpha + \beta\gamma)[\gamma m_t + \delta l_t + \gamma^2 \Delta_t^2/2] \\
&\quad - \beta\gamma[1 - \tau_t(2 - \tau_t) - \beta\gamma(1 - \tau_t)^2]v^2/2 \\
&\quad - [\alpha + \beta\gamma - (\alpha + \beta\gamma(1 - \tau_t))^2 - \beta\gamma\tau_t(2 - \tau_t)]\gamma^2 \Delta_t^2/2 \\
&= \ln \tilde{\kappa} + \delta(\ln l_{t+1} - \alpha \ln l_t) + (\alpha + \beta\gamma) \ln y_t \\
&\quad - \beta\gamma(1 - \beta\gamma)(1 - \tau_t)^2 v^2/2 - \mathcal{L}_\Delta(\tau_t)\gamma^2 \Delta_t^2/2,
\end{aligned}$$

hence the result, given the definitions of $\ln \tilde{\kappa}$, $\mathcal{L}_v(\tau)$ and $\mathcal{L}_\Delta(\tau)$.

Proof of Proposition 4. Substituting the optimal $l_t^i = l_t$ and $\nu_t^i = s$ into (11. A1), and denoting $\ln \kappa' \equiv \ln \kappa - (1 - r')w^2/2$, yields:

$$
\begin{aligned}
\ln V_t^i = {} & \rho \ln \kappa' + (1 - \rho) \ln (1 - s) + \rho\beta \ln s - (1 - \rho)l_t^\eta \\
& + (1 - \rho + \rho\beta)(1 - \tau_t)\delta \ln l_t + [\rho\alpha + (1 - \rho + \rho\beta)\gamma(1 - \tau_t)] \\
& \times \ln k_t^i + (1 - \rho + \rho\beta)[(1 - \tau_t) \ln z_t^i + \tau_t \ln \tilde{y}_t]. \quad (11.\text{A}4)
\end{aligned}
$$

Thus *conditional* on k_t^i, $\ln V_t^i$ is normally distributed, with variance $(1 - \rho + \rho\beta)^2$ $(1 - \tau_t)^2 v^2$. This implies:

$$
U_t^i \equiv \frac{1}{r}\ln E[(V_t^i)^r | k_t^i] = E[\ln V_t^i | k_t^i] + r(1 - \rho + \rho\beta)^2 (1 - \tau_t)^2 v^2/2. \quad (11.\text{A}5)
$$

Therefore, to obtain U_t^i one simply needs to replace in (11.A4) the term in $\ln z_t^i$ by $-(1 - \rho + \rho\beta)(1 - \tau_t)[1 - r(1 - \rho + \rho\beta)(1 - \tau_t)]v^2/2$. Finally, substituting in the value of $\tau_t \ln \tilde{y}_t$ from (11.A3) yields the claimed result, with

$$
\begin{aligned}
\bar{u}_t \equiv {} & \ln[(1 - s)^{1-\rho}s^{\rho\beta}] + \rho(\ln \kappa - (1 - r')w^2/2) \\
& + (\rho\alpha + (1 - \rho + \rho\beta)\gamma)m_t + (1 - \rho + \rho\beta)\gamma^2 \Delta_t^2/2. \quad (11.\text{A}6)
\end{aligned}
$$

Proof of Proposition 5. We can rewrite (11.21) as a second-degree polynomial in $x \equiv 1 - \tau$,

$$
P(x) \equiv x^2(\gamma^2\Delta_t^2 + Bv^2) - (\gamma(\ln k_t^i - m_t) - \delta/\eta)x - \delta/\eta = 0, \quad (11.\text{A}7)
$$

which always has two real roots of opposite sign. Since $\tau_t^i \leq 1$ necessarily, the relevant root is $x_t^i = 1 - \tau_t^i > 0$, and at that point $P'(x_t^i) > 0$. It is easy to compute τ_t^i explicitly, but for comparative statics one can simply use the implicit function theorem. Since $\partial P/\partial(Bv^2) > 0 > \partial P/\partial \ln k_t^i$ and $P'(x_t^i) > 0$, the theorem implies that $\partial x_t^i/\partial \ln k_t^i > 0 > \partial x_t^i/\partial(Bv^2)$. Similarly, $\partial x_t^i/\partial \Delta_t < 0$. Finally, $-\partial P/\partial(1/\eta) = \delta(1 - x)$, so $\partial x_t^i/\partial(1/\eta)$ has the sign of $1 - x_t^i = \tau_t^i$, or equivalently $\partial \tau_t^i/\partial(1/\eta)$ has the sign of $-\tau_t^i$. Finally, $\tau_t^i > 0$ if and only if $x_t^i < 1$, which means $P(1) > 0$, or $\gamma(\ln k_t^i - m_t) < \gamma^2\Delta_t^2 + Bv^2$.

Proof of Proposition 6. Let us index agents by their log-wealth, $\theta^i \equiv \ln k^i$, and denote its cumulative distribution function by $F(\theta)$. For any weighting scheme $\omega^i = g(\theta^i)$, the proportion of votes cast by agents with $\theta^i \leq \theta$ (more generally, their total political weight) is $G(\theta)/G(\infty)$, where $G(\theta) \equiv \int_{-\infty}^{\theta} g(z) \, dF(z)$. For an ordinal scheme, $g(z) = \omega(F(z))$, so $G(\theta) = \int_0^{F(\theta)} \omega(p) \, dp$. Given the single-crossing condition satisfied by preferences, the agent with log-wealth θ^* and rank $p^* = F(\theta^*)$ defined by $G(\theta^*)/G(\infty) = 1/2$ is clearly pivotal (see Gans and Smart, 1996). In the lognormal case $F(\theta) = \Phi((\theta - m)/\Delta)$, so if we define $\lambda \equiv \Phi^{-1}(p^*)$ then $\theta^* = m + \lambda\Delta$. This wealth level is the same as if the whole distribution of $\theta = \ln k$ were shifted up by $\lambda\Delta$. Let us now turn to the cardinal scheme $g(\theta) = e^{\lambda\theta}$. Simple derivations show that

$$G(\theta) = \int_{-\infty}^{\theta} e^{\lambda z} \, dF(z) = e^{\lambda(m+\lambda\Delta^2/2)} \cdot F(\theta - \lambda\Delta^2), \tag{11.A8}$$

hence $G(\theta)/G(\infty) = F(\theta - \lambda\Delta^2)$. The whole distribution is thus shifted by $\lambda\Delta^2$, and so is the solution to $G(\theta^*)/G(\infty) = 1/2$.

Proof of Proposition 7. The equilibrium tax rate is the one preferred by the agent with $\ln k_t^i - m_t = \lambda\Delta_t$, so claims (11.1) and (11.2) follow directly from the properties of τ_t^i established in Proposition 5. To establish the third claim let us rewrite that agent's first-order condition, $\partial U_t^i/\partial\tau = 0$, in terms of $x_t \equiv 1 - \tau_t$. By (11.A7) x_t is the unique positive root of the polynomial:

$$Q(x) \equiv x^2(\gamma^2\Delta_t^2 + Bv^2) - (\gamma\lambda\Delta_t - \delta/\eta)x - \delta/\eta = 0. \tag{11.A9}$$

Now, $Q'(x_t) > 0$ and $\partial Q/\partial\Delta_t = 2x^2\gamma^2\Delta_t - \gamma\lambda x$, so $\partial x_t/\partial\Delta_t$ has the sign of $\lambda - 2\gamma x_t\Delta_t$. Therefore $\partial\tau_t/\partial\Delta_t > 0$ if and only if $x_t > \lambda/2\gamma\Delta_t$. For $\lambda \leq 0$ this is always true, hence τ_t is strictly increasing in Δ_t. For $\lambda > 0$, on the other hand, the condition is equivalent to:

$$\Delta_t^2 Q(\lambda/2\gamma\Delta_t) = (\lambda/2\gamma)^2(\gamma^2\Delta_t^2 + Bv^2) - (\gamma\lambda\Delta_t - \delta/\eta)(\lambda\Delta_t/2\gamma)$$
$$- (\delta/\eta)\Delta_t^2 < 0$$
$$\Leftrightarrow R(\Delta_t) \equiv -(\lambda + 4\delta/\eta\lambda)\Delta_t^2 + 2(\delta/\eta\gamma)\Delta_t + \lambda Bv^2/\gamma^2 > 0.$$

This second-degree polynomial in Δ_t has two real roots of opposite sign. Denoting $\underline{\Delta}$ the positive one [with, clearly, $\partial\underline{\Delta}/\partial(Bv^2) > 0$], we conclude that $\partial\tau_t/\partial\Delta_t > 0$ if and only if $\Delta_t > \underline{\Delta}$. Thus τ_t is indeed U-shaped in Δ_t, and its limiting values at $\Delta_t = 0$ and as $\Delta_t \to \infty$ are readily obtained from (11.A9). Finally, recall that $\tau_t^i > 0$ if and only if $\gamma(\ln k_t^i - m_t) < \gamma^2\Delta_t^2 + Bv^2$; therefore:

$$\tau_t > 0 \Leftrightarrow \gamma^2\Delta_t^2 - \gamma\lambda\Delta_t + Bv^2 > 0. \tag{11.A10}$$

When $Bv^2 > \lambda^2/4$ the condition always holds, so $\tau_t > 0$. When $Bv^2 < \lambda^2/4$ there is a range $[\Delta', \Delta''] \subset (0, 2\lambda)$ such that $\tau_t < 0$ if and only if Δ_t is in that interval.

Proof of Theorem 1. Let us start with a lemma characterizing stable and unstable steady states.

Lemma 1. *A stable steady state is a point τ^* where the function $f(\tau)$ cuts the horizontal λ from above, or equivalently a point (Δ^*, τ^*) where the curve $\Delta = D(\tau)$ cuts the curve $\tau = T(\Delta)$ from above. An unstable steady state corresponds in each case to an intersection from below.*

Proof. The dynamical system (11.26) reduces to a one-dimensional recursion: $\Delta_{t+1} = \mathcal{D}(\Delta_t, T(\Delta_t))$. A fixed-point $\Delta^* = \mathcal{D}(\Delta^*, T(\Delta^*))$ is stable if and only if

$(d\mathcal{D}(\Delta_t, T(\Delta_t))/d\Delta_t)_{\Delta=\Delta^*} < 1$, or:

$$\mathcal{D}_1(\Delta^*, \tau^*) + T'(\Delta^*)\mathcal{D}_2(\Delta^*, \tau^*) < 1, \qquad (11.A11)$$

where $\tau^* \equiv T(\Delta^*)$ and a j subscript denotes a jth partial derivative. Now, the function $\tau = T(\Delta)$ is implicitly given by the first-order condition (11.24), or:

$$\psi(\tau, \Delta) \equiv (1 - \tau)\left(\frac{\gamma^2 \Delta^2 + Bv^2}{\gamma}\right) - \frac{\delta}{\eta\gamma}\left(\frac{\tau_t}{1 - \tau_t}\right) - \lambda\Delta = 0, \qquad (11.A12)$$

therefore $T'(\Delta) = -\{\psi_2/\psi_1\}(T(\Delta), \Delta)$ and the stability condition becomes:

$$\mathcal{D}_1(\Delta^*, \tau^*) - \left(\frac{\psi_2(\tau^*, \Delta^*)}{\psi_1(\tau^*, \Delta^*)}\right)\mathcal{D}_2(\Delta^*, \tau^*) < 1. \qquad (11.A13)$$

Next, recall from (11.28) that f is defined by: $f(\tau) - \lambda = \psi(\tau, D(\tau))/D(\tau)$, so that $f' < 0$ if and only if $\psi_1 + (\psi_2 - \psi/D)D' < 0$. Finally, $D(\tau)$ is defined by (11.27) as the (unique) fixed-point solution to $D(\tau) = \mathcal{D}(D(\tau), \tau)$; therefore: $D' = \mathcal{D}_2/(1 - \mathcal{D}_1)$. Substituting D' and using the fact that $\psi(\tau^*, \Delta^*) = 0$ at a steady state, this becomes:

$$f'(\tau^*) < 0 \quad \Leftrightarrow \quad \psi_1(\tau^*, \Delta^*)(1 - \mathcal{D}_1(\Delta^*, \tau^*)) + \psi_2(\tau^*, \Delta^*)\mathcal{D}_2(\Delta^*, \tau^*) < 0,$$

which is the same as (11.A13), hence the result in terms of the slope of f. Its translation into the condition that $T'(\Delta^*) > (D^{-1})'(\Delta^*)$ is immediate.

We now come to actually solving for steady states. It will be more convenient here to work with the variable $x \equiv \beta\gamma(1 - \tau) \in [0, \infty)$. Accordingly, let us define

$$\Delta(x) \equiv \sqrt{\frac{w^2 + x^2 v^2/\gamma^2}{1 - (\alpha + x)^2}} = D(\tau), \qquad (11.A14)$$

and rewrite the equation $f(\tau) = \lambda$ as

$$\varphi(x) \equiv x\left(\Delta(x) + \frac{Bv^2/\gamma^2}{\Delta(x)}\right) - \left(\frac{\beta\delta}{\eta\gamma\Delta(x)}\right)\left(\frac{\beta\gamma - x}{x}\right) = \lambda\beta. \qquad (11.A15)$$

A stable steady state is now an intersection of the function $\varphi(x)$ with the horizontal $\lambda\beta$, from below. Since $\phi(0) \leq 0$ (it equals $-\infty$ for $1/\eta > 0$, or 0 for $1/\eta = 0$) while $\varphi(1 - \alpha) = +\infty$, for any $\lambda > 0$ there is always at least one stable equilibrium $x \in (0, 1 - \alpha)$, with $0 < \Delta(x) < +\infty$. Moreover, the total number of intersections must always be odd, with n intersections from below (stable equilibria), alternating with $n - 1$ intersections from above (unstable equilibria). Multiple intersections ($n > 0$) will actually occur, for some non-empty interval of values of λ, if and only if $\varphi(\cdot)$ is *non-monotonic*. Indeed, since $\varphi'(0) > 0$ (this is easily verified from (11.A15)) and $\varphi(1 - \alpha) = +\infty$, non-monotonicity is equivalent to the property of having at least one strict local maximum, followed by one strict local minimum, in $(0, 1 - \alpha)$. Given the boundary values of φ, multiple equilibria then occur *if and only if* λ belongs to the range $[\underline{\lambda}, \bar{\lambda}]$, where

$$\begin{cases} \underline{\lambda} \equiv \beta^{-1} \min \{\varphi(x) | x \text{ is a strict local minimum of } \varphi(x)\} > 0 \\ \bar{\lambda} \equiv \beta^{-1} \max \{\varphi(x) | x \text{ is a strict local minimum of } \varphi(x)\} > 0. \end{cases} \quad (11.A16)$$

That $\bar{\lambda}$ and $\underline{\lambda}$ are both always positive follows from the fact that for $1/\eta = 0$, $\varphi(x) > 0$ for all $x > 0$ (see (11.A15)), while for $1/\eta > 0$, if $\varphi(x) < 0$ then $\varphi'(x) > 0$ necessarily. This last property can be verified directly from (11.A15) and (11.A17) below, or more intuitively by observing that if it were not true, there would be a subinterval of values of x where $\varphi(x) < 0$ and φ is not monotonic. This, in turn, would imply that there exist values of $\lambda < 0$ for which (11.A15) has at least two solutions. But such solutions are also intersections of the curves $\Delta = D(\tau)$ and $\tau = T(\Delta)$; the former is always decreasing, and we saw earlier that, for all $\lambda < 0$, the latter is always increasing. Multiple intersections are therefore impossible.

Theorem 1 will now be proved by characterizing the set $B \equiv \{B \geq 0 | \varphi$ is non-monotonic on $(0, 1 - \alpha)\}$, then studying its variations with the parameters v, w, and η.

Lemma 2. *Let* $1 - \alpha < 2\beta\gamma$. *The set* $B \equiv \{B \geq 0 | \exists\, x \in (0, 1 - \alpha), \varphi'(x) < 0\}$ *is a non-empty interval of the form* $B = (\underline{B}, +\infty)$ *with* $\underline{B} > 0$, *or* $B = [0, +\infty)$.

Proof. Let us differentiate (11.A15):

$$\varphi'(x) \equiv \frac{\varphi(x)}{x} + x\Delta'(x)\left(1 - \frac{Bv^2/\gamma^2}{\Delta^2(x)}\right) - \frac{\beta\delta}{\eta\gamma}\left[\left(\frac{1}{x} - \frac{2\beta\gamma}{x^2}\right)\frac{1}{\Delta(x)}\right.$$
$$\left. - \left(\frac{\beta\gamma}{x} - 1\right)\frac{\Delta'(x)}{\Delta^2(x)}\right]$$
$$= \Delta(x) + \frac{Bv^2/\gamma^2}{\Delta(x)} - \left(\frac{\beta\delta}{\eta\gamma\Delta(x)}\right)\left(\frac{\beta\gamma - x}{x^2}\right) + x\Delta'(x)\left(1 - \frac{Bv^2/\gamma^2}{\Delta^2(x)}\right)$$
$$- \frac{\beta\delta}{\eta\gamma}\left[\left(\frac{1}{x} - \frac{2\beta\gamma}{x^2}\right)\frac{1}{\Delta(x)} - \left(\frac{\beta\gamma}{x} - 1\right)\frac{\Delta'(x)}{\Delta^2(x)}\right].$$

Grouping terms, $\varphi'(x) < 0$ if and only if:

$$\frac{Bv^2}{\gamma^2}\left(\frac{x\Delta'(x)}{\Delta(x)} - 1\right) > \left(\frac{x\Delta'(x)}{\Delta(x)} + 1\right)\Delta^2(x)$$
$$+ \left(\frac{\beta\delta}{\eta\gamma}\right)\left(\frac{\beta\gamma}{x^2} + \left(\frac{\beta\gamma}{x} - 1\right)\frac{\Delta'(x)}{\Delta(x)}\right). \quad (11.A17)$$

We now establish the lemma through two intermediate claims.

Claim 1: If (11.A17) is satisfied for some $B \geq 0$ at some $x \in (0, 1 - \alpha)$, then $x\Delta'(x)/\Delta(x) > 1$. As a consequence, (11.A17) is satisfied at x for all $B' > B$.

Proof. If $\Delta'(x)/\Delta(x) - 1/x \le 0$ the left-hand side of (11.A17) is nonpositive, so on the right-hand side it must be that $\beta\gamma/x - 1 < 0$. But then:

$$\frac{\beta\gamma}{x^2} + \left(\frac{\beta\gamma}{x} - 1\right)\frac{\Delta'(x)}{\Delta(x)} > \frac{\beta\gamma}{x^2} + \left(\frac{\beta\gamma}{x} - 1\right)\frac{1}{x} = \frac{2\beta\gamma - x}{x^2}.$$

Since $x < 1 - \alpha < 2\beta\gamma$, this implies that the right-hand side of (11.A17) is positive, a contradiction.

Claim 2: There exists an $\hat{x} \in (0, 1 - \alpha)$ such that $x\Delta'(x)/\Delta(x) < 1$ on $(0, \hat{x})$ and $x\Delta'(x)/\Delta(x) > 1$ on $(\hat{x}, +\infty)$. As a consequence, for any $x > \hat{x}$, (11.A17) holds for B large enough.

Proof. Let us denote from here on $\omega \equiv v/\gamma w$. Since $\Delta^2(x) = w^2(1 + \omega^2 x^2)/(1 - (\alpha + x)^2)$,

$$\frac{\Delta'(x)}{\Delta(x)} = \frac{\omega^2 x}{1 + \omega^2 x^2} + \frac{\alpha + x}{1 - (\alpha + x)^2}. \tag{11.A18}$$

Therefore $x\Delta'(x)/\Delta(x) > 1$ if and only if

$$\omega^2 x^2(1 - (\alpha + x)^2) + x(\alpha + x)(1 + \omega^2 x^2) > (1 + \omega^2 x^2)(1 - (\alpha + x)^2)$$

$$\Leftrightarrow \quad \omega^2 x^3(\alpha + x) - (1 - (\alpha + x)^2) + x(\alpha + x) > 0$$

$$\Leftrightarrow \quad \omega^2 x^3(\alpha + x) + (\alpha + x)(\alpha + 2x) - 1 > 0.$$

This last expression is clearly increasing in x on $(0, 1 - \alpha)$, from $\alpha^2 - 1 < 0$ at $x = 0$ to $\omega^2(1 - \alpha)^3 + 1 - \alpha > 0$ at $x = 1 - \alpha$. This proves Claim 2 which, together with Claim 1, establishes that the set B is a nonempty interval of the form $(\underline{B}, +\infty)$ or $[\underline{B}, +\infty)$. Moreover, note that its complement, $\mathbb{R}_+ \setminus B \equiv \{B \ge 0 | \forall x \in (0, 1 - \alpha), \varphi'(x) \ge 0\}$, is a closed set because φ' is continuous in B at every point. This implies that either $B = (\underline{B}, +\infty)$ with $\underline{B} > 0$, or else $B = [0, +\infty)$, and thereby finishes to establish Lemma 2. From (11.A17)–(11.A18), moreover, it is clear that $\underline{B}$ depends on v, w, and η only through v/w and ηv^2; let it therefore be denoted as $\underline{B}(v/w; \eta v^2)$.

To conclude the proof of Theorem 1 as well as the additional claims in footnote 28 concerning the exact number of steady states, we shall make use of a last lemma.

Lemma 3. For $B < \underline{B}(v/w; \eta v^2)$, there is a unique, stable steady state. For $B > \underline{B}(v/w; \eta v^2)$ the same is true if $\lambda \notin [\underline{\lambda}, \bar{\lambda}]$, while for $\lambda \in [\underline{\lambda}, \bar{\lambda}]$ there are $n \in \{2, 3, 4\}$ stable steady states. Moreover, if $1/\eta$ is small enough then $n \le 3$, and if α is also small enough then $n = 2$.

Proof. By definition, for $B < \underline{B}(v/w; \eta v^2)$ the function φ is strictly increasing everywhere, so the steady state is unique. The same is true for $B = \underline{B}(v/w; \eta v^2) > 0$, since then $B = (\underline{B}, +\infty)$. The other measure-zero case, $B = \underline{B}(v/w; \eta v^2) = 0$, is too special to be of interest. Now, for $B > \underline{B}(v/w; \eta v^2)$, we saw earlier that there must be n stable equilibria and $n - 1$ unstable ones in the interval $(0, 1 - \alpha)$. To examine what values n can take, rewrite $\varphi(x) = \lambda\beta$ as

$$S(x) \equiv \left[x^2\left(\Delta^2(x) + \frac{Bv^2}{\gamma^2}\right) - \left(\frac{\beta\delta}{\eta\gamma}\right)(\beta\gamma - x)\right]^2 - [\lambda\beta x \Delta(x)]^2 = 0. \quad (11.A19)$$

By (11.A14), $\Delta^2(x)$ is a polynomial fraction in x whose numerator and denominator are both of degree 2. Multiplying the whole equation (11.A19) by the squared denominator of $\Delta^2(x)$, we therefore obtain a polynomial $S^*(x)$ of degree $2 \times (2 + 2) = 8$, which can have at most eight real roots. But we saw in the discussion following (11.A15) that $\varphi(x) = \lambda\beta$ must have an odd number of solutions on $(0, 1 - \alpha)$, with n intersections from above and $n - 1$ from below. The numbers of stable and unstable equilibria can therefore only be $(1, 0), (2, 1), (3, 2)$, or $(4, 3)$.

When $1/\eta = 0$ we can simplify (11.A19) by x^2, leaving for $S^*(x)$ only a polynomial of degree 6; this rules out $n = 4$. When, in addition, $\alpha = 0$, note from (11.A14) that $\Delta(x)$ depends on x only through x^2. As a consequence, the sixth-degree polynomial $S^*(x)$ is also a polynomial of degree 3 in x^2, so it has at most three real roots. This rules out $n = 3$. Finally, since the polynomial $S^*(x)$, like (11.A19), is continuous with respect to $1/\eta$ and α, so is (genetically with respect to the other parameters) its number of real zeroes in the interval $(0, 1 - \alpha)$. The preceding results therefore also apply for $1/\eta$ and α small enough.

This concludes the proof of Theorem 1.

Proof of Proposition 9. When $1/\eta = 0$ the condition for $\varphi'(x) < 0$, namely (11.A17), becomes

$$\frac{Bv^2}{\gamma^2} > \left(\frac{x\Delta'(x)/\Delta(x) + 1}{x\Delta'(x)/\Delta(x) - 1}\right)\Delta^2(x), \quad (11.A20)$$

with the requirement that the denominator must be positive. Using (11.A18), this can be rewritten as

$$B > \left(\frac{x^2 + \omega^{-2}}{x^3(\alpha + x) - \omega^{-2}(1 - (\alpha + x)(\alpha + 2x))}\right)$$
$$\times \left(\frac{x^2(2 - (\alpha + x)(\alpha + 2x)) + \omega^{-2}(1 - \alpha(\alpha + x))}{1 - (\alpha + x)^2}\right) \equiv \Gamma(x, \omega),$$

where $\omega \equiv v/\gamma w$. It is easily verified that the each of the bracketed functions is increasing in ω^{-2}, therefore

$$\underline{B}(\omega) \equiv \inf\{\Gamma(x, \omega) | x \in (0, 1 - \alpha) \quad \text{and}$$

$$x^3(\alpha + x) > \omega^{-2}(1 - (\alpha + x)(\alpha + 2x))\} \quad (11.A21)$$

is strictly positive, and decreasing in ω. Observe next that, as ω tends to infinity, $\Gamma(x,\ \omega)$ approaches $\Gamma(x,\ +\infty) = x(2 - (\alpha + x)(\alpha + 2x))/(1 - (\alpha + x)^2)$, whose infimum value on $(0, 1 - \alpha)$ is zero; therefore, $\lim_{\omega \to +\infty} \underline{B}(\omega) = 0$. Finally, for any x with $x^3(\alpha + x) > \omega^{-2}(1 - (\alpha + x)(\alpha + 2x))$, note that $\Gamma(x,\ \omega) > \omega^{-2}/(1 - \alpha^2)$, which tends to infinity as ω tends to 0. Therefore, $\lim_{\omega \to 0} \underline{B}(\omega) = +\infty$.

Proof of Proposition 10. Given lognormality, (11.29) becomes $\ln \kappa_t = m_t + \gamma \Delta_t^2/2 = (\ln y_t - \delta \ln l_t)/\gamma$, so substituting $\ln \tilde{\kappa}$ into the growth equation (11.15) yields

$$\ln y_{t+1} - (\alpha + \beta\gamma + \phi) \ln y_t$$
$$= \ln \bar{\kappa} + \delta(\ln l_{t+1} - (\alpha + \phi) \ln l_t) - \mathcal{L}_\nu(\tau_t)\nu^2/2 - \mathcal{L}_\Delta(\tau_t)\gamma^2\Delta_t^2/2,$$
$$(11.A22)$$

with $\ln \bar{\kappa} \equiv \beta\gamma \ln s - \gamma(1 - \gamma)w^2/2$. In a steady state, if $\alpha + \beta\gamma + \phi < 1$ the left-hand side equals $(1 - \alpha - \beta\gamma - \phi)$ times the output level $\ln y_\infty$; when $\alpha + \beta\gamma + \phi = 1$ it becomes equal to the asymptotic growth rate, $\lim_{t \to +\infty} \ln(y_{t+1}/y_t)$. As to the right-hand side, in a steady state with $\tau_t = \tau$ it becomes:

$$g_\infty(\tau) \equiv \ln \bar{\kappa} + \beta\gamma\delta \ln l(\tau) - \mathcal{L}_\nu(\tau)\nu^2/2 - \mathcal{L}_\Delta(\tau)\gamma^2 D(\tau)^2/2. \qquad (11.A23)$$

For $\alpha = 0$ we saw earlier that $\mathcal{L}_\Delta(\tau) = \mathcal{L}_\nu(\tau) = \beta\gamma(1 - \beta\gamma)(1 - \tau)^2$; therefore $\mathcal{L}_\nu(\tau)\nu^2/2 + \mathcal{L}_\Delta(\tau)\gamma^2 D(\tau)^2/2$ is strictly decreasing in τ. Now, with $1/\eta = 0$ the labour-supply term is constant, therefore $g_\infty(\tau)$ is strictly increasing in τ; this proves the proposition's first claim. Conversely, when $\beta\gamma = 1$, then $\mathcal{L}_\nu(\tau) = \mathcal{L}_\Delta = 0$; with $1/\eta > 0$, $g_\infty(\tau)$, like $\ln l(\tau)$, is then decreasing in τ, hence the second claim.

Proof of Proposition 11. Once agent i knows his productivity z_t^i, hence also his income $y_t^i = z_t^i(k_t^i)^\gamma(l_t^i)^\delta$ and his investment subsidy rate $\hat{e}_t^i/e_t^i = (\tilde{y}_t/y_t^i)^{\tau_t}$, his decision problem takes the form:

$$\ln V_t^i = \max_{l,\nu}\{(1 - \rho)[\ln((1 - \nu)y_t^i) - l^\eta] + (\rho/r')\ln[E_t(k_{t+1}^i)^{r'}]\ |k_{t+1}^i$$

$$= \kappa\xi_{t+1}^i(k_t^i)^\alpha(\hat{e}_t^i)^\beta\}$$

$$= \max_\nu\{(1 - \rho)\ln(1 - \nu) + \rho\beta \ln \nu\} + \max_l\{-(1 - \rho)l^\eta$$

$$+ (1 - \rho + \rho\beta(1 - \tau_t))\delta \ln l\}$$

$$+ \rho(\ln \kappa - (1 - r')w^2/2) + [\rho\alpha + (1 - \rho + \rho\beta(1 - \tau_t))\gamma] \ln k_t^i$$

$$+ (1 - \rho + \rho\beta(1 - \tau_t)) \ln z_t^i + \rho\beta\tau_t \ln \tilde{y}_t, \qquad (11.A24)$$

where $\nu_t^i \equiv e_t^i/y_t^i$ is the savings rate. Strict concavity in ν and l is easily verified, and the first-order conditions directly yield the stated results.

Proof of Proposition 12. Substituting the optimal $l_t^i = l_t$ and $v_t^i = s$ into (11.A24) and denoting $\ln \kappa' \equiv \ln \kappa - (1 - r')w^2/2$ yields:

$$
\begin{aligned}
\ln V_t^i = {} & \rho \ln \kappa' + (1 - \rho) \ln (1 - s) + \rho\beta \ln s \\
& - (1 - \rho)l_t^\eta + (1 - \rho + \rho\beta(1 - \tau_t))\delta \ln l_t \\
& + [\rho\alpha + (1 - \rho + \rho\beta(1 - \tau_t))\gamma] \ln k_t^i \\
& + (1 - \rho + \rho\beta(1 - \tau_t)) \ln z_t^i + \rho\beta\tau_t \ln \tilde{y}_t.
\end{aligned}
\tag{11.A25}
$$

Thus *conditional* on k_t^i, $\ln V_t^i$ is normally distributed, with variance $(1 - \rho + \rho\beta(1 - \tau_t))^2 v^2$. This implies:

$$
\begin{aligned}
U_t^i & \equiv \frac{1}{r} \ln E[(V_t^i)^r | k_t^i] \\
& = E[\ln V_t^i | k_t^i] + r(1 - \rho + \rho\beta(1 - \tau_t))^2 v^2/2.
\end{aligned}
\tag{11.A26}
$$

Therefore, to obtain U_t^i one simply needs to replace in (11.A25) the term in $\ln z_t^i$ by $-(1 - \rho + \rho\beta(1 - \tau_t)) [1 - r(1 - \rho + \rho\beta(1 - \tau_t))]v^2/2$. Finally, substituting in the value of $\tau_t \ln \tilde{y}_t$ from (11.A3) yields the claimed result, with:

$$
\begin{aligned}
\bar{u}_t \equiv {} & \ln[(1 - s)^{1-\rho}s^{\rho\beta}] + \rho(\ln \kappa - (1 - r')w^2/2) \\
& + (\rho\alpha + (1 - \rho + \rho\beta)\gamma)m_t + \rho\beta\gamma^2\Delta_t^2/2.
\end{aligned}
\tag{11.A27}
$$

Proofs of Theorem 2 and Proposition 13. By (11.37) and (11.38), $\bar{\lambda} > \underline{\lambda}$ if and only if

$$
B(\bar{\tau}) - B(0) - (C(0) - C(\bar{\tau}))\left(\frac{2}{v^2}\right) > \rho\beta\bar{\tau}\left(\frac{2 - \bar{\tau}}{v^2}\right)\gamma^2 D(0)D(\bar{\tau}),
\tag{11.A28}
$$

which yields Theorem 2, with

$$
\begin{aligned}
& G(\bar{\tau}, \ v^2/w^2) \\
& \equiv \rho\beta\bar{\tau}(2 - \bar{\tau})\gamma^2 \left(\sqrt{\frac{w^2/v^2 + \beta^2}{1 - (\alpha + \beta\gamma)^2}}\right)\left(\sqrt{\frac{w^2/v^2 + \beta^2(1 - \bar{\tau})^2}{1 - (\alpha + \beta\gamma(1 - \bar{\tau}))^2}}\right).
\end{aligned}
\tag{11.A29}
$$

Note that since $G(\bar{\tau}, \ v^2/w^2) > 0$, if $B(\bar{\tau}) - B(0) > \underline{B}$ then it must be that $\underline{\lambda} > 0$. Finally, both $\underline{\lambda}$ and $\bar{\lambda}$ are clearly increasing in $B \equiv B(\bar{\tau}) - B(0)$ and in $-(C(0) - C(\bar{\tau}))$ (hence in η). Since the common coefficient of these two terms is $1/(\bar{\tau}D(\bar{\tau}))$ in $\bar{\lambda}$, and $1/\bar{\tau}D(0)$ in $\underline{\lambda}$, Proposition 13 follows immediately.

REFERENCES

Ades, Alberto and Verdier, Thierry (1996). The rise and fall of elites: Economic development and social polarization in rent-seeking societies, *Centre for Economic Policy Research (London) discussion paper* 1495.

Aghion, Philippe and Bolton, Patrick (1997). A trickle-down theory of growth and development with debt overhang, *Review of Economics Studies*, 64 (2), 151–72.

Alesina, Alberto F. and Rodrik, Dani (1994). Distributive politics and economic growth, *Quarterly Journal of Economics*, 109 (2), 465–90.

Banerjee, Abhijit and Newman, Andrew (1993). Occupational choice and the process of development, *Journal of Political Economy*, 101 (2), 274–98.

Bénabou, Roland (1993). Workings of a city: Location, education, and production, *Quarterly Journal of Economics*, 108 (3), 619–52.

—— (1996a). Unequal societies. *National Bureau of Economic Research* (Cambridge, MA) *working paper 5583*.

—— (1996b). Heterogeneity, stratification, and growth: Macroeconomic implications of community structure and school finance, *American Economic Review*, 86 (3), 584–609.

—— (1996c) Inequality and growth, in Ben S. Bernanke and Julio J. Rotemberg (eds.) *National Bureau of Economic Research macro annual*, vol. 11. Cambridge, MA: MIT Press, 11–74.

—— (2002). Tax and education policy in a heterogenous agent economy: What levels of redistribution maximize growth and efficiency? *Econometrica*, 70(2), 481–517.

Bertola, Giuseppe (1993). Factor shares and savings in endogenous growth, *American Economic Review*, 83 (5), 1184–98.

Björklund, Anders and Jäntti, Markus (1997a). Intergenerational mobility of economic status: Is the United States different? Mimeo, Stockholm Institute for Social Research.

—— (1997b). Intergenerational income mobility in Sweden compared to the United States, *American Economic Review*, 87 (5), 1009–19.

Borjas, George J. (1995). Ethnicity, neighborhoods, and human-capital externalities, *American Economic Review*, 85 (3), 365–90.

Bourguignon, François and Verdier, Thierry (2000). Oligarchy democracy, inequality and growth. *Journal of Development Economics* 62, 285–313.

Casamatta, George, Cremer, Helmuth, and Pestiau, Pierre (2000). Political sustainability and the design of redistributive social insurance systems, *Journal of Public Economics*, 75, 314–40.

Clarke, George R. G. (1992). More evidence on income distribution and growth, *World Bank Policy, Research and External Affairs working paper 1064.*

Conway, Margaret M (1991). *Political participation in the United States*. Washington DC: U.S. Congressional Quarterly Press.

Cooper, Suzanne J. Durlauf, Steven N. and Johnson, Paul A. (1994). On the evolution of economic status across generations, *American Statistical Association Papers and Proceedings (Business and Economics Section)*, 50–58.

Couch, Kenneth A. and Dunn, Thomas A (1997). Inter-generational correlations in labor market status: a comparison of the United States and Germany, *Journal of Human Resources*, 32 (1), 210–32.

Deininger, Klaus and Squire, Lyn (1995). Inequality and growth: results from a new data set. Mimeo, World Bank.

Devarajan, Shantarayan, Swaroop, Vinaya and Zou, Heng-Fu (1993). What do governments buy? *World Bank Policy, Research and External Affairs Working Paper No. 1082.*

Durlauf, Steven N (1996a). A theory of persistent income inequality, *Journal of Economic Growth*, 1 (1), 75–94.

328   *R. Bénabou*

Durlauf, Steven N. (1996*b*). Neighborhood feedbacks, endogenous stratification, and income inequality, in William A. Barnett, Giancarlo Gandolfo, and Claude Hillinger, (eds.), *Dynamic disequilibrium modeling: Theory and applications. Proceedings of the Ninth International Symposium in Economic Theory and Econometrics.* Cambridge: Cambridge University Press, 505–34.

Edsall, Thomas B. (1984). *The new politics of inequality.* New York: Norton.

Epstein, Larry G. and Zin, Stanley E. (1989). Substitution, risk aversion, and the temporal behavior of asset returns: A theoretical framework, *Econometrica*, 57 (4), 937–69.

Erikson, Robert and Goldthorpe, John H (1992). *The constant flux: A study of class mobility in industrial societies.* Oxford: Clarendon Press.

Evans, William N. Oates, Wallace and Schwab, Robert (1992). Measuring peer effects: a study of teenage behavior, *Journal of Political Economy*, 100 (5), 966–91.

Feldstein, Martin S. (1969). The effects of taxation on risk taking, *Journal of Political Economy*, 77 (5), 755–64.

Fernández, Raquel and Rogerson, Richard (1998). Public education and the dynamics of income distribution: a quantitative evaluation of education finance reform, *American Economic Review*, 88 (4), 813–33.

Figini, Paolo (1999). Inequality, growth, and redistribution. Mimeo, Trinity College.

Galor, Oded and Zeira, Joseph (1993). Income distribution and macroeconomics, *Review of Economic Studies*, 60 (1), 35–52.

Gans, Joshua S. and Smart, Michael (1996). Majority voting with single-crossing preferences, *Journal of Public Economics*, 59 (2), 219–37.

Glomm, Gerhard and Ravikumar, B (1992). Public vs. private investment in human capital: endogenous growth and income inequality, *Journal of Political Economy*, 100 (4), 818–34.

Gradstein, Mark and Justman, Moshe (1997). Democratic choice of an education system: implications for growth and income distribution, *Journal of Economic Growth*, 2 (2), 169–84.

Grossman, Gene M. and Helpman, Elhanan (1998). Intergenerational redistribution with short-lived governments, *Economic Journal* 108, 1299–1329.

Jakobsson, Ulf (1976). On the measurement of the degree of progression, *Journal of Public Economics*, 5 (1–2), 161–8.

Jencks, Christopher and Mayer, Susan E (1990). The social consequences of growing up in a poor neighborhood, in Laurence E. Lynn and Michael G. H. McGeary (eds.), *Inner City Poverty in the United States.* Washington, DC: National Academy Press, 111–86.

Kakwani, Nanak C. (1977). Applications of Lorenz curves in economic analysis, *Econometrica*, 45 (3), 719–27.

Kanbur, S. M. (1979). Of risk taking and the personal distribution of income, *Journal of Political Economy*, 87 (4), 769–97.

Keefer, Philip and Knack, Stephen F. (1995). Polarization, property rights and the links between inequality and growth. Mimeo, World Bank.

Kreps, David M. and Porteus, Evan L. (1979). Dynamic choice theory and dynamic programming, *Econometrica*, 47 (1), 91–100.

Krusell, Per, Quadrini, Vincenzo and Ríos-Rull, José-Víctor (1997). Politico-economic equilibrium and economic growth, *Journal of Economic Dynamics and Controls*, 21 (1), 243–72.

Lindert, Peter H. (1996). What limits social spending? *Explorations in Economic History* 33 (1), 1–34.

Loury, Glenn C. (1981). Intergenerational transfers and the distribution of earnings, *Econometrica*, 49 (4), 843–67.

Manski, Charles F. (1993). Identification of social effects: The reflection problem, *Review of Economic Studies*, 60 (3), 531–42.

McCarthy, Nolan M., Poole, Keith T. and Rosenthal, Howard (1997). *Income redistribution and the realignment of American politics*. Washington, DC: American Enterprise Institute Press, 1997.

Meltzer, Alan H. and Richard, Scott F. (1981). A rational theory of the size of government, *Journal of Political Economy*, 89 (5), 914–27.

Musgrave, Richard A. and Thin, Tun (1948). Income tax progression 1929–48. *Journal of Political Economy*, 56 (6), 498–514.

Perotti, Roberto (1993). Political equilibrium, income distribution, and growth. *Review of Economic Studies*, 60 (4), 755–76.

—— (1994). Income distribution and investment, *European Economic Review*, 38 (3–4), 827–35.

—— (1996). Growth, income distribution, and democracy: What the data say. *Journal of Economic Growth*, 1 (2), 149–87.

Persson, Mats (1983). The distribution of abilities and the progressive income tax, *Journal of Public Economics* 22 (1), 73–88.

Persson, Torsten and Tabellini, Guido (1994). Is inequality harmful for growth? Theory and evidence, *American Economic Review*, 84 (3), 600–21.

—— (1996). Federal fiscal constitutions, part II: risk sharing and redistribution, *Journal of Political Economy*, 104 (5), 979–1009.

Piketty, Thomas (1995). Social mobility and redistributive politics, *Quarterly Journal of Economics*, 110 (3), 551–84.

—— (1997). The dynamics of the wealth distribution and interest rate with credit-rationing, *Review of Economic Studies*, 64 (2), 173–90.

Rodriguez, Francisco (1998). Inequality, redistribution and rent-seeking, *Ph.D. dissertation*, Harvard University.

Roemer, John E. (1998). Why the poor do not expropriate the rich in democracies: An old argument in new garb, *Journal of Public Economics*, 70 (3), 399–426.

Rosenstone, Steven J. and Hansen, John M (1993). *Mobilization, Participation and Democracy in America*. New York: Macmillan.

Rustichini, Aldo, Ichino, Andrea C., and Checchi, Daniele (1999). More equal but less mobile? Education financing and intergenerational mobility in Italy and the U.S, *Journal of Public Economics* 70 (3), 399–424.

Saint-Paul, Gilles (2001). The dynamics of exclusion and fiscal conservatism, *Review of Economic Dynamics*, 4, 275–302.

—— and Verdier, Thierry (1992). Historical accidents and the persistence of distributional conflicts, *Journal of the Japanese and International Economies*, 6 (4), 406–22.

—— —— (1993). Education, democracy and growth, *Journal of Development Economics*, 42 (2), 399–407.

Sala-i-Martin, Xavier (1996). A positive theory of social security, *Journal of Economic Growth*, 1 (2), 277–304.

Topa, Giorgio (2001). Social interactions and the spatial distribution of unemployment, *Review of Economic Studies*, 68(2), 261–95.

Weil, Philippe (1990). Nonexpected utility in macroeconomics, *Quarterly Journal of Economics*, 105 (1), 29–42.

Wolfinger, Raymond E. and Rosenstone, Steven J. (1980). *Who votes?* New Haven, CT: Yale University Press.

12

Unemployment, Specialization, and Collective Preferences for Social Insurance

JOHN HASSLER, JOSÉ V. RODRÍGUEZ MORA,
KJETIL STORESLETTEN, AND FABRIZIO ZILIBOTTI

12.1. INTRODUCTION

Two facts are the driving motivation behind this chapter. On the one hand, the average unemployment rate in Continental Europe is about twice as large as that of the US. Moreover, the duration of unemployment is substantially larger in Europe; more than 50 per cent of the unemployed in Europe have been unemployed for more than a year, while the corresponding figure for the US is a mere 10 per cent (see, for instance, Table 1 in Ljungqvist and Sargent, 1998). On the other hand, the generosity of the unemployment insurance (UI) remains substantially higher in most of Continental Europe than in the US. According to the summary measure of the OECD Data-base on Benefit Entitlements and Gross Replacement Rates, constructed as a weighted average of extent, duration and coverage of insurance for different types of workers, workers in Continental Europe enjoy government provided insurance that is more than three times higher than do workers in the US.[1]

The European unemployment problem has indeed been a major concern for economists over the last two decades, and the mainstream view suggests a positive relationship between UI and unemployment rate (see below). Against this background, exploring and trying to account for interactions between the labour-market and social insurance institutions seem imperative. In particular, one would like to understand why the US and Europe have chosen so markedly different approaches to the provision of social insurance.

---

[1] This finding is confirmed in Martin (1996). International comparisons of measures of replacement rates remain controversial, however. According to alternative measures, the differences are less dramatic, although in no case negligible. Nickell (1997) reports the benefit replacement ratio in the average Continental European country for the period 1989–94 to be 63.3 per cent and the benefit duration 2.1 years, whereas the corresponding measures for the US are reported to be 50 per cent and 0.5 years.

In this chapter, we argue that these differences are due to that in Europe, workers tend to be less mobile and more specialized (where 'specialization' is understood to be the existence of strong comparative advantages in some sectors, professions or geographical locations), while in the US, workers are more versatile; that is, they are more willing to change profession or residence. These differences in degrees of 'versatility' between European and American workers are not necessarily due to exogenous 'cultural' differences, but are likely to arise as the result of endogenous behaviour in the acquisition of human capital. In particular, European workers are more prone to acquire specialized skills, while US workers tend to acquire relatively versatile skills. These choices are affected by differences in institutional frameworks—little or no UI in the US, while generous UI in Europe. As a result, we observe different distributions of human capital across the Atlantic. These differences in the distributions of human capital, in turn, can explain the observed differences in social insurance institutions through a standard Political Economy channel.

Thus, the differences in labour-market performance and institutions across the Atlantic can be understood by the following interlinked mechanisms: (1) on the one hand, UI is generous in Europe because European workers have endogenously acquired attributes (human capital) making them more concerned about unemployment risk than US workers. Hence, European workers muster stronger political support for UI than American workers. (2) On the other hand, the existence of generous UI gives incentives to European workers to acquire more specialized human capital, associated with higher unemployment risk. American workers, faced with low UI, will instead tend to accumulate more flexible human capital featuring less risk.

The chapter is organized in the following way: Section 12.2 provides a survey on the literature of the effects of UI (taken as exogenous) on labour-market performance, and illustrates the main findings by the use of a standard search model. Section 12.3 surveys the literature by studying the reverse causality: the endogenous determination of UI, taking the labour market as exogenous. In Section 12.4, we study how these two directions of causality interact and can give rise to multiple steady states, accounting for the differences between the US and Europe. Finally, Section 12.5 presents a simple analytical model capturing the main essence of our arguments and Section 12.6 concludes.

12.2. IMPACT OF UI ON THE LABOUR MARKET

Unemployment insurance is an institution which, according to standard economic theory, affects the labour-market performance in a variety of dimensions. In particular, it increases the aggregate unemployment rate and compresses the earning distribution. In the Appendix, we show these effects to be the outcomes of standard search models.

As argued in the introduction, UI is substantially more generous in Europe than in the US. On the other hand, wage inequality is substantially higher in the US than in Europe. For instance, Freeman (1996) reports that, in Western Europe, a male worker in the bottom 10 per cent of the earning distribution earns 68 per cent of the median worker's income, whereas in the US, the corresponding figure is 38 per cent. In absolute terms, low-paid workers in Germany earn 2.2 times more than low-paid workers in the US. An interesting fact, consistent with the simple search model presented in the Appendix (where workers are *ex ante* identical), is that a large part of US earnings inequality is between observationally equivalent workers, i.e., workers of equal age, experience, gender, education, etc. (see Gottschalk, 1997; Levy and Murnane, 1992).

Given these observations, it would be tempting to relate the evidence that unemployment (especially long-term unemployment) is higher in Europe, while wage inequality is higher in the US, to differences in the regimes of UI. This conclusion encounters an objection, however. UI—and, more in general, welfare state institutions—were more generous in Europe than in the US already during the late 1960s and early 1970s, and, yet, the unemployment rate was lower in Europe than in the US at the time. Some recent papers have addressed this objection, arguing that, due to the nature of technological change in the last quarter of the century, the labour-market performance has become much more sensitive to pre-existing welfare state institutions (Ljungqvist and Sargent, 1998; Marimon and Zilibotti, 1999; Mortensen and Pissarides, 1999).

In the Appendix, we illustrate how these observations are indeed consistent with the simple search model once skill-biased technological change is added to the framework, which illustrates the key mechanisms in Marimon and Zilibotti (1999) (MZ) and Mortensen and Pissarides (1999). In particular, MZ calibrate their model and show that it can mimic salient features of the US and European labour markets in the last twenty years.[2] For instance, the two economies would, in the early 1970s, start with similar unemployment rates (4 per cent in the US and 5.5 per cent in Europe). Then, after the shock, the economies would reach two new steady states, such that the unemployment rate is almost unchanged in the laissez-faire economy, and twice as high as before the shock in the welfare state economy. The average duration of unemployment is also predicted to double in Europe, where about 30 per cent of the workers would experience an unemployment duration of more than 12 months. Wage inequality increases more in the laissez-faire than in the welfare state economy. An interesting feature is that, despite the higher unemployment, total output growth is very similar in the two economies. This is due to the fact that in the laissez-faire economy, there is higher employment, but also more mismatch, i.e., many workers are employed in activities where they do not have their comparative advantage.

An interesting implication of the analysis is that even though, in the case considered by MZ, a planner maximizing a utilitarian welfare function would choose zero benefits, the majority of workers in the welfare state economy would

---

[2] In particular, MZ assume job creation to be endogenous and determined in equilibrium, rather than assuming an exogenous wage offer distribution.

be hurt by a reduction of the unemployment benefits. That is, the majority of workers would rationally oppose dismantling the welfare state, even if anticipating that this were to increase unemployment and taxation. The elementary mechanism behind this result is described formally in the simple model presented in the Appendix. The intuition goes as follows. Assume that benefits are financed by labour income tax. When the economy is hit by the shock, workers holding a low-paid job (which is now even worse paid than earlier) realize that it becomes more attractive to move into unemployment and wait for a better opportunity. This is, however, prohibitively costly in an economy without UI (clearly, the point would be strengthened if workers were risk-averse). If generous benefits are available, however, poor workers can decide to quit their bad job and search for better opportunities. Thus, not only unemployed workers but also the 'working poor' prefer to live in a welfare state economy and will vote against removing unemployment benefits when the shock occurs. The 'rich' (well-matched) workers, instead, have more to lose from paying higher taxes and, although anticipating the possibility of becoming unemployed in the future, this event is discounted. Thus, there is, in general, a conflict of interests between different groups of workers.[3]

While MZ ignore distortions on the incentives for the unemployed to search, this is the main focus of the analysis in Ljungqvist and Sargent (1998) (LS). They make the important assumption that workers progressively acquire skills during their employment spells, and progressively lose skills during unemployment spells. Moreover, some of the skills acquired on-the-job are not general, implying that they are lost (become worthless) when the job in which a particular worker is employed is destroyed. The benefit rate is proportional to the wage obtained by a displaced worker in his last job. In this model, the extent to which UI distorts the incentives of a displaced worker to search for a new job depends on the characteristics of the displaced worker. In particular, incentives to search are most severely weakened for those workers who were earning high wages before displacement (hence with high benefits), but whose human capital was destroyed upon displacement. These workers will engage in an effortless and picky search strategy, and will not be deterred by the threat of losing skills while unemployed. Hence, their generous benefits will keep their reservation wage high. According to LS, the size of this group of workers in the labour force has increased substantially since the late 1970s. If this were the case, the effects of UI would be to dramatically increase the aggregate unemployment rate. This would explain why welfare state institutions were consistent with low unemployment in the 1960s, whereas they became associated with high unemployment in the 1990s. In fact,

---

[3] In MZ, the result is reinforced by the assumption that workers do not hold shares of firms, and that these are instead owned by a class of rentiers. Due to firing restrictions, firms offering 'bad jobs' are hurt by the increase in the reservation value of the 'poor' workers, and suffer a loss which does not affect any of the workers' utility. It is still true, however, that rich employed workers and firms prefer the laissez-faire environment, while poor employed and unemployed workers prefer to be in a welfare state economy.

LS show that a calibrated version of their model can account for the whole increase in European unemployment.[4]

But why would the economic environment have changed and, in particular, why would the probability of a worker losing skills upon displacement have increased? The argument here is that recent technological change (e.g. IT revolution) tends to make skills (associated with destroyed jobs) obsolete at a faster rate. Evidence in support of this claim is the observation of an increase in the variability of individual earnings in the US, as documented by, among others, Gottschalk and Moffit (1994). This suggests that the destruction of old and the accumulation of new human capital tend to occur more rapidly (note, though, that the same evidence is consistent with the argument of an increasing importance of mismatch, emphasized by MZ). In summary, the argument proposed by LS stresses that in order to achieve the same degree of equality through UI, the society must now pay a much larger cost in terms of unemployment and output per capita.

Another mechanism which may reduce the distortionary impact of UI is discussed by Acemoglu (2001), where job creation is endogenous and firms can decide to produce either good (high productivity) or bad (low productivity) jobs. The sunk cost of creating a good job is larger than that of creating a bad job. Due to *ex post* rent sharing, the equilibrium tends to have too low a proportion of good jobs. Thus, increasing unemployment benefits have a beneficial effect on the equilibrium composition of jobs, since the impact of the benefits, via the outside option effect, is more important for low wage than for high wage jobs. In fact, Acemoglu shows that benefits can increase the absolute number of good jobs created, and not only their proportion of the total number of jobs in the economy and, in some cases, be welfare improving (see also Acemoglu and Shimer, 1999, 2000).

12.2.1. Some Empirical Evidence

A large body of empirical literature has studied various aspects of displaced workers' behaviour. The data lend strong support to salient features of standard search theory. In particular:

(1) workers accumulate human capital through learning by doing, and large components of accumulated human capital are sector-specific, region-specific, and profession-specific;

(2) the geographical and sectoral mobility in Europe is substantially smaller than in the US. In particular, the search behaviour of agents with more 'specific' or 'specialized' human capital is very sensitive to the level of UI: higher UI benefits make specialized workers substantially more picky.

Standard search theory has the implication that workers suffering large wage losses upon accepting certain job offers should reject these offers if UI were

---

[4] See Haefke (1999) for a criticism of the LS argument in a model with endogenous job destruction.

more generous. Given that benefits are more generous in Europe than in the US, post-displacement wage losses should therefore be lower in Europe than in the US, which is confirmed by the data. A range of empirical studies suggests that displacement leads to 10–25 per cent wage losses in the US (see e.g. Jacobson *et al.*, 1993; Hamermesh, 1989; and Fallick, 1996 for reviews of the literature). In contrast, post-displacement wage losses upon re-employment seem to be relatively small in Europe. Leonhard and Audenrode (1995) document that displaced workers experience no wage loss in Belgium, and Burda and Mertens (2002) find very low post-displacement wage losses in Germany (i.e., full-time employed men displaced in 1996 and re-employed in 1997 suffered an average wage reduction of 3.6 per cent in comparison with those with no unemployment spell in that period). Using US data from the Continuous Wage and Benefit History, Meyer (1990) finds support for another important aspect of search theory; namely that higher benefits have a strong negative effect on the probability of exiting unemployment.

Let us now turn to evidence on sector-specific learning by doing. The effect of switching industries on the wage earning of displaced workers is well documented. For the US, Neal (1995) finds that workers switching industries after losing their previous job usually suffer much larger losses than observationally equivalent workers remaining in the same industry. On an average, the wage loss for a male worker changing industries is in the order of 15 per cent, while if staying, he would only suffer a loss in the order of 3 per cent. Moreover, wage losses increase with experience and tenure, and at a much more pronounced rate for those changing industries than for those remaining. Using the displaced workers survey (DWS), Topel (1990) shows that the wage fall associated with job displacement increases by 1.3 per cent for each extra year of tenure in the job from which the worker was displaced. General labour-market experience is substantially less important for the size of the wage loss. This evidence suggests that there is a significant on-the-job accumulation of human capital and that part of this human capital is lost if a worker switches industries.

As concerns the issue of whether UI affects the degree of sectoral mobility of workers, Fallick (1991), using the DWS, documents that higher UI 'retard the mobility of displaced workers between industries' (p. 234), i.e., reduces the rate at which displaced workers become employed in other sectors than the one in which they where laid off. In contrast, UI has little effect on re-employment rates in the same industry.

Moreover, on the relationship between the accumulation of 'specific' human capital and search behaviour, Thomas (1996) finds, using Canadian micro-data, that workers' average unemployment spells increase with tenure for UI recipients (increasing tenure to 5 years increases the unemployment spell by 18 per cent). Using the DWS, Addison and Portugal (1987) report similar findings. These findings are in line with our idea that more specialized (high tenure) displaced workers tend to be more selective in the search process, since they have more to lose from switching to jobs for which they are not qualified.

In summary, both the theoretical and the empirical literatures suggest that UI has strong effects on the labour-market outcomes. In particular, UI increases the unemployment rate and induces workers to acquire human capital associated with more specialized labour-market careers, which, in turn, make them less mobile.

12.3. POSITIVE THEORIES OF UI

The previous section argued that differences in the unemployment insurance institutions might be a major factor in explaining the large differences in unemployment rates and earnings inequality observed in Western Europe and the US during the last 25 years. A serious shortcoming of the literature discussed is that it treats UI as an exogenous institution, which begs the question 'why do countries choose, through their political process, such dramatically different levels of UI?'

A first possible answer could be that agents have different preferences in different countries, or that agents have different perceptions of the effects of different institutions on the economic performance (e.g., Piketty, 1995). An alternative approach is to provide a positive theory addressing why such different UI levels are observed across countries. To this end, a small but growing literature has instead taken labour-market behaviour as given and analysed precisely the social preferences over UI (Wright, 1986; Saint Paul, 1993, 1996, 1997; Di Tella and MacCulloch, 1995; Hassler and Rodríguez Mora, 1999; Pallage and Zimmermann, 1999, 2001).

A seminal contribution to this literature is due to Wright (1986), who explores the choice of UI in a median voter model where agents switch stochastically between being employed and unemployed. Since the median voter is employed, and the employment status is persistent, the employed face a trade-off between insurance against future unemployment spells on the one hand, and an expected transfer to the unemployed on the other.

Saint Paul (1993, 1996, 1997, and 1999) studies various politico-economic implications of unemployment, the labour-market, and labour-market regulation. Saint Paul (1993) investigates how reducing firing costs by means of a two-tier system may be politically feasible. Saint Paul (1996) argues that labour-market rigidities in European countries, including the underlying institutional regulations, can be understood as the outcome of political influence by incumbent employees, since policies increasing unemployment in many cases benefit these insiders and provide some empirical evidence. Saint Paul (1997) studies how labour-market status affects the preferences for the provision of a public good and subsidies, and explores the implied dynamics of government expenditures. Finally, Saint Paul (1999) inquires into the political support for employment protection legislation in a model where workers face a trade-off between employment protection and the adoption of new technology, which requires creative destruction.

Pallage and Zimmermann (1999, 2001) explore models with asymmetric information about the search effort of the unemployed. In particular, the unemployed are supposed to accept any relevant job offer, but since the insurance agency cannot observe the job offers, there is moral hazard in that the unemployed can turn down job offers without being detected. The workers are heterogeneous in skills and employment status, and vote over the unemployment benefits. The decisive voter—whose wage is typically below average—faces a trade-off between redistribution on the one hand and efficiency (more job offers accepted) on the other.

Hassler and Rodríguez Mora (1999) extend the work by Wright (1986) by introducing a capital market where agents can self-insure against the risk of experiencing unemployment by accumulating buffer stocks of savings. This precautionary saving can serve as a substitute for public UI and thus affect individual preferences and the level of UI chosen by the political system. However, the degree of substitutability between public UI and precautionary savings depends on the expected rate of turnover between employment and unemployment. If the duration of job and unemployment spells is low (high), i.e., turnover high (low), precautionary savings is a good (bad) substitute for UI. Thus, if UI is costly, for example because of distortionary taxation, individuals living in a world with high turnover would choose low benefits and instead use precautionary savings to insure against the relatively frequent, but short, spells of unemployment. On the other hand, if turnover is low (but not too low), the demand for UI will be high, even if it is costly. Since turnover is typically much lower in Europe than in the US, this mechanism can offer an explanation why most European countries have chosen much more generous UI schemes than the US. Interestingly, their model shows that a worker who could choose between low and high turnover rates (with higher wages with low turnover) would be more prone to choose low turnover *conditional on having a generous UI*. Thus, not only the institutional framework is determined by the characteristics of the agents, but these characteristics depend on the level of UI in a symmetrical manner. The political process and private behaviour complement each other and suggest the possibility of multiplicity.

Summing up, the theoretical literature on the determination of UI suggest that the demand for UI will differ with the characteristics of the agents; employed workers will demand less than unemployed workers. Similarly, workers facing high unemployment risk will demand more UI than workers facing low unemployment risk. Finally, workers expecting long spells of unemployment will demand more UI than other workers.

12.4. A UNIFIED THEORY OF SOCIAL INSTITUTIONS AND THE LABOUR MARKET

Sections 12.2 and 12.3 reviewed two strands of the literature, the former taking the UI system as given and analysing the impact on the labour market, and the latter taking the labour-market structure as given and exploring the resulting social preferences and political choices. The purpose of this section is to provide a unified theory of social institutions and the labour market. In particular, we provide a theory that can account for why two societies populated by rational agents may choose very different levels of UI, even if the economies are identical in terms of production technology and agents' preferences.

The reason why different political choices emerge in our work is that, in different countries, the identity of the agents who are politically preponderant varies. This diversity, in turn, originates endogenously from the institutions on which agents vote. Therefore, different outcomes can be sustained as stable steady-state equilibria. It is this complementarity between individual *behaviour* on the labour market and the *policies* collectively chosen which is the driving force in our theory. Explanations of persistently different structures of societies in terms of multiple steady states are present in a number of recent papers (Bénabou, 1998; Banerjee and Newman, 1993; Quadrini, 2000; Hassler *et al.*, 2003). A common feature in these papers is that multiplicity does not originate from missing markets or strategic complementarity (à la Cooper and John, 1988), but from the interplay between the agents' private decisions (determining their characteristics) and their collective choices, determining public policies and institutions.

In one recent paper in this stream of literature, Hassler *et al.* (1999), multiplicity instead arises in the context of unemployment and labour-market institutions. In this model, workers are risk averse, and acquire sector-specific skills while employed. Depending on their current labour-market conditions, some agents attach more value to UI than others, causing divergent political views about the degree of income taxation for financing UI. The unemployed naturally prefer a more generous insurance than the employed. However, their political influence is limited, since the employed are more numerous (as in Wright, 1986). Therefore, the focus of the paper is on the heterogeneity of preferences across groups of employed workers. In particular, more *specialized* workers, i.e., those with a pronounced comparative advantage for working in a particular activity, will tend to value insurance more highly than workers with skills of a more general nature. When displaced a specialized worker faces a trade-off between accepting *any* job—and suffering a wage cut with respect to pre-displacement wage—or waiting for a job offer where there is a comparative advantage—implying a longer unemployment spell. Specialized workers, therefore, tend to pursue picky search strategies which, endogenously, entail more risk. In order to hedge this risk, they prefer a more generous UI. The selective search, in turn, reinforces the degree of specialization among workers. If one has held the same job in a particular industry for a long time, one is likely to have developed a more pronounced comparative advantage than a worker having frequently changed jobs and industries. For example, a mature miner who has only been working in mining activities is bound to suffer large wage losses if switching to a different sector, as one's human capital is very industry-specific.

It is precisely this reinforcing interaction between specialization and preference for insurance which can give rise to multiple steady-state equilibria.

In particular, two economies with small or even no differences in preferences or technology may end up with very different political choices over social insurance and therefore, large differences in their economic performance. Consider an economy where highly specialized workers are politically preponderant. On the one hand, this economy features a strong political pressure for high insurance. On the other hand, given a generous UI, unemployed workers tend to be picky, in order to retain their skills in the sector where they have an initial comparative advantage. This will, in turn, increase the proportion of highly specialized workers and sustain the demand for high insurance. Hence, this economy may have a locally stable equilibrium outcome with low employment turnover, low mobility between industries (or occupations), small post-displacement wage losses (since job-searchers are 'picky'), and high unemployment. Conversely, consider an economy where most workers have little specialization. The majority of workers then attach a low value to UI, so that low benefits will be chosen in equilibrium. Less insurance reduces the incentive for unemployed workers to be picky which, in turn, suppresses the proportion of narrowly specialized workers, and undermines the support for a generous UI system. Thus, this economy may have another locally stable equilibrium outcome with a high employment turn-over, large post-displacement wage losses (since job-searchers are 'non-picky'), and low unemployment, where the majority is content with low benefits.

The main result in Hassler *et al.* (1999) is that a 'European' steady state with high unemployment, low employment turnover and high UI can coexist with an 'American' steady state with low unemployment, high employment turnover and low UI. Moreover, we show that a reasonably calibrated version of the model has two sustainable steady state equilibria. One steady state has an unemployment rate of 12.7 per cent, an average duration of unemployment of 23 months and a replacement ratio of 76 per cent, while the other steady state features an unemployment rate of 6.4 per cent, an average duration of unemployment of 4.5 months and a 24 per cent replacement ratio.

These results illustrate our general point that social insurance affects economic behaviour, which, in turn, feeds back on preferences over social insurance. It is important to note, however, that the notion of *specialization* goes beyond 'human capital accumulation'. We believe that the notion of 'specialization' should have a broader interpretation, capturing the idea that Europeans are less mobile and more specialized than Americans in more ways than one. Two alternative interpretations that we find particularly fruitful are *geographical* specialization and *educational* specialization.

The interaction between geographical specialization and UI demand has been analyzed in Hassler *et al.* (2001). With geographical specialization, we mean local networks, local knowledge, family ties and the distribution of house ownership. In these dimensions, the degree of heterogeneity in Europe is substantially larger than in the US. This statement embodies cultural heterogeneity—differences in language, work attitudes, corruption, business and work etiquette—as well as heterogeneity in tangible factors—differences in government regulations, welfare laws (e.g., that welfare claims are, in most cases, non-transferable across borders), etc.

Moreover, casual evidence suggests that the degree of discrimination against job applicants from other countries (and even regions within the same country) is larger in Europe than in the US.

Finally, our last interpretation of geographical specialization is the distribution of house ownership. Because of high transaction costs, house ownership implies a larger fixed cost of moving than for non-house owners, which should reduce geographical mobility.[5] Moreover, house owners should, given the larger risk they bear, be relatively more prone to support more generous UI. Thus, a country with a high fraction of owner-occupied housing should be expected to have a high unemployment rate. Indeed, Oswald (1997) shows that the fraction of owner-occupied housing is highly correlated with the unemployment rate across a sample of OECD countries.

When turning to *education* as specialization, what we have in mind is education as a risky human capital investment. Prospective students might choose to invest in specialized human capital assets yielding a high wage in one particular occupation, but low wages in others. Alternatively, they could pursue a more generalized education providing skills applicable to many occupations, and therefore paying an intermediate wage in many occupations. We believe the former (specialized) education to be more prevalent in Europe, manifested, for instance, in the German apprenticeship system. A general undergraduate degree—by far the most popular college education on either continent—represents what we mean by a more 'generalized' education.[6]

12.5. A SIMPLE MODEL WITH POLICY-BEHAVIOUR COMPLEMENTARITY

In this section, we illustrate the main points of Section 12.4 with the aid of a simple, highly stylized model featuring joint determination of policy and behaviour in the context of labour markets. The set up is that of an educational choice (related to our discussion in Section 12.4) where agents choose between a specialized education—featuring a high return while being subject to substantial

---

[5] Moreover, if an unemployed house owner in an economically depressed area contemplates moving to a more economically vibrant area, the value of her house will be low, relative to the cost of housing in the alternative residence. In this sense, house ownership magnifies the unemployment risk because moving away from a weak labour market becomes more costly. However, if UI is generous and has a long duration, the risk associated with house ownership becomes less threatening, and more workers should own their home. Thus, a generous UI should, over time, induce agents to accumulate assets—residential capital—embodying risk that is highly correlated with unemployment risk.

[6] There is direct evidence that college education serves as an insurance against unemployment risk. For instance, Hubbard *et al.* (1995) argue that less educated agents face a substantially riskier income stream than do college graduates. In particular, they find that the variance of shocks to individual

unemployment risk—or a more generalized education, embedding an insurance against unemployment, since skills are more generally applicable.

The model is a standard overlapping-generations model with no capital markets and no private insurance. Individuals live for three periods and are identical at birth. In the first period of life, each individual chooses $s^i \in \{f, r\}$ in order to maximize expected life-time utility, given by

$$\ln c_{2, t+1} + \beta \ln c_{3, t+2} \tag{12.1}$$

for an individual born in period t.

Individuals work and receive a stochastic wage w^i in the second and third periods of their lives

$$w^i = \begin{cases} 1, & \text{if } s^i = f \\ \omega \geq \dfrac{1}{p}, \text{with probability } p & \text{if } s^i = r \\ \gamma < 1, \text{ with probability } (1 - p) & \text{if } s^i = r. \end{cases} \tag{12.2}$$

We think of this as representing an economy with a trade-off between flexibility and productivity. The interpretation of s^i is that it represents an investment decision that individuals make when young, which cannot be reversed later without a cost. Here, we simplify by assuming this cost to be high enough to always deter reversal.

If an individual chooses f, we say that she becomes of type *flexible*, which means that she can readily adapt to shocks that are non-symmetric with respect to different sectors or jobs. If the choice is $s^i = f$, the wage is unity and if a negative productivity shock hits her sector (job), she can easily find a new job with equal pay. If, on the other hand, $s^i = r$, it is costly or impossible to find a new job. Thus, she experiences an income loss of $\omega - \gamma$. Individuals who have chosen $s^i = r$ are thus said to be of type *rigid*. We index unemployment by $(1 - p)$ times the number of rigid individuals. The key feature of $s^{i,j}$ are that it is a state variable affecting the probability distribution of shocks later in life, and thus preferences over different insurance schemes.[7]

At the beginning of each period, before individual wages are revealed, a political decision mechanism uses simple majority voting to decide on the level of UI, with a replacement ratio denoted $b \in [\gamma/\omega, 1]$. The insurance applies to all active workers, who are the only participants in the political process. Each generation is

---

income, conditional on previous earnings, is twice as large for agents with high school only, compared to agents with a college degree.

[7] Alternatively to an educational choice, one could think of s^i as representing other choices entailing a trade-off between specialization and flexibility, such as whether to buy a house or rent an apartment.

of identical size. The insurance is financed via a proportional tax on income, denoted τ. The insurance system is assumed to work under a balanced budget requirement.

So, given b and τ, the three possible values for net income are $1 - \tau$, $(1 - \tau)\omega$ and $b(1 - \tau)\omega$. When $b = \gamma/\omega$, taxes are zero and incomes are i, ω and γ, and when $b = 1$ then are $1 - \tau$, $(1 - \tau)\omega$ and $(1 - \tau)\omega$. Note that UI both provides insurance and transfers resources from flexible to rigid.

12.5.1. Steady-state Equilibria

Let us now restrict the analyses to steady-state equilibria. For simplicity, we make the following tie-breaking assumption; if all old individuals (representing 50 per cent of the electorate) vote for some benefit level, that level is implemented. We will show that both a full insurance, high unemployment and a no insurance, zero unemployment equilibrium may co-exist.

Consider first the old generation, who have already chosen s. These individuals will not be forward-looking when choosing voting behaviour, since they will soon disappear from the scene. If they are flexible, they have nothing to gain from the insurance, so voting $b = \gamma/\omega$ weakly dominates all other voting strategies. On the other hand, if they are all rigid, they have a risk-reduction motive for insurance, and the insurance is at least actuarially fair (the expected pay-off is zero if all working individuals are rigid and positive otherwise). Thus, voting $b = 1$ is weakly dominating.

Now, consider the middle-aged individuals. Clearly, if they all are flexible (rigid), they cannot manipulate the voting outcome the following period, since that outcome is then perfectly determined by the type of the middle-aged. As for the old, the strategy to vote for zero insurance if flexible and full insurance if rigid, then weakly dominates all other strategies.

Finally, let us consider the young. Clearly, the optimal choice of s depends on the expectations of the young regarding future benefits. However, in period t, the young can perfectly infer the value of b_{t+1}, if all current middle-aged are of the same type. Benefits in period $t + 2$, on the other hand, are not predetermined in period t, since they depend on choices made in t and $t + 1$.

Consider first a potential steady-state equilibrium, denoted SSE_0, where all individuals are flexible and benefits are zero. This is a steady-state equilibrium if no young individual wants to deviate by choosing to become rigid. Consider a deviation in period t and note first that $b_{t+1} = \gamma/\omega$ but b_{t+2} is possibly large. Let us first analyse the payoffs for the two alternatives, deviating and not deviating for any out-of-steady-state belief about b_{t+2}. Denoting the payoff to the deviator and the non-deviator U_0^d and U_0, we see that

$$U_0^d \leq p \ln \omega + (1 - p) \ln \gamma + \beta \ln(1 - \tau_{t+2})\omega$$
$$= (p + \beta) \ln \omega + (1 - p) \ln \gamma + \beta \ln(1 - \tau_{t+2})$$

where the inequality is strict unless $b_{t+2}=1$. On the other hand,

$$U_0 = \ln(1) + \beta \ln(1 - \tau_{t+2})$$
$$= \beta \ln(1 - \tau_{t+2}).$$

(12.4)

Thus, SSE_0 exists regardless of out-of-equilibrium beliefs if

$$(p + \beta) \ln \omega + (1 - p) \ln \gamma < 0.$$

(12.5)

Consider now the potential steady-state equilibrium SSE_1, where all individuals are rigid and benefits are 1. Then, $b_{t+1}=1$, and

$$U_1^d \leq \ln(1 - \tau_{t+1}) + \beta \ln 1 = \ln(1 - \tau_{t+1}),$$

(12.6)

and

$$U_1 \geq \ln(1 - \tau_{t+1})\omega + \beta(p \ln \omega + (1 - p) \ln \gamma)$$
$$= \ln(1 - \tau_{t+1}) + (1 + \beta) \ln \omega + \beta(1 - p) \ln \gamma.$$

(12.7)

where the inequalities are strict unless $b_{t+2} = \gamma/\omega$. Thus, deviating by choosing to be flexible is dominated if

$$(1 + \beta) \ln \omega + \beta(1 - p) \ln \gamma > 0.$$

(12.8)

As we see, (12.5) and (12.8) can both be satisfied. If they are, both the full insurance-rigid and the no-insurance-flexible steady-state equilibria exist simultaneously, regardless of out-of-equilibrium beliefs.

12.5.2. Policy Persistence

Let us conclude this section by analysing the dynamic stability of our two equilibria. In other words, we want to see if the equilibria show policy persistence in the sense that if an economy is in one equilibrium, it tends to remain there.

Consider first SSE_0. If all young individuals choose to become rigid, they will certainly be able to implement full insurance but not until they become old. Clearly, if (12.5) is satisfied, there is an incentive to deviate from such a concerted action to break out of SSE_0, which therefore is persistent. Similarly, if the economy is in SSE_1, if all young individuals choose to become flexible, the benefits will go to zero after two periods. However, if (12.8) is satisfied, the individual incentives will be against this and, hence, SSE_1 is also persistent. Note also that discounting is important for stability since policy changes take time and do thus incur a cost in the short run but a gain in the long run.

In conclusion, this simple model exhibits some form of policy-behaviour complementarity; individuals tend to choose to be flexible (rigid) if current benefits are low (high), and if individuals have previously chosen to be flexible (rigid), they want low (high) benefits. The policy choice depends on aggregate state variables and is thus predetermined in every period. This is a stylized representation of the mechanism discussed at more length in Section 12.4. The model entails a number of simplifications which can be relaxed such as, for instance, the fact that the choice of specialization is irreversible. As shown in our previous work (Hassler *et al.*, 1999), most of these simplifications are inessential for the main argument to go through.

12.6. CONCLUSIONS

In this chapter, we have surveyed some recent literature discussing (i) the effect of unemployment insurance on labour-market performance; and (ii) the determination of preferences for social insurance, given an exogenous labour-market behaviour. We have argued that a unifying general equilibrium approach— where both policy and agents' behaviour are jointly endogenously determined— is fruitful. In particular, this approach can help explain the large differences across labour-market performance and institutions in the US and Europe, without resorting to exogenous structural differences in these economies, other than different initial distributions of agents. The general mechanism driving the results has been labelled policy-behaviour complementarity. In the context of our particular application, we thus mean that individuals tend to choose to be flexible (rigid) if current benefits are low (high), and if individuals have previously chosen to be flexible (rigid), they want low (high) benefits.

An insight from our analysis is that social insurance institutions are naturally persistent. For instance, generous UI today enhances the conditions for generous UI tomorrow. Thus, a policy reform involving reduced UI in Europe should be met by strong initial opposition. But, as the new levels of UI over time change the distribution of the labour force, this opposition will fade and the political support for the reform will increase. We have argued, however, that a UI reform involving reduced benefits in Europe is not necessarily welfare improving, even if this reform were to decrease unemployment substantially.

APPENDIX

UI and the Labour-Market: Implications of a Simple Search Model

The purpose of the Appendix is to illustrate, with the use of a simple search model, two fundamental effects of UI on the labour-market; that unemployment benefits increase unemployment and reduce wage inequality.

Consider an economy populated by *ex ante* identical risk neutral workers. In each period, each worker can be either employed or unemployed. If unemployed, she receives the unemployment benefit b, and suffers a search cost $\sigma(c)$, where $\sigma(0) = 0$, $\sigma' > 0$ and $\sigma'' > 0$, and c is the time devoted to search. Moreover, at the Poisson arrival rate $p(c) = \lambda c^\varepsilon$ (where $\varepsilon < 1$), she receives a wage offer $\omega(x) = w - ax$ drawn from a uniform distribution, where $x \in [0,1]$ and $w > a$. If the offer is accepted, she moves into employment and receives the wage $\omega(x)$, until a separation occurs. Separations arrive at the exogenous rate s. The value function for an employed worker, $W(x)$, who has accepted an offer paying the wage $\omega(x)$ satisfies

$$rW(x) = \max\{w - ax + s(U - W(x)), rU\}$$

whereas the value of being unemployed U, is given c, satisfies

$$rU = b - \sigma(c) + p(c) \int_0^1 \max\{W(x) - U, 0\}\, dx.$$

Workers face interesting decision problems only when unemployed. In particular, each of them will have to decide (i) the optimal search effort level, c^*, and (ii) the cut-off level, $\bar{x}$, such that wage offers paying more or equal to (less than) $\omega(\bar{x})$ are accepted (rejected). The cut-off is found by equating $W(\bar{x}) = U$. This yields, after some algebra

$$w - a\bar{x} - b + \sigma(c) = \frac{\bar{x}p(c)}{r + s + p(c)\bar{x}}\left(w - \frac{a\bar{x}}{2} - b + \sigma(c)\right) \qquad (12.A1)$$

or, equivalently

$$w - b + \sigma(c) = a\bar{x}\frac{r + s + \lambda c^\varepsilon \bar{x}/2}{r + s} \qquad (12.A2)$$

which shows that, conditional on c, an increase in benefits, b, reduces $\bar{x}$ (the unemployed become more picky).

We then need to determine the optimal search effort, c^*. This is found by setting c so as to maximize welfare of the unemployed. The solution yields

$$\sigma'(c) = p'(c) \int_0^{\bar{x}} (W(x) - U)dx$$
$$= p'(c)\bar{x}\frac{w - a\bar{x}/2 - b + \sigma(c)}{r + s + p(c) \cdot \bar{x}}. \qquad (12.A3)$$

From 12.A1–12.A3, recalling that $p(c) = \lambda c^\varepsilon$, we obtain

$$\sigma'(c) \cdot c/\varepsilon - \sigma(c) = w - a\bar{x} - b. \qquad (12.A4)$$

Using 12.A2–12.A4, we obtain

$$\sigma'(c) \cdot c^{1-\varepsilon} = \frac{a\bar{x}^2}{2} \frac{\varepsilon\lambda}{r+s}. \tag{12.A5}$$

Equations 12.A4 and 12.A5 define the equilibrium. Note that an increase in b will induce the unemployed workers to become pickier (lower $\bar{x}$) and exert a lower search effort.

This simple model has implications on unemployment and wage inequality. Assume the total mass of workers to be one. In this economy, unemployment is determined by the following differential equation:

$$\dot{u}_t = s \cdot (1 - u_t) - \lambda c^{\varepsilon} \bar{x} \cdot u_t$$

which yields the steady state

$$u_t^S = \frac{s}{s + \lambda c^{\varepsilon} \bar{x}}.$$

Thus, high benefits increase unemployment by reducing the outflow from unemployment, and increasing the average duration of unemployment. Simple extensions can be constructed, emphasizing the effects of b on long-term unemployment. We will only sketch the argument here. Assume that, with the positive arrival rate ξ, an unemployed worker loses her skills and becomes unemployable. If we maintain the assumption that benefits are unlimited over time, then we have that the value of being long term unemployed in b/r.[8] The value function of the unemployed becomes, in this case,

$$(r + \xi) U = b(1 + \xi/r) - \sigma(c) + p(c) \int_0^{\bar{x}} (W(x) - U)\, dx.$$

It should be intuitive that, in this case, high benefits increase both unemployment and the share of long-term unemployment.

UI also affects the equilibrium wage inequality. By shrinking the range of job offers regarded as acceptable, benefits decrease the inequality between fortunate and unfortunate workers (recall that $a\bar{x}$ is a measure of the spread of the age distribution). The comparative statics of this simple model therefore illustrates two effects of UI on the labour market outcome: unemployment benefits increase unemployment and reduce wage inequality.

Skill-biased Technological Change

The purpose of this section is to illustrate how our simple search model can be consistent with the observations that both Europe and US featured low

---

[8] In order to avoid that all workers eventually become long-run unemployed, we need to abandon the assumption that workers are infinitely lived, and assume that each worker faces a positive probability of death, and that each newborn enters the labour force as unemployed (as in Blanchard, 1985).

unemployment and low wage inequality in the 60s and 70s, while the US have experienced rising wage inequality but little change in unemployment during the 1980s and 1990s. In contrast, European countries have experienced rising unemployment but little change in wage inequality. The key change relative to the simple search model in this Appendix is to add skill-biased technological change to the framework.

Consider, first, a version of the simple model constructed above where search effort is inelastically supplied (thus, set $\sigma(c) = 0$ and $p(c) = p$). Let two economies be different in the UI regime only. For simplicity, assume that in an 'American' laissez-faire economy $b = 0$, whereas in a 'European' welfare state economy $b = b^{WS} > 0$. Furthermore, assume that parameters are such that $w - b^{WS} > a\frac{r+s+p/2}{r+s}$, implying that, in both economies, $W(1) > U$. This means that, in both economies, agents will always accept any job offer, and the two economies have the same unemployment rate $(u^S = s/(s+p))$ and wage inequality.[9] Next, assume that both economies are hit by a common shock changing the wage offer distribution. In particular, after the shock, agents in both economies face the wage offer distribution $\omega(x) \in [\gamma w - \tilde{a}x]$, where $\tilde{a} \equiv (a + 2(\gamma - 1)w)$. Note that, under this assumption, the expected wage does not change (in particular, $\bar{\omega} = w - a/2$), but its variance increases. MZ refer to a shock of this type as 'mismatch-biased' and argue that this is related to what other papers have referred to as 'skill-biased' technical change. This shock enhances the relative value for a worker finding the right match, or, equivalently, increases the cost for an agent of accepting an unsuitable job. Assume, further, that

$$b^{WS} > \gamma w - \tilde{a}\frac{r+s+p/2}{r+s} > 0.$$

In this case, it is easy to see that in the laissez-faire equilibrium, all jobs will continue to be accepted, whereas in the welfare state economy, unemployed workers will decline all job offers paying a wage $\omega(x)$ such that $x > \bar{x} \equiv \left[\sqrt{(r+s)^2 + 2p(\gamma w - b)} - (r+s)\right]/2$. Thus, on the one hand, the unemployment rate will remain unchanged in the laissez-faire economy, whereas it will increase in the welfare state economy. More precisely, unemployment will increase in this economy from $u^{S0} = s/(s+p)$ to $u^{S1} = s/(s+p\bar{x})$. The inequalizing nature of the shock will, on the other hand, unambiguously increase wage inequality in the laissez-faire economy, whereas this will be partially offset in the welfare state economy by the changes in the search behaviour of the unemployed.

---

[9] In a more elaborated model where job creation is endogenous and wages are determined by Nash bargaining, b would also affect unemployment through its effect on the equilibrium wage rate (outside option effect). See MZ.

REFERENCES

Acemoglu, D. (2001). Good jobs versus bad jobs, *Journal of Labour Economics*, 19, 1.

—— and A. Shimer (1999). *Journal of Political Economy*, 107(5), 893–928.

—— and R. Shimer (2000). Productivity Gains from Unemployment Insurance, *European Economic Review*, 44(7), 1195–12.

Addison, J. and P. Portugal (1987). On the distributional shape of unemployment duration, *Review of Economics and Statistics*, 69, 520–26.

Banerjee, A. and A. Newman (1993). Occupational choice and the process of development, *Journal of Political Economy*, 101 (2), 274–98.

Bénabou, R. (1998). *Unequal Societies: Income Distribution and the Social Contract*, mimeo, New York University.

Blanchard, O. (1985). Debt, deficits, and finite horizons, *Journal of Political Economy* 93, 223–47.

Burda, M. and A. Mertens (2002). Wages and workers displacement in Germany, *Labour Economic* (forthcoming), CEPR discussion paper 1869.

Cooper, R. and A. John (1988). Coordinating coordination failures in Keynesian models, *Quarterly Journal of Economics*, 103 (3), 441–63.

Di Tella, R. and R. MacCulloch (1995). The determination of unemployment benefits, *Oxford Applied Economics discussion paper series* 180.

Fallick, B. C. (1991). Unemployment insurance and the rate of re-employment of displaced workers, *Review of Economics and Statistics*, 73 (2), 228–35.

—— (1996). A review of the recent empirical literature on displaced workers, *Industrial and Labor Relations Review*, 50 (1), 5–16.

Freeman, R. B. (1996). Towards an apartheid economy? *Harvard Business Review*, 115–121.

Gottschalk, P. (1997). Inequality, income growth, and mobility: The basic facts, *Journal of Economic Perspectives*, 11 (2), 21–40.

—— and R. Moffit (1994). The growth of earnings instability in the US labor market, *Brookings Papers on Economic Activity*, 217–72.

Haefke, C. (1999). The European unemployment puzzle: The importance of bargaining and endogenous job destruction in a dynamic matching model, unpublished manuscript.

Hamermesh, D. S. (1989). What do we know about worker displacement in the United States? *Industrial Relations*, 28 (1), 51–9.

Hassler, J. and J. V. Rodríguez Mora (1999). Employment turnover and the public allocation of unemployment insurance, *Journal of Public Economics* (forthcoming).

—— —— K. Storesletten, and F. Zilibotti (1999). Equilibrium unemployment insurance, *CEPR working paper* 2126.

—— *et al.* (2001). A Positive Theory of Mobility and Insurance (CEPR discussion paper 2964).

—— *et al.* (2003). The Survival of the Welfare State, *American Economic Review*, forthcoming.

Hubbard, R. G., J. Skinner, and S. P. Zeldes (1995). Precautionary savings and social insurance, *Journal of Political Economy*, 103 (2), 360–99.

Jacobson, L. S., R. J. LaLonde, and D. G. Sullivan (1993). Earnings losses of displaced workers, *American Economic Review*, 83 (4), 685–709.

Krusell, P. and A. A. Smith (1998). Income and wealth heterogeneity in the macroeconomy, *Journal of Political Economy*, 106 (5), 867–98.

Leonhard, J. and M. V. Audenrode (1995). The duration of unemployment and the persistence of wages, *CEPR discussion paper* 1227.

Levy, F. and R. J. Murnane (1992). U.S. earnings levels and earnings inequality: A review of recent trends and proposed explanations, *Journal of Economic Literature*, 30 (3), 1333–81.

Ljungqvist, L. and T. Sargent (1998). The European unemployment dilemma, *Journal of Political Economy*, 106, 514–50.

Marimon, R. and F. Zilibotti (1999). Unemployment vs. mismatch of talents reconsidering unemployment benefits, *Economic Journal*, 109(405), 266–91.

Martin, J. P. (1996). Measures of replacement rates for the purpose of international comparisons: A note, *OECD Economic Studies*, 26, 99–115.

Meyer, B. D. (1990). Unemployment insurance and unemployment spells, *Econometrica* 58, 757–82.

Mortensen, D. and C. Pissarides (1999), Unemployment responses to skill-biased shocks: The role of labor market policies, *Economic Journal* 109(405), 242–61.

Neal, D. (1995). Industry-specific human capital: Evidence from displaced workers, *Journal of Labor Economics*, 13 (4), 653–77.

Nickell, S. (1997), Unemployment and labor market rigidities: Europe versus North America, *Journal of Economic Perspectives*, 11 (3), 55–74.

Oswald, A. J. (1997). The missing piece of the unemployment puzzle, mimeo, University of Warwick.

Pallage, S. and C. Zimmermann (1999), Heterogenous labor markets and the generosity towards the unemployed: An international perspective, *CREFE working paper* 88.

―――― (2001). Voting on unemployment insurance, *International Economic Review*, 42(4), 903–23.

Piketty, T. (1995). Social mobility and redistributive politics, *Quarterly Journal of Economics*, 110 (3), 551–84.

Quadrini, V. (2000). Growth, learning and redistributive policies, *Journal of Public Economics* (forthcoming).

Saint Paul, G. (1993). On the political economy of labor market flexibility, *NBER Macroeconomic Annuals*.

―――― (1996). Exploring the political economy of labor market institutions, *Economic Policy*, 23, 265–300.

―――― (1997). Voting for jobs: Policy persistence and unemployment, *CEPR discussion paper* 1428.

―――― (1999). The political economy of employment protection, *CEPR discussion paper* 2109.

Thomas, J. M. (1996). An empirical model of sectoral movements by unemployed workers, *Journal of Labor Economics*, 14, 126–53.

Topel, R. (1990). Specific capital and unemployment: Measuring the costs and consequences of job loss, *Carnegie Rochester Conference Series on Public Policy*, 33, 181–214.

Wright, R. (1986). The redistributive roles of unemployment insurance and the dynamics of voting, *Journal of Public Economics*, 31 (3), 377–99.

Index

Printed in the United States
By Bookmasters